AN INTRODUCTION TO THE HEBREW PROPHETS

THE PROPHETS AS PREACHERS

GARY V. SMITH

Nashville, Tennessee

In honor of three of God's wonderful gifts:

Dorothy Putnam, my mother-in-law
Susan Smith, my wife
Christine Brunko, my daughter

4216-10
0-8054-1610-2

Dewey Decimal Classification: 224
Subject Heading: BIBLE. O.T. PROPHETS
Library of Congress Card Catalog Number: 94-18068

Library of Congress Cataloging-in-Publication Data

Smith, Gary V., 1943–.
The prophets as preachers : an introduction to the Hebrew prophets / Gary V. Smith
p. cm.
Includes bibliographical references and index.
ISBN 0-8054-1610-2
1. Bible O.T. Prophets—Criticism, interpretation, etc.
2. Prophecy (Christianity). 3. Preaching I. Title
BS1505.6.P69S55 1994
224'.06—DC20 94-18068
CIP

Contents

List of Illustrations

Abbreviations

AB	Anchor Bible
ABD	*Anchor Bible Dictionary*
ANET	*Ancient Near Eastern Texts*
AUSS	*Andrews University Seminary Studies*
BA	*Biblical Archaeologist*
BAR	*Biblical Archaeologist Reader*
BASOR	*Bulletin of the American Schools of Oriental Research*
BBC	Broadman Bible Commentary
BBR	*Bulletin of Biblical Research*
Bib	*Biblica*
BKAT	Biblischer Kommentar Altes Testament
BSac	*Bibliotheca Sacra*
BTB	*Biblical Theology Bulletin*
BZ	*Biblische Zeitschrift*
BZAW	Beihefte zur Zeitschrift fur die alttestamentliche Wissenschaft
CBC	The Cambridge Bible Commentary on the New English Bible
CBQ	*Catholic Biblical Quarterly*
CC	Continental Commentary

CTR	Criswell Theological Review
DSB	Daily Study Bible
EBC	Expositor's Bible Commentary
EJ	*Evangelical Journal*
Enc	*Encounter*
EvQ	*Evangelical Quarterly*
ExpT	*Expository Times*
FOTL	Forms of Old Testament Literature
HAR	Hebrew Annual Review
HAT	Handbuch zum Alten Testament
HBD	*Holman Bible Dictionary*
Her	*Hermenia*
HUCA	*Hebrew Union College Annual*
IB	*Interpreter's Bible*
ICC	International Critical Commentary
IEJ	*Israel Exploration Journal*
Int	*Interpretation*
IntCom	Interpretation Commentary: A Bible Commentary for Teaching and Preaching
ISBE	*International Standard Bible Encyclopedia*
ITC	International Theological Commentary
JAOS	*Journal of the American Oriental Society*
JBL	*Journal of Biblical Literature*
JETS	*Journal of the Evangelical Theological Society*
JJS	*Journal of Jewish Studies*
JNES	*Journal of Near Eastern Studies*
JSOT	*Journal for the Study of the Old Testament*
JSOT Sup	Journal for the Study of the Old Testament, Supplement Series
JSS	*Journal of Semitic Studies*
JTS	*Journal of Theological Studies*
KAT	Kommentar zum Alten Testament
LBBC	Laymen's Bible Book Commentary
LXX	Septuagint
NAC	New American Commentary
NCBC	New Century Bible Commentary
NICOT	New International Commentary on the Old Testament

OTL	Old Testament Library
OTS	*Oudtestamentische Studien*
OTWSA	Die Ou Testamentiese Werkgemeenskap in Suid-Afrika
PEQ	*Palestine Exploration Quarterly*
RevExp	*Review and Expositor*
RTR	*Reformed Theological Review*
SBT	Studies in Biblical Theology
SEÅ	*Svensk exegetisk arsbok*
ST	*Studia theologica*
SWJT	*Southwestern Journal of Theology*
TB	*Tyndale Bulletin*
TBC	Torch Bible Commentary
TDOT	*Theological Dictionary of Old Testament*
TLZ	*Theologische Literaturzeitung*
TOTC	Tyndale Old Testament Commentary
TS	*Theological Studies*
TZ	*Theologische Zeitscrift*
UF	*Ugarit-Forschungen*
VT	*Vetus Testamentum*
VTSup	*Vetus Testamentum, Supplements*
WEC	Wycliffe Exegetical Commentary
WBC	Word Bible Commentary
WTJ	*Westminster Theological Journal*
ZAW	*Zeitschrift für die alttestamentliche Wissenschaft*

Preface

The prophetic books are witnesses to God's attempt to transform the lives of people in Israel and the ancient Near Eastern world. Transformation was possible because God's messengers, the prophets, were willing to communicate ideas that would change the way their audiences thought about the world, about the gods/God, about themselves, and about other people. The inspired prophets challenged the deceptions within the socially developed culture of the listener and called them to transform their thinking.

This introduction does not focus on the composition of prophetic books like other introductions. This introduction uses communication theory and the sociology of knowledge to analyze the prophets. Those familiar with the prophets, communication theory, and sociology of knowledge will recognize my great debt to past studies. My prayer is that this study will awaken a new appreciation of the prophetic ministry.

I wish to thank Bethel Theological Seminary for providing a semester sabbatical to work on this project. I also want to thank Ken Goudy who introduced me to the sociological approach of Berger and Luckmann and the many students who have encouraged and challenged my thinking along the way.

Introduction

The Old Testament prophets changed lives. They continue to change lives. How is such amazing change possible? That is the basic question we seek to answer in this study.

The Old Testament prophets were God's messengers to Judah and Israel. They declared God's words to common men and women, wealthy kings and judges, and large groups at public events. The prophetic books are the written record of what the Spirit directed the prophets to communicate to their audiences. Some prophets condemned those who oppressed the poor, while others provided spiritual answers for the difficult questions of everyday life. God's messengers challenged audiences to transform their behavior so that they could enjoy the blessing of God's presence.

The Hebrew prophets addressed people who lived hundreds of years ago, but their words contain theological principles that are applicable to each new generation of readers. The description of God's holiness (Isa. 6) and the challenge to trust in God's power and promise (Isa. 7) have relevance in this modern world of uncertainty. The prophets' faithfulness to God's calling sets an example to all who desire to proclaim God's word today.

Before a person can understand and benefit from the prophetic messages, the reader needs a basic understanding of:

1) when each prophet spoke,
2) what was the political, social, and spiritual context,
3) who was in the prophet's audience, and
4) why this audience needed this message.

The answers to these questions lead to more detailed inquiries about the structure of each book, the interpretation of literary forms of speech, the meaning of imagery and symbolic language, and the theology of their messages.

Modern scholars have developed several methods of looking at compositional issues (source criticism, form criticism, and redaction criticism)[1] which focus attention on the development and authorship of prophetic oracles. This book addresses these issues from time to time in footnotes, but the primary goal of this study is to examine how God used the prophets to transform the thinking and behavior of Israelite people.[2] This requires an:

a) analysis of persuasion in prophetic communication;
b) investigation of the theology of prophetic messages; and
c) a sociological study of the process of transforming the way people think and act.

This introductory study of transformation discusses how these three dynamic factors influence the process of change. It includes an examination of theories about the nature of

1. These approaches are surveyed by J. Barton, *Reading the Old Testament* (Philadelphia: Westminster, 1984).

2. We prefer a more wholistic method of looking at structure and find most compositional theories unconvincing. A review of these approaches seems unnecessary, for they do not further the sociological and communicative methods pursued in this study.

communication and social change (chaps. 1—2) and the application of this theoretical framework to the prophet's transformational messages (chaps. 3—18). The study ends (chap. 19) with some principles that characterize prophetic ministry. Some of these issues raise questions about the way God's messengers should communicate God's message to audiences today. At the end of each chapter questions related to the theological and practical implications of each prophet's experience are raised. These should encourage the reader to participate in the real-life dilemmas that the prophets faced.

Chapter 1

Communication that Transforms

Everyone would like to change something or transform some policy. Some people do not like early morning classes; others dread going to dentists; and most wish they did not have to pay so many taxes. How does one go about changing these unpleasant experiences? A child can be warned with a strong "NO!" Wrong behavior can be corrected with an appropriate punishment, but how does one change the way adults or governments think and behave? Employers may provide job training to increase productivity or offer monetary incentives to affect the behavior of employees. A teacher can motivate adults in an educational setting by offering a letter grade for good performance. But how does one bring about change in another person's beliefs or attitudes where there is freedom to choose between two or three different views?[1]

---

1. S. W. Littlejohn and D. M. Jabusch, *Persuasive Transactions* (Glenview, Ill.; Scott, Foresman, 1987), 7, claimed that "Choice is therefore important in distinguishing persuasion from coercion." G. Cronkhite, *Persuasion: Speech and Behavioral Change* (New York: Bobbs-Merrill, 1969), 4–6, believe threats bring about change but do not change beliefs or behavior; they merely mandate mechanical compliance.

It may seem impossible to bring about some changes, yet people do change in small ways all the time. Most people are unconsciously affected by a multitude of subtle pressures. Change occurs because of social pressures like the desire for approval, the psychological need to avoid conflict, or in response to an emotional appeal. People desire to learn better ways to meet their needs and are open to suggestions that are persuasively presented. Technological innovations are quickly accepted because they make life easier, but habits are more difficult to alter.

Persuasion was one of the key tools Old Testament prophets used to transform the way people acted.[2] By orally communicating with their audiences, they motivated some to reconsider the way they thought about themselves, God, and their relationship with God and others. If they would transform their way of thinking (repent), God would restore His relationship with them. If the people would forsake the customs of the nations and follow God's ways, His covenant would continue.

The Role of Communication

Prophetic Communication

The prophets functioned as spokesmen for God (Ex. 7:1–2; Jer. 1:4–10)[3] so their main role was to communicate God's words to others. As God's messengers, they were not interested in just declaring the truth.[4] Their purpose went far beyond the goal of simply repeating what they heard.

2. Persuasion is simply an attempt to change the behavior or thinking of another person.

3. For a survey of scholarly research on the prophets see G. M. Tucker, "Prophecy and the Prophetic Literature," *The Hebrew Bible and Its Modern Interpreters,* eds. D. A. Knight and G. M. Tucker (Chico, Calif.: Scholars Press, 1985), 325–68, or G. V. Smith, "Prophets, Prophecy," *ISBE* III (Grand Rapids: Eerdmans, 1986), 986–1004.

4. J. F. Ross, "The Prophet as Messenger," in *Israel's Prophetic Heritage,* ed. B. W. Anderson and W. Harrelson (New York: Harper and Row, 1962), 98–107. F. B. Craddock, *Overhearing the Gospel* (Nashville: Abingdon, 1978), 19, says the preacher is not just trying "to say the word, to tell the truth, but to get the truth heard, to effect a new hearing of the word."

The prophets were preachers who communicated God's words in order to transform their audience's thinking and social behavior.[5] They were not primarily concerned with writing a record of an historical period, an eschatological chart of future events, or a systematic presentation of their theology. They were real people attempting to communicate urgent messages to friends, and even to some enemies. They were persuading people to look at life in a radically different way (Jer. 3:6–13). They offered hope to the hopeless and a realistic assessment of the nation's weakness to the country's proud military leaders (Amos 6:1–14). They encouraged people to look at themselves from God's perspective and not conform to the prevailing political perspective of the day because of social pressures. They exhorted people to put off their old ways, to take an oath to change, and to transform their lives by breaking new ground (Jer. 4:1–4).

Models of Communication

Communication is the ongoing process in which a source person transmits an intended meaning to a receiving person in order to elicit a response from the listener.[6]

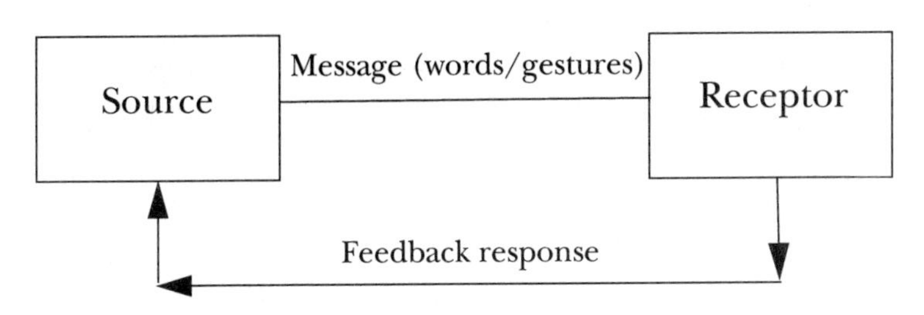

5. T. J. Overholt, *Channels of Prophecy: The Social Dynamics of Prophetic Activity* (Minneapolis: Fortress, 1989), 6–11, properly critiques those who focus only on the prophetic giving of the message and ignore the social dynamics of prophecy.

6. J. E. Baird, *Speaking for Results: Communication by Objectives* (New York: Harper and Row, 1981), 7–8, lists about a dozen different definitions of communications which emphasize one or more of the aspects in the definition used here. Compare K. O. Gangel and S. L. Canine, *Communication and Conflict Management* (Nashville: Broadman Press, 1992), 23–46. J. D. Baumann, *An Introduction to Contemporary Preaching* (Grand Rapids: Baker, 1972), 13, has a similar definition of communication in preaching.

Since people have unique personalities, life experiences, and perceptions of the world, the dynamics of communication vary from conversation to conversation. This three-step communication process (sending-receiving-responding) takes place over a period of time and through a series of events. Burke envisions a complete conversation as a drama with acts, scenes, agents, agency, and purpose.[7] Since most communication involves a series of interactions between two people, a helical model illustrates the dynamics of communication.[8]

The Helical Model of Communication

	Speaker A	Speaker B
Step 1	A	B
Step 2	A	B
Step 3	A	B

These models of communication diagram some regular traits of conversation, but most people have also experienced the unpredictable dynamics of communication. A woman you do not know may say, "Watch out for the car!" You may hear her words, but not be sure she is talking to you. You look again and notice she is looking at you and pointing frantically to your left. Now you realize she is trying to warn you of danger. Quickly, you respond to avoid the car unexpectedly backing up toward you. Then you thank the woman.

The process only took seconds, but it involved the transmission of a meaningful idea through words and gestures so that the listener could understand the warning and take action. If you continued thinking the stranger was speaking to someone else, communication would not occur. If you un-

7. K. Burke, *A Grammar of Motives* (Cleveland: Meridian, 1962), 547. E. Berne, *Games People Play* (New York: Grove, 1964) compares communication to a game.

8. Baird, *Speaking for Results,* 14–16.

derstood the words to be, "Watch out for the star," miscommunication would occur.

Successful communication involves the reception of the intended idea from the source person.[9] Sounds and gestures convey an intended meaning that may or may not be correctly interpreted. If the message does not make sense to the listener or is interpreted to mean something unintended, a breakdown occurs in communication.[10] Barriers to communication might include: noise which distorts or interrupts the message, ignorance about the topic, or preconceived attitudes about the speaker. A poorly structured speech, unsupported claims, or exaggerated conclusions may also interfere with communicating ideas effectively.

Theological Communication

Communication theory does not address the theological dimension in this process, but it does provide a helpful examination of human interaction.[11] The divine factor must be added to the communication paradigm, for both God and the messenger play key roles in convincing listeners to change their thinking. Messengers cannot control or limit God's work, but they need to be aware of the human factors which influence good communication. This will comple-

9. Concerning the controversy over the source of meaning (the world, language sign, or what most people believe), see the options outlined by C. Kraft, *Communication Theory for Christian Witness* (Nashville: Abingdon, 1983), 110–15.

10. A fuller discussion of the communication model can be found in D. Ehninger, B. Gronbeck, R. McKerrow and A. Monroe, *Principles and Types of Speech Communication,* 10th ed. (Glenview, Ill.: Scott, Foresman, 1986), 5–17, or E. Bormann and N. Bormann, *Speech Communication: An Interpersonal Approach* (New York: Harper and Row, 1972), 18–36.

11. D. J. Hesselgrave, *Communicating Christ Cross-Culturally* (Grand Rapids: Zondervan, 1991), 42–43, distinguished between the primary (divine), secondary (Paul), and tertiary (Timothy) sources of a communication. See also R. D. Hughes, *Talking to the World in the Days to Come* (Nashville: Broadman Press, 1991) for different roles a speaker may take and how the role taken can affect communication.

ment God's work in the listener's mind, rather than discourage it.

When the divine factors are inserted at two points in this communication framework, a more complete model of prophetic discourse is portrayed. The impact of the transcendent power on the communication process is difficult to quantify, but prophetic texts insist on God's part in communication (Mic. 3:8; Ezek. 11:5).

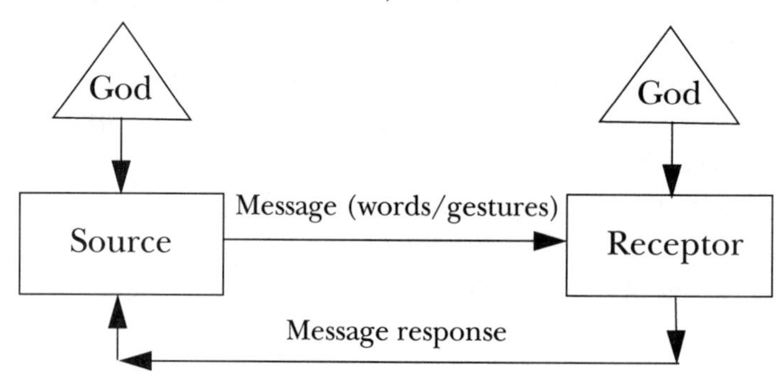

The prophets transmitted God's message to their audiences to elicit a response. After the listener decoded these words (reproducing the speaker's intended meaning), the mysterious influence of God worked in the receptor's mind to bring about conviction and the will to act.[12] The audience may choose to respond to human persuasion and the divine working either positively, with neutrality, or negatively.

Prophetic Cross-Cultural Communication

The prophets spoke to Israelites as well as foreigners from diverse cultural backgrounds. These people spoke several languages, had different laws, and followed unique social customs. They honored many gods and worshiped in a variety of ways. This cultural diversity was most evident when a prophet went to preach in a foreign city like Nineveh (Jon. 3:1–9), but it also existed in Israel itself. Not all the residents

12. Baumann, *Contemporary Preaching,* 277–91, has a chapter on the role of the Holy Spirit in bringing about change in the life of the person who hears the word of God.

in Israel were Jews, and Israelites themselves differed from one another. Some grew up with rural values, while others were impacted by commercial practices in the city. A noble, a judge, or a priest in Jerusalem had a social status of privilege and wealth that poor nomadic shepherds in the Sinai desert did not share. Laws, family custom, and religious commitments varied from group to group and family to family.

Culture is defined as "the cumulative deposit of knowledge, experience, meanings, beliefs, values, attitudes, religions, concepts of self, the universe . . . hierarchies of status, expectations, spacial relations, and time concepts acquired by a large group of people."[13] Culture is the learned behavior and thought patterns shared by a group of people. Although one can speak in a general way of an Israelite culture, it is more helpful to recognize that many subcultural groups existed within Israel. These smaller groups were the primary units that defined norms and behavior. They were the sources of information that provided paradigms for understanding the social, spiritual, and natural world.[14]

Cultural differences need to be minimized if two people from different cultural groups are going to communicate. This can be done by finding common points of mutual identification that provide a basis for the transmission of shared meanings. For the word "knife," the cultural context of a woodcarver calls to mind a very positive image of a favorite and much-loved tool. The word "knife" makes a mother think immediately of a dangerous object that might hurt her child. The greater the social, behavioral, philosophical, and linguistic diversity between individuals, the greater the potential for misunderstanding not only what is connoted (the secondary meaning of a word), but also what is denoted (the

---

13. R. E. Porter, "An Overview of Intercultural Communication" in L. A. Samovar and R. E. Porter, *Intercultural Communications: A Reader* (Belmont, Calif.: Wadsworth, 1972), 3.

14. C. H. Dodd, *Perspectives on Cross-Cultural Communication* (Debuque: Kendall/Hunt, 1977), 31–41, outlined the importance of group membership and its production of a subculture.

main meaning of a word). The diagram illustrates the nature of the cross-cultural communication process.

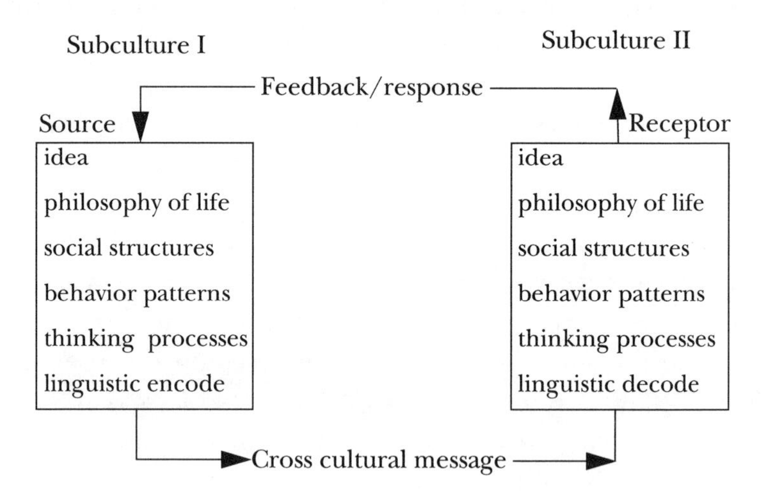

The meaning of an idea intended by the source person passes through several cultural filters that define the encoded words in a culturally specific way. When the receptor hears these words, they are decoded and passed through a different series of cultural filters that may produce a meaning not identical to the idea the source intended. If a messenger does not recognize and compensate for the different cultural or social background of a listener, that person may not accurately understand the intended meaning. For cross-cultural communication to take place, the speaker must know how the audience thinks and then must use terms that fit that frame of reference.[15] For example, a four-year-old would probably not understand the philosophical arguments for the existence of God, but might believe in God from a story about God's creation of humans.

The prophets did not need to address all of the unique cultural perspectives represented in their audiences, but they did need to speak so people could understand them.

15. Hesselgrave, *Communicating Christ Cross-Culturally,* 163–73, has a somewhat similar seven dimensional framework for cross-cultural communication.

Many prophets mentioned how their view of the world contrasted with the cultural perspective of the listening group. Jeremiah reminded his Judean audience of their Baalism, using Baalistic imagery and illustrations (Jer. 2). Ezekiel corrected those who blamed the sinfulness of their parents and the injustice of God for their problems (Ezek. 18:1–29) by showing they were guilty and God was just. The cultural gap between the prophets and their audiences complicated the process of transmitting ideas, making it more difficult to convince people to reject their cultural patterns and accept new ideas from the prophets.

Communication to Bring About Transformation

Transformations involve significant change, alteration, or a major development. Transformations may alter the external form, texture, or looks of an object or person; but the most dynamic changes are internal variation. Changing clothes brings a minimal differentiation in the way a person looks, but information can change the way people think or behave. Minor alterations in the way people think take place on a daily basis. If a new discovery or a different way of looking at life proves to be advantageous, people will gladly change. Political philosophies or religious beliefs are usually deeply connected to the self-identity of a person and are more difficult to change.

The prophets desired to transform the way their audiences thought about themselves, their world, and the supernatural powers that controlled both. They wanted to change the norms that governed people's social relationships, to alter their sinful desires to fulfill their own wishes, and to bring their lives into line with God's will. Although many Israelites listened to the prophetic message and allowed God to transform their thinking, some refused to believe what God said.

The Failure to Communicate

Why do some people continue to worship idols generation after generation? Why do people cling to their old ways and not change their social behavior? Why was it so difficult for the prophets to transform the way the Israelites thought about God? Why did the message of God which the prophets communicated bring about so little change? Several reasons explain why people do not change.

Because God Did Not Speak

Knowledge is liberating, powerful, and the basis for successful transformation. A lack of knowledge leads to fear, ignorance, failure, and an inability to take control of life. Parents teach their children how to act in order to transform their behavior from the selfishness of a two-year-old to the maturity of a high school graduate. Colleges provide detailed information required by various professions in order to change an unqualified freshman into a highly qualified employee. Spiritual knowledge about God's ways frees one from the fear of an unknown God who acts capriciously and without principle.

Before one can change, a person must hear about an alternative way of understanding life. Before a prophet can communicate God's way to live, God must reveal knowledge about His plans for a group of people and send a prophet to deliver that message. True prophets waited until they received divine knowledge from God. Receiving a divine message was a prerequisite because it gave the prophets purpose and authority. If the prophets were to be trusted, if they hoped to maintain their prophetic role as messengers of God, their advice and predictions had to be true. If God did not speak, prophets had no transforming, divine word to proclaim.

References to the infrequency of revelations from God during the time of the judges (1 Sam. 3:1), at the time of the destruction of the northern nation of Israel (Amos 8:11–12), and during Judah's exile (Ps. 74:9; Ezek. 7:26) show that Israel did not always have a new word from God. Since Eli and his sons despised God and were under God's punishment, they were not qualified to receive a message from God (1 Sam. 2:27–36).[16] Israel and Judah rejected God's word

16. R. W. Klein, *1 Samuel* in *WBC 10* (Waco: Word, 1983), 27–28, 32.

through the prophets for many years, so God did not send any new messages at the time of their destruction (Ezek. 7:23–27). The false prophets deceptively claimed to have a word from God, even when He did not speak (see 1 Kings 22; Jer. 28).

Because No Messenger Will Speak

If transformation is to take place, a prophet must be willing to communicate the divine will when God reveals it. Knowledge kept secret has no liberating force. God's ability to change superstition and misguided behavior is frustrated if the audience never hears His wisdom.

The life of Naaman, the Syrian general who had leprosy, illustrates the importance of sharing what one knows about God (2 Kings 5). This valiant warrior had won numerous battles for Syria, yet the dreaded disease of leprosy was slowly eating away his flesh. His professional role as a soldier was brilliant, but his life was miserable because he knew no cure for this disease. A young Israelite girl, captured during one of Naaman's battles, knew a prophet of God in Samaria who could cure leprosy (5:2–4). This information would not help Naaman if the Israelite girl did not tell him about the prophet Elijah. After Naaman came to Elijah, the prophet communicated information about how to be healed of leprosy. Naaman needed to dip seven times in the Jordan River; an illogical act that would only humiliate a man of his stature (5:10–12). Once his servants persuaded Naaman to act on the prophet's advice, God miraculously healed him. As a consequence, his belief system and actions were transformed. Instead of worshiping and serving the Syrian gods, Naaman said, "Now I know that there is no God in all the earth, but in Israel" (5:15). Naaman's life was transformed because a young girl spoke about a prophet who could heal him and because a prophet willingly told a pagan what to do.

The failure to communicate stifles the possibility of transformation. Therefore, God (the primary source) sent Ezekiel (the messenger) to the stubborn sons of Israel (those receiving) to communicate the message God had spoken

(Ezek. 2:3–4). Ezekiel was to "speak my words" (2:7; 3:4) whether the people listened or not (2:5; 3:11). Jeremiah introduced his message in chapter 2 with "the Word of the Lord came unto me saying." Micah announced a message of judgment against God's covenant people in chapter 6 by calling them to "Hear what the Lord is saying." In Isaiah 3:16 the prophet simply said, "The Lord said," but Amos shouted to the sinful Israelites, "Thus says the Lord" (Amos 2:6). These "messenger formulas" are a reminder of the prophets' willingness to speak God's message. Their words testify to the prophets' communication of God's word. If they did not speak, how would people hear the divine communication?

Because the Speaker Is Not Credible

A person dressed in ragged clothes, using poor grammar, and espousing questionable medical procedures could try to communicate a new cure for cancer to a group of doctors; however, the lack of a credible messenger might obscure the brilliant medical treatment. New information is usually accepted or rejected on the basis of answers to a few simple questions. People ask, "Who said it? Why should I believe what they said? What significance does it have to my life?" People ignore those who do not know what they are talking about, but people's lives are transformed when information comes from credible people who know what they are saying.

Since the time of Aristotle, teachers of rhetoric and communication have recognized the disadvantage of not being a credible speaker. Aristotle defined rhetoric as "the faculty of discovering the means of persuasion in reference to any subject whatsoever."[17] Aristotle believed that one key means of persuasion was *ethos,* a term which describes the influence that a speaker's credibility has on the listener's acceptance of what is said. The factors which support a strong persuasive ethos for Aristotle were "intelligence, character, and good will."[18] Whitehead's recent study of rhetoric con-

---

17. Aristotle, *Rhetoric,* I. 2.

18. L. Cooper, *The Rhetoric of Aristotle* (New York: Appleton-Century, 1932), 8–9.

cluded that a listener would accept a speaker's words if the speaker demonstrated "trustworthiness, competence, dynamism, and objectivity."[19] A speaker of high status with a likable personality who identifies with an audience has more persuasive power.[20]

When people in the Old Testament heard the prophets speaking, they would, consciously or unconsciously, assess the credibility of the speaker. They would be more open to the prophetic messenger who spoke with conviction, demonstrated trustworthiness, identified with the past history or present problems of the audience, and testified to being called by God to the role of a prophet (a status position).

The Israelites did not want to be deceived; they did not want to make fools of themselves by believing something that could not be supported. They wanted to know who the prophets were and where they got their information. Were their words derived from their own imagination (Jer. 23:16, 23)? Were they mouthing political propaganda, or were these the words of God? If the listeners believed the prophet was not trustworthy, honest, or objective, they would not accept what was said (Jer. 43:1–5). These examples show that God's words will seldom transform people's thinking if the messenger has no credibility.

Because the Listener Will Not Believe

Communication is an unpredictable task. God can reveal a powerful message of hope, and a credible messenger can willingly communicate the message in an effective manner; but the listeners may still refuse to respond to the message. The audience may fail to believe and change because

19. J. L. Whitehead, "Factors of Source Credibilty," *Quarterly Journal of Speech* 54 (1966), 65–72, or H. Hazel, *The Power of Persuasion* (Kansas City: Sheed and Ward, 1989), 14–29.

20. W. A. Linkugel and E. C. Buehler, *Speech Communication for the Contemporay Student* (New York: Harper and Row, 1975), 70–78; B. E. Bradley, *Fundamentals of Speech Communications: The Credibility of Ideas* (Dubuque: Brown, 1974), 134–52; K. Burke, *A Rhetoric of Motives* (New York: Prentice-Hall, 1950), 55, stress the importance of identifying with the audience.

they enjoy what they are doing, because their friends do it, or because they misinterpret the message.

When Jehoshaphat visited Ahab, the two kings decided to recapture the city of Ramoth-gilead (1 Kings 22:1–4). After receiving a promise of victory from the four hundred prophets in Ahab's court, Jehoshaphat wanted to hear what a prophet of Yahweh would say. Micaiah, the prophet of God, claimed that Israel would be scattered and be like sheep without a shepherd (1 Kings 22:17); that is, Ahab would die, and the nation would be leaderless. Ahab refused to believe Micaiah's negative prediction and put the prophet in prison. Micaiah was not trusted because he never said anything positive about Ahab (1 Kings 22:8, 18). The king believed that God spoke to the four hundred prophets who predicted victory. Micaiah communicated God's words, and they were fulfilled (1 Kings 22:29–36). These true words, however, did not help Ahab because he would not believe them.

The human and the Divine mysteriously interact in the decision-making process. God sends His messengers to assist in the spiritual battles for the allegiance of all who listen. In the end, individuals are responsible for their actions because each person can choose to accept or resist God's prompting.

The Possibility of Persuasion

Many actions can improve the likelihood of success in communication. Messengers cannot control all the factors which bring about a changed life, but when God sends a messenger to deliver a message, He usually provides an opportunity to persuade the listener. Following the basic principles of effective persuasion makes transformation possible.

Of course, the prophets had no classes on persuasive techniques or communication theory like preachers have today. They naturally observed the culturally defined rhetorical patterns that parents, friends, politicians, teachers, and religious leaders used to convince others to change. One prophet was a better persuader than another; some audiences were more open to new ideas than others; at times God's convicting power moved with greater force than at other times. Although success was not totally dependent on the prophet's skills, the messenger played a pivotal role in the persuasion process. Since the attitudes of the listeners, the personalities of the prophets, and the controversial issues differed, the prophetic messengers used a variety of persuasive techniques. Nevertheless, some common factors influence most persuasive encounters.

Understanding the Audience Permits Persuasion

Since their audiences lived in diverse circumstances, prophets needed to know something about the cultural behavior, beliefs, needs, and attitudes of the audience to speak intelligently to them.[21] What were their political leanings? Did the people have a need for peace and security? Did they honor Israel's God and believe that He was in control of nature? Did they see nothing wrong with praying to God and also enjoying the sensuous ritual at Baal temples?

These factors carry varying weights of influence on the persuasion process. Central beliefs, strong interests, core values, and physical needs were harder to change than peripheral values, nonessential needs, momentary interests, or socio-psychological needs.[22] Persuasive interaction, logical argumentation, and demonstrating the truthfulness of a claim can bring about change, so the wise speaker becomes aware of the audience to increase the potential for transformation.

When Elijah went to persuade Ahab to recognize Yahweh rather than Baal, he needed to understand the attitudes and behavior of his audience. He could not destroy his credibility by accusing them of worshiping Ra, the Egyptian sun

---

21. Baird, *Speaking for Results,* 35–43, defines and explains the significance of each factor.

22. M. Rokeach, *Beliefs, Attitudes, and Values* (San Francisco: Jossey Bass, 1968) discusses some of these key motivational factors, while Ehninger, Gronbeck, McKerrow and Monroe, *Principles and Types of Speech Communication,* 106–7, explain Maslow's hierarchy of needs.

god, because no one in his audience believed in this god. He needed to know the weaknesses of their worldview in order to demonstrate God's superiority in a convincing way.[23]

Elijah was aware of Ahab's marriage to Jezebel, the daughter of the king of Sidon. He knew Ahab built a temple to Baal in the city of Samaria (1 Kings 16:29–34). Elijah approached Ahab in the context of a three year drought that had already undermined the power of Baal, the fertility god (1 Kings 17:1; 18:1). The people were hungry not only for grain but also for the blessings of the god/God who controlled the rain. Elijah demonstrated fairness by setting up equal sacrificial situations for Baal and Yahweh. Everyone agreed to the appropriateness of the challenge (1 Kings 18:23–24). Elijah strengthened the effectiveness of his case by soaking his wood and sacrifice with water (1 Kings 18:33–35) before the lightning from heaven consumed the sacrifice, wood, altar stones, and water (1 Kings 18:38). Elijah's case was further supported by God's answer to his prayer for rain. The people who heard what Elijah said and saw what God did were persuaded to confess, "The Lord, He is God" (v. 39). The message and the miraculous drama supporting it directly affected those who were willing to change their thinking.

Evidence that Supports the Claim, Produces Persuasion

Most people need a reason to change their behavior or beliefs. An emotional appeal to fear, a promise of reward, trust in the integrity of a friend, or the logical relationship between cause and effect may motivate a person to accept another person's claims.[24] People are often easily persuaded on minimal evidence when the issues are not that central to the person's identity or belief system. It is extremely difficult to change a person's opinion about things that are integral

23. L. Bronner, *The Stories of Elijah and Elisha* (Leiden: Brill, 1968).

24. Motivational theory is discussed in D. McClelland, *Human Motivation* (Glenview: Scott, Foresman, 1985); J. Houston, *Motivation* (New York: Macmillan, 1985).

to one's core beliefs. The reasons that carry the greatest impact vary from person to person and culture to culture. Thus what appears to be logical and persuasive evidence to one person will be irrelevant to someone in another cultural context.

Aristotle believed that rhetoric brought persuasion through ethos, pathos, and logos.[25] Ethos relates to the credibility of the person speaking; pathos refers to the emotional appeal of the speaker; while logos describes the logical nature of the argumentation. Although logic is often associated with syllogisms or truth tables, this view is too restricted for understanding social relationships. Since persuasive conversations often omit assumptions or leave certain premises unstated, the logical connections are not always obvious or explicit.[26] Although some rhetorical arguments can be broken down to a claim (Israel is sinful) based on evidence (Israelites worship Baal) that is supported by a warrant (the worship of Baal is sinful),[27] the transformation of the listener is not assured by including each of these items. People can stubbornly reject a tightly knit logical argument for changing behavior, while on another occasion they might quickly change on the basis of rather flimsy evidence. Persuasion is a communicative process that is heavily weighted by the evidence that supports the claims of the messenger, but the effect of the arguments are dependent on their acceptability into the world view and social setting of the listener.

Prophetic oracles frequently attempted to motivate people to change their thoughts and actions by giving a series of reasons why they should transform their actions. The logical reason why the political and religious leaders of Jerusalem

---

25. Aristotle, *Rhetoric*, I. 2.

26. Aristotle, *Rhetoric*, I. 2, called the looser logic of rhetorical arguments enthymemes to contrast them with the syllogisms of a strict logical approach.

27. This model is explained in D. Ehninger, *Influence, Belief and Argumentation: An Introduction to Responsible Persuasion* (Glenview, Ill.: Scott, Foresman and Co., 1974), 10–89, or S. Toulmin, *The Uses of Argument* (Cambridge: Univ. Press, 1958), 97–104.

should believe Micah's predictions was the evidence against them. Because they abhorred justice, shed innocent blood, were violent, accepted bribes, and performed religious duties for a price, God would destroy the city of Jerusalem (Mic. 3). Using a little different logic, Haggai encouraged his listeners to continue building the temple by reminding them that God's Spirit was with them; He would shake the political powers that stopped the building progress and would fill the temple with glory (Hag. 2:4–9).

The prophet Amos presented the case for the judgment of Judah with a fairly logical argument (Amos 2:4–5). His introductory, "Thus says the Lord," identified the authority behind his message. The evidence for his claim that God would punish Judah was based on "three transgressions of Judah and four" (2:4). To further substantiate his general evidence, Amos specified the type of transgressions ("because they have rejected the law of the Lord and did not keep his statutes; but their lying leaders led them astray")[28] and spelled out the punishment the nation would experience ("I will send fire on Judah and it will consume the palace-fortresses of Jerusalem"). In this case the logic made sense, and Amos's Israelite audience was easily persuaded.

Many types of evidence are persuasive, but not all are logical. The discussion of how social pressure legitimates the acceptance of behavior, values, and other cultural patterns is examined in the next chapter.

The Spirit Brings Change

The prophets knew that effective communication was ultimately dependent on the work of God's Spirit in the heart of the speaker and the listener. Micah said very little about how this mysterious power operated in the listener, but he knew that he was "filled with power, with the Spirit of the Lord, with justice and courage to declare to Jacob his rebellion" (Mic. 3:8). This was an "indefinable extension of [God's] personality which enabled him to exercise a myste-

28. G. V. Smith, *Amos* (Grand Rapids: Zondervan, 1989), 77, 80.

rious influence upon mankind."[29] Most passages do not identify a direct causal link between the Spirit and the prophet's power and courage, but a connection is implied in some cases (1 Kings 22:23; Ezek. 11:5).

The Spirit also had a key role in the life of the listener. Ezekiel realized that God's Spirit would transform lives in the future. God "will put a new spirit within them" (Ezek. 11:19–20) and take away their stubborn heart of stone. After years of disobedience, the Spirit will "cause you to walk in my statutes" (Ezek. 36:27). No matter how technically competent, communication will not persuade people unless the Spirit is actively producing an openness to the ideas that are communicated and a conviction that change is necessary.

Theological and Social Implications

God's messengers today are sent to transform the way people think and act. The messenger must listen to the way people talk about their world so that the cross-cultural, cross-generational, and cross-economic barriers do not inhibit the transfers of ideas. The messenger must be a credible witness in the subculture where the message is delivered. Thus one would dress differently, use different illustrations, and employ different logical arguments to gain acceptance in different groups. Social acceptance of ideas that are not popular in society will rarely take place if the arguments for them are not well supported. Messengers need to realize that success in preaching ultimately depends on the Holy Spirit, but that is no excuse for sloppy communication skills.[30]

The hermeneutical task of interpreting the prophets involves not only the analysis of their theology but also their so-

29. A. R. Johnson, *The One and the Many in the Israelite Conception of God* (Cardiff: Univ. of Wales, 1961), 16.

30. L.M. Perry, *Biblical Preaching for Today's World* (Chicago: Moody, 1973), 160; Baumann, *Contemporary Preaching,* 277–90; D. L. Hamilton, *Homiletical Handbook* (Nashville: Broadman Press, 1992), 19–29; R. A. Mohler, Jr., "A Theology of Preaching" *Handbook of Contemporary Preaching,* ed. Michael Duduit (Nashville: Broadman Press, 1992), 13–20.

cial interaction with their audiences through communication. Their messages were not lifeless abstract dissertations on hypothetical issues. They were talking to real people about what they should do, how they should think, and why they should transform their lives. By witnessing their methods of communication, today's messengers can learn how to persuade people in our culture.

Questions for Discussion

1. Describe why you might reject the message of a person from another religion.
2. Explain why you might be open to accepting the ideas described in this chapter.
3. What might you do to increase your credibility if you were speaking to: (a) a group of teenagers; (b) a Muslim?
4. Why do you sometimes have difficulty communicating with people from a different generation?
5. What role does the Spirit play in decision making?

Chapter 2

The Social Dimensions of Transformation

People may decide to study more, to exercise regularly, to save money every month, or to stop some bad habit. Even though the decision to make a new start is made in complete seriousness, often the process of transforming behavior ends in frustration. This may be due not to unwillingness or stubbornness, but to a failure to incorporate the new practice into their present world. Integration requires the acceptance of a new behavior into the existing social context.

When a person persuasively communicates a message to an audience, a potential for change exists. When the listeners become aware of the message and accept the arguments of the messenger, the process of transformation can begin. Change usually does not happen instantly. Transforming the way people think and act is a complex process which may involve redefining an entire worldview and readjusting social relationships. Sometimes change is welcomed, but at other times it is difficult and painful.

Even if people are persuaded that they ought to tell the truth, it will be hard to break the habit of telling little white lies. They are part of the way some people have always thought; they are acceptable social behavior among friends. It is hard to change because fabricated stories protect oneself and one's friends from embarrassment. Attempts to change may bring such strong social disapproval that people will do what they know is wrong to maintain their relationships with others.

When the prophets tried to persuade the people of Judah to reject their evil ways and return to God, they faced some of the same issues. Their audiences had a different way of looking at reality; their cultural context gave social approval to behavior patterns the prophets rejected. The prophets described these changes as repentance, a rejection of the old ways, and the creation of a new heart (Jer. 3:13; Ezek. 11:19). God empowered these spiritual transformations, but they required changes in human relationships which sometimes frustrated God's work.

To understand the human side of the process of transformation, it is necessary to look at the social setting of the prophetic messengers and their audiences so that one can trace the dynamic process of change. This will reveal how each group described its culture and structured its society. Knowledge of the roles people play and an understanding of social stratification will show how transformation interrupts previously established cultural norms and existing social relationships.

The Growing Concern About Social Context

Most early studies of the prophets contained remarks about the historical setting of individual prophets and an occasional comment about the social evils the prophets condemned (Amos 2:6–8; Mic. 7:1–6).[1] Few included an analysis

1. G. A. Smith, *The Book of the Twelve Prophets* I (New York: Armstrong, 1906), 136–37.

of how the prophet's social location affected a particular message or what social role the prophet filled in Israelite society. The organization of Israelite society, the nature of social interaction, and the social implications of prophetic calls for transformation were not addressed.

Form Critical Contributions

Gunkel's form critical studies included a study of the social setting (*Sitz im Leben*) of various types of literature, as well as the social location of the prophets who used these literary works at a later time.[2] This led Mowinckel to place some prophets (Joel, Habakkuk, and Isaiah) in the temple beside the priests at a hypothetical New Year Festival where Yahweh was crowned king.[3] Von Waldow connects the salvation oracles in Isaiah with a temple setting, while Reventlow thinks Jeremiah was a covenant mediator in the temple.[4]

Wolff connects Hosea's social background to Levitical circles, Micah to the elders of the city of Moresheth, and Amos to clan wisdom.[5] Gerstenberger finds a connection between the woe oracle and wisdom literature, while Whedbee sees a strong wisdom influence in Isaiah.[6] These studies hypothesize significant social connections, but they are sometimes based on minimal amounts of evidence and do not

---

2. H. Gunkel, "Fundamental Problems of Hebrew Literary History," *What Remains of the Old Testament* (London: Allen and Unwin, 1928), 60–62.

3. H. S. Mowinckel, *The Psalms in Israel's Worship* II (Nashville: Abingdon, 1962), 53–73. The prophetic connection with worship at the temple was further supported by A. R. Johnson, *The Cultic Prophet in Ancient Israel* (Cardiff: University of Wales, 1944) and A. Haldar, *Association of Cult Prophets Among the Ancient Semites* (Uppsala: Almqvist and Wiksell, 1945).

4. H. E. Von Waldow, *Anlass und Hintergrund der Verkündigung des Deuterojesja,* Dissertation, Bonn, 1953; H. Reventlow, *Liturgie und Prophetisches Ich bei Jeremia* (Gütersloh: G. Mohn, 1963).

5. H. W. Wolff, "Hoseas geistige Heimat," *TLZ* 91 (1956), 83–94, and *Micah the Prophet* (Philadelphia: Westminster, 1981), 3–25.

6. E. Gerstenberger, "The Woe-Oracle in the Prophets," *JBL* 81 (1962), 249–63, and J. W. Whedbee, *Isaiah and Wisdom* (Nashville: Abingdon, 1971).

address the social changes required in the transformation process.

Sociological Inquiries

Wilson's comparative anthropological study of the nature of prophetic activity, the social location, and the social function of the prophets makes several important advances.[7] Using comparative material, Wilson examines the characteristic behavior of spirit possession and stereotypical behavior patterns. He emphasizes the role that a support group plays in recognizing an intermediary.[8] He adopts the anthropological distinction between central and peripheral intermediaries.

The Social Function of Prophets
Central Intermediaries
- support the ruling political and cultic policies
- maintain social stability
- want gradual change in social order
Peripheral Intermediaries
- oppose those in power
- call for radical social changes
- want immediate justice for the powerless [a]

a. Wilson, *Prophecy and Society*, 69–73, 83.

Wilson's testing of this reconstruction in his treatment of Ephraimite (Israelite) and Judean prophecy follows earlier critical reconstructions and do not relate these sociological insights to the prophetic transformation of Israelite culture through persuasive communication.

Petersen's sociological study of the role of the prophets casts doubts on some of Wilson's conclusions. In contrast to

7. R. R. Wilson, *Prophecy and Society in Ancient Israel* (Philadelphia: Fortress, 1980), 2.

8. Ibid., 32–51, 58–59.

Wilson, Petersen thinks that few prophets had support groups. Petersen prefers to talk of levels of role involvement (from full to noninvolvement) to describe the conduct of a person in a social setting. Petersen divides prophets into central and peripheral and connects prophetic titles to these roles.[9]

Name	Role	Place
"man of God"	peripheral role	Israelite
"prophet"	central role	Israelite
"seer"	central role	Judean

Petersen, like Wilson, connects these prophets to different traditions by adopting earlier critical conclusions. (Mosaic tradition is Israelite and Davidic tradition is Judean).[10]

Hanson's study of the rise of the apocalyptic movement recognizes that different groups had different ways of looking at the world along with distinctive religious beliefs which supported their own social status.[11] He employs Mannheim's contrast between a) the "ideological" thinking of the ruling class which focused on self-preservation, and b) the "utopian" mentality of the disadvantaged who hoped for the end of present inequities and the creation of their own vision of social order.[12] Hanson's examination of Isaiah, Ezekiel, and Zechariah distinguishes between a) the ruling Zadokite

9. D. L. Petersen, *The Roles of Israel's Prophets* in *JSOTSup* 17 (Sheffield: JSOT Press, 1981), 44–45, 64–69. He follows ideas from I. Lewis, *Ecstatic Religion: An Anthropological Study of Spirit Possession and Shamanism* (Harmondsworth: Penguin, 1971).

10. Petersen, *Roles of Israel's Prophets,* 70–71, 79–84. See J. Muilenburg, "The 'Office' of the Prophet in Ancient Israel," *The Bible in Modern Scholarship,* ed. J. Hyatt (New York: Abingdon, 1965), 229–49.

11. M. Weber, *Sociology of Religion* (Boston: Beacon, 1964), 46–67, 106; P. D. Hanson, *The Dawn of Apocalyptic* (Philadelphia: Fortress, 1975), 214.

12. K. Mannheim, *Ideology and Utopia, An Introduction to the Sociology of Knowledge* (New York: Harcourt, Brace and Co., 1936), 40; See Hanson, *Dawn of Apocalyptic,* 213.

priests who supported the restoration program in Ezekiel 40—48, and b) the disenfranchised visionary Levites whose apocalyptic ideas were found in Isaiah 60—62. Those in power were pragmatists who regulated the cultic life of the nation in order to maintain their privileged holy position, while the reforming visionaries wanted the whole nation to share in this holy status.

Using concepts from Berger and Luckmann's approach to the sociology of knowledge, Brueggemann sees the prophetic message as a radical liberating response to the royal consciousness that arose during the monarchy. Solomon's establishment of a bureaucratic and militaristic empire (based on heavy taxation) led to oppression, the development of an affluent class, and the establishment of a static religion that functioned to support the political interests of those in power.[13] The prophetic message imagined an alternative of economic equality, justice, and accessibility to God. The prophetic role involved criticizing the royal consciousness, expressing grief over the bankruptcy of its view of life, and imagining the possibility of a new alternative through God's power.[14] Applying this schema to the canonical shape of Isaiah, Brueggemann saw Isaiah critiquing the self-serving royal ideology of the powerful in 1—39. The prophet embraced the pain of the oppressed and returned to past traditions for comfort in 40—55, and then released social imagination to envisage the world from an alternative perspective of freedom in 56—66.[15]

Developing a Sociological Methodology

Not all fields of sociological research interact with issues of the social setting and its structural order, the function

13. W. Brueggemann, *The Prophetic Imagination* (Philadelphia: Fortress, 1978); See P. L. Berger and T. Luckmann, *The Social Construction of Reality: A Treatise in the Sociology of Knowledge* (Garden City: Doubleday, 1966).

14. Brueggemann, *The Prophetic Imagination* (Philadelphia: Fortress, 1978), 44–79.

15. W. Brueggemann, "Unity and Dynamic in the Isaiah Tradition," *JSOT* 29 (1984), 89–107.

which tradition plays in legitimating behavior, and how new theological ideas bring about transformation. Biblical scholars have usually chosen a single sociological method of looking at social life (Marxist, structuralist, behavioralist, conflict, or interactionist theory) and then applied it to a portion of the Bible. This approach enhances inner consistency, limits research to a defined area, and provides a diagnostic tool to attack a specific problem (role theory, ecstatic behavior, social stratification, etc.). The danger is that one may try to explain too much on the basis of a theory designed to deal with only a limited area of social reality. Since no one theory deals with all aspects of the social world (some focus on the structural system of society while others treat conflict and interaction), Fredrichs proposes a multiple-paradigm approach.[16] Ritzer concludes that the multiple-paradigms should include theories that deal with various levels of social reality:

1. Objective social structures and systems (law, class, roles)
2. Social action and subjective reality (ideas, values)
3. Macro-sociological issues (group generalizations)
4. Micro-sociological matters (individual behavior)[17]

Another concern is the tension between theories that emphasize social determinism and those that allow human freedom and creativity. One needs to employ theories that deal with human behavior from the subjective side that permit human freedom, as well as the objective side that exert deterministic social pressure on behavior.[18] Berger and

16. R. Fredrichs, *A Sociology of Sociology* (New York: Free Press, 1970).

17. G. Ritzer, *Toward an Integrated Sociological Paradigm* (Boston: Allyn and Bacon, 1981), and *Contemporary Sociological Theory* (New York: Knopf, 1983), 306–12.

18. J. Turner finds a convergence between T. Parsons' functionalism and H. Blumer's symbolic interactionism. R. Collins's approach to conflict borrows insights from Weber, Marx, Durkheim, and phenomenologists. R. Collins, *Conflict Sociology* (New York: Academic Press, 1975), 1–45.

Luckmann, whose work will be a major source for the methodology used in this study, attempt to develop a multiple-paradigm approach.[19]

However, adopting sociological principles brings potential dangers as well as benefits. On the positive side stands the prospect of obtaining a more complete picture of Israelite prophets. An uncritical use of sociology can lead to misunderstandings and reductionistic tendencies. Since everyone employs a combination of recognized and hidden assumptions, it is important to test new approaches with caution, openness, and attention to the underlying theory.[20] As long as theoretical principles serve rather than rule the interpreter's analysis, they play a beneficial role.

The Sociology of Knowledge

The sociology of knowledge as developed by Berger and Luckmann is the starting point for the methodology applied to the Hebrew prophets in this study. Their phenomenological approach is a part of a larger group of methodologies called the "sociologies of everyday life."[21] They focus on inter-

19. Berger, *Social Construction,* 16–18, uses Mead's contribution to symbolic interactionism, the phenomology of A. Schutz, and the studies of Weber, Marx, and Durkheim. G. Ritzer, *Contemporary Sociological Theory,* 209–12, does not believe that Berger and Luckmann were very successful in their attempt to integrate these different approaches.

20. G. A. Herion, "The Impact of Modern and Social Science Assumptions on the Reconstruction of Israelite History," *JSOT* 34 (1986), 6–7, 11–14, critiqued the tendency to let theory control the data rather than allowing the data to modify the theory.

21. J. D. Douglas, ed., *The Sociologies of Everyday Life* (Boston: Allyn and Bacon, 1980) provides a survey and evaluation of the various approaches within the sociology of everyday life. Four or five *sub-methods* are found within this broad approach to sociology: symbolic interactionism, labeling theory, dramaturgical analysis, phenomenology and ethnomethodology, and existential sociology. These approaches are a response to weakness in structural-functionalist sociologists.

Phenomenology is a philosophical approach which relies on an individual's own conscious view of the phenomena of life and tries not to cloud it with a foreign, possibly prejudiced modern or western interpretation. E. Herssurl is the founder of this philosophy, and A. Schutz, *The Phenomenology of the Social World* (Evanston: Northwestern Univ. Press, 1967) developed the sociological use of phenomenology.

action between people in everyday life, with what people think and do, and in the meanings that people themselves give to interaction. They believe that meanings are partially regulated by a commonly accepted stock of knowledge and partially open to individual (unpredictable or new) ideas or behavior.

Three central dialectical concepts govern the development of social order and the transformation of thinking and behavior in Berger and Luckmann's approach.

1. People become aware that the subjective meanings that people give to their sociocultural setting are part ofobjective reality (the social process of objectivication).
2. People accept the socially defined objective reality around them as their own view of the world (the social process of internalization).
3. People themselves create and project new meanings, thus changing the understanding of reality (the social process of externalization).[22]

At this point the process repeats itself, for these new ideas are objectified and then internalized by other people. This approach maintains that common everyday knowledge of the world is primarily derived through social interaction with the existing cultural definitions (social determinism), but that people can be innovative, creative, and propose new meanings (individual freedom). Although Berger and Luckmann try to be integrative, in actuality they emphasize the individual subjective nature of social life and say little about large-scale objective social structures or human externalization.

1. Objective Reality: The Social Setting

Socially constructing a view of reality. Because knowledge of objects, language, and institutions is primarily derived through social interaction with other members of one's

22. Berger, *Social Construction,* 61.

group, each person's understanding of the world is initially defined by what is meaningful to the group. *Objectification* is the social process of becoming aware of the subjective meaning that other people give to the objects, linguistic symbols, and institutionalized patterns of behavior in a social setting.[23] This learning process allows the child to identify the various parts of the environment and to name each part. Parents and siblings teach the common facts of everyday life: "This is dirt which you should not eat; those things flying in the sky are birds." This knowledge enables the person to understand the world of that society—their "socially constructed view of reality." This means that an interpretation of a prophet's behavior or message must be based on the prophet's and his audience's cultural objectifications about their world.

The prophets interacted with the knowledge they shared with their audiences. Isaiah referred to a donkey and ox, drew on the cultural view that these were not smart animals, and then created an analogy contrasting the wisdom of dumb animals with Israel's foolish rejection of God (1:3). He and his audience shared a common language that gave meaning to these objects and ideas.

Similar yet different views of reality. Social pressure encourages a unified view of a group's objective world but each person's experience with nature, with other people, and with God/the gods is different. This meant that each person operated both on the basis of unique individual understandings of objective reality and on the basis of the dominant cultural worldview. The meaning attached to parts of reality varied according to the role, social status, occupation, and outlook of parents and peers. On account of this, a prophet's socially constructed view of the world was partially consistent with the prevailing cultural climate of the day, yet uniquely different from every other person.

Both Elijah and the worshipers of Baal believed a divine power sent rain. Elijah thought Yahweh, the God of Israel, was responsible for rain (1 Kings 17:1–7; 18:1–2,41–46),

23. Ibid., 21–22, 35–38.

while the prophets of Baal claimed that Baal was in charge of fertility and rain. To understand this story, the interpreter needs to appreciate the prophet's knowledge of the world, how his perspective differed from his audience, and the dynamic interaction of these conflicting ideas.[24]

Roles and institutions. In the process of learning about the socio-cultural world, each person discovers that humans order life into typical structured patterns of behavior to make sense out of the enormous amount of information they interact with every day. Data concerning nature, social interaction, and religious beliefs are categorized in different ways. When these habitual ways of doing things become part of a group's structured order of objective reality, they are "institutionalized."[25] Although institutionalized patterns are very powerful, an individual can choose to exhibit deviant behavior.

Berger and Luckmann focus on the individual *process* of objectification rather than the structures of society, which are the *results* of objectification (a structural-functionalist emphasis).[26] This is partially due to their opposition to conceiving any part of reality as a nonhuman creation.[27] However, people may not know about the process of forming laws, roles, or worship practices in the past. Some will understand that these are humanly created institutions, while others (young children) will not. Part of the prophets' and the sociologists' role is to unmask the binding cultural forces, to free

---

24. L. Bonner, *The Stories of Elijah and Elisha as Polemics Against Baal Worship* (Leiden: Brill, 1968).

25. Berger, *Social Construction,* 53–55, has a very broad (and unusual) view of institutions because he believes they can refer to the mutual acceptance (thus it has control over action) of typical patterns of behavior (defined by past behavior) by at least two people rather than a group. I do not follow Berger and Luckmann but believe it is a group practice.

26. Ibid., 47–88.

27. For example, Berger accepts marriage as a humanly agreed upon arrangement between two families or persons, but he rejects the reification of marriage as a false elevation of an element of culture into a structure (natural or divine) that is beyond human control. See Berger, *Social Construction,* 88–91.

people to act creatively and responsibly, not as powerless pawns.

Common knowledge about the structure of society gives unity and security to social interaction because everyone in the group knows what is expected and accepted. Instead of being bombarded with random and chaotic data, the thousand phenomena of life are ordered into patterns that function in ways meaningful to that cultural group. This is particularly true in interpersonal relationships where people take on typical role patterns of behavior within each institution that a society establishes.[28] Even a person's identity is related to the roles that person embodies (for example, a father role), and interpersonal relationships are circumscribed by role expectations. If people were not aware of male roles, female roles, leadership roles, or religious roles, they would have no social order. Interpersonal relationships would be in chaos. Children might demand to be treated as adults, or fathers might act like unmarried men. Society and culture are ordered on the basis of a common acceptance of well-defined role patterns.

Each prophet's writings reveal the way life was ordered around structured role expectations. References to economic, religious, and social behavior assume an accepted way of doing things. The roles of the king, priest, prophet, and rich person follow set guidelines accepted in that time period. The prophets criticized the priests who failed to carry out their role or follow institutionalized religious patterns (Mal. 1:6—2:9).

2. Subjective Reality: The Internalization of Legitimate Traditions

The role of language. Subjective thinking and interpretation are possible because people are self-conscious and gifted with the ability to use language.[29] Language enables people

28. Petersen, *Roles of Israel's Prophets,* 16–34, or J. P. and M. L. Hewitt, *Introducing Sociology* (Englewood Cliffs, N.J.: Prentice-Hall, 1986), 45–50.

29. A brief survey of G. H. Mead's *Mind, Self and Society* is given in Ritzer, *Contemporary Sociological Theory,* 162–66. It has served as a foundation for Berger and Luckmann as well as those of the school of Symbolic Interactionism.

to (a) identify and remember the phenomena of objective reality, (b) interact socially on the basis of commonly accepted linguistic signs, (c) legitimate a group's institutional patterns, and (d) conceptualize the symbolic universe (abstract or philosophical thinking), including transcendent forms of reality beyond the concrete forms people see and touch.

The world is understood first (and most fundamentally) when a group develops a common way of describing the phenomena of its experience. To internalize a shared knowledge of objective reality, a group must agree to designate certain linguistic signs (its language) to represent objects, actions, and institutional patterns. By internalizing these meanings, a child accepts a group's meanings into its subjective world. Because of language, people can meaningfully discuss both tradition (what happened many years ago) and experience (what went on yesterday at a friend's house). Because of language, people can also think, choose, abstract, and imagine new things.

Dreams, parables, or drama represent a second level of subjective reality, the world of make-believe. Although a nightmare may seem real while a person is asleep, as soon as that person wakes up, it becomes obvious that the dream was all in the mind. Abstract philosophical thinking and religious experience are part of a third level of reality, called the "symbolic universe." This knowledge transcends the natural order and includes spirits, God/gods, and abstract economic, social, and philosophical theorizing.[30] The symbolic universe legitimates a group's view of the world. It enables a group to (a) maintain its worldview, (b) integrate the various components of its worldview, and (c) explain or justify behavior.[31]

The prophet Habakkuk had philosophical beliefs about the way God ruled the world. These abstractions formed a unified way of thinking, a symbolic universe that provided clues for interpreting daily life. Because unjudged political violence in his society could not be explained or integrated into his theory of divine justice, he cried out to God for an

30. Berger, *Social Construction,* 92–104.
31. Ibid., 92–96.

explanation (Hab. 1:1–4). Other prophets tried to transform their audience's thinking by showing that their symbolic universe was based on faulty thinking (Jer. 7:1–15).

Legitimation brings internalization. Every social context contains both patterns which order behavior and oral or written traditions that justify them (their legitimations). Legitimations cause people to internalize a group's view of objective reality and make it their own. For a child, a person's say-so is enough to legitimate acceptance of the view that fire is dangerous. Later in life, it may take threats or logical arguments to legitimate behavioral change. Legitimations include traditions that explain how and why the group's ancestors established an institutional pattern (the tradition about Adam and Eve in Genesis 2 justifies marriage patterns), or myths that link the changes of the seasons with the activity of the gods (the Baal and Anath epic from Ugarit).[32] These traditions exert a powerful force on individuals, causing them to internalize the group's cultural meanings. Each group, of course, has its own traditions which legitimate their cultural patterns it accepts.[33]

When discussing these issues, Berger and Luckmann seem to place an unbalanced amount of weight on the influence of society in determining meanings, defining institutions, and regulating social interaction. They place too little emphasis on human freedom. The prophets indicate that humans have the ability to innovate, imagine, choose, and modify their behavior and thinking.[34] Berger "brackets out"

32. J. B. Pritchard, ed., *ANET* (Princeton Univ., 1954), 129–41.

33. Berger, *Social Construction,* 61, 71, 92.

34. P. Berger, *Invitation to Sociology: A Humanistic Perspective* (Garden City, New York: Doubleday, 1963), 122–50, deals with the problem of freedom. He sees signs of freedom in a person's choosing between world-views, the subjective need to accept objectifications, deviance, role distancing, and "bad faith." Nevertheless, he was skeptical of claims of freedom and does not give genius and true innovations much of a place in his approach. Berger admits that one can postulate freedom in those who "step outside" (he calls this "ecstasy") the normal expectations of social order, but claims that it is impossible to demonstrate freedom scientifically. This criticism is not true of all who use the sociology of knowledge. For example, see W. Stark, *The Sociology of Knowledge* (Glencoe: Free Press, 1958), xi, 141–45.

human freedom because of his phenomenological approach, but this is inconsistent with most people's perception of everyday life. Adults may perform routine social expectations without much thinking or creativity (social determinism), but people do freely choose to accept cultural viewpoints or interpret life in new ways (social freedom). Some individuals are more secure and willing to risk rejection by challenging conventional ideas, while others are more traditional. Social conditions (education, travel, economic status), sex, religion, age (teenagers tend to assert their freedom), and cultural ideals (some cultures value new ideas) have a role in influencing each person's response to social patterns and their own freedom.

The power of tradition and experience. One of the prophet's roles was to legitimate a particular way of thinking and acting, one consistent with God's view of reality (a part of their symbolic universe). The prophets used two major methods to legitimate their worldview. First, the prophets retold past traditions: for example, God's power in creating the world occurs in Isaiah 40:25–26 (possibly using tradition from Gen. 1:16; Ps. 89:11; 147:4); the garden of Eden is a key idea in Isaiah 51:3 (see Gen. 2:8–10); God's acts of judgment on Sodom appear in Isaiah 13:19 (see Gen. 19:24–25; Deut. 29:23); and allusions to the flood are in Isaiah 54:9 (see Gen. 9:11, 15). These traditions explain the Israelite way of life, justify various cultural practices, and integrate the past with the present, the divine with the human, and the individual parts of life with the whole. The prophet was attempting to transform the people's thinking by renewing their minds according to God's standards (see Rom. 12:2).

A second method of legitimating a group's view of reality was to appeal to experience. Isaiah condemned trust in idols because they cannot tell about the past or the future, or do anything good or evil (Isa. 41:21–24; 44:6–8). Experience dictates that idols are merely pieces of wood, fashioned by humans. One piece of a tree was made into an idol, but the rest of the tree was burned. Experience proves that trees cannot answer prayers (Isa. 44:9–22). Idols cannot even walk;

they have to be carried. Idols cannot speak or deliver from disaster (Isa. 45:5–7); but God makes plans, tells what the future will be, and then does it (Isa. 45:9–11). Because Israel's God appeared to Moses at the burning bush (Ex. 3) and His glory and voice were seen and heard at Mount Sinai (Ex. 20; Deut. 5), the Israelites experienced God as a person and as a real power.

Communicating legitimations persuasively. In convincing the Israelites to internalize the divine perspective, the prophets employed traditional forms of speech which the people understood. If a prophet chose to use the covenant lawsuit form (Mic. 6), the various components of the speech would be partially dictated by the traditional socio-cultural understanding of the secular lawsuit in the court. The content, however, would be tailored to God's lawsuit against Israel for breaking the patterns set down in the nation's covenant with God. The prophet Micah used the nation's traditions of God's care for Israel (Mic. 6:3–5, see the traditions in Ex. 3—4; 14—15; Num. 22—24) to show that the people's view of God's requirements (Mic. 6:6–7) were not consistent with His demands (Mic. 6:8). Micah said that the cultural pattern they used was missing the key ingredients (justice, lovingkindness, and humility). An understanding of the forms of speech from Israel's cultural setting and the theological traditions within them provide a background for explaining the prophet's method of communication.

These prophetic messages were needed because of (a) problems caused by the development of the monarchy, (b) the urbanization and militarization of the nation, (c) the emergence of a wealthy upper class, and (d) the nation's contact with Canaanite religion and social institutions. With these changes came new moral values, altered role definitions, and a weakening of social solidarity among tribal members.

Many Israelites chose not to follow their fathers' traditional way of life. In response, the prophets tried to convince them to change their behavioral patterns and to transform their way of thinking about how the world really works.

Sometimes the prophets did not have many supporters,[35] however they did not allow their culture to determine the meaning of life, nor did they uncritically accept its social customs. Instead, they attempted to mold their society into a new form. The prophets gave new words of judgment and new messages of hope to bring about a new understanding of how God rules the world.

3. New Theological Understandings: Applying Externalizations to a Setting

People can produce a new understanding of reality; they can *externalize* new ideas or behaviors that are not determined by their social environment.[36] Thus, when the prophets spoke God's word, they not only called the people back to their theological roots (past tradition), they also introduced new ideas. They gave new meaning to words like *harlotry* (Hosea), a new understanding of a role (Jer. 23:9–40; Mic. 3:8), new perspectives on the meaning of covenant promises (Amos 3:1–2; 9:7), and new interpretations of institutionalized behavior patterns (Amos 5:21–24). Because the audience had the freedom to think about these new prophetic ideas, some accepted them (internalization), thus transforming their thinking and action.

The divine source of externalizations. The biblical text shows that the prophets thought not every aspect of life was determined by their historical and social setting.[37] In addition to social forces, there was personal genius, innovations,

35. Berger's discussion on the need for a "plausibility structure" for support may be generally true, but does not seem to hold for the innovative, imaginative, or religious pioneer. See Berger, *Social Construction,* 153–56.

36. Ibid., 104. His view of externalization is critiqued and expanded in an unpublished paper by W. M. Lafferty, "Externalization and Dialectics: Taking the Brackets Off Berger and Luckmann's Sociology of Knowledge," presented at the annual meeting of the American Sociological Association, August 26, 1975.

37. J. P. and M. L. Hewitt, *Introducing Sociology,* 88, and G. A. Herion, "The Impact of Science Assumptions," *JSOT* 34 (1986), 10–18, avoid the deterministic problems by allowing some individual freedom.

imagination, and free will, plus divine or demonic factors influencing people's action.

Any reference to God as a real force in human activity is a stumbling block for sociologists, for most social methodologies (including the sociology of knowledge) exclude God.[38] This is partially because sociologists see religion as a humanly constructed system of beliefs and practices. Most who believe in the God of the Bible might agree that this is true of ancient Mayan religion, but it is not true of their beliefs. This is because the divine origin of beliefs is always a matter of faith. Since sociology is a science that cannot prove or disprove the divine origin of religious beliefs, it should properly limit itself to describing what religious people believe and how they interact. Too many sociologists flatly state that God did not speak (a faith statement that sociology is unable to prove) and that religion is a projection of the human mind.[39] It is impossible for a social scientist to determine that God really did not act or that a prophetic word actually was not from God. It is not legitimate to ignore a person's convictions that a god/God has spoken, for these beliefs are a part of what motivates behavior in that person's worldview. Sociology should look at what an individual does and says in all areas of life and not make statements about ul-

---

38. For an extended discussion of these problems see: T. F. Best, "The Sociological Study of the New Testament: Promise or Peril," *Scottish Journal of Theology* 36 (1983), 181–94; B. W. Anderson, "Biblical Theology and Sociological Interpretation," *TToday* 42 (1985), 296–306; and R. Wilson, *Sociological Approaches to the Old Testament* (Philadelphia: Fortress, 1984), 28–29, 81–83. D. Tidball, *The Context of the New Testament: A Sociological Analysis* (Grand Rapids: Zondervan, 1984), 11–22, 137–42, discusses this issue in some detail and specifically refers to Berger's approach in the sociology of knowledge. In *The Sacred Canopy: Elements of a Sociological Theory of Religion* (Garden City: Doubleday, 1967), 175–88, Berger concludes that religion and God are human projections. His *A Rumor of Angels* (Garden City: Doubleday, 1969), 49–95, suggests there is something more beyond man, but it is only a rumor. Order, play, hope, justice, and humor are "signals of transcendent reality" in the empirical world of mankind. On page 88 he affirms the Old Testament conception of a wholly other God (not in man or in the natural reality of man).

39. Berger, *The Sacred Canopy*, 180, makes such a statement.

timate truth or faith claims. A fine line divides the legitimate task of unmasking or debunking false perceptions and the illegitimate task of denying the possible existence of transcendent reality.[40]

An analysis of the world of the prophets and their audiences cannot ignore their beliefs about God. Those beliefs determined people's understanding of their setting (God gave them the land), the development of social traditions (God designed their tradition), and their understanding of the future (God determines it). To understand a person's own cultural view, one must allow for an explanation that includes divine or demonic action. Berger and Luckmann's acknowledgment of the importance of the "symbolic universe" leaves room for including a divine view of reality within it. (Political, philosophical, and social legitimations are also part of the symbolic universe.)[41]

The need for externalizations. The prophets' new ideas were needed because the nation's historical situation was in constant flux due to political events. Weather changes caused yearly fluctuations in the economic prosperity of various subgroups, and statehood deteriorated tribal and family solidarity. Israel was impacted by increased religious and cultural influences from Phoenicia, Assyria, and Babylonia, plus the people's endemic rebellion against the discipline required to serve God.

As the prophet Hosea looked at his setting in Israel, he saw that the priests were leading the people astray by neglecting their priestly role (Hos. 4:4–10), the kings were depending on other nations instead of God (Hos. 7:8; 8:8–10), and the people were worshiping idols of Baal and involved in sacred prostitution (Hos. 4:11–15; 11:2; 13:1–2). The merchants were using deceitful scales to oppress the poor (Hos. 12:7–8). Hosea proclaimed that these practices were accepted because the people had no experiential knowledge of

40. R. Perkins, *Looking Both Ways: Exploring the Interface between Christianity and Sociology* (Grand Rapids: Baker, 1987), 1–39, and Berger, *Invitation to Sociology,* 38–39.

41. Berger, *Social Construction,* 92–128.

God. Their perception of His covenant stipulations was faulty, for the people had no love for God or truth, and no real commitment to their covenant relationship with God (Hos. 4:1). Because the nation's Mosaic traditions were no longer a guide for proper behavior, the nation internalized a Canaanite view of life that was inconsistent with God's past revelation. This change in Israel's beliefs caused a change in their relationship to God. Hosea did not accept the legitimations supporting Baalism. He externalized a fresh understanding of God's relationship to Israel.

His new message included both negative words of judgment and positive words of hope. Hosea believed that God withdrew from them because of their sin (Hos. 5:6). God would chasten them because they rejected a relationship with Him (Hos. 5:2). God would pour out wrath on them, and they would suffer the effects of a devastating war (Hos. 5:8–14; 2 Chron. 28). In addition to this negative message, Hosea added a positive word of hope concerning Israel's setting after their judgment. The nation will eventually acknowledge its guilt (internalizing Hosea's view) and seek God. They will return to God and know Him (Hos. 5:15—6:3; 14:1–8). These two messages described a future reality for the nation and explained why these new situations will come about.

This investigation into Hosea illustrates how interpreters can examine the objectifications in each audience's worldview to understand the socially constructed view of reality with which the prophets interacted. A study of the prophet's messages reveal externalizations which challenged the status quo of the day and suggested a new way of looking at life. These new ideas were legitimated through persuasive communication so that the audience would internalize God's message and transform their lives.

Theological and Social Implications

Changing people's lives begins with the messenger's persuasive communication of God's word (externalization). If the modern messenger is a credible person who can persuade an audience through logic and legitimate the message by drawing on accepted traditions or earlier experience, some people will alter their worldview and internalize the message. Since socially accepted cultural norms and behavior patterns naturally resist change, it is not always easy for those hearing the message to transform their old habits. Regardless of the response, the messenger must faithfully deliver the message, yet recognize that it is God who sovereignly works to produce results that will glorify His name.

Although our language, culture, and audiences are different from the prophets, the process of transformation is similar. We address audiences deeply influenced by the social mores and cultural understanding of modern life. Our audience's socially constructed view of reality is often at odds with God's Word and in need of transformation. The process of change begins when we externalize a new view of reality to our listener. When the audience becomes aware of God's ways (objectification), the Spirit of God can begin to speak to the listener's heart. If the claims of Scripture are legitimated and if we are credible messengers who communicate persuasively by identifying with the needs of our audience, some will internalize the message and establish a new relationship with God. This will transform these people's worldview and change their social behavior. They will reject old cultural patterns and roles and establish new habits and new social relationships.

Questions for Discussion

1. What could you say to legitimate the idea that God loves everyone?
2. What are the objectifications that have been accepted as part of the socially constructed worldview of the people in Hosea?
3. What externalization (the new idea) from God did Hosea speak?
4. How did the people's internalization of this message transform their behavior?

Divided Monarchies
Scale of Miles
0
25
50
Scale of Kilometers
0
25
50
75
Judah (Southern Kingdom)
Israel (Northern Kingdom)
Area Possibly Included under Israel's Control
Beirut
Phoenicia
Sidon
Damascus
Aram
Ijon
Mt. Hermon
Dan
Tyre
Kedesh
Hazor
Acco
Kinnereth
Sea of Kinnereth
Hannathon
Ashtaroth
Golan
Mt. Carmel
Mt. Tabor
Yarmuk River
Edrei
Dor
Megiddo
Jezreel
Lo Debar
Taanach
Beth Shan
Mt. Gilboa
Ramoth Gilead
Ibleam
Jordan River
Jabesh Gilead
Samaria
Tirzah
Mahanaim
Socoh
Mt. Ebal
Penuel
Mt. Gerizim
Shechem
Jabbok River
Zarethan
Succoth
Aphek
Shiloh
Ammon
Mediterranean Sea
(Great Sea)
Joppa
Israel
Rabbah of the Ammonites
Bethel
Gezer
Gibeon
Heshbon
Aijalon
Jericho
Bezer
Beth Shemesh
Jerusalem
Mt. Nebo
Medeba
Ashdod
Gath
Azekah
Bethlehem
Jahaz
Libnah
Kedemoth
Ashkelon
Mareshah
En Gedi
Dead Sea (Salt Sea)
Gaza
Dibon
Lachish
Hebron
Aroer
Arnon River
Philistia
Brook of Besor
Wilderness of Judah
Arad
Moab
Beersheba
Kir Hareseth
Wadi el-Arish
Judah
Zered River
Zoar
Tamar
Kadesh Barnea
Bozrah
Arabian Desert
Edom
Desert of Paran

Chapter 3

Amos: The End Has Come!

Introduction

How does a person tell someone that he/she will die very soon? Is it better to keep silent and say nothing, or is there a moral obligation to speak up? If it is possible to avoid death, someone needs to say something. But how does one break the bad news to a person who thinks everything is great? What does one do if the person rejects the truth and turns against the messenger?

The prophet Amos could have kept silent about Israel's troubles; instead, he chose to tell the nation that its days were numbered. God will destroy Israel! It will end! The king will die! The army will be humiliated! The people will live in exile!

This message was almost unbelievable to Israelites, but Amos had the responsibility of persuading his audience of their impending doom. The nation's trust in military power, ritual at the temples, and chosen status would not prevent God's judgment.

Amos, like God's messengers today, must communicate what God said, whether it is popular or unpopular. If God has roared like a lion against a nation's sin, the messenger must speak (3:8). If the end is at hand, the people must be warned.

Social Setting

The Historical Context

Amos lived during the reign of Jeroboam II, king of Israel (1:1). At this time Egypt was weakened by internal division, and Assyria was preoccupied with Urartu to the north. This made it possible for Israel and Judah to become powerful nations.[1]

	Judah	Israel	Egypt	Assyria
King	Uzziah	Jeroboam II	XXII Dynasty	Ashur-dan
Power	strong	strong	weak	weak

In Judah, where Amos was born and socialized, King Uzziah reinforced Jerusalem's walls and equipped his elite army of 307,500 with the finest implements of war (2 Chron. 26:1–15). Uzziah brought great prosperity and status to Judah (Isa. 2:7; 3:16–24). A similar situation developed in the northern nation of Israel. King Jeroboam II extended Israel's northern borders to Hamath (6:14) as Jonah prophesied (2 Kings 14:23–27). Israel's military power and prosperity was at its height during Amos's ministry; thus his ministry was in the latter part of Jeroboam's reign (765–760 B.C.).[2] Evidence of a severe earthquake at Hazor coincided

1. J. Bright, *A History of Israel,* 3rd ed. (Philadelphia: Westminster, 1972), 252–55. Compare D. B. Redford, *Egypt, Canaan, and Israel in Ancient Times* (Princeton: Princeton University Press, 1992), ch. 12, 312–64.

2. J. H. Hayes, *Amos the Eighth-Century Prophet: His Times and His Preaching* (Nashville: Abingdon, 1988), 26–27.

with this date, for Amos spoke "two years before the earthquake" (1:1).[3]

The Structure of Social Order

To address the needs of his time, Amos had to understand how people thought in Samaria, the capital of the northern nation (3:9–15; 4:1–13; 6:1–14) and at the central temple at Bethel (7:1–9; 10–17). Their way of looking at the world gave meaning to life and provided a context for interpreting social interaction.

The political power in Israel was centralized in the king, his bureaucratic officials, and his army (2 Kings 14:25). Amos did not personally interact with the king, question the legitimacy of his power as the leader of a nation separate from Judah, or condemn his military conquests. Instead, he addressed the wealthy bureaucratic leaders, the "noted men of the first of the nations" (6:1). At times Amos spoke to the whole nation (Isaac in 7:9,16; Jacob in 3:13; 7:2; Joseph in 5:15; 6:6, and Israel). In other situations he mentioned smaller groups like the wealthy women of Bashan (4:1) or the secure ones in Samaria (6:1).

The main civic institution that Amos identified was the law court. The court was entrusted with maintaining order, protecting the rights of the innocent, and preserving justice (Ex. 23:1–8; Deut. 25:1–3). It did not uphold justice (2:6, 8; 5:10, 12) for people were being sold into slavery for small debts.

The population was sharply divided into two socioeconomic groups: the wealthy upper class and the poor lower class. This process of social stratification began in the prosperous days of David and Solomon (1 Chron. 11; 23—27; 1 Kings 9:15–22; 12:1–4). The wealthy in Samaria owned luxurious palace-fortresses (3:9–12; 4:1–2; 5:11), summer and winter homes (3:15), and enjoyed opulent feasts (6:4–6). Some families were dominated by powerful women (4:1);

---

3. Y. Yadin et al., *Hazor II: An Account of the Second Season of Excavation, 1956* (Jerusalem: Magness, 1960) 24–26, 36–37.

others were controlled by unscrupulous merchants (8:4–6). Amos's sermons interacted with the ideology of these groups.

Some in the lower class were farmers (5:11; 8:4–6), but Amos did not interact with them or incite them to revolt. There is no reference to a support group for Amos from the lower class. Amos predicted the fall of the whole nation, not just the upper class.

The state temples at Bethel and Dan and the high places at Gilgal and Beersheba provided spiritual identity to the nation (5:5; 8:14). Amaziah had the role of (high) priest at Bethel, where he served under the authority of Jeroboam II (7:10). His ability to prevent Amos from speaking to the people who came to worship at the temple suggests that Amaziah was able to control the cultural perspective espoused at temple functions (7:12–13). The traditional sacrifices and songs were celebrated (4:4–5), but the worship included the recognition of other gods (5:25; 8:14).

The Social Location and Role of the Prophet

Amos learned about the socially ordered world of language, objects, and institutions through his family and peers in a setting quite different from the urban centers of Samaria and Bethel. As he learned Judean Hebrew, he internalized the meaning of words like justice, understood the role of the judge, read the nation's traditions in the law, and came to believe in God.[4]

Part of the prophet's view of life was conditioned by his geographic location in Tekoa (1:1), a small country village about ten miles south of Jerusalem. Although a rural place, it was within walking distance of the temple and royal court. Tekoa was one of the fortified military encampments along Judah's southeastern border (2 Chron. 11:5–12). Because soldiers lived at Tekoa, schools were probably available. Amos's social interaction with soldiers provided him with

4. Berger and Luckmann, *The Social Construction of Reality: A Treatise in the Sociology of Knowledge* (Garden City: Doubleday, 1976), 19–23, 34–37.

knowledge about the military affairs of other nations and introduced him to the war oracle[5] which he mimicked in Amos 1—2. Tekoa was situated on the borderline between the hilly pastures to the west and the dry mountainous wasteland to the east. Amos worked with sheep and cared for sycamore trees, possibly a grove near the Dead Sea (a couple miles east of Tekoa). The metaphors and illustrations in the book (the roar of the lion, 3:4; the sieve for cleaning grain, 9:9; ploughing with oxen, 6:12) point to a person who understood rural life and was shaped by that social environment. However, Amos was not an ignorant peasant; his messages show familiarity with covenant, hymnic, legal, and wisdom traditions.[6]

Amos's occupation was defined by the rare word for shepherd in 1:1 (*noqed*). In Ugaritic this word referred to a manager of temple shepherds rather than the ordinary shepherd who herded sheep.[7] For this reason Kapelrud concluded that Amos functioned as a cultic official. A study of this term in Akkadian, Ugaritic, and Hurrian caused Craigie to conclude that these shepherds had no sacred role in temple services.[8] This evidence suggests that Amos was an educated person with managerial responsibility, probably with middle class status.[9]

Amos's occupation as a manager of shepherds was abruptly interrupted when God called him as a prophet. Amos went from his native land of Judah to communicate God's word to the people in Israel. They had different cul-

---

5. See footnotes 22 and 23 on pp. 55 and 56.

6. H. W. Wolff, *Amos the Prophet: The Man and His Background* (Philadelphia: Fortress, 1973), 138, sees clan wisdom influences in his use of numbered sayings "for three . . . and for four," use of a woe oracle, and short proverbial sayings in 3:3–8.

7. J. B. Pritchard, ed., *ANET* (Princeton: Princeton Univ., 1954), 141.

8. A. S. Kapelrud, *Central Ideas in Amos* (Oslo: Aschehoug, 1956); P. Craigie, "Amos the *NOQED* in Light of Ugaritic," *Studies in Religion* 11 (1982), 29–33. S. M. Paul, *A Commentary on the Book of Amos* in *Her* (Minneapolis: Fortress, 1991), 34, finds no evidence of a cultic role for Amos.

9. Wilson, *Prophecy and Society in Ancient Israel* (Philadelphia: Fortress, 1980), 268, suggested that Amos was a member of the upper class and possibly a part of the religious establishment in Jerusalem. This is based on the unlikely assumption that Amos was the "chief" of the shepherds.

tural patterns of behavior and theological beliefs that conflicted with what God told Amos (7:14). Amaziah told Amos "the seer" (*hozeh*) to go make his living in Judah.[10] Amos responded: "I am not a prophet (*nabi'*), nor the son of a prophet," but a shepherd (7:14–15).

Interpreters have understood this passage in two different ways. Some concluded that Amos was not filling the role of a professional cultic prophet, "a seer" who made his living by prophesying; rather he made his living by managing sheep. Others held that Amos said, "No, I am a prophet, the disciple of a prophet."[11] The second view is less plausible, for nothing indicates that Amos was a member of a prophetic guild from either the royal court or the temple in Jerusalem.[12]

Amos provided a social legitimation for his function as a messenger of God by pointing to his call (7:14). He believed that God had commanded him to prophesy in Israel. The messenger formulas ("thus says the Lord," or "declares the Lord") at the beginning and end of many oracles show that he fulfilled this role. Apparently, Amaziah expected Amos to speak only positive messages to maintain the existing institutional practices and authority figures in Israel.[13]

As an orator Amos displayed creative ways of thinking. He wrote in pairs in the oracles against the nations in 1:3—2:16 and paired the visions in 7:1—9:4. Amos drew on literary forms of speech common in his setting (hymn, vision, disputation, judgment oracle, woe oracle, and salvation oracle).

---

10. Seers were sometimes associated with roles in the royal court of Judah (1 Chron. 21:9; 2 Chron. 9:29; 19:2) or with singing in the temple in Jerusalem (1 Chron. 25:5; 2 Chron. 29:30), but elsewhere the word was used fairly synonymously in parallelism with the term prophet (Isa. 29:10). See D. Petersen, *The Roles of Israel's Prophets,* 51–58.

11. The first interpretation is accepted by J. Mays, *Amos* (Philadelphia: Westminster, 1969), 136–38, while S. Cohen, "Amos Was a Navi," *HUCA* 32 (1961), 175–78, supported the second. G. F. Hasel, *Understanding the Book of Amos: Basic Issues in Current Interpretations* (Grand Rapids: Baker, 1991), 42–47, surveyed the issues on this question.

12. Petersen, *The Role of Israel's Prophets,* 58, believes that Amaziah was identifying Amos as a Judean "seer," which is different from the role of the Israelite prophet.

13. These were characteristics of the central prophet. Amos was behaving more like a peripheral prophet.

Amos interacted with several theological traditions that his audience would accept as authoritative (Sodom and Gomorrah in 4:11; the exodus in 2:10; 9:7). These legitimated his worldview and demonstrated how his audience misunderstood God's past instruction.[14] By publicly unmasking the discontinuity between the audience's thinking and these authoritative Israelite traditions, Amos put social pressure on his audience to resolve the internal dissonance between these two worlds.

Social Interaction

The Book of Amos

Amos may have preached additional messages while in Israel or later in Judah, but present evidence limits study to the canonical form of the Book of Amos. Some scholars hypothesize a redactional history for the text, but others maintain the unity of the book.[15] The prophet's sermons can be divided into three major sections:[16]

I. Judgments on the Nations 1:1—2:16
   A. Oracles against the nations 1:1—2:3
   B. Oracles against Judah and Israel 2:4–16
II. Verification of God's Judgment on Israel 3:1—6:14
   A. Behind every result is a cause 3:1–8
   B. Confirmation of Israel's punishment 3:9—4:3
   C. Israel is unwilling to return to God 4:4–13
   D. A lament over Israel, the dead nation 5:1–17
   E. Woe oracle concerning false hopes 5:18–27

---

14. A key ingredient of the approach of the sociology of knowledge was that people produce their social world. Berger, *Social Construction*, 62. M. D. Carroll, *Context for Amos* (Sheffield: JSOT, 1992), 64–71, makes good use of Berger's approach to the sociology of knowledge.

15. Hayes argues for the unity of the book while Wolff finds five redactional levels in Amos. S. M. Paul, *Amos* in *Her*, 16–26, 288–89, argues against those who deny that Amos wrote certain passages in the book.

16. G. V. Smith, *A Commentary on the Book of Amos* (Grand Rapids: Zondervan, 1988), 7–9.

F. Woe oracle concerning false security 6:1–14

III. Visions and Exhortations of the End 7:1—9:15

A. Compassion instead of judgment 7:1–6

B. Destruction, not forgiveness 7:7–17

C. Wailing at the end, not forgiveness 8:1–14

D. No sinner can escape God's judgment 9:1–10

E. Epilogue: restoration after judgment 9:11–15

By applying concepts from communication theory and the sociology of knowledge to the interaction between Amos and his audience, it will be possible to study how Amos transformed the thinking of his audience.

I. Judgments on the Nations 1:3—2:16

The *oracles against the nations* address the setting of six foreign nations (1:3—2:3) and then the situation in Judah and Israel (2:4–16). The oppressive social policies of neighboring states gave the prophet an opportunity to critique unacceptable patterns of conduct in a context which was not threatening to his Israelite audience.

It is impossible to reconstruct each nation's historical or cultural situation, but Amos provided some information on their military and nonmilitary practices. He described the Syrian and Ammonite strategy to mistreat those defeated in war. Barbarity replaced respect for the defenseless.[17] Philistia and Tyre engaged in kidnapping "whole masses of captives in order to deliver them over to Edom" for a quick profit at the slave market (1:6, 9).[18] Each nation was accused

---

17. A similar trend toward inhumanity was found in the annals of the Assyrian king Ashur-nasir-apli II: "I burnt many captives from them. I captured many troops; I cut off of some their arms (and) hands; I cut off of others their noses, ears, and extremities. I gouged out the eyes of many troops. I made a pile of the living (and) one of the heads. I hung their heads on trees around the city. I burnt their adolescent boys (and) girls." A. K. Grayson, *Royal Assyrian Inscriptions* II (Wiesbaden: Harrassowitz, 1976), 126.

18. I. Mendelsohn, *Slavery in the Ancient Near East* (New York: Oxford, 1949). This cannot refer to taking prisoners of war, for biblical (Deut. 20:10–11) and extra-biblical texts never condemn taking prisoners of war.

of deviant behavior that Amos and his audience deemed worthy of judgment.

Wright suggests that these nations injured God's people and broke the norms of the Israelite covenant, a covenant they were under during the reign of David and Solomon (150 years earlier).[19] This explanation seems unlikely, for Tyre's covenant (1:9) was political (1 Kings 5:1; 9:12–13), not theological. In addition, the text does not say that these acts were committed against Israel (see 2:1–3).

These nations broke their own social and moral standards (not Israelite traditions). Anthropologists and sociologists have found that all communities develop ordered rules that define roles and regulate how members of society relate to one another. These norms of conduct identify acts which are right (pleasing to the gods) and those which are wrong.[20]

Ancient Near Eastern texts reveal some of these norms. The Egyptian "Protestations of Guiltlessness" recognized that violence, lies, mistreatment of the poor, murder, adultery, covetousness, blasphemy, cheating in the weighing of grain, and pride were wrong.[21] International treaties of Hittite and Assyrian origin included agreements not to plunder the other nation's towns, massacre its citizens, or disturb its dead.[22] These texts demonstrate that these acts of oppression were deviant behavior in their own social world (see Rom. 1:18—2:16). The Israelites listening to Amos would have internalized Amos's point of view and endorsed his announcement of judgment.

To communicate his message, Amos crafted his sermon using the literary pattern of "war oracles" (probably

---

19. G. E. Wright, "The Nations in Hebrew Prophecy," *Encounter* 26 (1965), 236, notes the mention of "covenant of brotherhood" in 1:9 and "brother" in 1:11. M. E. Poley, *Amos and the Davidic Empire* (New York: Oxford, 1989), 66–74, thinks Amos was trying to support the reunification of the Davidic empire.

20. J. P. and M. L. Hewitt, *Introducing Sociology*, 43–67, describes how roles, groups, and institutions develop norms and values that guide behavior in society.

21. Pritchard, *ANET*, 34–36.

22. J. Barton, *Amos's Oracles against the Nations* (Cambridge: Cambridge Univ., 1980), 51–61; Pritchard, *ANET*, 199–206.

heard in the military camp at Tekoa).[23] These speeches were given before a battle, after consulting the Urim and Thummim (Judg. 20:23–28), to assure the people of God's protection and their enemies' defeat (Num. 24:15–24).[24] Amos had the freedom to externalize a new organization of this form (note the pattern of paired oracles)[25] and a unique ending which made it much more powerful than a common war oracle.

Amos's message, which he attributed to the Lord's prompting,[26] contained key theological and social principles which were part of his symbolic universe: God is sovereignly in control of all nations; He holds all people accountable on the basis of conscience and their communities' understanding of right and wrong behavior; God's punishment is particularly severe on nations and rulers who misuse their power to mistreat the weak.

Amos's sermon predicted a new social setting for these foreign nations. Their end had come; God would destroy them. Because the Israelites accepted the application of these theological principles to their enemies, Amos was able to use the logic of these concepts when he addressed Israel's violence.

---

23. A. Bentzen, "The Ritual Background of Amos 1:2—2:16," *OTS* 5 (1948), 132–41, believed this speech was made at a cultic ceremony, but Wolff, *Joel and Amos* in *Her* (Philadelphia: Fortress, 1977), 144–47, rejects Bentzen's evidence from Egyptian execreation texts.

24. D. Christensen, *Transformations of the War Oracle in the Old Testament* (Missoula: Scholars Press, 1975), 38–48.

25. The indictment is short, and the punishment is long in the first two oracles, but the exact opposite was true of the next two oracles. Also note the repetition of vocabulary in 1:5 and 1:8. The structure of these oracles followed a regular pattern of:

a) Messenger formula: "thus says the Lord"
b) Indictment: "for three transgressions . . . and for four"
c) Punishment: "therefore I will send fire"
d) Divine confirmation formula: "says the Lord"

26. The sociologies of everyday life accept the view of the speaker and attempt to see how each part of his world fits in his social construction of reality without trying to make an ultimate judgment concerning whether God really did speak. Amos believed God spoke, and that determined his social behavior and thinking.

The seventh oracle (2:4–5) condemned Judah for rejecting the law of the Lord, that source of transcendent knowledge which defined proper behavior for God's chosen people. Instead of following the tradition given in the Torah, the leaders told lies that led the people astray (see Isa. 3:12; 9:15–16; 28:15). Such acts of deviance became more likely when traditions were divorced from everyday life and other cultural options were legitimated by authority figures.[27] When the Israelite audience agreed that God should judge Judah for not keeping the law, Amos was able to use this conclusion to evaluate Israel's social behavior and theological beliefs.[28]

This long sermon came to a climax in the final message against Israel (2:6–16). The accusation was based on (a) the oppressive behavior of the powerful and wealthy (2:6–8); (b) their rejection of God's gracious acts on behalf of His people; and (c) their rejection of God's messengers (2:9–12). The wealthy violated the traditional patterns of behavior legitimated by the nation's theological traditions. They sold the poor as slaves because of small debts, trampled the helpless into the dust, and sexually abused their servants (2:6–8). Such deviations would usually be perceived as moral depravity, mental illness, or ignorance, but many Israelites accepted them.[29] These sinful people did not internalize the nation's traditions that taught them to maintain the poor with an open hand of generosity, for God had freed them from slavery in Egypt (Deut. 15:7–15). Israel forgot the traditions about God's care for them when they were weak in Egypt (Ex. 14—15), how He graciously led them in the wilderness and defeated the Amorites (2:9–10; see Num. 13).

27. Berger, *Social Construction*, 62.

28. Hasel, *Understanding the Book of Amos*, surveys different approaches to the composition of Amos. T. R. Hobbs, "Amos 3:1b and 2:10," *ZAW* 81 (1969), 384–87; T. J. Findley, *Joel, Amos, Obadiah* in *WEC* (Chicago: Moody Press, 1990), 159–60; and W. Rudolph, *Joel-Amos-Obadja-Jona* in *KAT* XIII, 2 (Gütersloh: G. Mohn, 1971), 120–21, conclude that these verses were not late Deuteronomic additions.

29. Berger, *Social Construction*, 66.

Amos's sermon came to the shocking conclusion that Israel was no better than the heathen. The end had come for Israel and its powerful army (2:13–16). This devastating message externalized a new view of reality. God was going to do the unimaginable!

II. Verification of God's Judgment on Israel 3:1—6:14

Since this message was so out of touch with what the strong military position of the nation seemed to indicate, many Israelites did not find it easy to accept Amos's message. He needed to justify his claim. Amos unmasked three areas of incongruity in their behavior (a) the powerful abused the poor (3:1—4:3), b) the people's worship was unacceptable (4:4–13), and (c) the nation depended on false hopes (5:11—6:14).[30]

In his first sermon (3:1—4:3) Amos described the setting of the rich in their palace-fortresses in Samaria (3:9–11; 4:1). Their world of objective reality included winter and summer homes, a luxury usually enjoyed only by kings (3:15).[31] Their great houses were made of expensive cut stone (5:11; 6:11) and filled with furniture with exotic ivory inlays (3:15). The upper class gained and maintained its social status through violence (3:9–10). They crushed the poor (4:1), imposing heavy rents and taxes (5:11).[32]

---

30. Amos 5:1–17 dealt with all three of these topics, but its lamentation style with its emphasis on death causes one to link it more closely with chap. 6.

31. S. Paul, "Amos III:15: Winter and Summer Mansions," *VT* 28 (1978), 358–59.

32. B. Lang, "The Social Organization of Peasant Poverty in Biblical Israel," *JSOT* 24 (1982), 47–63, believed the problem in Israel was a rent capitalism system.

"The lion has roared—who will not fear?" (Amos 3:9). This Assyrian statue of a roaring lion is from Calah (Nimrud).

Amos wanted to transform his audience's interpretation of the nation's traditions (3:1–2). They had reified their deliverance from Egypt (Ex. 14:1—15:17) and their election to be God's people into an absolute guarantee of divine protection disconnected from covenant behavior (Ex. 19:5–6; Deut. 7:6–9).[33] Amos did not reject their tradition, but he used a disputational form of speech to criticize their logic (3:1–8).

Amos introduced a new logical understanding of covenant tradition. He maintained that *behind every result is a cause* (3:1–8), that privilege means accountability (and in this case punishment), not automatic blessing (3:2). God's previous grace was not an eternal guarantee, for His blessings were tied to keeping the covenant and living according to His standards. The nation's twisted reification of "orthodoxy" eliminated the dynamic of a trusting relationship with God, while falsely clinging to the expectation of privilege. Amos *reconfirmed Israel's punishment* (3:9—4:3) by expanding his description of God's plan to send an army to destroy Israel's fortresses, altars, and wealth (3:11–12, 14; 4:3–4). Their world would end.

The second sermon focused on *Israel's unwillingness to return to God* (4:3–12). Amos mimicked the social role of a priest (compare Lev. 23:2,4; Joel 1:14; 2:15–16) by giving a sarcastic call to worship (4:4–5). He boldly labeled Israel's acts of worship as transgression. They performed empty institutionalized rituals to increase their social status. The audience was the wealthy upper class, for Amos described them as offering extra sacrifices and giving their tithe every third day. God was concerned with internal qualities like justice, love for God, and humility (Deut. 6:5; Amos 5:24; Mic. 6:6–8), not in hypocritical public displays of piety (6:5). Ritual was meant to be a graphic symbol to help the worshipers meet God. When they did not turn their hearts to God, their worship became a mockery. God hated and would not accept

33. Berger, *Social Construction*, 89–90.

worship from a life devoid of righteousness or from people who worshiped other gods (5:21–26; 8:14).[34]

In spite of being chastened again and again with curses[35] (no food, no rain, plagues), the people did not truly turn to God. These chastenings could be seen as divine "therapy" to destroy a deviant cultural view of reality and its legitimations.[36] Because Israel did not learn from these experiences, Amos announced that God, the Creator of the universe, who knew their every thought, whom they had sung about in their hymns, would meet them in judgment (4:12–13).[37]

Amos *lamented over Israel, the dead nation* (5:1–17) to convince his audience of the seriousness of their future state.[38] The people of Samaria believed the popular reified tradition: "God will be with us" (5:14, see traditions like Deut. 31:6–7; Josh. 1:5). Amos tried to shake their security and transform their understanding. "God will be with us" is no guarantee of blessing. The nation was doomed to death; only the remnant who sought God and practiced justice would live (5:4–6, 14–15) when God passed through their midst (5:17; in Ex. 11:4; 12:12, God passed through Egypt in judgment).[39]

---

34. S. Gevirtz, "A New Look at an Old Crux: Amos 5:26," *JBL* 87 (1968), 267–76, denies any reference to the worship of star gods, but Sakkuth and Kiyyun do correspond to terms used by people in Mesopotamia who worshiped Saturn, the god Ninurta.

35. Wolff, *Joel and Amos*, 213, compares these chastenings to the curses in Lev. 26; Deut. 28; and 1 Kings 8. D. Stuart, *Hosea-Jonah WBC 31* (Waco: Word, 1987), xxxii–xl, categorizes these curses from Deuteronomy and Leviticus.

36. Berger, *Social Construction*, 114–15.

37. J. Crenshaw, *Hymnic Affirmations of Divine Justice* (Missoula: Scholars Press, 1975) questions the authenticity of this hymn and the others in 5:8–9 and 9:5–6. In contrast to Crenshaw, it would seem natural for Amos to use a hymn that the people knew in order to remind the audience of the power of the God who would meet them. See Hasel, *Understanding the Book of Amos*, 83–89.

38. J. De Waard, "The Chiastic Structure of Amos 5:1–17," *VT* 27 (1977), 170–77, suggests a solution to the structural problem by proposing a chiastic structure. See G. V. Smith, "Amos 5:13: The Deadly Silence of the Prosperous," *JBL* 107 (1988), 289–91.

The third sermon contained *woe oracles concerning false hopes* (5:18–27) and *false security* (6:1–14).[40] Amos confronted those who relied on the nation's traditions about the day of the Lord (5:18–20), their own wealth (6:1–7), and the nation's military might (6:8–14). These wealthy officials lived in beautiful homes and enjoyed lavish banquets (6:4–6). They naturally interpreted objective reality in very positive images. In their pride (6:6–8) they ignored the nation's social chaos. They had no reason to be proud; their riches were gained through shameful treatment of the poor and military victories determined by God's grace (2 Kings 13:4–5; 14:25–27). These oppressors deceived themselves with a nationalistic ideology based on a false understanding of the source of their blessings.

Amos attempted to transform the basis for their security by correcting their understanding of the day of the Lord (5:18–20). They had internalized the view that God would save His people and judge their enemies. Amos did not deny that the day of the Lord would come, but he externalized a new theological application of this tradition, transforming it into a day of darkness for Israel.[41] He pronounced a woe on Israel because they would soon be in a new setting beyond Damascus (5:27); the sumptuous banquets of the wealthy would end (6:7), the secure homes would be smashed to pieces (6:11), and lamentation would fill the nation (5:1–3, 16–17).

God's blessings were not automatically granted to heirs of true theological tradition. God's blessings were reserved for people who feared His words (3:7–8), returned to Him with all their heart (4:6–11), worshiped Him (4:4–5,12; 5:4–6), acted justly (5:14–15), grieved over those less fortunate

39. A. V. Hunter, *Seek the Lord: A Study of the Meaning and Function of the Exhortations in Amos, Hosea, Micah, and Zephaniah* (Baltimore: St. Mary's Seminary, 1982), 61–65, discusses ways of understanding this offer of hope at a time of judgment.

40. J. Williams, "The Alas-Oracles of the Eighth Century Prophets," *HUCA* 38 (1967), 75–91.

41. M. Weiss, "The Origin of the Day of Yahweh Reconsidered," *HUCA* 37 (1966), 29–72.

(6:6), and rejected attitudes of pride and self-sufficiency (6:8–14).

III. Visions and Exhortations of the End 7:1—9:15

The final section of the book dealt with the social role Amos assumed when he was called to be a prophet (7:10–17), five visions concerning Israel's judgment (7:1–9; 8:1–3; 9:1–4), and a final message of hope (9:11–15).

Amos's five visions dramatized God's judgment and gave the prophet insight into the future. The first pair of visions picture God's *compassion instead of judgment* (7:1–3, 4–6). A great fire and a huge swarm of locusts gave Amos a graphic picture of God's power. Amos was overcome with compassion and interceded for his sinful brothers. In response, God surprisingly (in light of earlier statements of judgment) and graciously stopped the judgment. The second pair pictures *wailing at the end, not forgiveness* (7:7–9; 8:1–14), for God determined to spare the nation no longer. He would bring King Jeroboam, the temple, and the people of Israel to an end.

The last vision described the destruction of the temple and emphasized that *no sinner can escape God's judgment* (9:1–4). Each of these visions was a visual legitimation of Amos's earlier statements. God created the world and controlled it (9:5–6; see Ps. 24:1–2), so He has the power to determine what will happen on the earth. How can anyone hide from the eyes of this sovereign God (see Ps. 139:1–9)?

Just before the final positive message, Amos advanced a new understanding of Israel's exodus from Egypt (Ex. 14—15). Amos proposed that God did not act either in judgment or grace on the basis of people's past exodus experience. He acted on the basis of personal response to Him. Just as He extended His grace to Israelites and non-Israelites (9:7), so His judgment would fall on all sinners, even Israelites (9:10). Although it was popular to think that calamity would never touch Israel (9:10), Amos externalized a conflicting view. God's great sieve of justice would separate the righteous from the wicked (9:9). Amos tried to transform the people's illusory ideology by presenting a new look at the social, political, and divine forces at work in the world.

Amos's book ended with an *epilogue of restoration after judgment* (9:11–15). Although Amos's communication was primarily negative, his symbolic universe included the hope of restoration.[42] Although many Israelites wanted God's kingdom to come, Amos's final sermon announced that it would become a reality only some day in the future. God will rebuild the kingdom of David as promised in the Davidic covenant (see 2 Sam. 7:8–17). At that time "all the nations of the earth will be blessed" (Gen. 12:1–3) when they submit to the Lord (9:12). Then God would restore Israel (9:14), pour out His covenant blessings on the land, and cause it to produce abundantly (compare Lev. 26; Deut. 28:1–14). Amos did not fully describe this new setting, but later prophets provide additional details about this glorious kingdom.[43]

Theological and Social Implications

Anyone who proclaims that the end is at hand is in danger of being ignored or silenced. Many feel that only radical fools talk this way, that the day of "fire and brimstone" preaching is past. No one can deny the theological orthodoxy of what Amos said. God is sovereignly in control of the nations; He judges those who proudly trust in military strength or violently oppress others. Who can defend the Israelites who refused to meet God in worship, who based their faith on false hopes, who defrauded the poor?

How would an audience today accept a sermon on God's judgment on our nation for our failures? It would

---

42. Wolff, *Joel and Amos*, 352–53, believes a later Judean redactor added these verses, but certainly the northern tribes would have had similar hopes based on their earlier association with David (Hos. 1—3; 2 Sam. 19:43; 1 Kings 11:30–38). See Hasel, *Understanding the Book of Amos*, 105–20, or Paul, *Amos*, 288.

43. D. H. Odendaal, *The Eschatological Expectations of Isaiah 40—66 with Special Reference to Israel and the Nations* (Philadelphia: Presbyterian and Reformed, 1970), 171–85.

probably not be real popular, because few want to hear criticism.

Great communication skills are required if one hopes to transform the way people think and act. Effective communicators get their listeners to accept their principles before they apply them (Amos 1—2), use logic (3:1–8), sarcasm (4:4–5), and repetition (4:6–11) to make their points. An audience will listen to those who weep for them rather than yell at them (5:1–17), who intercede on their behalf (7:1–6), and who balance the bad news with the good (9:11–15). The messenger must use the best means to persuade some. The unpopularity of a message does not excuse the messenger from speaking, but it will test the messenger's character and speaking ability.

Questions for Discussion

1. How can you warn another person that the end is near, without sounding like a fanatic?
2. How can Amos's opposition to social injustice be an example to preachers today?
3. Can you identify the sociocultural differences between Amos's and his audience's understanding of worship (4:4–5; 5:21–17) and wealth (6:1–7)?
4. What communication techniques helped Amos persuade his audience in chapters 1—2?

Chapter 4

Hosea: Can Anyone Love a Prostitute?

Introduction

Can anyone explain the subjective reasons why one person loves another person? It is far easier to describe why one does *not* love a member of the opposite sex. Most people are not immediately attracted to an unclean, self-centered, deceitful, and mean individual. If people are going to commit themselves to another person for the rest of their lives, they want to be sure that person loves them and will dedicate their life to the relationship. Many people would recoil at the thought of marrying a prostitute or restoring a marriage relationship with a spouse who spent the last year working as a male or female prostitute.

Some might conclude that prostitutes are despicable and not capable of a deep love commitment to another person. Their sin is somehow less tolerable, more offensive, less forgivable, and more loathsome than other sins. Shading the truth, cheating on a test, not bothering to tithe, or unfaithfulness to God do not seem to be as serious. Yet God views all sins as unholiness, treacherous acts which undermine a relationship, a

Hosea disapproved of Israel's kings depending on Assyria for protection. The above relief from the black obelisk of Shalmaneser III shows Jehu of Israel bringing tribute to the king of Assyria.

breaking of a love commitment to Him, a prostituting of loyalties.

In spite of their great unfaithfulness, God loved the sinful people of the world so much that He willingly forgave their acts of prostituting themselves to self-interests, fame, fortune, pleasure, drugs, work, or popularity. In this sinful condition of unfaithfulness, no qualities made people attractive; no good reasons explained God's love. But God still loved! The ugliness of sin exposed the exceeding greatness of God's love.

The prophet identified with God's feeling of grief and anger over an unfaithful covenant partner and with God's great love for His people. How often do God's messengers today identify with this view of sin? If they do not, will they not minimize the mysterious wonders of God's great love?

Social Setting

The Historical Context

Hosea lived during the time of Jeroboam II, king of Israel, and Uzziah, Jotham, Ahaz, and Hezekiah, the kings of Judah (1:1). Historical allusions suggest that the prophet's ministry extended from about 755 to 725 B.C. During these years Israel's political and military status suffered a great reversal. The nation's position of power and prosperity under Jeroboam II totally collapsed shortly after 725 B.C.[1]

---

1. J. Bright, *A History of Israel,* 267–77, or G. I. Davies, *Hosea* in *NCBC* (Grand Rapids: Eerdmans, 1992), 25–29. Compare D. Redford, *Egypt, Canaan, and Israel in Ancient Times* (Princeton: Princeton University Press, 1992), ch. 12, 312–64. R. L. Cate, "Hosea, An Annotated Bibliography," *SWJT* 36 (1993), 38–41, surveys recent literature.

The prophet preached in Israel in three different settings.

	Judah	Israel	Assyria	Egypt
Early	Uzziah strong	Jeroboam II strong	Ashur-dan weak	XXII Dynasty weak
Middle	Jotham weak	Pekah weak	Tiglath-Pileser III strong	XXII Dynasty weak
Late	Ahaz weak	Hoshea weak	Sargon II strong	XXII weak

The earliest context preceded the death of Jeroboam II, the great grandson of Jehu (1:4).[2] Signs of the prosperous days of this strong military ruler (2 Kings 14:25) are found in the positive statements about the land being full of wool, flax, wine, silver, and gold (2:8–13). The wealthy lived in great fortresses (Amos 3:15; 5:11) and had a false sense of security in their military power (Amos 6: 13, 12–14).

The second period was a time of economic depression and military weakness. Several kings were assassinated (7:7; 8:4), and anarchy was common in Israel (2 Kings 15:8–38). The Assyrian king Tiglath-pileser III (745–727 B.C.) added to the nation's woes by requiring tribute (2 Kings 15:19, 29). In 734–732 B.C. he defeated Israel (and Syria) for trying to force the Judean king Ahaz to join an anti-Assyrian coalition (2 Kings 15:27–29; 16:5–9; Isa. 7; 2 Chron. 28). The terror in Israel during this war was reflected in the sounding of the alarm (5:8–11; 8:1)[3] and Israel's defeat (5:14).

---

2. Hosea 1:4 predicted the end of the dynasty of Jehu (Jeroboam II) because of the violent sins he committed in the valley of Jezreel (2 Kings 9—10).

3. F. I. Andersen and D. N. Freedman, *Hosea* in *AB* 24 (Garden City: Doubleday, 1980), 34, 401–04, dated 5:8–11 in the early days of Uzziah, but D. Stuart, *Hosea-Jonah* in *WBC* 31 (Waco: Word, 1987), 100, relates it to the Syro-Ephraimite war.

Although the third period was a little less chaotic because of King Hoshea's skill in making prudent alliances with Egypt and Assyria (8:9; 9:3; 12:1; 2 Kings 17:4), eventually Assyria grew wise to his treachery and destroyed Israel (2 Kings 17:5–6). The Book of Hosea did not describe this final disaster (722/721 B.C.), but Hosea probably lived through it.

The Structure of Social Order

Hosea lived in the northern nation of Israel. The capital city of Samaria and the temples with the golden calves had a dominant cultural effect on the behavior and beliefs in Israel. Hosea's and his audience's view of objective reality was influenced by foreign policy, political intrigue among leaders, and the syncretistic religious teaching of priests. Hosea was familiar with agriculture (2:5–12; 4:16; 5:14; 7:14; 8:7, 9; 9:2,10; 10:1, 4,11–13) and used animal and nature metaphors (God is like a shepherd in 13:5 and a bear in 13:8).

Hosea's sermons drew from the social patterns regulating marriage, the naming of children, family life, agricultural ways of making a living, the slave market, temple worship, and war. Many cultural patterns in Israel were influenced by Baalism because the people accepted its ways of understanding nature, social mores, and divine power. To communicate effectively to his audience, Hosea creatively interacted with the ritual and theological beliefs in the mythology of Baalism.[4]

The mythology and ritual of Baalism contained a worldview that had some similarities with Hebrew views (otherwise no Israelites would believe any of it), but it included many ideas which contradicted their ancient traditions. The people thought Baal was a god (2:13, 17; 11:2), the divine power that blessed the land with fertility (2:5, 8–9; 7:14). Using sexual metaphors, Baal provided fertility through giving rain to

---

4. See Pritchard, "Poem about Baal and Anath," *ANET*, 129–42, and the description of their religious beliefs in J. A. Dearman, *Religion and Culture in Ancient Israel* (Peabody: Hendrickson, 1992), 35–39, 69–78. P. A. Kruger, "Yahweh and the Gods in Hosea," *J. Sem* 4 (1992), 81–97, analyzes religious life in Hosea's audience.

the land, the mother goddess. He gave people fruitfulness (many children; 9:10–14), for he was "*baal*," the "master, husband." The people offered sacrifices to both God and Baal (2:13; 4:13; 10:1; 11:2), and the temple ritual included sexual acts which imitated and celebrated Baal's acts of bringing fertility. Their harlotry was both physical (with prostitutes) and spiritual (with other gods).

The Social Location and Role of the Prophet

Little is known about the prophet's place of birth, his social status, or his occupation before he became a prophet. The frequent references to Ephraim (5:3, 5, 11–14; 6:4, 10; 7:1, 8, 11) and cities in the northern nation indicate that Hosea lived and delivered his sermons in Israel.[5] Hosea was a younger man of marriageable age when the Lord asked him to represent the relationship between God and Israel by marrying a woman of harlotry (1:2). He experienced the joys of marriage and children (1:2–6), but he also had heartaches, for his wife Gomer was unfaithful to him (2:2–7).[6] Hosea's love for his wife was supremely expressed in his purchase of her from the hopeless condition of slavery (3:1–3). Through

5. Samaria in 7:1; 8:5–6; 10:5,7; 14:1 or Bethel (or Beth-Aven) in 4:15; 5:8; 10:5; 12:5.

6. Some believe that the woman in chap. 3 is not Gomer but another woman since her name is not given. This reading of the text seems unlikely, for it spoils the analogy that God is going to bring about a renewal of His relationship with Israel, His first wife. God's instructions that Hosea marry a prostitute offend some scholars who hypothesize that the whole episode is a parable, vision, or drama rather than actual events in the life of the prophet. This is possible, but the story sounds like a biographical account. It is also questionable whether this solution actually reduces the moral problem in chap. 1 or 3. Those who see a historical basis for Hosea 1—3 divide into several groups. Some believe Gomer was (a) a regular temple prostitute, (b) one who submitted one time to the immoral bridal rites at a Canaanite temple, (c) pure when she married Hosea, but later unfaithful to Hosea, or (d) a woman who was immoral before and after her marriage to Hosea, but not a temple prostitute. The last view seems the best approach. For a discussion of these issues with full bibliographic details, see H. H. Rowley, "The Marriage of Hosea," *Men of God* (London: Nelson, 1963), 66–97; D. Stuart, *Hosea-Jonah* in *WBC* 31 (1987), 22; W. A. VanGemeren, *Interpreting the Prophetic Word* (Grand Rapids: Zondervan, 1990), n. 21, 457–58.

these experiences Hosea learned about God's deep love for Israel and His anguish over the nation's rejection of His love.[7]

It is unlikely that Hosea was employed as a baker of bread (7:4–7) or a Levite.[8] Hosea claimed to be a prophetic watchman filled with God's Spirit, but some Israelites considered him a crazy fool (9:7). When he communicated God's message to his audience, Hosea skillfully tried to persuade his listeners to transform their Baalistic cultural perspective. His use of literary forms of speech were fragmentary and not identical with their structure in other prophets.[9] It appears that he used parts of a covenant lawsuit (4:1; 12:2). He also used judgment speeches (8:1–3; 13:1–3), oracles of salvation (1:10–11; 14:4–8), and exhortations to repent (6:1–3; 14:1–3).

Within these sermons, theological traditions were employed to justify his accusations against the nation, identify the basis for Israel's traditional beliefs about reality, and support the prophet's new theological message.[10] These tradi-

---

7. See A. J. Heschel, *The Prophets*, vol. I (New York: Harper and Row, 1962), 44–52, or G. W. Anderson, "Hosea and Yahweh: God's Love Story (Hosea 1—3)," *RevExp* 72 (1975), 425–36.

8. H. W. Wolff, *Hosea* in *Her* (Philadelphia: Fortress, 1974), 79–80, 144, connects Hosea with the Levitical priests. G. A. F. Knight, *Hosea* (London: SCM, 1960), 13, believes that Hosea was a baker. See S. M. Paul, "The Image of the Oven and the Cake in Hosea 7:4–10," *VT* 18 (1968), 114–20.

9. Andersen and Freedman, *Hosea* in *AB* 24, 71–73, 315-16, do not find form critical studies helpful in their analysis of Hosea. Their conclusions seem overly pessimistic, for there is some influence from the covenant lawsuit.

10. Traditions employed included allusions to: a) the story about the destruction of Sodom in 11:8 (see traditions in Gen. 14:8 and Deut. 29:23); b) the life of Jacob in 12:3–4, 12 (see Gen. 25:23–26; 28:5; 29:18–20; 32:22–32; 35:9–15); c) the exodus from Egypt in 8:13; 9:3; 11:1, 5; 12:9, 13; 13:4 (see Ex. 4:22; 14:13–31); the wilderness journey in 2:14; 9:10; 12:9; 13:5–6 (see traditions in Num. 25:1–15; Lev. 23:39–44; Deut. 8:1–20; 32:10); the Ten Commandments in 4:2 (see Ex. 20:1–17); the Achan story at the valley of Achor in 2:15 (see the tradition in Josh. 7:26); the abuse of the Levite's concubine in Gibeah in 9:9; 10:9 (see the story in Judg. 19—20); the sins of Jehu in 1:4 (see 2 Kings 9—10); and possibly the preaching of Amos in 8:14 and 11:10 (see Amos 1:2; 2:4–5). See W. Brueggemann, *Tradition and Crisis* (Richmond: John Knox, 1968), 26–54, for an expanded discussion of these and other references to ancient Israelite traditions.

tions reminded his audience of their parents' experiences with God, integrated past failures with present problems, and explained why their behavior was not consistent with God's earlier revelation.

Social Interaction

The Book of Hosea

The Hebrew text of Hosea's sermons is difficult, but some of the unusual spellings may be dialectical peculiarities rather than textual corruptions.[11] The flow of thought from paragraph to paragraph is not always easy to follow, but the larger segments of the book are broadly organized around cycles of accusations, punishments, and offers of hope.[12] Rhetorical signs of repetition, inclusions, and chiasms were employed to mark the beginning and end of some paragraphs (2:4–15; 7:3–7; 8:9,13; 9:10–17; 11:5, 11).[13]

Some commentators question the authenticity of passages of hope and a number of the references to Judah,[14] but others consider them to be a genuine part of the message of the prophet. The English arrangement of the text can be outlined into four main sections:[15]

---

11. Because of textual or philological problems, one will find considerable differences in the translation and interpretation of some verses (see 4:4; 5:2; 7:16; 9:13; 11:7; 12:8). Andersen and Freedman, *Hosea* in *AB* 24, 66–67, attempt to deal with these as peculiarities of the language of the northern nation of Israel rather than as textual corruptions.

12. Note the repetition of the theme of restoration at the end of each major section of the outline.

13. Andersen and Freedman, *Hosea* in *AB* 24, 133–38, 140, 322, 452, 502, 517–20, 539, 575; E. M. Good, "The Composition of Hosea," *SEÅ* 31 (1966), 29, 35, 37, 46–47.

14. Andersen and Freedman, *Hosea* in *AB* 24, 59, 73, do not reject the references to Judah. G. I. Emmerson, *Hosea, An Israelite Prophet in Judean Perspective* in *JSOTSup* 28 (Sheffield: JSOT Press, 1984) carries out a detailed analysis of the Judah passages and retains most of them. R. E. Clements, "Understanding the Book of Hosea," *Rev. Exp* (1975), 405–23, feels that the references to Judah are secondary.

15. Several Hebrew chapter divisions differ from the English translations. Chap. 2 in the Hebrew begins at 1:10 in the English. In Hebrew, chap. 12 begins at 11:12 in the English and 14 begins at 13:16 in the English.

I. Prostitution in the Family of God and Hosea 1:1—3:5
   A. Hosea's family symbolizes God's broken family 1:1—2:1
      1. Prostitution destroys the families 1:2–9
      2. Future restoration of God's family 1:10—2:1
   B. Contending with harlotrous wives 2:2–15
      1. Efforts to remove prostitution 2:2–15
      2. Future restoration of God's covenant 2:16–25
   C. Restoration of the families of Hosea and God 3:1–5
      1. Love brings Hosea's wife back 3:1–3
      2. Love brings Israel back to God 3:4–5
II. Prostitution Comes from No Knowledge of God 4:1—6:6
   A. Declaration of a covenant lawsuit 4:1–3
   B. Charges against the priest and worship 4:4–19
   C. Judgment/war, for the leaders do not know God 5:1–14
   D. Restoration possible if you seek to know God 5:15—6:6
III. Prostitution Contradicts Loyal Devotion to God 6:7—11:11
   A. Charges against leaders for social sins 6:7—7:7
   B. Charges of turning to other nations, not God 7:8—8:14
   C. Metaphors of total destruction 9:1—10:15
   D. Restoration is possible because of God's love 11:1–11
IV. Prostitution Brings Deceitfulness with God 11:12—14:9
   A. Charges of deceitfulness, like Jacob 11:12—13:6
   B. Total destruction of the nation 13:7–16
   C. Restoration is possible if they return to God 14:1–9

In these sermons Hosea attempted to persuade his audience to transform their thinking and behavior and not be conformed to the cultural patterns of those who followed Baal.

I. Prostitution in the Family of God and Hosea 1:1—3:5

The prophet shared his experiences with his unfaithful wife to demonstrate how *Hosea's family symbolizes God's broken family* (1:2—2:1). The action moved from an unfaithful marriage/covenant relationship (1:2–9), to attempts to reconcile the relationship (2:2–15), to the reestablishment of the covenants (3:1–5). Thematic continuity (using the word harlotry) and the repeated sin, punishment, restoration cycle unified this sermon.[16]

To communicate the depths of God's hatred for Israel's Baalism, Hosea compared the nation's sins with his wife's. Hosea married a prostitute, for God's covenant wife Israel was full of harlotry (1:2).[17] The people thought that their pursuit of other lovers (gods) who could provide their earthly needs (2:5) was not inconsistent with their covenant relationship. They even called Yahweh "my Baal, my husband," confusing the distinction between God and Baal (2:16).

Hosea viewed this prostitution as a rejection of himself as husband and of God as covenant partner. This was a shameful act (2:2, 5) that was inconsistent with the exclusive social expectations of a married woman in that culture (Ex. 20:14). To restore these marriage/covenant relationships, the husbands *contended with their harlotrous wives* (2:2–25). The offending parties (Gomer and Israel) were exhorted to reject prostitution (2:2) and act according to the norms of their Hebrew traditions.[18] They refused to respond to these

---

16. Good, "The Composition of Hosea," *SEÅ*, 29.

17. Gomer represented Israel who is unfaithful to God, not the "pure" nation with whom God established a covenant relationship at Sinai. Wife of harlotry characterized her at this time; it is not a retrospective conclusion based on later experience.

18. J. L. Mays, *Hosea* in *OTL* (Philadelphia: Westminster, 1969), 36, sees chap. 2 as a divorce setting but believes the purpose of the court case was to reconcile the marriage relationship.

acts of reconciliation, ceased to function according to the social requirements of a family member (1:9; 2:2), and ended up in slavery (3:1, 4). They forgot about God's acts of grace in the exodus and wilderness (2:14–15).

Hosea and God responded to this harlotry by giving their wives a new theological understanding of the facts of life. God uncovered their lewdness, put an end to their joyful festivals, and removed the supposed blessings of prostitution (2:9–13). For many Israelites, the myth-ritual approach of Baalism presented an ordered view of the world that was socially accepted as an accurate explanation of the forces of nature that interacted to make the world function. God's action demonstrated that it was an inappropriate social understanding of nature. Similarly, Hosea's wife found out that joy, security, and love were not fulfilled through prostitution; it led to slavery (3:1–3).

The unfaithfulness of the one covenant partner contrasted starkly with the overwhelming love of Hosea and God. Their love made possible the *restoration of the families of Hosea and God* (3:1–5). Hosea externalized a totally undeserved word of hope. Gomer is loved and restored (3:1–3). In like manner, God announced Israel's restoration and the coming of the Davidic king (1:11; 3:5; see the promise in 2 Sam. 7:12–16).[19] The people will acknowledge the Lord, and He will affectionately respond to them (2:20–21) when the covenant relationship is renewed (2:17–23). The curse symbolized in the children's names (1:4–9) will be reversed (2:1; 2:22–23); *Lo-ammi* "not my people" will become *Ammi* "my people." God's plan for the future[20] was an amplification of the blessings outlined in the nation's tradition (Deut. 28:1–14; 2 Sam. 7:12–16).[21]

---

19. Some considered all of 3:5 or at least the phrase "David your king" to be a later Judean addition to the text (Wolff, *Hosea* in *Her* 57); but, as Andersen and Freedman (*Hosea*) conclude, it is not inconsistent with the eschatology of other prophets (Amos 9:11–15; Isa. 2:1–4; Jer. 23:5).

20. D. E. Gowan, *Eschatology in the Old Testament* (Philadelphia: Fortress, 1986), 21–37, 97–104, discusses the promise of restoration of the people to the land, the eschatological king, and the transformation of nature at the end of time.

21. Stuart, *Hosea-Jonah* in *WBC* 31, xxxi-xlii, 62, 68.

Hosea's personal testimony of his experiences with Gomer was a powerful illustration of the spiritual message he shared with his audience. He was not able to stop Gomer's self-destruction, but his preaching might persuade some Israelites to avoid the same foolish and heartbreaking mistake.

II. Prostitution Comes from No Knowledge of God 4:1—6:6

Hosea's sermon began with a rhetorical surprise, God gave a *declaration of a covenant lawsuit* (4:1–3) against His own people.[22] The structure was developed around a series of accusation and punishment statements. The historical setting is tied to the Syro-Ephraimite war (734–732 B.C.);[23] the land and its people were in mourning because society was in disorder (4:3). Social relationships were controlled by deception, murder, stealing, adultery, and bloodshed (4:2). Truthfulness, loyal devotion to others, and an intimate relationship with God were not a part of the people's objectifications about social relationships (4:2).

What was the reason for this crisis? How could Hosea persuade his audience that his criticisms of Israel's behavior were legitimate? Hosea brought *charges against their priests and worship* (4:4–19). The priests did not teach the traditional religious values. They rejected the standards of social order found in the covenant. The priests forgot God's law and its understanding of the world (4:5–6,10). The people followed the ideology of Baalism, accepted the prostitution of its ritual, shared its cultural worldview, and rejected God's ways (4:6).

The priests' failure to fulfill their role in society resulted in the perversions of the people's relationships to each other and to God (4:9, 15). The acceptance of theological and ethical ideas from Baalism led to the corruption of worship.

---

22. H. B. Huffmon, "The Covenant Lawsuit in the Prophets," *JBL* 78 (1959), 285–95, or G. E. Wright, "The Lawsuit of God," *Israel's Prophetic Heritage*, ed. B. W. Anderson, (New York: Harper and Row, 1962), 26–67.

23. In this war Syria and Ephriam (Israel) attacked Judah (2 Chron. 28; Isa. 7).

Wine weakened their resistance to nontraditional ideas. Soon they worshiped idols, sacrificed to Baal, and committed adultery with temple prostitutes (4:11–14). They stubbornly resisted God and centered their lives around harlotry (4:16–19; 5:5).

Hosea depicted the nation's behavior as a rejection of the Hebrew cultural view of life (4:1–2, 6, 10; 5:4; 6:3, 6) found in God's law.[24] These traditions legitimated Hosea's view that Baalism was deviant behavior. Loyalty, love, and a personal commitment to God were central to a covenant relationship, but these were not characteristic of Israelite behavior.[25]

Since the Israelites lived according to the ideological conceptions within Baalism and forgot the law of God, Hosea externalized a view of the future that was new and foreign to many in his audience. He pictured *judgment/war, for the leaders did not know God* (5:1–14). The conclusion to the first part of this covenant lawsuit was: Israel and even Judah[26] are guilty and will be punished. God will forget them (4:6), shame them (4:7), punish them (4:9), and withdraw from them (5:6). Military defeat and exile will come (5:8–14), and no one will deliver them.

Amazingly, this section did not close on a note of hopelessness. Hosea looked at the new theological setting of Israel after the nation's judgment (similar to Hos. 3).[27]

24. Hosea 4:2 draws on Ex. 20:7–15; Deut. 5:6–21; for stipulations about cult prostitutes in 4:13, see Deut. 23:17; on the moving of boundary stones in 5:10, see Deut. 27:17.

25. J. L. McKenzie, "The Knowledge of God," *JBL* 74 (1955), 22–27.

26. Wolff, *Hosea* in *Her,* 89, 100, and Mays, *Hosea* in *OTL,* 77, 84, believe 4:15 and 5:5 are late additions by a Judean editor. Andersen and Freedman, *Hosea* in *AB* 24, 371, 393, accept as authentic the negative references to Judah in 5:9, 12, 14 and 6:4 in light of the mention of the "tribes of Israel" in 5:9.

27. Mays, *Hosea* in *OTL,* 87–88, believe that 6:1–3 is a song of penitence which the people sang. Wolff, *Hosea* in *Her,* 116–17, thinks the priests sang it. Hos. 6:4–6 was God's response that their repentance falls short of God's expectations. Andersen and Freedman, *Hosea* in *AB* 24, 327–30, took 6:1–3 as a true statement of faith that chronologically took place after the judgment of 6:4–6.

Restoration is possible if you seek to know God (5:15—6:6). Some day in the distant future, the nation will seek God, return to the Lord, desire to know Him (5:15—6:3), and accept His transcendent point of view. Unfortunately, that time is future. Consequently, God called out in anguish as a rejected lover (6:4; see 11:8 at the end of the next section), because the people had no loyal devotion or a meaningful relationship with God (6:6).

III. Prostitution Contradicts Loyal Devotion to God 6:7—11:11

In the preceding sermonic re-creation of a court case the differences between the covenant partners were not resolved. Consequently, Hosea continued his sermon using the lawsuit format to bring *charges against the leaders for social sins* (6:6—7:7). The nation's worship and political actions demonstrate disloyalty to God's covenant standards (8:1–14).

The historical setting was connected to events just after the Syro-Ephraimite war in the reign of Hoshea ben Elah. Violence and anarchy was the norm, for Hoshea and several earlier kings assassinated the kings who ruled before them in order to rise to power (2 Kings 15:10–30). Although Hoshea brought some stability by his political deals with Egypt and Assyria (2 Kings 17:4), eventually the Assyrians found out about his conspiracies.

Hosea legitimated his claim that Israel's leaders broke the covenant (6:7) by pointing to acts of murder (6:8–9; 7:6–7), harlotry (6:10), deception (7:1), robbery (7:1), lying (7:3), and adultery (7:4; similar to chapter 4:1–2). These sins involved the priests (6:9) and princes (7:3–6) in high levels of leadership. These leaders were so perverted that they thought that God would not see that their deeds were inconsistent with His covenant stipulations (7:2); therefore, they did not even bother to call out to God for direction (7:7).

Hosea strengthened his case by bringing *charges of turning to other nations, not God* (7:8—8:14). The leaders naively mixed with Egypt and Assyria, not even realizing that this was a turning from dependence on God, a giving of devotion to other nations (8:8–10). They also blindly worshiped the golden calves rather than Yahweh (8:4b–6; 10:5; 11:2; see 1 Kings 12:25–32) and turned sacrificing into sinning (8:11–13).

To persuade his audience, Hosea legitimated his analysis of the nation's perverse state by showing that their behavior was inconsistent with the nation's traditional standards of behavior. The people did not internalize the standards in the covenant (8:1, 12; probably referring to Ex. 20—23). They forgot about their personal relationship to God (8:14). They ignored warnings against making alliances with other nations (8:4; see Ex. 23:32–33; Deut. 7:2), against trusting in a large army (10:13; see Deut. 17:16), and against appointing kings not chosen by God (8:4; see Deut. 17:14–15).[28] They forgot about God's love in delivering them from Egypt (11:1, 4; see Ex. 14—15), His care for them in the wilderness (11:3–4; see Deut. 8), and their shameful deeds at Baal-peor (9:10; see Num. 25). This society was not loyally devoted to their covenant partner with all their heart (Deut. 6:5). They prostituted their love to others. If they planted deeds of righteousness, they would reap the fruit of loyal devotion (10:12).

Because they had no loyal devotion to God, Hosea introduced his audience to a new theological understanding of their future using *metaphors of total destruction* (9:1—10:15). God will remember their iniquity (7:2; 8:13; 9:9) and destroy them (7:12–13). Their calf idols will be broken in pieces (8:5–6; 10:2, 8); their allies will not help (8:10); and their cities will burn with fire (8:14; 10:14; 11:6). They will have no joyful day of feasting (9:1–9); instead, they will endure a day of punishment (9:7). God will love them no more (9:15); therefore, God will depart from them (9:12) and not make them fruitful (9:11–17). The nation will return to their condition of slavery (8:13; 9:3, 6) and go into exile in Assyria (11:5).

---

28. A. Gelston, "Kingship in the Book of Hosea," *OTS* 19 (1974), 86–96.

Amazingly, Hosea did not close this section of the covenant lawsuit on this note of hopelessness. He looked toward the new theological setting of the nation after their judgment (compare the end of 1—3 and 4:1—6:6). Punishment was deserved, but *restoration is possible because of God's love* (11:1–11). In anguish, God cried out (11:8; compare 6:4). He would not totally destroy His people (11:9). The future plans of God included the return of His people to the land and the transformation of their behavior (11:10–11). This experience would give them a new conception of God's power, for He would no longer be a lion who destroyed them (5:14), but a lion who roared as He defeated their enemies (11:10). Israel would no longer act like a silly dove running off to Assyria (7:11), but would return to her nest (the land of Israel) fearing God (11:11).

IV. Prostitution Brings Deceitfulness with God 11:12—14:8

Hosea preached his final sermon toward the end of Hoshea's reign (shortly before 722/721 B.C.).[29] Hosea reminded the people that God still had a case against them (12:2). The sermon began with *charges of deceitfulness, like Jacob* (11:12—13:6).

The people dealt with God in deceitful ways (11:12). Their political policies were deceptive because they promised loyalty to both Egypt and Assyria (12:1). Their social behavior oppressed the poor through the use of deceptive weights (12:7). Their wealth deceptively led some to believe they did nothing wrong (12:8), and their sacrifices to Baal deceived them (12:11; 13:1–2).[30] These deceptions led to

29. J. Limburg, *Hosea-Micah* in *IntCom* (Atlanta: J. Knox, 1988), 47, dates this section just before 722 B.C.

30. The reference to Judah in 12:2 was changed to Israel by Mays, *Hosea* in *OTL,* 161–62, and Wolff, *Hosea* in *Her,* 206, but there seems to be no need to eliminate a negative reference to Judah. Andersen and Freedman, *Hosea* in *AB* 24, 605–06, maintain the text as it is in the Hebrew. They interpret the mention of Judah in 11:12 as an accusation of following after other gods rather than as a positive statement that contrasts with the wicked behavior of Israel.

pride, a sense of self-sufficiency, and a forgetting of God (13:6).

God rejected this deceptive approach to life. It resembled the behavior of their forefather Jacob "the deceiver."[31] Their tradition warned against using deceptive weights (12:7; see Lev. 19:36) and excluded alliances with other nations (12:1; see Deut. 7:2; 17:16). These traditions legitimated Hosea's thinking against the people for their ways were inconsistent with the norms God had communicated. Their behavior did not make sense, for God delivered them from Egypt, cared for them in the wilderness, and sent prophets to reveal His will to them (12:9–10, 13; 13:4; see traditions in Ex. 3—19).

Hosea externalized a new way of looking at Israel. Because the nation was full of deception, God would no longer act in compassion, but would be a destructive lion in their midst (13:7–8, 14). This would produce a *total destruction of the nation* (13:7–16). They would have no king to save their cities (13:9–11). Their land would be dry without fertility (13:15, Baal would be impotent). An enemy would plunder their riches (13:15) and kill their children and wives (13:16). This experience would demonstrate the deceptive nature of the dominant cultural understanding of the world.

Following the pattern established in the earlier parts of the lawsuit, Hosea ended this sermon with a promise that *restoration is possible if they return to God* (14:1–9). The first paragraph called the people to repentance (14:1–3), while the second promised salvation (14:4–8).[32] After repenting, the people would recognize Yahweh as God, see the sinfulness of

31. On the use of the Jacob tradition from Gen. 25:26 (the birth story); 32:22–32 (his wrestling with the angel); 35:10–15 (his meeting with Esau), see E. M. Good, "Hosea and the Jacob Tradition," *VT* 16 (1966), 137–51; W. C. Kaiser, "Inner Biblical Exegesis as a Model for Bridging the 'Then' and 'Now' Gap: Hos. 12:1–6," *JETS* 28 (1985), 33–46; G. V. Smith, "Alienation and Restoration: A Jacob-Esau Typology," *Israel's Apostasy and Restoration*, ed. A. Gileadi (Grand Rapids: Baker, 1988), 165–74.

32. A. V. Hunter, *Seek the Lord* (Baltimore: St. Mary's Seminary, 1982), 167–74.

their prostitution, and acknowledge the powerlessness of other nations and idols (14:1–3). They would see that God heals the sinner, loves His people, gives them fertility, and looks after them (14:4–8).

An epilogue to the wise reader (14:9, Israel was unwise in 13:13) was appended to these sermons. The wise person who reads these sermons will understand what Hosea's messages mean, will realize God's ways are right (compare Deut. 10:12; Prov. 10:29), and will apply these things to daily living.

Theological and Social Implications

Hosea's sermons lay a great deal of blame for Israel's condition at the feet of its political and religious leaders. They did not teach the people the covenant and did not help them see that their behavior was inconsistent with wholehearted loyal devotion to God. Since the politicians and priests forgot about the nation's past traditions, the people conformed their thinking and behavior to the dominant Baalistic culture of their day. The syncretism of Israel's ancient faith was so complete that the people deceived themselves into thinking everything was fine, even though they did not acknowledge Yahweh as their sole God.

Like Hosea, the messenger of God today needs to evaluate the secular culture's domination over the religious and social structures of modern society. All too often it appears that syncretism and pluralism is the politically correct posture of many religious institutions. Its power has affected definitions of the family, approved forbidden sexual behavior, and promoted economic prosperity over moral responsibility.

If preachers today hope to acknowledge God's power over their lives and desire to remain loyally devoted to Him, they will need to identify and confront the deceptive love for self that parades as religion in society. This syncretism of divided loyalty is prostitution in God's eyes. This prostitution should grieve the modern messenger as much as it tormented Hosea and God. God's kingdom is not threatened by this rebellion, but His judgment will come if repentance does not.

Transformation will only come to God's people when His messengers are convinced of God's utter hatred of sin and His deep desire to forgive the prostitutes of this world. Although His love is not deserved, it is available to all who seek Him.

Questions for Discussion

1. Compare and contrast Hosea's marriage and God's covenant relationship with Israel. Why is marriage such a good picture of the human relationship to God?
2. How can a person today communicate the seriousness of sin? What evidence of sin could be used to evaluate our society's relationship to God?
3. How could a person persuade people of God's great love? How could a person's personal experience help convince a person who thinks God is not a God of love?

Chapter 5

Jonah: Should God Be Compassionate to Everyone?

Introduction

Should God be merciful to a murderer? Is there any place for compassion on child molesters? Should a just God have mercy on those who refuse to love and obey Him? Should the violent Assyrians who destroyed nations throughout the ancient Near East receive compassion from God? Would it not be more just for God to destroy those who commit such atrocities?

Yes, it is true. God's punishment of these sinful people would establish justice, but God does not take pleasure in the death of the wicked (Ezek. 18:2–3). God wants all people to come to know the truth and repent of their evil ways (1 Tim. 2:4). Therefore, in unbelievable patience God will frequently send a prophet to warn undeserving people of their impending doom. Would anyone want Him to act with less compassion on themselves?

The prophet Jonah, and preachers today, sometimes have trouble understanding why God is so compassionate to people who do not deserve mercy. They question why God waits so long to destroy the wicked. God could just send fire from heaven to destroy them (Luke 9:54). Sometimes it seems that God's compassion almost undermines His claims to justice. Life would be a lot easier if He did not have compassion on everyone.

Social Setting

The Historical Context

Jonah did not refer to any king in this book, but a brief comment in 2 Kings 14:25 preserved his Israelite background. In the early years of King Jeroboam II (around 790–780 B.C.) Jonah predicted that Jeroboam II would expand Israel's borders.[1] The date for Jonah's trip to Nineveh is unknown, but it probably took place around 780 B.C. in a period of Assyrian weakness.[2]

The Structure of Social Order

Jonah's worldview recognized ethnic (being a Hebrew, 1:9), political (3:2), and religious (fearing the God of heaven, 1:9) differences between people as meaningful cultural identifying markers. The story is centered around social relationships on a ship and in Nineveh, the Assyrian capital. A man who functioned in the role of captain controlled the ship on a commercial voyage to deliver cargo to the foreign

---

1. This was before the ministries of Amos and Hosea. Early in Jeroboam II's reign, Jonah saw the rise of his kingdom. But twenty years later Amos (7:1–17) predicted the destruction of Jeroboam's nation.

2. D. Stuart, *Hosea–Jonah* in *WBC* (Waco: Word, 1987), 446, places Jonah's visit to Nineveh in the reign of Asshur-dan III (773–756 B.C.). See the treatment of this period in B. Mazar, "The Aramean Empire and Its Relations with Israel," *Biblical Archaeologist Reader 2* (Garden City: Doubleday, 1964), 142–45; W. W. Hallo, "From Qarqar to Charchemish: Assyria and Israel in the Light of New Discoveries," *Biblical Archaeologist Reader 2* (Garden City: Doubleday, 1964), 162–68; D. Redford, *Egypt, Canaan, and Israel in Ancient Times* (Princeton: Princeton Univ. Press, 1992), chap. 12, 312–64.

A coin from the time of Mattathias Antigonus, last of the Hasmoneans (40-37 B.C.). The obverse shows the table of the tabernacle; the reverse, the menorah.

port of Tarshish. This leadership position gave him authority over the ship, its cargo, the sailors under his command, and the passengers on board (1:3–6). Consequently, Jonah had to make an economic payment to ride the ship and had to obey the captain (1:3, 6). The sailors believed in gods who could bring judgment and were acquainted with the custom of casting lots to identify a guilty person (1:5–7). The sailors were from a different culture (possibly Phoenicia) and structured objective reality different than Jonah.[3] Still, they understood Jonah's confession. They also offered appropriate behavioral responses to God when He compassionately delivered them from the storm (1:15–16).

In a quite different setting, an Assyrian king and his nobles set political and social policies to control behavior in Nineveh (3:6–7). Nineveh was a large commercial and military center for the Assyrian empire. Its army was renowned for its violence (1:2; 3:8; Nah. 3:1–4). The people internalized a cultural worldview different from Jonah and followed their own patterns of fasting, confession of wrongs, and turning away from evil (3:5–9). In spite of the potential for misunderstanding between people from different cultural backgrounds, communication was possible, and God transformed the lives of many people.

The Social Location and Role of the Prophet

Jonah was from the Israelite town of Gath-hepher (north of Nazareth) in the tribal territory of Zebulon (Josh. 19:13). Jonah was a prophet (2 Kings 14:25), a Hebrew who feared Israel's God (1:9). He probably spoke Aramaic, the international trade language, in Nineveh and had the economic resources to afford the cost of a ticket to distant Tarshish.[4] Jonah's age, marital status, and associations with other prophets remain unknown.

The prayer in 2:2–9 reproduced the main elements of a prayer of thanksgiving, suggesting that the prophet was well aware of the literary forms of speech from the nation's hym-

---

3. P. Berger and T. Luckmann, *The Social Construction of Reality: A Treatise in the Sociology of Knowledge* (Garden City: Doubleday, 1966), 76–79, 85–88, describe how different roles and occupations involve people in separate cultures with distinctive vocabularies and perspectives.

4. Mazar, "The Aramean Empire," 140–42, believes that Aramaic became the official language of business during or shortly after the reign of Ben-hadad II. The Book of Jonah has several Aramaic words in it. G. M. Landes, "Linguistic Criteria and the Date of Jonah," *Eretz Israel* 16 (1982), 147–82, believed that some "Aramiaic" words in Jonah were actually Phoenician.

nic traditions.[5] The phraseology in this hymn picked up earlier theological traditions.[6] These traditions helped form Jonah's way of looking at the world. They enabled him to communicate to his Israelite readers in meaningful ways.

The startling irony of the story is that Jonah helped two foreign groups (the sailors and the Ninevites) change their thinking about God and the world around them, but he was unwilling to internalize a new view of God's compassion (4:1–11). Jonah received God's compassion when he was thrown into the sea (2:1–9), but he did not believe that God should be compassionate on everyone—especially not on the people of Nineveh.[7]

Social Interaction

The Book of Jonah

The book is unusual in that it has only one short prophetic message (3:4). Its main concern was the prophet's own struggle with traditional beliefs about God's compassionate yet just rule of the world.[8] Some have questioned the

5. C. Westermann, *The Praise of God in the Psalms* (Richmond: John Knox, 1961), 102–12, or J. Limburg, *Hosea–Micah* in *IntCom* (Atlanta: J. Knox, 1988), 146.

6. J. Magonet, *Form and Meaning: Studies in the Literary Techniques in the Book of Jonah* (Sheffield: Almond Press, 1983), 44–49, 65–84, gives a detailed study of these quotations. These include: the wickedness of Nineveh coming up to God in 1:2 (see the Sodom story in Gen. 18:20–21); God's creation of the sea and the dry land in 1:9 (see Gen. 1:9–10; Ps. 95:5); God having compassion (see Ex. 32:12); God's mercy on the people of Nineveh in 3:10 (see Ex. 32:14); the character of God in 4:2 (see Ex. 34:6); and numerous phrases in the prayer in 2:2–9 (see Ps. 42:8; 103:4; 120:1; 142:4). See also J. Limburg, *Jonah* in *OTL* (Louisville: Westminster: John Knox, 1993), 64–70.

7. Berger, *Social Construction*, 95–100, sees the more abstract understanding of the world in a person's symbolic universe as a key factor in ordering, integrating, and legitimating a person's meaningful interpretation of experiences. Conflicts between experience and a symbolic universe required new explanations or changes in one's understanding of life.

8. T. E. Fretheim, "Jonah and Theodicy," *ZAW* 90 (1978), 227–37.

historical nature of the book, the unity of certain parts (particularly the poem in chapter 2), and dated the book much later than the time of Jeroboam II,[9] because the book has Aramaic vocabulary, surprising ironic twists, and verses that parallel other prophetic texts (compare Joel 2:13 and Jon. 4:2). Traditionally, the story was understood as an historical account of events in Jonah's life, but some now classify it as a satire or parable.[10] The text is divided into two main sections:

I. Compassion of God for Disobedient Jonah 1:1—2:10
   A. Rejection of God's calling by Jonah 1:1–16
   B. Salvation of the Lord came to Jonah 1:17—2:10
II. Compassion of God for Repentant Nineveh 3:1—4:11
   A. Compassion of God came to Nineveh 3:1–9
   B. Rejection of compassion to Nineveh 3:10—4:11

The narrative provides the reader with a snapshot of the social world of Jonah, some sailors, and the people of Nineveh. The participants in each setting thought and acted on the basis of their own culture. New experiences presented them with the choice of transforming their socially derived

---

9. J. M. Sasson, *Jonah* in *AB* 24b (New York: Doubleday, 1990), 16–27, discusses these issues. G. M. Landes, "The Kerygma of the Book of Jonah," *Int* 21 (1967), 3–31, and Magonet, *Form and Meaning*, 43, argue for the authenticity of the poem in 2:2–9. H. W. Wolff, *Obadiah and Jonah* in *CC* (Minneapolis: Augsburg, 1986), 76–78, prefers a late date. We follow Stuart, *Hosea–Jonah* in *WBC* 31, 432–42, who takes a traditional date. Compare T. Lescow, "Die Komposition des Buches Jona," *BN* 65 (1992), 29–34.

10. M. Burrows, " The Literary Category of the Book of Jonah," *Translating and Understanding the Old Testament*, eds. H. T. Frank & W. L. Reed (Nashville: Abingdon, 1970), 80–107, and Wolff, *Obadiah and Jonah* in *CC*, 80–84, believe the book is a satire while L. C. Allen, *Joel, Obadiah, Jonah, and Micah* in *NICOT* (Grand Rapids: Eerdmanns, 1976), 177, considers the book a parable. Since real life is full of ironies, this characteristic does not make the book an unhistorical parable. K. M. Craig Jr., *A Poetics of Jonah; Art in the Service of Ideology* (Columbia: University of South Carolina, 1993), develops Jonah's literary srtategies.

worldview on the basis of new experiences and new theological understandings.

I. Compassion of God for Disobedient Jonah 1:1—2:10

The structure of the narrative action moved from the *rejection of God's calling by Jonah* (1:1–16) to a hymn of thanksgiving for God's deliverance (1:17—2:10).

Hebrew tradition affirmed that God communicated His plans through those having the role of a prophet (1:2; Ex. 7:1–2; Deut. 18:18). When Jonah received a divine call to speak God's words, he understood his prophetic role, but he did not want to go to Nineveh. He did not reject God's evaluation of Nineveh. He—and most Israelites readers—fully agreed that Nineveh was a wicked and violent city that should be judged —like Sodom in Gen. 18:20–21—.[11] Although the Assyrians were their enemies in the earlier days of Jehu,[12] more recently the Assyrians had delivered Israel from years of Syrian oppression (2 Kings 10—13). Thus Jonah's objection to God's command was not motivated by political loyalties, but rather by his concept of divine justice.[13]

He was a Hebrew (1:9), and his view of the way God operated was socially determined by the principles he learned during socialization as a child.[14] In his social context, justice meant the wicked were punished, compassion was extended only to the righteous. Jonah knew that God was patient, but

---

11. Contrast Abram's response to the judgment of Sodom in Gen. 18:22–33.

12. Although the Bible does not record the event, Jehu was defeated by Shalmaneser III in 841 B.C. See J. Pritchard, ed., *ANET* (Princeton: Princeton Univ. Press, 1954), 279–81.

13. T. E. Fretheim, *The Message of Jonah* (Minneapolis: Augsburg, 1977), 19–26, deals with the key theological issues raised by the book. He notes that Jonah is quite positive toward the sailors and offered to die that they might live; thus the issue of the book was not a Jew/Gentile problem.

14. Berger, *Social Construction*, 129–37. Socialization is internalizing the culturally-determined objective view of reality that defines the world in meaningful ways.

he believed that justice would not bring compassion to the evil Ninevites.

Jonah's rebellion moved through several stages. First he attempted to flee from the presence of God (1:3, 10), a foolish act which contradicted Hebrew traditions concerning the universal presence of God (see Ps. 139:7–12). Later, in the midst of a storm, the prophet admitted his sin (1:10–12) and accepted punishment in order that God might have compassion on the heathen sailors (1:12; a compassionate attitude toward non-Israelites). The storm brought about a new understanding of his responsibility and began to transform his will.

The sailors functioned as a fitting (and ironic) contrast to the behavior and beliefs of Jonah. Although they worshiped other gods (1:5) and initially had no knowledge of Israel's God, they recognized that the storm was an act of Jonah's God (1:4–6, 14). They were astonished that Jonah would purposely reject a divine instruction (1:10) and were concerned about divine justice when they threw the prophet overboard (1:14). Fearing Yahweh, they sacrificed to Him after the sea was calm (1:16). These heathens were more in tune with the behavior God desired than Jonah.

While in the sea, the *salvation of the Lord came to Jonah* (1:17—2:10). Jonah thanked God for His compassion and salvation (2:6–10), realizing that God delivered him from death by sending the great fish (1:17—2:1).[15] The prophet's prayer of thanksgiving described his setting in very traditional language (Ps. 69:1–2; 42:7).[16] As he sank to the bottom of the sea (2:2–3, 5–6a), he found himself standing at the threshold of death.[17] At that point he gained new insight

15. G. M. Landes,"The 'Three Days and Three Nights' Motif in Jonah 2:1," *JBL* 86 (1967), 446–50, traces the reference to three days in the fish to a Sumerian myth which said it takes three days to travel to the underworld.

16. Other psalms of thanksgiving include Pss. 30; 34; 116. They usually included an introduction, a rehearsal of the difficult situation they were delivered from, a remembrance of their deliverance, and a conclusion (including a vow to praise).

17. D. L. Christensen, "The Song of Jonah: A Metrical Analysis," *JBL* 104 (1985), 225–29, shows how the repetition of vocabulary helped convey meaning.

concerning what it meant to be away from the presence of God (2:4; see 1:3). Consequently he looked to God for deliverance (2:7a; see Ps. 142:4).[18] He personally experienced an unjust application of God's compassion.[19] Jonah's new theological perspective was evident in his promise to praise God (2:8–9).[20]

II. Compassion of God for Repentant Nineveh 3:1—4:11

The second half of the book was structured to mirror the first half in several ways. Both chapters 1 and 3 began with a sending of the prophet to Nineveh (1:1–3; 3:1–2), while 2 and 4 contained prayers of Jonah (2:2; 4:2). The *compassion of God on Nineveh* (3:1–9) and on Jonah (1:17—2:10) was emphasized in the middle chapters, while the narrative began and ended (1 and 4) with Jonah rejecting God's compassion on Nineveh.

The social relationships of the people of Nineveh were ruled by violence (3:8); they acted against the moral conscience within every person and in rebellion against God. Jonah's message to the people of Nineveh externalized a new vision of the future that was foreign to their thinking.[21] God would destroy them in forty days (3:4). This new knowledge legitimated a change in their belief system and social behavior. Amazingly, the king and the people chose to internalize this new view of their future. They repented of their

18. J. Ellul, *The Judgment of Jonah* (Grand Rapids: Eerdmans, 1971), 43–46, believes the fish was a means of destruction of Jonah rather than his salvation.

19. A. Lacoque & P. E. Lacocque, *The Jonah Complex* (Atlanta: John Knox, 1981), 53–60, calls this movement from death to life a resurrection, but Jonah never spoke in these terms.

20. J. S. Ackerman, "Satire and Symbolism in the Song of Jonah," *Traditions in Transformation: Turning Pounts in Biblical Faith,* eds. B. Halpern & J. D. Levenson (Winona Lake: Eisenbrauns, 1981), 221–27, thinks the song of thanksgiving has signs of self-centeredness. We believe there was a change in Jonah's heart.

21. Berger, *The Sacred Canopy: Elements of a Sociological Theory of Religion* (Garden City: Doubleday, 1967), 4–8.

evil ways, changed the commonly accepted behavioral patterns of violence (a process of alternation or conversion), and hoped that God might be compassionate (3:5–9).

Jonah surprisingly returned to the attitude of chapter 1 and *rejected God's compassion on Nineveh* (3:10—4:11). As the prophet sat somewhere east of the city of Nineveh in a hot and arid area (4:5–8), the forty days expired. The repentant city of Nineveh was spared. Jonah realized that God's compassion and freedom to respond to human action caused Him to act in mercy (3:10). This divine act was consistent with Israel's traditions (4:2; Ex. 34:6) and Jonah's own personal experience (1:17—2:10), but Jonah was angry with God because these wicked people did not deserve God's compassion. Apparently God thought that justice would be furthered more by the living testimony of the transformed people of Nineveh than by their death. In addition, the people of Nineveh repented! Why should God not change His plans to destroy the nation (see Jer. 18:1–10)?

Jonah's request to die (see similar traditions in 1 Kings 19:4) contradicted his prayer for deliverance in the fish and is almost incomprehensible.[22] Did Jonah want to die because he feared that some might call him a false prophet? No, his problem was with God and His freedom to grant compassion for reasons beyond human reason. Although Jonah had a head knowledge of how God acted (4:2), the integration of this truth into concrete experience was extremely difficult. It was impossible to understand how the justice, compassion, and freedom of God interacted. In a passionate fit of anger Jonah struck out at the senselessness of life in a world run on the basis of divine behavior beyond human understanding.[23]

22. The failure of Elijah to bring down the worship of Baal may explain some of his despair, but Jonah despaired because his ministry was more successful than he wanted.

23. Jonah's response was not that different from the parent who questions God and the purpose for living after the senseless death of a child. The experience does not match the parent's concept of the justice of God. Anger is a frequent response when one feels God has not played the game of life fairly.

To bring some sense of order to Jonah's understanding of the divine operation of justice and compassion, God gave Jonah the joy of a shady plant. Then He removed it (4:5–8). God taught Jonah something about His ways by causing Jonah to experience both the compassion and judgment of God. Jonah was happy with God's compassion (giving the plant) and angry at His judgment (killing the plant). Simply put, Jonah was for compassion (to the insignificant plant; 4:9), and so was God (to 120,000 people in Nineveh; 4:10). This final drama demonstrated that God's ways were sometimes mysterious, but they were not totally beyond finding out. God's acts were a mirror of His justice and compassion, but His freedom to rule the world left a blurred image that required trust, not just human knowledge.

Theological and Social Implications

The prophet Jonah, and the messenger today, must not second-guess God's desire to bestow His compassion on others. God will (and does) act in justice against sin, but His great love for every person in the world causes Him to wait patiently, to give graciously, to forgive mercifully, and to accept compassionately even the most unworthy people in the world. To experience the grace of God and not be willing to tell others of His compassion is a tragedy all must avoid. Messengers of God can neither limit the grace of God nor control its distribution, but they can prevent God's grace from having an effect on their own lives.

Nineveh, Jonah, and God's messengers today have the free will to change the way they think and behave. They can reject God's plan for political, social, or theological reasons. They can try to run from God's demands, but they cannot escape from God's sight or overturn His goals. When they reject God's way, God may compassionately but firmly transform their thinking. It may not be the just thing to do, but who can argue against the compassion of God?

Questions for Discussion

1. Identify a person or group that does not deserve the compassion of God.
2. What was Jonah's understanding of God's compassion that he picked up from the culture and theological traditions of his day?
3. According to God's view of things: What persons or nations deserve compassion?
4. How does the justice of God fit in with His compassion?

Chapter 6

Micah: Justice Will Reign

Introduction

Ancient Near Eastern people believed in the justice of God/the gods. Different cultures define justice in different ways, but a widespread expectation believes that divine powers control the world on the basis of principles of right and wrong. Injustices may exist now, but in the end justice will prevail.

In the real world where people live, injustices are not uncommon. They happen every day, to people in every social class. Injustice involves an abusive use of power where one person forcibly takes advantage of another. Societies construct norms of acceptable and unacceptable behavior and provide institutions to enforce these norms, but people deviate from these standards and do not treat one another justly.

What can or should a messenger of God do about injustice? Will pleasant talk about God's love transform the abuse of power and cause people to treat others fairly? Should a person just ignore the problem? Does it do any good to rant and rave or to lead a march against injustice? The prophets did not avoid the issue of justice, and the modern messenger should not fail to address the implications of justice. God was not silent about the unjust, and He did not forget those who suffered unjustly.

Social Setting

The Historical Context

Micah's ministry was divided into three separate historical settings: a) the difficult days of the weak Kings Jotham and Ahaz; b) the good times of independence and reform under the righteous King Hezekiah; and c) the disastrous years of Manasseh's reign. His prophetic career began a few years before the fall of the northern nation of Israel in 722/721 B.C. (2 Kings 17) and continued until a few years after the defeat of the Assyrians at Jerusalem in 701 B.C. (from 725– 695 B.C.)[1]

	Judah	Israel	Assyria	Egypt
Early	Ahaz weak	Hoshea weak	Tiglath-pileser III strong	XXV Dynasty weak
Middle	Hezekiah strong	in exile	Sennach-erib strong	XXV Dynasty weak
Late	Manasseh weak	in exile	Sennach-erib, Esarhad-don strong	XXV Dynasty weak

The earliest context (1:5–6) placed Micah in Jerusalem during Ahaz's reign (2 Chron. 28). Judah faced the eco-

1. Micah 1:1 mentioned Jotham, but nothing in the book seems to come from his time. Maybe Micah was born in his reign.

nomic pressure of paying tribute to the Assyrian King Tiglath-pileser III (2 Kings 16; 2 Chron. 28) and the religious malaise of rampant idolatry (1:5–7; 2 Kings 16:3–4).

Sargon II came to Judah in 720 and again in 714–711 B.C. to conquer cities in the Philistine plain, the area of Micah's home town of Moresheth.[2] Micah lamented for the cities of this area (1:10–16) and for the nation's royal city, for a similar calamity would soon reach Jerusalem's gates (2:1–2, 8–9; 3:1–12).

After Hezekiah gained political independence from Assyria and instituted religious reforms, the Assyrian king Sennacherib threatened to totally destroy Jerusalem with more than 185,000 troops in 701 B.C. (Isa. 36—38; 2 Kings 18—19; 2 Chron. 32). In the midst of these events Micah encouraged the suffering Judeans with words of hope and deliverance (4:1—5:15).

The last few years of Hezekiah's rule are hidden.[3] In Hezekiah's final years, his son Manasseh became a co-regent and began to turn the nation away from God. This could account for Micah's negative descriptions of social behavior in 6:3–5, 9–11 and his despair in 7:1–6, 10.[4]

---

2. Some relate the list of towns in 1:10–16 to the towns that the Assyrian King Sennacherib conquered in 701 B.C., but the reference to Gath argues for an earlier date around 720–711 B.C. as L. C. Allen, *The Books of Joel, Obadiah, Jonah and Micah* in *NICOT* (Grand Rapids: Eerdmans, 1976), 242, suggests.

3. J. Bright, *A History of Israel* 3d ed.(Philadelphia: Westminster, 1981), 286–88, and his *Excursus* I on 298–309, propose that Sennacherib had a second campaign against Judah around 689 B.C., but this reconstruction is questionable. See D. Redford, *Egypt, Canaan, and Israel in Ancient Times* (Princeton: Princeton Univ. Press, 1992), 351–58.

4. The dating of chaps. 6—7 to the period of Manasseh was first suggested by H. Ewald, *Die Propheten des Alten Bundes* (Gottingen: Vandenhoeck and Ruprecht, 1840), 327. Allen, *Joel, Obadiah, Jonah and Micah* in *NICOT*, 250–52, put chap. 6 earlier between 722 and 701 B.C. and 7:8–20 in the post-exilic era, while J. L. Mays, *Micah* in *OTL* (Philadelphia: Westminster, 1976), 130, 138, 145, 150 and 158, relates most of 6—7 to an exilic or post-exilic setting. H. W. Wolff, *Dodekapropheton Micha* in *BKAT* XIV/4 (Neukirchen-Vluyn: Neukirchener Verlag, 1982), 142–45, points to Deuteromistic circles after the exile. W. Rudolph, *Micha-Nahum-Habakuk-Zephanja* in *KAT* XIII 3 (Gütersloh: Gütersloher Verlaghaus, Gerd Mohr, 1975), 113–14, points to the reign of Ahaz.

The Structure of Social Order

Micah was aware of his audience's sociocultural conception of objective reality, and their political, economic, and religious institutions. His messages interacted with this social order, but his vision of the future was not encased by its limitations. He was open to God's creative work and was able by faith to imagine a future situation quite distinct from his setting.

This political world included nations (Judah, 1:9; Babylon, 4:10; Assyria, 5:5) and cities (Samaria and Jerusalem, 1:5), as well as the rulers (Omri, 6:16) and armies that controlled political events. Time was marked by the rule of kings (1:1), and history commemorated the conflicts between nations (1:5–6, 16; 6:4–5; 7:15). Some powerful leaders had an exaggerated view of their political security among the nations and an unrealistic view of divine justice. Consequently, they did not believe Micah's prophecies of Jerusalem's destruction (2:6–7). Several times Micah interacted with a group of upper class bureaucratic Judean rulers (3:1–3, 9; 7:3). These politicians and judges (3:11; 7:3) were responsible for administering social order, but they corrupted government. They took advantage of the poor, and did not defend individual rights or establish justice (3:9).

The Syro-Ephramite war (734–732 B.C.) and the tribute Ahaz paid the Assyrians (2 Chron. 28:5–8, 17–21) weakened Judah's socio-economic situation. Some Israelites oppressed the dispossessed refugees who fled south after the defeat of Israel (2:8).[5] Social relations deteriorated as upper class people schemed to maintain their status by taking property from the poor (2:1–2, 9) and by abusing the rights of the innocent in court (3:1). King Hezekiah encouraged a return to covenant principles to regulate social and religious behavior (2 Chron. 29:1–16; 30: 1–9; 2 Kings 18: 1–7), but at the end of Micah's ministry, Manasseh reverted to the evil policies of Ahaz and Ahab (6:12, 16; 7:2; 2 Kings 21:3). Violence gov-

5. M. Broshi, "The Expansion of Jerusalem in the Reigns of Hezekiah and Manasseh," *IEJ* 24 (1974), 21–26.

erned social relations. People could no longer even trust in the strong bonds of family loyalty (7:5–6).

Some naively believed that God would never bring judgment on Jerusalem because the Lord was in their midst (2:6–7; 3:11). False prophets legitimated this belief by promising peace to the wealthy (3:5, 11). Though these people worshiped at the temple, many were confused about the purpose of sacrifices (6:3–8).

The Social Location and Role of the Prophet

The Book of Micah did not include detailed information on Micah's former occupation or his social status before he became a prophet. His early years were spent in Moresheth (1:1; likely the Moresheth-Gath in 1:14). This country village in the Philistine plain was about six miles from the major military fortress of Lachish. Micah's view of objective reality was made up of the Hebrew words his parents used, the roles typified in his rural social environment, and the local cultural patterns of behavior. During the years of primary socialization, he internalized these sociocultural meaningful ways of thinking and acting by making them his own.[6] His birth at Moresheth might suggest a lower class rural setting, but his writings assume some education. Rudolph believes that Micah was a landowner in Moresheth, not a poor man.[7] Kapelrud and Beyerlin conclude that he was a cult prophet, while Wolff thinks that his attack on the injustices of the leaders (3:1–4, 9–11) suggests Micah had the social role of village elder.[8] These diverse viewpoints illustrate the breadth of

---

6. P. Berger and T. Luckmann, *The Social Construction of Reality: A Treatise in the Sociology of Knowledge* (Garden City: Doubleday, 1966), 129–37.

7. W. Rudolph, *Micha-Nahum-Habakuk-Zephanja* in *KAT* XIII 3, 1975), 22–23.

8. A. S. Kapelrud, "Eschatology in the Book of Micah," *VT* 11 (1961), 392–405; W. Beyerlin, *Die Kulttraditionen Israels in der Verkündigung des Propheten Micah,* Freant 54 (Gottingen: Vandenhoeck und Rupsecht, 1959); H. W. Wolff, *Micah the Prophet* (Philadelphia: Fortress, 1981), 3–25.

Micah's knowledge of his world and his ability to enter the thought patterns of various subgroups, not his role.

Micah based his understanding of his social identity on his call to a prophetic role (3:8). As a prophet, he believed the source of his power was the Spirit of the Lord. His messages were based on the principle of justice, courage characterized his delivery, and his goal was to cause people to recognize their sins (3:8). These facets stood in sharp contrast to the social identity of other prophets (3:5–7) and in opposition to the theological standards of the leaders of his day (2:1–2; 3:1–3, 9–11; 6:10–12; 7:2–3). This alternate approach to the prophetic task (a deviant view in his social setting) indicates that Micah was not supported by the dominant plausibility structures (political, religious, or social) in society.[9] Micah did not try to maintain the present social or religious structures; instead he tried to transform the popular beliefs of his audience (2:6–7; 6:6–8; 7:10). Micah probably did receive some support from Hezekiah during his reforms.[10]

Although Micah talked a lot about justice, he was not a hard and uncaring person. He cried and lamented (1:8–9; 7:1–6) as he reflected on the wicked state of the nation. He also spoke of the glorious kingdom that God would establish (4:1–8) and sang God's praise for His eternal love and forgiveness (7:18–20).

As a messenger of God, Micah demonstrated literary skill in weaving similar themes together in the judgment and hope sections.[11] He played with words as he repeated them within paragraphs.[12] In 1:10–16 he cleverly created puns on the name of each city to describe its punishment.

---

9. Berger, *Social Construction*, 154–56.

10. An elder, at the time of Jeremiah, reported that Hezekiah did not kill Micah but responded positively to Micah's preaching (Jer. 26:17–19).

11. J. T. Willis, "The Structure of the Book of Micah," SEÅ 34 (1969), 5–42. Themes include just retribution, captivity, an invading army, the fall of the capital city, and complete destruction.

12. J. T. Willis, "The Structure of Micah 3—5 and the Function of Micah 5:9–14," *ZAW* 81 (1969), 191–214. For example: "and now" in 4:9, 11 and 5:1; "drip, prophesy, say" in 2:6 and 11; "head" in 2:13 and 3:1; "in that/the last day" in 4:1 and 4:6.

Micah borrowed literary forms of speech from his cultural setting. These included the lament, oracles of woe, salvation and judgment oracles, plus the covenant lawsuit. These cultural means of expression enabled him to communicate with the people of that time. He employed older theological traditions to justify his accusations against his audience and give authority to his words of hope. These included God's opposition to bribery (3:11; see Ex. 23:8), the exodus (6:4; see Ex. 3—15), and the Balaam story (6:5; see Num. 22—24).

Social Interaction

The Book of Micah

Although some commentators question the authenticity of chapters 4—7, recent authors conclude that Micah spoke most of these sermons.[13] The book can be outlined into three major sections:[14]

- I. The Coming of God in Power to Bring Justice 1:1—2:13
  - A. God's coming will bring destruction 1:1–16
    1. Judgment on Israel for idolatry 1:1–7
    2. Lament over coming disaster on Judah 1:8–16
  - B. Reasons for the coming judgment 2:1–11
    1. The powerful steal property 2:1–5
    2. The powerful reject God's word 2:6–11
  - C. God will come to gather a remnant 2:12–13

---

13. Rudolph, *Micha-Nahum-Habakuk-Zephanja,* KAT XIII3, 25, and Allen, *Joel, Obadiah, Jonah and Micah* in *NICOT* 241–52, believe Micah wrote all the book except 4:1–4; 5:6–8; 7:8–20). According to H. W. Wolff, *Micah: A Commentary* in *CC* (Minneapolis: Augsburg, 1990), 12–14, and Mays, *Micah* in *OTL,* 23, the sayings that can be attributed to Micah are primarily in chaps. 1—3.

14. For a detailed discussion of the major options proposed for the structure of the Book of Micah see D. G. Hagstrom, *The Coherence of the Book of Micah* (Atlanta: Scholars Press, 1988).

II. Just Leadership Will Come to Zion 3:1—5:15
- A. Removal of evil leaders 3:1–12
  1. Unjust judges rejected 3:1–4
  2. False prophets quieted 3:5–8
  3. Corrupt leaders removed 3:9–12
- B. Zion delivered and ruled by a just leader 4:1—5:15
  1. Final exaltation of Zion with God as king 4:1–8
  2. Zion's affliction and deliverance 4:9—5:9
  3. Transformation of a sinful society 5:10–15

III. Coming to God in Humility, Justice, and Hope 6:1—7:20
- A. Lawsuit for not coming to God in God's way 6:1–16
- B. Coming to God for hope in times of despair 7:1–20
  1. Lamentation over an evil society 7:1–6
  2. Hope in God's promises and love 7:7–20

With this background material, it is possible to examine the prophet's social interaction with his audience to discover how he persuaded them to transform their lives.

I. The Coming of God in Power to Bring Justice 1:1—2:13

Micah began his preaching by announcing his theme that God was coming from His place to bring justice to the earth (1:3). *God's coming would bring destruction* (1:2–16) to Samaria and Jerusalem. Micah then explained why God was judging them (2:1–11) and how He would gather a remnant after judgment (2:12–13).

Micah saw how the people in Samaria and Jerusalem adopted ideas from their non-Hebrew neighbors (1:5–7). Frequently when contrary views of reality exist, the more powerful segment of society will try to liquidate the competitive social traditions, its institutions, and the legitimations that support its cultural approach to reality. However, if the alternate ordering of reality is seen as only a small modification, the dominant society may decide to integrate the two approaches.[15] Since the time of Solomon, Judah had preferred the option of integrating Canaanite ways for both he and Ahab gave official approval to the worship of the fertility god Baal (1 Kings 11; 16:29–33). Soon these religious practices at the Baal temples became the norm at the "high places" in Judah under King Ahaz (1:7; 2 Kings 16:4).

Micah's sermon confronted this situation by repeating Israelite theophany traditions (see Pss. 18:7–19; 97:1–5) concerning the power of the God of Israel (1:2–4).[16] The nation's early traditions[17] identify Yahweh as God with sovereign power and justice over all nations. Not even the mountains can resist His power and His holiness. These traditions brought into question ideologies about the existence, power, and worship of Baal. Although the pluralistic nature of most urban centers like Samaria and Jerusalem allowed for some theological diversity,[18] Baalism threatened the heart of Hebrew thought. To undermine this syncretistic perspective, Micah gave a new point of view that was not determined by his social context. God would remove the social mechanisms (ritual, priests, prostitutes, high places) which supported this alternate view of life (1:6–7).

A few years later Micah identified with his audience's mourning by weeping in deep sorrow (1:8–9) over the Assyrian defeat of towns in the Philistine plain.[19] This lament gave Micah credibility in the eyes of his audience (1:10–16), for

15. Berger, *Social Construction,* 116–24.

16. D. R. Hillars, *Micah* in *Her* (Philadelphia: Fortress, 1984), 19–20, focuses on the theophany background to 1:2–4, while Mays, *Micah* in *OTL* 40 and R. L. Smith, *Micah-Malachi* in *WBC* (Waco: Word, 1984), 16, find a prophetic lawsuit here. J. T. Willis, "Some Suggestions on the Interpretation of Micah 1:2," *VT* 18 (1968), 372–79, discusses the universalistic references in 1:2.

17. Berger, *Social Construction,* 92–97. These two powerful forces can determine social behavior and legitimate views about the gods/God in the symbolic universe of a group.

18. Ibid., 125–26.

19. J. B. Pritchard, ed., *ANET* (Princeton: Princeton Univ. Press, 1954), 284–87.

he sorrowed with them over the death of friends and relatives.[20] Nevertheless, the people of Jerusalem were not persuaded to internalize the warnings of this lament, for they had confidence in their military might (1:13).

Micah tried to persuade his Judean audience that all was not well for them. He justified his claims in a woe oracle and a disputation, giving the *reasons for the coming judgment* (2:1–11) of Jerusalem. Micah accused Judah's powerful leaders of stealing property (2:1–2, 8–9) to maintain their status. They took goods from defenseless travelers and those escaping the ravages of war (2:8). Heavy Assyrian taxation (2 Kings 16:7–18) and the burden of a huge immigrant population from Israel around 721 B.C. placed great financial demands on Judah,[21] but this social behavior was unjust.

By faith Micah imagined a new theological and social setting.[22] He believed that God was scheming to turn the tables on those who robbed by robbing them of their houses and land (2:3), their blessing of rest in the land (2:10),[23] and their right to inherit tribal land (2:5, see Num. 34:13). If these abusive individuals would not transform their behavior, God would give their land to godless nobodies (2:4). Now it was the audience's choice. They could internalize Micah's persuasive sermon or reject his message from God.

In self-defense, the audience refused to believe that God would do these things (2:6).[24] Instead, they maintained their own understanding of life by quoting what their proph-

---

20. Hillars, *Micah* in *Her,* 24–28, provides extensive textual notes on the problems associated with reconstructing the puns in 1:10–15, using the names of these towns.

21. Broshi, "Expansion of Jerusalem," *IEJ* 24 (1974), 21, finds archaeological evidence for a tremendous growth in this period. He believed that refugees from Israel comprise a large percentage of these people.

22. Berger, *Social Construction,* 104. In sociological terms, Micah externalized a new view of reality.

23. P. D. Miller, "The Gift of God: The Deuteronomic Theology of the Land," *Int* 22 (1969), 451–61; W. C. Kaiser, "The Promise Theme and the Theology of Rest," *BSac* 130 (1973), 135–50.

24. Berger, *Social Construction,* 130. Believing involves the social process of internalizing something meaningful from another's view of reality into one's own worldview.

ets taught (3:5).[25] The Spirit of God was patient, not vindictive.

Micah unmasked this deceptive way of thinking about God by giving a more complete understanding of God's justice. Indeed, God is patient and good, but only to the just (2:7). Their one-sided view led to false conclusions about their security (2:11).

These words about Jerusalem's destruction brought into question the very future of Judah, but Micah assured his audience that God is faithful to His promises. On a future day *God will come to gather a remnant* (2:12–13) from those judged.[26] God, the King, will lead His people to freedom to their land (2:13).

II. Just Leadership Will Come to Zion 3:1—5:15

The next sermons were a series of judgment oracles about the *removal of the evil leaders* (3:1–12) who ruled Jerusalem during the early years of Hezekiah. Micah communicated God's perspective on the unjust judicial system. It was designed to protect justice, but acts of social deviance by officials led to a fundamental problem. The judges did not know what justice was; they inhumanely treated the weak. Instead of interacting with people on the basis of the social standards set forth in the covenant traditions of Israel (Ex. 21—23), these leaders hated good and loved evil.

The second part of this sermon (3:5–8) addressed the roles of the prophets and diviners in Judah. They were not enlightened by externalizations provided by God's Spirit. They were not filled with courage to tell the truth, nor guided by principles of justice (3:8). They proclaimed positive or negative messages on the basis of their imagination and the

25. Wolff, *Micah* in *CC*, 75, concludes that those objecting to Micah were the military and civil officials he condemned in 2:1–5, while Allen, *Joel, Obadiah, Jonah and Micah* in *NICOT*, 292–94 thinks his opponents were false prophets.

26. Instead of understanding this to be a true prophecy by Micah, A. S. van der Woude, "Micah in Dispute with the Pseudo-prophets," *VT* 19 (1969), 244–60, takes this oracle to be a quotation of the false prophets who promised blessings.

size of the payments they received (3:5).[27] Micah's behavior legitimated the superiority of his motives, gave his message greater authority, and increased its persuasive power.

Micah's concluding evidence indicted all the political and religious leaders (3:9–12). The politicians' social conscience saw no problem with shedding human blood to get a building project done. They condoned violence and encouraged bribery in courts. Priests and prophets served to make a big salary.[28] Yet, these same people had a sense of assurance that God would never destroy Jerusalem, for God dwelt in Zion's temple (3:11; see Ps. 46:4). The dissonance between social behavior and theological beliefs exposed a reified world disconnected from human behavior.[29]

Micah envisioned a day when God would destroy Jerusalem and His temple (3:12). He tried to persuade the leaders to recognize that their security was deceptive. They foolishly believed that God's justice would not bring judgment on them.

A few years later King Hezekiah carried out a great religious and social reform (2 Chron. 29—31). Jerusalem was under Assyrian siege (in 701 B.C.) and the future seemed hopeless (Isa. 36—37). Micah preached a series of salvation oracles that contrasted Jerusalem's present problems with the future *deliverance of Zion and its rule by just leaders* (4:1—5:15). Micah reminded the faithful that God cared for Jerusalem and would rule over it (4:1–8). He externalized a new vision of Jerusalem inspired by insight from God's plan.[30] This constructed a new "utopian" picture of religious and social order.

---

27. G. Stansell, *Micah and Isaiah: A Form and Tradition Historical Comparison* (Atlanta: Scholars Press, 1988), 67–82, examines Micah's opposition to the popular prophets of his day.

28. The priests and prophets were supposed to teach the law of God (see Lev. 10:11; 33:10); courts were to have no bribery (see Ex. 23:8; Deut. 27:25).

29. Berger, *Social Construction,* 89. When reality is disconnected from human activity and viewed as an unchangeable divine will (God is patient), reification takes place. Although God is patient, His patience is directly connected to human behavior.

30. Berger and Luckmann's view of externalization, that process by which people create new social knowledge, is underdeveloped in *Social Construction,* 104.

It justified the people's faith in God and encouraged them to endure their suffering under the Assyrian siege.

Using traditional songs about Zion (Ps. 46—48), God's universal rule (Ps. 96—99),[31] and a prophetic oracle[32] (see Isa. 2:2–4), Micah described Zion's glorious future. Yahweh would be there teaching (4:2), transforming the worldview of Jews as well as Gentiles. All violence and war would end as God righteously judged between nations (contrast 3:1–4,10–12). Then true prosperity will come (4:4), and the exiled remnant of Israel and Judah will come back to Zion (4:6–7), for God will be King forever (4:8). On account of this hope, King Hezekiah and the faithful resisted the popular thoughts and social patterns of their culture and walked in God's ways (4:5).

This great prophecy transformed the people's hopelessness, but the Assyrians were still besieging Jerusalem. What was the relationship between the nation's present difficult situation with Assyria and its future days of glory? Three small paragraphs (4:9–10, 11–13; 5:1–9) contrast what was happening "now" (4:9, 11; 5:1) with what will happen.[33] Now Judah was writhing in pain ("like a woman giving birth"); her leaders and troops could not deliver her (4:9–10).[34] In the future God would deliver the remnant (4:10; 5:7–8) and de-

---

31. These early traditions concerning the future hope of Zion were reviewed in J. J. M. Roberts, "The Davidic Origin of the Zion Tradition," *JBL* 92 (1973), 329–44, and G. von Rad, "The City on a Hill," *The Problem of the Hexateuch and Other Essays* (New York: McGraw-Hill, 1966), 232–42.

32. E. Cannawurf, "The Authenticity of Micah IV:1–4," *VT* 13 (1963), 26–33, believes Micah wrote this oracle and Isaiah used it. Th. C. Vriezen, "Prophecy and Eschatology," *VTSUP* 1 (1953), 213, concludes that Isaiah wrote this oracle and Micah borrowed it, while Allen, *Joel, Obadiah, Jonah and Micah*, 243–44, suggests that both Isaiah and Micah used an earlier oracle.

33. J. T. Willis, "Micah IV:14–V:5-A Unit," *VT* 18 (1968), 529–47, and "Structure of Micah," *ZAW* 81 (1969), 191–214, give a detailed treatment of questions relating to the structure of this section.

34. The reference to Babylon in 4:10 has produced all kinds of difficulties. Mays, *Micah* in *OTL* 26, 104–6 thinks it came from the exilic period, but certainly these people knew that some Israelite exiles in 721 B.C. were sent into exile in Babylon (2 Kings 17:24) and had heard about Merodach-baladan's overtures to form an alliance with Hezekiah (2 Kings 20:16–18).

feat their enemies (4:13; 5:5–6, 9). Expectations would be fulfilled, but not for the present wicked society.

To legitimate his words about a future ruler (the Messiah) of Israel, Micah introduced Davidic traditions (2 Sam. 7:8–16; Hos. 3:5; Ps. 89:35). A child would come from the Davidic city of Bethlehem (1 Sam. 17:12). Through the power of God, he would shepherd the remnant as well as all the nations of the earth (5:4). These words of hope challenged thoughts of despair during the Assyrian crisis. Micah's message transformed the people's misunderstanding of God's plan for Judah (4:12).

The last paragraph (5:10–16) complements 4:1–8.[35] It outlines the social changes that would take place in a future setting.[36] It focuses on the removal of the sources of false hope. Through divine insight Micah was able to imagine the end of trust in military forces and fortifications (no war; see 4:3–4), the end of false gods and false prophets (God would teach the people His ways; 4:1–2), and the end of opposing nations (God would judge between nations; (see 4:3, 7–8). In that day the divine plan will exist on earth.

III. Coming to God in Humility, Justice, and Hope 6:1—7:20

The final sermons came from a later period. Jerusalem was wicked and full of violence (6:12; 7:2). Its dishonest political leaders forgot about God (6:3; 7:3) and did not remember what was required to worship God. This reflected the situation when Manasseh reigned (2 Kings 21). Micah's sermon was a *lawsuit for not coming to God in God's way* (6:1–16).[37]

---

35. E. Nielsen, *Oral Tradition* (London: SCM, 1954), 86, also sees a correspondence between 4:1–4 and 5:10–15.

36. J. T. Willis, "The Authenticity and Meaning of Micah 5:9–14," *ZAW* 81 (1969), 353–67, believes these changes reflect the reform of Hezekiah, but the references to the removal of horses and chariots (5:10–11) hardly apply to what Hezekiah did.

37. Smith, *Micah-Malachi* in *WBC* 32, 5, sees a relationship between Amos 8:5–6 and Micah 6:10–12; thus he dates chap. 6 before 722 B.C. Allen, *Joel, Obadiah, Jonah and Micah,* 249–52, dates 6:9–16 between 722 and 701 B.C. F. C. Burkitt, "Micah 6 and 7: A Northern Prophecy," *JBL* 45 (1926), 159–61, connects both chapters to an Israelite rather than a Judean setting.

The covenant lawsuit followed cultural patterns of the court where witnesses were called, evidence was presented against the accused, a defense was given, and a verdict reached.[38] Micah reminded his audience how God kept His part of the covenant relationship (6:3–5). He delivered them from Egypt (see Ex. 3—15), sent them leaders (Moses, Miriam and Aaron, Ex. 4:10–14; 15:20–21; Ps. 77:20), saved them from the plan of Balak and the curse of Balaam (see Num. 22—24), and led them through the flooding Jordan river (Josh. 2—4). These acts were done so that the people would know God's justice and grace (6:5).

In the final days of Hezekiah, when Manasseh began to take control of Judah, the people did not maintain their covenant relationship (6:3). A different cultural worldview was accepted (2 Kings 21). Some thought they could please God by offering more sacrifices (a thousand rams) or more precious possessions (a firstborn son). This maintained an external level of continuity with the institutionalized patterns for sacrificing (see Ex. 23:15; 34:20; Lev. 1—5), but this approach to coming to God was a radical change from what God required.

Micah condemned the nation's mechanistic ideology of ritual sacrifices (see Isa. 1:10–17; Amos 5:21–24). To come into the presence of God, a person must pattern life around principles of honesty, justice, love for neighbor, fear of the Lord (Ps. 15:1–5), a pure heart (Ps. 24:1–6), a deep love for God (Deut. 6:5), loyal devotion to the covenant stipulations (Deut. 4:13; 1 Sam. 15:22), and a humble submission to God (Lev. 16:31). These traditions legitimated Micah's call for the nation "to practice justice, to continually love being kind, and to walk humbly with your God" (6:8).

The prophet communicated a new theological message to the people because the nation's behavior and theology did not match God's requirements (6:8).[39] Instead of receiv-

---

38. The structure and use of the prophetic covenant lawsuit are treated by G. W. Ramsey, "Speech Forms in Hebrew Law and Prophetic Oracles," *JBL* 96 (1977), 45–58.

39. This is the social process of externalization, proposing a new view of reality that is not socially determined.

ing God's covenant blessing, the nation would be desolate (6:13–16).

The record of Micah's ministry ends with a personal lament about *coming to God for hope in times of despair* (7:1–20). In great sorrow the lamenter described the troubles of the nation (7:1–6) and then came to God for hope (7:7–20). Initially, it seems that the lamenter is the prophet. However, the confession of sin (7:9) could indicate that the city of Zion might also use this lament when it recognized its sinful condition and came to God for help (compare Hos. 6:1–3).[40]

The setting of the lament (7:1–6) was a time of great discouragement and loneliness for the righteous (compare Elijah traditions in 1 Kings 19:4, 10). The reform of Hezekiah was over, and godly behavior patterns changed (7:1–2).[41] With the loss of the righteous community, the plausibility structures which maintained the social world of the prophet crumbled. This threw his subjective understanding of reality into confusion.[42] Bribery and bloodshed were everywhere, and the normal security and social cooperation in family structures were absent (7:3–6). People mocked those who trusted God (7:10).

At this point Micah remembered laments from the Psalms (Pss. 13:5; 31:14; 55:16; 71:14) about waiting on God. Because God is willing to hear those who come to Him (7:7–8), Micah's negative view of his setting faded into the background. The repetition of traditional beliefs, ritual formulas, and prayers were common ways of maintaining the subjec-

40. Mays, *Micah* in *OTL*, 151, thought the speaker was the city of Zion (6:9) which turned to God for help. J. T. Willis, "A Reapplied Prophetic Hope Oracle," *VTSUP* 26 (1974), 64–76, believes this was originally a northern oracle. Hillars, *Micah* in *Her*, 89–90, concludes that the reference to northern cities could be due to the author's interest in reestablishing the united Davidic empire.

41. Some date 7:7–20 to an exilic period because the walls of the city were already destroyed and in need of rebuilding (7:11) and the nation was in exile (7:12). Since Micah told of the destruction of Jerusalem, the exile of its people (1:12, 16; 2:3–4; 3:12), and a restoration in the future (4:1–8, 10, 13; 5:2–9), it would be odd to deny that he could predict the future rebuilding of Jerusalem.

42. Berger, *Social Construction*, 155.

tive reality of one's identity and worldview in times of distress.[43] Micah recognized that God would bring about justice and destroy their enemies (7:9–10; see Pss. 17:2; 43:1). Remembering earlier traditions about God's desire to build Jerusalem (see Amos 9:11–15; Ps. 69:35–36), extend its boundaries (Ps. 80:11–12), and save people from all nations (see Mic. 4:2–4) strengthened his confidence.

These claims so overwhelmed the prophet that he boldly prayed, "do it now, fulfill Your promises, shepherd Your people, establish Your rule as in the days of David!" (7:14). When God answered yes (7:15), Micah broke forth in a hymn of praise (7:18–20). Now he saw God as He really was; he understood something of the plan of God. Thus he praised God because He would solve the problem that separated God and mankind. God would pardon sins (7:18–19; see Ps. 103:12), maintain His lovingkindness forever, have compassion on the remnant of His people, and keep His promises to Abraham (7:20). Although objective reality was full of despair, Micah's vision of God transformed his thinking.

Theological and Social Implications

Preachers not filled with the Spirit of God, not bold enough to talk about justice and sin (3:8), unwilling to weep for those facing judgment (1:8–9), and fearful of loneliness and disappointment will not walk in the steps of Micah. They will emphasize the patience of God (2:7) and the security of God's presence (3:11). They will be more concerned with maintaining their own good paying jobs (3:5, 11). They will not encourage change because they will not see the danger that is coming. They will not attempt to transform the people's behavior because they will ignore God's standard of justice which reveals the need for change. They will not imagine the hope that the future holds.

43. Ibid., 154–55.

Micah knew that justice comes to the earth whenever God comes in power. It is His sovereign reign which the messengers of God proclaim. They weep and warn when they hear that the power of God's justice may bring destruction on sinful people (1:2–7). They oppose those who oppose God's standards of justice (3:1–4) and encourage those who suffer while waiting for God's righteous reign (4:1–8). Although preachers who follow the prophets do not always have success (7:1–2), in the darkness of despair they can have confidence knowing that God hears their cries (7:7–15). They can rejoice in God's everlasting love which removes the sins that separate people from God (7:18–20).

Questions for Discussion

1. Give three examples where Micah's message of justice was different from his audience's view of justice.
2. What principles of effective communication are demonstrated in Micah's sermons?
3. What issues of justice need to be addressed in your social context? What are the cultural differences between your worldview and those who do unjust things today? How could one possibly communicate with these people in a persuasive way?

Chapter 7

Isaiah: Can You Trust God?

Introduction

Why do people trust one person, but not trust another? Often the decision to believe what a person says, and the behavioral responses that follow, are based on past experiences, as well as an understanding of a person's character. These factors produce confidence that the person will do what is promised. Trust allows people to be secure because someone reliable is in control of the final results. Fear is removed; hope is possible.

Trusting God can produce some of the same benefits, but many people are not sure what He will do for them. Others prefer to trust in their own abilities to do what is logical or expedient. Security is controlling the most votes. Fear is removed by manipulating the causes;[1] confidence is having no question about who will win.

1. E. W. Conrad, *Reading Isaiah* (Minneapolis: Fortress, 1991), 36–40, focuses on the "fear not" of trust.

Isaiah did not argue against logical thinking or pretend that trusting God will always be easy, but he knew that those who put their trust in humans were deceiving themselves.[2] The prophet, and God's messengers today, must open the eyes of the blind so that they can see the inadequacies of trusting in human resources. People need to know that Yahweh, the Holy One, is King, the Creator, the Redeemer, the Power that controls history, the everlasting God who strengthens the weak. God is trustworthy!

Social Setting

The Historical Context

Isaiah lived at the same time as the prophet Micah, during the reign of Uzziah, Jotham, Ahaz, and Hezekiah, kings of Judah (1:1). Uzziah sought the Lord and was blessed with great military strength (2 Chron. 26:1–15).[3] The land was full of gold, horses, and pride (2:7–22). The upper class women wore high fashions (3:16–24), and their husbands oppressed the poor (3:14–15; 5:7–9). People thought they did not need to trust God.

In Ahaz's reign (chaps. 7—12) political and social conditions were much worse. Ahaz worshiped foreign gods (8:19; 2 Kings 16), oppressed the lower class (10:1–2), and refused to trust God (7:1–12). God punished the nation by sending Rezin, king of Syria, and Pekah, king of Israel, to defeat Judah (the Syro-Ephramite war; 2 Chron. 28). The Assyrian king Tiglath-pileser III rescued Ahaz from this situation, but he levied heavy taxes on Ahaz.[4]

---

2. J. N. Oswalt, *The Book of Isaiah: Chapters 1–39* in *NICOT* (Grand Rapids: Eerdmans, 1986), 193–96.

3. J. Milgrom, "Did Isaiah Prophesy During the Reign of Uzziah?" *VT* 14 (1964), 164–82. This time is parallel to the days of Hosea (1:1–4) who prophesied in the northern nation of Israel during the prosperous days of Jeroboam II.

4. M. E. W. Thompson, *Situation and Theology: Old Testament Interpretations of the Syro-Ephraimite War* (Sheffield: Almond, 1982), 22–24.

Prosperous time	Uzziah
Syro-Ephramite war Tiglath-pileser strong	Ahaz
Sennacherib's war	Hezekiah
Essarhaddon strong	Manasseh

Much of Isaiah 13—39 relates to Sennacherib's attack on Jerusalem during the reign of Hezekiah (701 B.C.). Historians have reconstructed this event in different ways,[5] but there is little argument over the general political setting. Hezekiah charted a course independent of Assyrian policy (2 Kings 18:7, 13; Isa. 36) and in opposition to the religious patterns of his wicked father Ahaz (2 Kings 18:1–14). In response the Assyrians conquered all of Judah except Jerusalem (Isa. 37:32–37).[6] During this crisis Isaiah gave the nation reasons to trust God.

Hezekiah maintained the independence of Judah, but his son Manasseh submitted to the Assyrian King Esarhaddon, encouraged the worship of other gods, and oppressed the people of Judah (2 Kings 21; 2 Chron. 33). Some of the messages of hope found in 40—66 may date from the early years of his era (see Mic. 6—7).

The final chapters of Isaiah picture the destruction of Babylon, the appearance of the Persian King Cyrus, and the

5. The different ordering of the events in Isaiah 36—39, 2 Kings 18—20, 2 Chronicles 29—32, and the annals of Sennacherib (J. B. Pritchard. ed., *ANET* [Princeton: Princeton Univ. Press, 1954), 287–88) led to the development of five or six distinct ways of understanding the setting in Isaiah 36—39. See the detailed explanation of these theories in B. S. Childs, *Isaiah and the Assyrian Crisis* (London: SCM, 1967) or R. E. Clements, *Isaiah and the Deliverance of Jerusalem: A Study in the Interpretation of Prophecy in the Old Testament* (Sheffield: *JSOTSup* 13 1980). See recently D. Redford, *Egypt, Canaan, and Israel in Ancient Times* (Princeton: Princeton Univ. Press, 1992), 352–58.

6. Sennacherib claimed he took 200,150 people captive in Judah, plus many animals and a large payment of tribute. See Pritchard, ed., *ANET*, 288, and 2 Kings 18:14–16.

return of the remnant to Jerusalem (44:24—45:13; 46—47). Life in exile caused some to question God's power, their status as God's chosen people, and God's love for them (40:27; 49:14; 54:4–8). Isaiah challenged people not to fear other nations or gods, but to trust God. He will accomplish His plan of deliverance (42:9; 43:18).

The Structure of Social Order

The objective parts of the world that structured life into interrelated parts included smaller nations like Syria and Israel, who formed an anti-Assyrian coalition (7:1–8) and large empires like Assyria and Babylon. The social stratification in these nations included kings, princes, wisemen, soldiers, the wealthy daughters of Zion, craftsmen, shepherds, widows, and merchants. These groups developed a social order, but could not completely control conditions in their nation, for nations destroyed nations (13:17–19).

Pro-Egyptian groups in Judah thought their political status was dependent on help from foreign horses and chariots (31:1–3). Isaiah believed God planned political order and military victories. His plans ordered history and challenged secular political theory (14:24–27; 37:26; 46:10–11). A nation's military power was nothing to God (40:15–17).

The institutionalized activities at the temple (1:10–15) included sacrifices and prayers by unrepentant people (43:23–24; 59:1–3). God's house was supposed to be a house of prayer, but it was profaned (56:1–7). Levitical norms directed people to humble themselves and care for the oppressed on fast days (58:3–7). God's word provided structure and meaning for people, but many ignored it or listened to false prophets (8:19–20; 30:9–11).

The Social Location and Role of the Prophet

Isaiah gave minimal information on his family.[7] His wife was called a prophetess (8:3),[8] and their children had symbolic names: Shear-jashub (7:3 "a remnant will return") and Maher-shalal-hash-baz (8:3 "the spoil speeds, the prey hastens"). Isaiah's sermons addressed both the needs of the common people of Jerusalem and the fears of Kings Ahaz and Hezekiah (7, 37—39). Some hypothesized that Isaiah functioned as a royal scribe (in the wisdom traditions), while others traced his roots to the worldview of the temple.[9] His vocabulary reflected knowledge of temple, wisdom, covenant, and royal ideology. This diversity argues against limiting his cultural background to one social group.[10] Isaiah functioned as a central prophet in Hezekiah's reign, but as a peripheral prophet in the time of Ahaz.[11] Isaiah rejected the status quo of political and social conditions. God transformed the prophet's understanding of himself, his people, and the holiness and power of God (6:1–13). In externalizing this new message to his audience,[12] Isaiah used drama (7:3; 8:1–3; 20:1–5; 38:21) and drew upon a rich storehouse of experience to communicate God's plan effectively.

As an orator or preacher, Isaiah used imaginative metaphors, subtle allusions, and double meanings. Rhetorical studies of Isaiah have produced a new appreciation of the lit-

---

7. Amoz is identified in rabbinic tradition (Bab. Tal. Megilla 10b) as the brother of King Amaziah (the father of Uzziah). This would mean that Isaiah was related to the royal family and this might explain why he had access to kings.

8. C. B. Reynolds, "Isaiah's Wife," *JTS* 36 (1935), 182–85. Prophetess could mean she had a prophetic gift or simply that she was the wife of a prophet.

9. J. J. Schmitt, *Isaiah and His Interpreters* (New York: Paulist, 1986), 9–60, supports a wisdom background.

10. P. Berger and T. Luckmann, *The Social Construction of Reality: A Treatise in the Sociology of Knowledge* (Garden City: Doubleday, 1966), 3, 15, 19–28, believe that a person's view of reality is based on the worldview of the people in their social context.

11. R. R. Wilson, *Prophecy and Society in Ancient Israel* (Philadelphia: Fortress, 1980), 271–74.

12. Berger, *Social Construction*, 52, 104, defines externalization as the process of introducing new ideas into reality that were not part of a person's social context.

erary and persuasive skills of the author.[13] The prophet employed traditions concerning creation, the exodus, the covenant, and David.[14] Davies traces Isaiah's use of traditions from legal, wisdom, and prophetic sources,[15] while Clements connects traditions in the first part of Isaiah to those in the second half.[16] These traditions legitimate Isaiah's critique of the popular world view of his day.[17]

Isaiah employed literary forms of speech that were familiar in the social setting of his audience. Although Westermann, Melugin, and Schoors present somewhat different conclusions on the forms of speech in 40—66, all find disputations, salvation oracles, servant songs, and trial speeches.[18]

---

13. J. Muilenburg, "The Book of Isaiah," *IB* 5 (Nashville: Abingdon, 1956), 382–93, focuses on the literary characteristics while Y. Gitay, *Prophecy and Persuasion: A Study of Isaiah 40—48* (Bonn: Linguistica Biblica, 1981) emphasizes persuasion.

14. These traditions included creation in 40:22, 26, 28; 51:16 (see traditions from Gen. 1); the garden of Eden in 51:3 (Gen. 2:8); the flood in 54:9–10 (see Gen. 7:10—9:17); the life of Abraham in 41:8; 51:2 (Gen 12:1–3; 17:1–21); Sodom and Gomorrah in 1:10; 3:9; 13:19 (see Gen. 19:24–26); Israel's bondage in Egypt in 10:24; 52:4 (Ex. 1:8–14); the exodus in 11:15; 43:2, 16; 51:10; 63:11 (see Ex. 14—15); the Sinai covenant in 51:16; 56:4 (Ex. 19—24); the wilderness journey in 43:19–20; 48:21 (Ex. 16—18; Num. 11—14; 20); sacrificial worship on the sabbath in 1:10–16; 56:1–8 (Ex. 20:8–11; Lev. 1—6); laws on bribery in 5:23 (see Ex. 23:8); Israel's battle with Midian in 9:4; 10:26 (Judg. 7—8); and the rule of David in 9:6–7; 11:1–5; 16:5; 55:3–4 (from traditions in 2 Sam. 7:11-16; Pss. 89; 132).

15. E. W. Davies, *Prophecy and Ethics: Isaiah and the Ethical Traditions of Israel* (Sheffield: *JSOTsup* 16, 1981), 12–39, while J. Begrich, *Studien zu Deuterojesaja* (Munich: Kaiser, 1969) finds Isa. 40—66 to be dependent on certain psalms.

16. R. E. Clements, "Beyond Tradition-History: Deutero-Isaianic Development of First Isaiah's Themes," *JSOT* 31 (1985), 95–113, traces themes of the blindness of Israel, divine choosing of Israel, and other less dominant ideas.

17. W. Brueggemann, "Unity and Dynamic in the Isaiah Tradition," *JSOT* 29 (1984), 89–107, makes the same point. His thoughts about "embracing the pain" are less convincing.

18. C. Westermann, *Isaiah 40—66,* OTL (Philadelphia: Westminster Press, 1969), finds the salvation oracle (41:17–20; 43:16–21); the disputation (40:12–31; 49:14–26); the trial speech against the nations (41:1–5;43:8–15) and against Israel (43:22–28; 50:1-3); the royal oracle (44:25–45:7); servant songs (42:1–4; 49:1–6); and the song of praise (42:10–13; 48:20–21; 49:13; 52: 9–10). The prophet used the woe oracle (5:8–23; 28:1—33:24); songs (5:1–6; 12:1–6); and oracles against the nations (13—23). T. C. Butler, *Isaiah* in *LBBC* 10 (Nashville: Broadman Press, 1982) uses forms of speech to describe the prophet's relation to his audience in each section of the book.

Social Interaction

The Book of Isaiah

Isaiah included sermons he preached and messages he wrote to help later generations trust in God. Some suggest that an unknown prophet ("Second Isaiah" and some add a "Third Isaiah") or later disciples of Isaiah added supplementary oracles to this collection because 40—66 mentions exilic events.[19] Others feel it would be unusual for this later prophet to just vanish from the memory of the Jews and for his messages to be attached to another prophet's work. They thought the book was the work of one person.[20] The book can be outlined into seven sections.[21]

I. Trusting God or Trusting Yourself 1:1—6:13
   A. Introductory indictment of Judah 1:1–31
   B. Exaltation of God and humbling of the proud 2:1—4:6
   C. Song of the abandoned vineyard 5:1–7
   D. Woe oracles 5:8–30
   E. Isaiah is transformed by the King 6:1–13
II. Trusting God or Testing God 7:1—12:6
   A. Judgment on God's people 7:1—8:22
   B. Gladness when God's kingdom is established 9:1–7

---

19. See the explanation and basis for this theory in C. Westermann, *Isaiah 40—66* in *OTL*, 3–30. D. R. Jones, "The Tradition of the Oracles of Isaiah of Jerusalem," *ZAW* 67 (1975), 226–46, follows S. Mowinckel, DieKomposition des deuterojesajanischen Buches'; *ZAW* 49 (1931), 87–112, 242–60, who believes Isaiah's disciples edited and collected these messages.

20. R. K. Harrison, *Introduction to the Old Testament* (Grand Rapids: Eerdmans, 1969), 769. D. Carr, "Reaching for Unity in Isaiah," *JSOT* 57 (1993), 61–80, analyzes recent studies of the unity of Isaiah.

21. A. Gileadi, *The Apocalyptic Book of Isaiah* (Provo: Hebraeus, 1982), 171–85, presents a unique view of the structure and unity of Isaiah. He finds a bifid structure (1—33; 34—66), emphasizing the four themes of apostasy, judgment, restoration, and salvation.

C. God's judgment on proud Samaria and Assyria 9:8—10:34
D. The true source of hope 11:1–16
E. A song of comfort and salvation 12:1–6

III. Trusting God's Plan for the Nations 13:1—27:13
A. Humbling of the proud and exaltation of God 13:1-27:1
1. Humbling of the nations 13:1—23:18
2. Exaltation of God 24:1—27:1
B. Song of the protected vineyard 27:2—13

IV. Trusting God or Other Nations 28:1—39:8
A. Woe oracles 28:1—31:9
B. Judah will be transformed by a King 32:1—33:24
C. Judgment on the nations 34:1–17
D. Gladness when God's kingdom is established 35:1–10
E. God's judgment on the proud Assyrians 36:1—37:38
F. The true source of hope 38:1—39:8

V. Trusting God for Deliverance 40:1—48:22
A. Deliverance from other gods 40:1—44:23
B. Deliverance from Babylon 44:24—48:22

VI. Trusting in God for Salvation 49:1—55:13
A. The Servant will bring salvation 49:1—53:12
B. Promise of salvation to those who seek 54:1—55:13

VII. Trusting in God for Restoration 56:1—66:24
A. Restoration after turning from evil 56:1—59:21
B. Glory of restoration 60:1—62:12
C. Final judgment and restoration 63:1—66:24

This outline will provide a literary context for examining the prophet's sermons and understanding his persuasive attempts to transform his audience's thinking and behavior.

I. Trusting God or Trusting Yourself 1:1—6:13

All these sermons came from the period of Uzziah, except the *introductory indictment against Judah* (1:1–31). During the Syro-Ephraimite war (734–732 B.C.) in Ahaz's reign, the nation was like a wounded soldier; all its territory was captured except Zion (1:5–8, see 2 Chron. 28:5–20).[22] This judgment came because the people did not follow God's covenant instructions on social, political, and religious issues (1:2–4). They had less common sense than a donkey (1:3)! Murder instead of justice became the accepted norm, and no one defended the orphan or widow (1:21–23). Some people thought they were pleasing God with their sacrifices (1:10–15, 29), but God rejected their offerings.

Using a covenant lawsuit,[23] Isaiah tried to persuade the nation to internalize new values and transform its meaningless worship at the temple, for God wanted pure hearts, just action, and covenant loyalty (1:16–20).[24] Isaiah externalized a new vision of the future. God will purify the nation (1:20, 24, 29–31), but restore those who trust God. Then Zion will be characterized by righteous behavior (1:18, 24–25).

Having set the book's overall theological direction, Isaiah collected some early sermons from Uzziah's reign (chaps.

---

22. Because of the severity of the destruction pictured in 1:5–8, H. Wildberger, *Isaiah 1—12* in *CC* (Minneapolis: Fortress, 1991), 21, concludes the setting was after the Assyrian attack against Hezekiah in 701 B.C. but the spiritual apostasy was not as fitting. It seems better to connect this to the spiritual conditions during the reign of Ahaz. J. D. W. Watts, *Isaiah 1—33* in *WBC* (Waco: Word, 1985), 17–21 believes this refers to a battle against the northern nation of Israel (not Judah) before 721 B.C.

23. Davies, *Prophecy and Ethics*, 40–64, 90–112. He found covenant traditions, but doubts that wisdom or Amos traditions were employed. H. B. Huffmon, "The Covenant Lawsuit in the Prophets," *JBL* 78 (1959), 288–95, provides background for the covenant lawsuit.

24. Berger, *Social Construction*, 130–31. Internalization is the social process of accepting an idea or behavior as part of a person's own meaningful worldview.

2—6).[25] In this time of economic and political power, Isaiah's first sermon contrasted the future *exaltation of God and the humbling of the proud* (2:1—4:6). Isaiah warned about following the socially constructed worldview of their neighbors who believed false prophets and worshiped idols (2:6–8). God's people were not to multiply military and financial assets (2:7; Deut. 17:16–17) or be proud (2:9–11).

To encourage a change in the people's worldview, Isaiah contrasted two new theological settings: a day when Jerusalem will be holy (2:2–5; 4:2–6) and a day when God will pour out His anger on Judah (3:1–24). On that future day of the Lord (2:2–4; 4:2–6), when the splendor of God's glory appears, He alone will be exalted. Every false source of trust and pride (trees, fortified cities, and idols) will disappear.[26]

God will fulfill his royal Zion promises (see Pss. 46—48; 96—99[27] and traditions like Mic. 4:1–4).[28] God Himself will come to Zion to teach His people and the nations His ways. This primary resocialization or "alternation" will transform people.[29] Their view of the world will then conform with God's new vision of life. War will end, and God will judge

---

25. R. Davidson, "The Interpretation of Isaiah 2:6ff," *VT* 16 (1966), 1–7, and Watts, *Isaiah 1—33* in *WBC* 24, 34, takes the reference to Jacob to refer to the northern nation of Israel, not Judah, but this is foreign to the rest of Isaiah 2—5. Milgrom, "Did Isaiah Prophesy During the Reign of Uzziah?" *VT* 14, 164–72, believes that the lack of any reference to the enemy who will destroy Judah, which is found later in prophecies in the time of Ahaz (7:17–20; 8:4; 10:5–34), indicates that Isaiah 2—5 were from the time of Uzziah.

26. Isaiah used earthquake and theophany imagery in 2:19, 21 to describe the destruction when the majesty of God's splendor appears. See J. Hayes, *Isaiah: The Eighth-Century Prophet: His Times and His Preaching* (Nashville: Abingdon, 1987), 83–87.

27. These traditions are described in J. J. M. Roberts, "The Davidic Origin of the Zion Tradition," *JBL* 92 (1973), 329–44, and G. von Rad, "The City on a Hill," *The Problem of the Hexateuch and Other Essays* (New York: McGraw-Hill, 1966), 232–42.

28. E. Cannawurf, "Authenticity of Micah 4:1–4 (cf. Isa. 2:2–4)," *VT* 13 (1963), 26–33 believes Micah wrote this oracle and Isaiah used his tradition. Th. C. Vriezen, "Prophecy and Escatology," VTSup(1953), 213 thinks Isaiah wrote it and Micah used it, while L. C. Allen, *Joel, Obadiah, Jonah and Micah* in *NICOT* (Grand Rapids: Eerdmans, 1976), 323, suggests that both Isaiah and Micah used an earlier source.

between nations. The Branch, the Messiah,[30] will be in Zion (4:2a, not ineffective leaders as in 3:1–12); the land will be fruitful and God will purge all sin (4:3–4). God's glory will dwell in this new creation to protect His people (4:5–6).

Isaiah communicated God's deep disappointment with Judah in a short symbolic agricultural *song of the abandoned vineyard* (5:1–7).[31] Judah was a vineyard that had special care and everything needed to grow good grapes (5:1–2). Unexpectantly only worthless grapes were found, so it was destroyed.

Isaiah lamented the behavior of the wealthy in a series of *woe oracles* (5:8). They enjoyed elaborate banquets with excessive wine (5:11–12), obstructed justice in the court (5:23), and drove people into slavery (5:7–8).[32] They were proud, claimed to be wise (5:21), rejected the social patterns of behavior in the covenant laws (5:24), and mocked God (5:19). When the Holy One comes, He will be exalted and will humble the proud leaders of Jerusalem (5:15–16). God will defeat their army (5:26–30) and send them into exile (5:13).

In the final section *Isaiah himself was transformed by God* (6:1–13) in the year that King Uzziah died, (6:1). Since Isaiah was preaching before Uzziah's death (chaps. 2—5) this event was not Isaiah's original call. It was a later commissioning for a new role.[33] Although Isaiah was already a prophet, as he stood before the holy God, he saw his own uncleanness and Judah's sin-

---

29. Berger, *Social Construction*, 157–58, 163–73, calls a conversion experience "alternation because it requires a person to alter one's identity and primary ways of viewing what happens in the world.

30. O. Kaiser, Isaiah in *OTL*, 1—12, 2d ed. (Philadelphia: Westminister, 1983), 85–86 refers the "sprout, branch" to the fertility of the land, parallel to the next clause "fruit of the earth." This fits the poetic parallelism well but ignores the use of this root in Davidic traditions (2 Sam. 23:5; Ps. 132:17). See J. Baldwin, "*Semah* as a Technical Term in the Prophets," *VT* 14 (1964), 93.

31. J. T. Willis, "The Genre of Isaiah 5:1–7," *JBL* 96 (1977), 337–62.

32. Davies, *Prophecy and Ethics*, 65–89, traces the legal background of these abuses.

33. C. R. Seitz, *Isaiah 1—39* in *IntCom* (Louiville: J. Knox, 1993), 55, does not see this as Isaiah's inaugural call. K. Koch, *The Prophets I* (Philadelphia: Fortress, 1983), 113, questions whether this was a call narrative while R. Knierim, "The Vocation of Isaiah," *VT* 18 (1968), 41–68, shows that there was a mixture of a vision of judgment and vision of call in chap. 6.

fulness (6:5). This vision of God legitimated his belief in God's kingship (6:1, 5) and holiness (Lev. 19:2). When he saw God's glory, he realized the nation could not exist before a holy God without either forgiveness (6:6–7) or judgment (6:5, 9–11).

God transformed Isaiah's understanding of His two-stage plan for Judah. First the blind will become more blind because the people refused to repent of their sinful ways (6:9–10). This will result in the destruction of the nation (6:11–12). In the second stage, a holy seed will appear (6:13). Now Isaiah had a clear view of God's strategy and the role he would play within this plan.

II. Trusting God or Testing God 7:1—12:6

Isaiah preached these messages during the Syro-Ephraimite war (734–732 B.C.) in Ahaz's reign. The material was structured with alternating judgment (7:1—8:22 and 9:8—10:34) and hope themes (9:1–7 and 11:1—12:6). Three false perspectives (Ahaz's, Israel's, and Assyria's) were exposed in the negative sections, while a great messianic hope unfolded in the positive messages.

The negative sermons described the *judgment on God's people* (7:1—8:22). This happened when Syria and Israel (also called Ephraim) attacked Judah because she did not join an anti-Assyrian coalition (7:1–9).[34] The people of Judah felt helpless (7:1–2), but Isaiah externalized a new divine perspective of hope.[35] Calm can replace fear because God will defeat Israel and Syria (7:3–4,7–9). Isaiah's interaction with Ahaz challenged him to accept the viewpoint of the divine King, but King Ahaz would not trust in God's ability to control his enemies (7:11–12).[36] Ahaz trusted in the military power of Assyria (2 Kings 16:7).

---

34. M.E.W. Thompson, *Situation and Theology: Old Testament Interpretations of the Syro-Ephraimite War* (Sheffield: Almond, 1982), 13–21, relates Isaiah 17:1–11 and Hosea 5:8—7:16 to this period.

35. Berger, *Social Construction,* 104, sees externalization as man's attempt to construct new meanings into reality. This creative activity was an imaginative attempt to believe what God said in this hopeless context.

36. C. A. Evans, "On Isaiah's Use of Israel's Sacred Tradition," *BZ* 30 (1986), 95, finds a play on the root 'mn "believe, establish" in 7:9 and the Davidic covenant in 2 Sam. 7:16. Thus Ahaz's unbelief nullified the Davidic covenant.

Pictured above is a relief dating from 1000-800 B.C. of a six-winged figure who resembles the seraphim described in Isaiah 6:2.

Later Isaiah confirmed this vision by writing on a tablet Maher-shalal-hash-baz "The spoil speeds, the prey hastens"(8:1–2). This was his son's name and symbolized that Syria and Israel would be Assyria's booty (8:3–4). Judah could not rejoice at her enemies' destruction (8:6), for Judah rejected God, that gentle stream of water. Consequently, Judah also would face the destructive flood of Assyria (8:8; 7:17–25).

The central question is: Whose view of the world can one trust? Isaiah heard and followed instructions from the Lord and so rejected the political and military worldview of Judah (8:11). His sermon exhorted people not to be slaves to the fears of the popular view of political reality (8:12–13). Those who believed God waited for Him to fulfill His plans (8:16–18), but those who rejected God's word foolishly looked for explanations from mediums and witches. They suffered in darkness without the light (8:19–22).[37]

The prophet also described *God's judgment on proud Samaria and Assyria* (9:7—10:34). The leaders in Samaria were arrogant (9:9); the people foolishly boasted that they were invincible (9:10). The leaders did not seek the Lord; the prophets deceived the people (9:13–16). The courts did not protect the poor (10:1–2). God's judgment of these nations was a warning that Judah should not follow similar social patterns (9:17; 10:3–4).

The Assyrians in pride declared their strength, wisdom, and control of history (10:8, 13, 15), but they did not understand God's purpose to use them only as instruments of His wrath against Israel (10:5–7).[38] Isaiah revealed God's plan to destroy the glory of Assyria (10:12, 16–19, 24–34) and cause a remnant of Israelites who trusted in Him to return to the land (10:20–22).[39] Judah should not fear Assyria, but trust in the Holy and Mighty One of Israel.

---

37. Thompson, *Situation and Theology*, 36–42, emphasizes the contrast between faith and unbelief in this section.

38. Pritchard, *ANET*, 275–301, gives examples from Assyrian texts which demonstrate their proud attitude.

39. G. Hasel, *The Remnant: The History and Theology of the Remnant Idea from Genesis to Isaiah* (Berrien Springs, Mich.: Andrews University Press, 1980), 96–98.

These negative messages of gloom contrasted with the climactic news of *gladness when God's kingdom is established* (9:1–7). Defeat will vanish in face of joy over a son from David's line.[40] This righteous ruler will be a light, a source of joy and victory (see Ps. 132:16–18), an eternal ruler on the throne of David (2 Sam. 7:16; Ps. 89:27–29). This Davidic ruler will be a Wonderful Counselor (see 28:29), Mighty God (see 7:14), Everlasting Father (10:21), and Prince of Peace (see Mic. 5:4–5). The social interaction and behavior of the Davidic king will be radically different from Judah's present ruler. Earlier Isaiah predicted that a young woman (implying a virgin) will have a son called Immanuel "God is with us" (7:14). Some probably saw this as a reference to the birth of Ahaz's son Hezekiah or Isaiah's son in 8:3, but the traditions concerning "God's presence with" the Davidic ruler (9:6; 11:1; 2 Sam. 7:9, 12–16; Ps. 89:20–29) suggest that Isaiah associated Emmanuel with messianic motifs (Matt. 1:23 connected it to Jesus' birth).[41] This ruler will be a son of Jesse (David's father, compare 9:7; 2 Sam. 7:8–16), *the true source of hope* (11:1–9). He will have the spirit of God, wisdom, counsel, and knowledge (11:1–2; see traditions in 1 Sam. 16:13). This will enable Him to rule according to divine standards of justice and righteousness (11:3–5; see Ps. 72:1–4; Isa. 9:7). This will transform the secular royal ideology of Israel.[42]

The Messiah will function as a signal (compare 5:26; 30:17) to the nations as well as to the Jews exiled in other lands (11:10–11). With a new exodus (11:14, 16),[43] Judah's

---

40. M. E. W. Thompson, "Israel's Ideal King," *JSOT* 24 (1982), 79-88, thought this oracle offered hope to Israel after its terrible defeat by Assyria, but Isaiah spoke to Judah.

41. P. D. Wegner, *An Examination of Kingship and Messianic Expectations in Isaiah 1—35* (Lewistown: Mellen, 1992), 62–135, has a detailed discussion of these issues. See J. A. Moyter, *The Prophecy of Isaiah* (Downers Grove: InterVarsity, 1993), 84–87, or the survey of views in E. E. Hinson, *Isaiah's Emmanuel* (Philadelphia: Presbyterian and Reformed, 1978).

42. M. Tate, "King and Messiah in Isaiah of Jerusalem," *RevExp* 65 (1968), 409–21 emphasized this contrast. Wegner, *Messianic Expectation,* 217–69 gives a detailed treatment.

enemies will be destroyed. Then Judah will sing praise to God for His salvation; they will trust Him and joyfully make known His name throughout the earth (12:1–6).

III. Trusting God's Plan for the Nations 13:1—27: 13

Most of the sermons in 13—23 are "burdens" against nations.[44] Three themes were emphasized: the humbling of the proud nations (13:11; 14:13–14; 16:6; 23:9; 25:11), God's exaltation, and Zion's establishment (14:1–3,32; 16:5; 17:7; 19:19–25; 24:14–16,23—25:9; 26:1–19).

Isaiah's Jewish audience thought their only hope was to trust in the military power of other nations, so the prophet told them about God's *humbling of the nations* (13–23).[45] In the burden against Babylon (13:1—14:23), Isaiah's sermon was legitimating a policy of nonalliance with Babylon. Babylon will not save Judah from Assyria. God will not bless Merodoch-baladan's revolt (in 704 B.C.),[46] for the Babylonians were arrogant and ruthless (13:9, 11, 19; 14:4–6, 20–21) and their king proudly claimed the status of king of the

43. B. W. Anderson, "Exodus Typology in Second Isaiah," *Israel's Prophetic Heritage* (New York: Harper, 1962), 177–95, and G. Widengren, "Yahweh's Gathering of the Dispersed," *In the Shelter of Elyon: Essays on Ancient Palestinian Literature,* eds. W. B. Barrick and J. R. Spencer (Sheffield: *JSOTSUP* 31, 1984), 227–45, treat these themes in some detail.

44. Isaiah 13:1; 14:28; 15:1; 17:1; 19:1; 21:1,11; 22:1; 23:1.

45. S. Erlandsson, *The Burden of Babylon: A Study of Isaiah 13:2—14:23* (Lund: Gleerup, 1970), 48–54, 64, outlines several different ways of analyzing 1—39. S. Mowinckel, *Jesaja-disiplene. Propheten fra Jesaja til Jeremia.* (Oslo: Forlagt Ar. H. Aschoug, 1925), believes that 13—27 were a unit, and O. Kaiser, *Isaiah 13—39* in *OTL* (Philadelphia: Westminster, 1974), xi thinks it would be a mistake to make a large break between 13—23 and 24—27.

46. Erlandsson, *The Burden of Babylon,* 160–66, argues that this chapter refers to an Assyrian king who ruled the province of Babylon. He does not think it referred to the conquest of Babylon by the Persians in 539 B.C. He connects it to the Assyrian attack on Jerusalem in 701 B.C. R. Clements, *Isaiah 1—39* in *NCBC* (Grand Rapids: Eerdmans, 1980),132, dates the chapter to 540 B.C. and the fall of Babylon by the Persians. Watts, *Isaiah 1—33* in *WBC* 24, 189 believes this was a defense of the divine stategy to cause the Assyrians to defeat Judah.

gods (14:12–14). Their destruction will be their day of the Lord. Babylon's king will no longer wage war (14:4–7),[47] but will enter the world of the dead (14:9–21).

Isaiah contrasted Judah's hope with Babylon's hopelessness (14:1–3). The transcendent plan included judgment for Judah (and Babylon), but it also predicted compassion on Judah, their return to the land, and the coming of the nations to Judah. Isaiah's persuasive sermon was based on God's plan for the nations.[48] Judah's leaders needed to transform their understanding of how to survive the present Assyrian threat. They must trust God who rules the nations, not the military leaders who try to control the future with alliances.

This sermon led to a long series of burdens. In the year that King Ahaz died, Philistia rejoiced because a powerful king from the north died (14:29). Judah was tempted to join Philistia in revolt, but Isaiah knew Philistia's joy would soon end (14:31—Sargon II regained order in 711 B.C.). Isaiah encouraged Hezekiah to reject the social pressure to become allies with Philistia for God will protect Zion (14:32).

The burden against Moab (15:1—16:14) came from the same general period.[49] The people mourned earlier judgments (15:1–9), but Moab was still full of pride (16:6); consequently there will be more weeping (16:7–12). Isaiah's

---

47. W. S. Prinslov, "Isaiah 14:12–15. Humiliation. Hubris, Humiliation," *ZAW* 93 (1981), 432–38, and D. E. Gowan, *When Man Becomes God. Humanism and Hubris in the Old Testament* (Pittsburgh: Pickwick, 1975), 66–67, deal with the mythical traditions used in this passage and the sin of pride.

48. Watts, *Isaiah 1—33* in *WBC* 24, 213–16; T. Vriezen, "Essentials of the Theology of Isaiah," *Israel's Prophetic Heritage,* eds. B. W. Anderson and W. Harrelson (New York: Harper, 1962), 128–46; and Conrad, *Reading Isaiah,* 53–82, discuss the divine plan in the theology of Isaiah.

49. W. Rudolph, "Jesaja XV-XVI," *Hebrew and Semitic Studies Presented to G. R. Driver* (Oxford: Clarendon, 1963), 130–43, relates this defeat to the destruction of Moab by Jeroboam II in 2 Kings 14:25, but most placed it somewhere between 715–701 B.C.

sermon was legitimating a policy of independence from Moab.

The burdens about Damascus and Ephraim (17:1–14) came during the Syro-Ephraimite war in 734–732 B.C. God will destroy their fortified cities (17:1, 3, 9), for they trusted in idols (17:8). In the future all nations will worship Israel's God (17:7, 10).

The burden about Cush or Egypt (18:1—20:6) came when the new Cushite King Shabako sent emissaries to ask Hezekiah to join those revolting against Assyria.[50] Isaiah knew that civil war would tear Egypt apart (19:2, 4), its idols and sources of insight would fail (19:3); therefore, it was senseless to trust in Egypt. To discourage Judean acceptance of this alliance, Isaiah walked around naked, symbolizing Egyptians going into exile (20:2–4).

A second reason for rejecting an Egyptian alliance was drawn from the final era of Egyptian (and Assyrian, 19:23–25) history. In the future God will deliver the weak Egyptians (19:16–22, like Israel in Ex. 3—15).[51] In that day Assyrians, Egyptians, and Israelites will worship God together in Zion (18:7; 19:23–25). Since Egypt and Assyria will one day accept God, why should Judah now reject God and foolishly depend on Egypt or fear Assyria?[52]

The burdens against Babylon (21:1–10), Dumah (21:11–12), and Arabia (21:13–17) are rather obscure. Although some ate and drank at ease, thinking that Babylon and her allies (Elam and Media) would be victorious,[53] Isaiah saw visions of Babylon failing. Judah should not depend on these nations.

---

50. Kaiser, *Isaiah 13—39* in *OTL*, 91, agrees with this context for Isaiah 18, but misdates 19 in the Persian period.

51. Erlandsson, *The Burden of Babylon,* 76–80 picks up several verbal connections with the exodus tradition.

52. Berger, *Social Construction,* 92–95, describes how legitimations like these justify behavior and a person's view of the world.

53. Ibid., Erlandsson describes the history of this period and believes Elam and Media were in an alliance against Assyria around 700 B.C. Oswalt, *Isaiah 1—39,* in *NICOT,* 392, thinks that Elam and Media were fighting against Babylon.

The sermon against Judah (22:1–25) was connected to events surrounding Sennacherib's attack on Jerusalem.[54] Although some died and others became captives, Jerusalem was full of laughter and joy (22:1–3,12–13) when Assyria withdrew to fight Egypt (2 Kings 18:9; Isa. 37:9). Isaiah saw this joy as a false perception of their condition. They trusted in weapons of war and not the divine plan (22:8, 11). Isaiah called for repentance (22:12).

Isaiah's sermon about Tyre (23:1–18) pictured an ancient, proud, and beautiful metropolis; a powerful trading city with merchants as wealthy as princes. The city had powerful colonies throughout the Mediterranean and an impregnable defensive location on an island (23:7–9). This human view of Tyre would change. God's strategy was to remove Tyre's pride (22:8–9). This was another warning not to trust in alliances.

Isaiah concluded this series of sermons on foreign nations with a description of the *exaltation of God* (24:1—27:1) after the humbling of all mankind. Scholars have different opinions of the literary genre (eschatological or apocalyptic), structure, unity, and date of this sermon.[55] Some signs point to continuity between 13—23 and 24—27 so it probably came from this period.[56] The cities mentioned in 13—23 were typified in the condemnation of "a city" (24:10,12;

---

54. J. T. Willis, "Historical Issues in Isaiah 22:15–25," *Bib* 74 (1993), 60–70, discusses the historical issues.

55. W. R. Millar, *Isaiah 24—27 and the Origin of Apocalyptic* (Missoula: Scholars, 1976), 1–22; Kaiser, *Isaiah 13—39* in *OTL*, 173–79; B. Otzen, "Traditions and Structures of Isaiah XXIV-XXVII," *VT* 24 (1974), 196–206; and G. W. Anderson, "Isaiah 24—27 Reconsidered," *VTSUP* 9 (1963), 118–26, offer a survey of different views on each of these questions.

56. Kaiser, *Isaiah 13—39* in *OTL*, xi, and Clements, *Isaiah 1—39* in NCBC, 196-97, see a close connection between 13—23 and 24—27. In contrast O. Plöger, *Theocracy and Eschatology* (Richmond: John Knox, 1968), 54, believes 24—27 were a distinctive section which cannot be compared to the oracles against the nations. On the apocalyptic character of these chapters see J. Oswalt, "Recent Studies in the OT Eschatology and Apocalyptic," *JETS* 24 (1981), 189–302.

25:2–3; 26:5). Both 13—23 and 24—27 foresaw the humbling of the proud, the exaltation of God, and the universal rule of God.[57]

The social setting was not identified. The sociological analyses by Plöger, Hanson, and Millar found a ruling class (including priests) in conflict with another group of visionary Jews who were eschatological in orientation, but this rests on meager evidence.[58] The setting was explained in the lament in 26:7–19.[59] Other nations ruled over God's people in the past (26:13), but these were defeated (26:14). Now God had increased the borders of Judah (26:15). In spite of this, their present enemy created stress (26:16–18). Jews longed for God to teach the wicked nations that He is God (26:8–10). This lament fits Hezekiah's reign which had both a spiritual revival (26:7–9,13) and an attack on Jerusalem by Sennacherib (see the connection with 37:3, 20).

The prophet summarized God's ultimate plan for the nations in 24:1—27:1. His strategy will involve two phases: a destruction of the present world to delegitimate its institutions and philosophy, to delegitimate its institutions and philosophy, and the introduction of new plausibility structures that support the new world that God will create.[60]

The first phase will devastate everything on the surface of the earth and end the religious, economic, and social patterns that previously governed behavior (24:1–2, see Isa. 13:5, 9). God will remove the proud (24:4; 25:11, see 2:9–22).

---

57. Humbling of the proud in 13:11, 19; 14:12–14; 16:6, 14; 17:4; 23:9 and 24:4, 21,23a; 25:2, 10–12; 26:5–6, 11; the exaltation of God in 14:32; 16:5; 17:7; 18:7; 19:19–25; and the universal rule of God in 24:14–16a, 23; 25:1, 3, 9; 26:13,15. Day of the Lord and Sheol themes are strong in the opening (13:6–13; 14:8–11, 5–21) and closing sections (24:1–13, 16a–22; 26:14, 19).

58. Plöger, *Theocracy and Eschatology*, 57–67; Millar, *Isaiah 24—27*, 115–17; P. D. Hanson, *The Dawn of Apocalyptic* (Philadelphia: Fortress, 1979), 313–14.

59. Kaiser, *Isaiah 13—39*, 210.

60. Berger, *Social Construction*, 148–63, sees the importance of key officials sharing their subjective view of the world to help others to maintain what is acceptable and reject other views as deviant.

This would bring an end to laughter and "the typical fortified city" (24:10–12; 25:2,10–12). This will shake the natural world to its core (24:18); it will bring heavenly powers and earthly kings low (24:22–23). The old world will end.

A transformed world will take its place. God will reign as King in Zion (24:23, see 2:2–4); people from the ends of the earth will sing hymns to glorify God (24:14–16a; 25:1, 3; 26:1). They will enjoy a feast on God's mountain, with no more sickness, death, or dragon (25:6–8; 26:19; 27:1). People will be righteous and trust God (26:1–4). This new world provided a perspective from which to endure Judah's present situation.

In light of this hope Isaiah sang a *song of the protected vineyard* (27:2–13) to replace the earlier "Song of the Abandoned Vineyard" (5:1–7). Although God cared for both vineyards (both symbolized God's people), the future vineyard will have peace, much fruit, and no wrath from God (27:2–6). The former "city" was abandoned (27:10–11), but in the future people will worship God at Jerusalem (27:12–13).[61]

IV. Trusting God or Other Nations 28:1—39:8

In a series of *woe oracles* (28:1—31:9; like the woe oracles in 5:8–30 after the song of the vineyard), the prophet preached to those who still did not trust God. Isaiah spoke these sermons in Hezekiah's day when the Assyrians were attacking Palestine.

Isaiah reminded his audience of the situation in Israel before its destruction in 721 B.C. Israel was ruled by proud leaders, priests, and prophets who were blinded by their drunken stupors (28:1, 7–8). They mocked the prophet's instructions (28:9–10) and did not understand God's plan to destroy them (28:2–3, 11) or His promise of a future king over the remnant (28:5–12).

---

61. Plöger, *Theocracy and Eschatology*, 73–75, and Clements, *Isaiah 1-39*, 220–21, interpret this passage to be about the fall of the Northern Kingdom of Israel, but this rips it from the context of 24—27.

Isaiah maintained that Judah was just as bad as Israel, for their leaders scoffed at Isaiah's warning, foolishly claimed that death would never get them, and deceived themselves with lies (28:14–15). The leaders were so blind that God shut their eyes so that God's vision would be sealed from them (29:9–12, see 6:9–10).[62] They talked like they honored God, but these were just memorized words without meaning (29:13). They thought God would not see their ruthlessness (29:15, 20–21). They even accused God of not knowing how to run the world (29:16).

To convince his audience to transform their thinking, Isaiah claimed that these socially acceptable ways of thinking in Judah were inconsistent with the divine plan. God interacted with mankind on the basis of His precepts of justice and their trust in Him. They did not have as much sense as the simplest farmer who plows and harvests in the right season (28:23–29). Contrary to popular opinion, God will destroy the proud city of David, the place of the altar (28:21; 29:1–8).

In spite of this terrible future, God will one day open the eyes of the blind. Then the needy will rejoice in God's abundance, and oppression will end (29:17–21). The people's thinking will be transformed, for they will accept God's ways, know His truth (29:24), and sanctify His name (29:22–23).

The prophet lamented Judah's rejection of God's plan (30—31). An alliance with Egypt was not part of God's strategy; it contradicted their tradition (30:1, 9–10; 31:1). The people preferred pleasant words rather than negative ones from a holy God, oppression and military strength rather than a quiet trust in God (30:10–11, 15–17; 31:1). Trust in Egypt will cause shame and no profit. Egyptians were mere men, not God (31:2–3).

As a lion protecting its prey, God will protect Zion if she will return to Him and get rid of her false gods (31:4–9). Then He will be gracious and will teach them His ways (30:19–22, see traditions in 2:2–4). Prosperity will return to

---

62. Thompson, *Situation and Theology*, 15–17; 50–51, discuss different ways of looking at God's hardening.

the land, and God will heal and transform His people (30:26).

Just as Isaiah's vision of the glory of God transformed his thinking and actions (6:1–13), so *Judah's will be transformed by the king* (32:1—33:24), when the Lord demonstrates His power in their midst.[63] Isaiah described an ideal future time when a righteous ruler will reign with justice (32:1–2, see Messianic ideas in 9:6–7). Using wisdom imagery[64] Isaiah told how the Spirit will open the eyes of the spiritually blind, the fool will change his ways, and the nobles will make noble plans (32:2–8). Righteousness and security will come (32:15–20).

Judah required major changes before this could happen. Therefore, Isaiah urged the complacent people of Jerusalem to mourn over the coming destruction of Judah (32:9–14). Finally, the people internalized the idea that God might not protect them (33:8).[65]The people wept (33:7–9), pleaded for grace, glorified God's name, and confessed that He was the only source of justice, salvation, and wisdom (33:5–6). This was a total change from their old socially developed way of looking at things. Now their view was consistent with the transcendent perspective. Now God could fulfill His promise and turn Assyria into chaff (33:10–11). Now He could rule as King (33:17, 22) and deliver them from Assyria (37:18–21, 30–38).

---

63. This happened after Hezekiah's payment of tribute to Sennacherib (2 Kings 18:13–16) and just after Rabshakah's last call for surrender before the Assyrian seige (36:1–20). J. B. Payne, "The Effect of Sennacherib's Anticipated Destruction in Isaianic Prophecy," *WTJ* 34 (1971), 22–38.

64. Kaiser, *Isaiah 13—39*, 321, and most others recognize this wisdom connection, but there is no need to date it in a post-exilic period. Hezekiah and his court were known to have a strong interest in wisdom (see Prov. 25:1).

65. Berger, *Social Construction*, 114, 129–32. Having denied or nullified the political view of the blind in Isaiah 30—31, Isaiah now enables some to accept into their frame of reference the divine perspective. This changes their pride and manipulation into weeping and trusting in God's salvation. True transformation was accomplished.

Consequently, Isaiah announced that God would bring *judgment on all nations* (34:1–17). The oracle initially mentioned the small nation of Edom (34:4, 6), but its climactic position at the end of 28—33 and its reference to all nations (34:1–2) suggests that Edom was a symbol of all nations (compare the use of Edom in Isa. 63:1–6; Obad. 15–21).[66] In justice, God the warrior will sacrifice the nations (symbolized by Edom). The earth will burn from fire and brimstone (34:9) and be left to wild animals and weeds (34:10–15; see 13:21–22). Isaiah assured his audience that God's Spirit would accomplish this (34:16–17).

In sharp contrast to the slaughter and desolation of the nations was the *gladness when God's kingdom is established* (35:1–10). God's plan will transform Zion into a place of rejoicing when she sees the majesty of God (35:2; see 30:23–25; 33:17,21). God will heal those with blindness (35:5–6) and provide a safe highway for the redeemed to come to Zion (35:7–10).

Isaiah proclaimed *God's anger on the proud Assyrians* (36:1—37:38) who surrounded the city of Jerusalem (2 Kings 18—20, 2 Chron. 29—32 and the Annals of Sennacherib in *ANET,* 288).[67] The Assyrians had captured most of Judah, and Hezekiah had paid back taxes to Sennacherib.[68] The dialogue contrasted the views of the Assyrian commander Rabshakah (36:1–20; 37:8–13) and God's plan (37:6–7, 21–38). Hezekiah was caught between these two strategies. Should he submit to Assyria or trust God (37:1–4)?[69] Rabshakah's purpose was to change Hezekiah's understanding of reality so that the king would internalize the Assyrian point of view

---

66. J. Muilenburg, "The Literary Character of Isaiah 34," *JBL* 59 (1940), 339–65, and M. Pope, "Isaiah 34 in Relation to Isaiah 35 and 40—66," *JBL* 71 (1952), 243, see Edom as a representative.

67. See H. H. Rowley, "Hezekiah's Reform and Rebellion," *Men of God* (Edinburg: Nelson, 1963), 98–132; Childs, *Isaiah and the Assyrian* ; Clements, *Isaiah and the Deliverance of Jerusalem JSOT Sup 13,* and Redford, *Egypt, Canaan, and Israel,* 351–58, for a discussion of the historical and literary problems as well as some possible solutions to these difficulties.

68. It does not seem to be necessary to hypothesize a second campaign to account for all the events in this story as J. Bright, *A History of Israel,* 3rd ed. (Philadelphia: Westminster, 1981), 298–309.

and submit to Assyria without a battle. To undermine any possible sources of Israelite confidence, Rabshakah rationally argued that:

(a) he Jews did not have enough military power to withstand the Assyrian army (36:5);

(b) any strategy that put hope in the Egyptian army would bring injury rather than help (36:6; 37:9, this was consistent with Isaiah's words in 18:1—19:17; 30:1–5; 30:1–3);

(c) God sent Assyria to destroy Judah (36:10);

(d) the Jews should not blindly accept the words of a political leader who was apt to deceive his followers with promises that God will deliver them (36:14–15; 37:10); and

(e) none of the gods of the other nations had delivered their countries from the Assyrians (36:18–20; 37:11–13).

To counteract any "misinformed propaganda" by Hezekiah about the brutal treatment that the people would receive, Rabshakah made a bargain (36:8) and promised peace and prosperity (36:16–17).

In light of such overwhelming evidence and the social pressure of the Assyrian army around Jerusalem, few options were available. Hezekiah could accept the Assyrian worldview (like his father Ahaz in 7:1–10) or ask God to prove that Yahweh, not the Assyrian gods, were all-powerful. Hezekiah lamented his situation in sackcloth; he recognized his inability to rescue the nation from Assyria. He cried out to the living God for hope (37:1–4). Hezekiah internalized God's perspective in spite of this Assyrian crisis.

---

69. Berger, *Social Construction,* 109, 115, 119, notes that the strongest arguments for one worldview do not always win the hearts of the listeners. The person or group having the most power will often impose their will on others rather than allowing them to choose the best reasons. This is not always bad, for Hezekiah's reform was a top down movement, not a grass roots turning to God.

He believed that the Creator of the heavens and the earth is still the ruler of all the kingdoms, that He is God and is enthroned in the temple in Jerusalem (37:16; see Ps. 24:1–2; 74:12–17; 99:1).[70] Hezekiah requested deliverance so that God's name might be glorified by His victory (37:17–20).

Isaiah's response contrasted God's view of reality with the Assyrian perspective (37:21–35). God saw Assyria raising herself in pride against the holy God of Israel, reproaching God by claiming, "I have done this and I have done that," when in fact it was God who made it possible for Assyria to defeat other nations (37:23–28). God will defeat the Assyrians and save Jerusalem for His sake and for the sake of His servant David (37:6–7, 30–35). That night God struck down 185,000 Assyrian troops, and the remaining troops returned home.

In spite of these victories Hezekiah still needed to learn more about *the true source of hope* (38:1—39:8; parallel to 2 Kings 20; 2 Chron. 32:24–26, 31).[71] The approaching death of Hezekiah (38:1) indicated that Hezekiah was not the true hope for Judah (contrast 11:1—12:6). Although God extended the life of Hezekiah and produced a miraculous sign because Hezekiah walked in a pattern consistent with God's wishes (38:3–8), God was the only true source of hope for Judah. Salvation and life came from the Giver of life who delivered Hezekiah from death by sickness (38:6, 20). God does not honor the proud who attempt to live by political alliances or human riches (39:2). Ultimately,

---

70. Clements, *Isaiah and the Deliverance of Jerusalem,* 72–89, draws the Zion tradition from the later period of Josiah, but this reconstruction was built on the supposed legendary character of this passage and provides no theological tradition for Hezekiah to base his decision on. Certainly he knew of the Davidic promises, covenant traditions, hymnic songs of praise to God, and ideas associated with God's presence in the temple at Jerusalem.

71. Chapter 38 is hard to place (it seems to be before 39:1), but 39 is clearly out of chronological order, for the time of Merodach-baladan's visit was while Hezekiah still had riches to show off (39:2) and when he was thinking about the possibility of an alliance with Babylon against Assyria (probably 703 B.C.).

Hezekiah was not the answer for Judah; salvation was in the Lord.

V. Trusting God for Deliverance 40:1—48:22

The setting of Isaiah's audience is problematic because there are few specific historical details. Because of the reference to Cyrus (44:28—45:1) this material could be post-exilic; but there is no lamenting over the fall of Jerusalem as in Lamentation, and there are inconsistencies between Isaiah's vision of the future and the actual setting in post-exilic times. These factors make it difficult to place the author in exile.[72]

The first sermon dealt with Judah's hope of *deliverance from other gods* (40:1—44:23). Judah needed comfort, had paid dearly for her sins (40:1–2), and wondered if God cared for her (40:27). The people were afraid and not sure if God would deliver them (41:10–14, 20; 43:1, 5; 44:8). The people were blind (42:16, 18–20; 43:8; see 29:9; 32:3–4) and were unwilling to obey God's law; therefore, God would destroy their land (42:18–25; 43:5–6, 14; 44:26–28).[73]

Isaiah legitimated a new social understanding of reality by transforming the people's perception of who God was and what His plan was for dealing with their problems. Judah needed a new view of God (they ignored earlier instructions, 42:19–24).[74] When other nations conquered God's people, Judah's reified belief in Zion's unconquerability was destroyed (Ps. 46; 48; 132).[75] God now appeared to be not as

---

72. R. N. Whybray, *Isaiah 40—66* in *NCBC* (London: Oliphants, 1975), 20–23, and Westermann, *Isaiah 40—66*, 3–6, date the book around the time of Cyrus (550–539 B.C.) E. J. Young, *The Book of Isaiah*, vol. III (Grand Rapids: Eerdmans, 1972), 17, believes the prophecies come from Isaiah before the exile.

73. Conrad, *Reading Isaiah*, 83–102, makes a distinction between the "we" passages (42:24a which refers to the faithful survivors of the exile) and the "they" passages (42:24b which refers to a idolatrous and disobedient community).

74. Berger, *Social Construction*, 110–11; 156, shows how the repetition of tradition helped to maintain a person's worldview.

75. Ibid. Berger sees reification as the social process of attributing absolute status to a belief (God will protect Judah) by ignoring the human factor (protection is based on human faithfulness).

powerful as other gods. Isaiah attacked these popular opinions by showing that the nations, idols, and kings were nothing before God (40:12–26). The Creator measured the heavens; He put the stars in orbit; He has unlimited strength (40:12–28).

Isaiah also interacted with the people's false views of other gods in a court trial (41:1–29; 43:8–13).[76] The idols were invited to announce what they had done or will do, but they could not answer (42:5–7, 21–24). The idols were made by craftsmen from a tree. One part of the tree was burned, but the rest of the tree was worshiped (44:12–17). People who followed idols have lost touch with reality and have a deceptive view of how the world works (44:18–20). In contrast, Yahweh is the King of Israel, the only God, the first and the last. He created, spoke, and acted (44:6). Those who trust in God can gain strength for their trials (40:29–31) and insight from His promises and character (41:20). The reason for God's punishment was Judah's sin, not God's weakness or injustice (40:2; 42:22–25; 43:27).

Isaiah gave other sermons that provided reasons for accepting a new understanding of the world in salvation oracles.[77] God will allow Israel's captives to come home (43:1–7). God controlled events in former days (known from their traditions), and He will do similar things in a new day (43:18–21). God's "former things" were a persuasive reinforcement to maintain the nation's faith.[78] His "new things" justify a change from skepticism to faith in God.[79] He will redeem, for they are still His chosen servants who were created to glorify His name (43:1–7; 43:21). Their world will be transformed when God leads the blind servants out of the

---

76. R. J. Clifford, "The Function of the Idol Passages in Second Isaiah," *CBQ* 42 (1980), 450–64, believes the idol passages were meant to be a contrast to make Isaiah's image of God more vivid. This is true, but it ignores their function in legitimating a new social understanding of the idols and God in Israel's belief system.

77. For a detailed study of the salvation speeches see R. Melugin, *The Formation of Isaiah 40—55, BZAW,* 1976, 13–27, or E. W. Conrad, "Second Isaiah and the Priestly Oracle of Salvation," *ZAW* 93 (1981), 234–46.

78. Gitay, *Prophecy and Persuasion,* 34–49, analyzes the use of persuasion (the emotional, rational, and ethical appeal) in each oracle. His rhetorical study is a valuable complement to a sociological study.

darkness (41:17–19; 42:14–17; 43:14–21; 44:3–4). God will forgive their sins (43:25; 44:22) and pour out His Spirit on them (44:3).

Finally, in the first servant song, God promised to send a special chosen Servant in whom His soul delighted (42:1, see Davidic traditions in 1 Sam. 13:14). This Servant will establish justice in the earth (42:1–4; see 9:6–7; 32:1; 33:5–6). He will be a light to Israel and the nations, to open the eyes of the blind and bring glory to God (42:6–8, see 9:1–2). Some identified this Servant with a prophet or God's blind servant Israel, but the characteristics of this servant go beyond either (compare with messianic traditions).[80]

In the second section Isaiah described Judah's *deliverance from Babylon* (44:24—48:22). The Israelites were obstinate children who quarreled (45:9–10; 46:8, 12; 48:4, 8) and refused to follow God's laws (48:17–18). They swore by God's name, but righteous behavior was not characteristic of their lives (48:1–2). The people were unwilling to accept God's ways (45:9–10), but followed the explanations of diviners and wise men (44:25).

To persuade the people to reject their foolish deviant thinking[81] and internalize God's plan, the prophet preached that God had already chosen a king named Cyrus to be His shepherd (44:28; 45:1). God will cause him to sub-

---

79. B. S. Childs, *The Old Testament as Scripture* (Philadelphia: Westminster, 1979), 311–38, thinks the former things refer to the prophecies in Isaiah 1—39, and R. E. Clements, "Beyond Tradition History: Deutero-Isaianic Development of First Isaiah's Themes," *JSOT* 31 (1985), 95–113, agrees C. R. North, "The 'Former Things' and the 'New Things' in Deutero-Isaiah," *Studies in Old Testament Prophecy* (Edinburgh: T & T Clark, 1957), 111–26, believes the former things refer to the exodus or earlier victories by Cyrus.

80. An extensive survey of different interpretations of the servant is found in H. H. Rowley, "The Servant of the Lord in the Light of Three Decades of Criticism," *The Servant of the Lord and Other Essays* (London: Nelson, 1952), 1–57; C. C. Kruse, *The Servant Songs: Interpretive Trends Since C. R. North* (Guilford, Ct., 1978); J. D. W. Watts, *Isaiah 34—66,* in *WBC* 25 (Dallas: Word Books, 1987), 115–18, with recent bibliography.

81. Berger, *Social Construction,* 119–28. To gain social disapproval of the Babylonian worldview, Isaiah classified it as a deviant, sick way of looking at reality; then he justified his claim with appropriate evidence like any good preacher.

due nations (45:1–2) and build Jerusalem and the temple (44:26–28; 45:13). The foreign nations who worship other gods will come to Israel with gifts and a humble spirit, for every knee will confess that He is God and glorify Him (45:20–25; see traditions in 2:2–4; 19:19–25). These announcements justified a change in Israel's thinking. Why refuse to trust God if He will accomplish these redemptive acts for Israel?[82]

The prophet reinforced this position in Isaiah 46—47. What would happen to the gods and nations which appeared so powerful?[83] The Babylonian chief god Bel (also called Marduk) and Nebo (Nabu, the one who determined people's destiny) would be impotent; they would not save anyone (46:1–2). Idols of wood and metal which cannot speak are nothing when compared to God (46:5–7; see 40:12–31). Babylon would soon lament its demise and go into exile (47:1–15). Babylonian wisdom and its astrologers were deluded and self-centered (47:10–13). God's past faithfulness legitimated the people's trust in His future acts of salvation (46:8–13).

The prophet closed this section with some harsh words about Israel's present state and her need to transform her thinking and action. Although some people called themselves the people of Zion and claimed to trust God (48:1–2), others were very rebellious and obstinate (48:4, 8). Israel should have learned from her past failures to accept God's instructions; then they would have enjoyed the blessings of God (48:17–19). In the future they will rejoice when God delivers them from Babylon (48:14–15,20–21).

VI. Trusting in God for Salvation 49:1—55:13

These sermons were centered around the servant of the Lord who will establish justice and salvation to bring a new

82. C. Stuhlmueller, *Creative Redemption in Deutero-Isaiah* (Rome: Pontifical Institute, 1970) provides an extensive study of the redeeming and creative activities of God in Isaiah.

83. Gitay, *Prophecy and Persuasion*, 191–209, describes some of the persuasive techniques Isaiah used.

order to the world (49:1–13; 50:4–11; 52:13—53:12). These give little evidence of the polarization of the nation into the religio-political parties that Hanson finds.[84] The main social groupings were those faithful to God and those who were not.

The sermons point to a time when the land will be desolate and the people will feel alone (49:17, 19–20; 54:7) because they think God has forsaken them (49:14; 54:6).

Isaiah's sermon reminded his audience that *the Servant who will bring forth salvation* (49:1—53:12) will transform the world's orientation to justice, bring salvation to the nations (49:1, 6–7; see 42:1–13), and bring the people of Israel back to God (49:5–6). His task will seem like a futile waste of time because He will be despised, beaten, and killed (49:7; 50:6; 53:2–9). Nevertheless, He will be faithful to His task, and God will vindicate Him (49:3; 50:5, 7–9). One day kings and rulers will honor the servant (49:7; 52:12, 15).

One might conclude that the Servant was a foolish prophet who got what He deserved (53:4b) or was a symbol of Israel who suffered in exile,[85] but the Servant humbly died for other people's sins, not His own (53:4–9). Since God's justice was satisfied through His offering of Himself as a sin offering (53:10–12b), He provided salvation for others by dying in their place (53:11–12; the New Testament identified Jesus as this Servant in Mark 10:34; Matt. 8:17; Acts 8:32–37). The identity of the servant was partially hidden, but opened to the eye of faith.[86] Salvation through the servant was possible for those who trusted God (49:8–13).

The salvation oracles between the servant songs (49:14—50:3; 51:1—52:12) justified a change of heart. God loved them and had a plan for their future. God did not di-

---

84. Watts, *Isaiah 34—66* in *WBC* 25, 199–200, discusses different ways of interpreting the various parties.

85. Some still conclude that the servant was one of the prophets, possibly Isaiah, Jeremiah, or Moses or a corporate symbol of the nation Israel. See note 73.

86. The New Testament authors connected the servant songs to the life and death of Jesus. See Matthew 12:18–21; Luke 2:32; Acts 13:47; 26:23.

vorce them (49:14; 50:1–3), but will gather them together again. Then they will recognize that He is God (49:15–26; see traditions in 45:14–25).

The second series of salvation speeches (51:1—52:12) encouraged those who trusted God (51:1, 7) to maintain their present worldview, to remember how God was faithful to His promises to Abram (51:2–4; see Gen. 12:1).[87] They can have confidence in God for He will redeem His people from bondage (51:3–16). Zion will joyfully awaken with those returning from captivity (52:1–5). God will reign in Jerusalem (52:7–10).

The final section *promised salvation to those who seek God* (54:1—55:13). Isaiah encouraged Israel to shout for joy because her desolate and barren state will soon end; she will have many children in Jerusalem (54:1–3). To legitimate this understanding of their future, Isaiah reminded them that God's oath to have compassion and restore Israel was just as sure as the oath to Noah (54:9–10, see Gen 8:21—9:16). The prophet pictured new Jerusalem richly adorned with precious jewels (54:11–17), the people being taught by God (see 2:2–4), and righteousness governing all behavior. This will be the heritage of those who choose to trust and serve God.

Isaiah believed the time had come for the wicked to accept God's vision. The concluding evangelistic sermon (55) challenged the people to reject their present worldview and accept God's offer of grace, forgiveness, and blessing.[88] He offered a free gift that could not be purchased (55:1–2). Acceptance will bring life and the fulfillment of God's eternal covenant with David (see 2 Sam. 7:8–16; Ps. 89:27–37). Acceptance meant seeking God's way (55:6–7), turning from the misunderstandings of their own social understanding of reality, and having their minds transformed by God's higher

87. Berger, *Social Construction,* 116–22, notes that the rehearsal of past traditions is an effective method of maintaining one's social defined worldview of a group.

88. Westermann, *Isaiah 40—66* in *OTL,* 286–87, sees the conclusion in 55 matching the introduction in 40:1–11.

thoughts and ways (55:8–9). God promised salvation and blessing, and He will keep His word (55:10–13).

VII. Trusting in God for Restoration 56:1—66:24

These sermons were divided into three parts: (a) 56—59 were a series of judgments, laments, and salvation oracles which called the wicked to turn from their sins; (b) 60—62 looked at the future glory of the restored community; and (c) 63—66 gave a final judgment of the evil nations, plus laments and salvation oracles concerning God's final restoration of His people. This section has a chaiastic structure.[89] Some hypothesized a "Third Isaiah" in a new setting, but this is unnecessary because the same themes in 40—55 are in 56—66.[90]

Details concerning the nation's setting are abundant, but it is difficult to tell whether this is a present or future setting. Hanson's sociological analysis finds two conflicting groups struggling in Jerusalem in the post–exilic era. One was an oppressed and disillusioned Palestinian group of visionary eschatologists who followed Isaiah's teaching (their ideas are in 60—62 and some of the laments), while the other group was made up of realists returned from exile who followed the Zadokite priests and the program described in Ezekiel 40—48.[91] Hanson's interpretations does not seem to be supported by 56—66.

Initially, Isaiah preached about *restoration after turning from sin* (56:1—59:21). The judgment speeches invited the nations (the beasts in 56:9) to destroy the blind watchmen

---

89. G. J. Polan, *In the Ways of Justice toward Salvation* (New York: P. Lang, 1986), 14–16, or E. Charpentier, *Jeunesse du Vieux Testament* (Paris: Fayard, 1963), 78–80.

90. For a discussion of these issues, see Westermann, *Isaiah 40—66* in *OTL*, 296–308, who finds a "Third Isaiah" or J. D. Smart, *History and Theology in Second Isaiah: A Commentary on Isaiah 35, 40—66* (Philadelphia: Westminster, 1965), 229–39, who does not.

91. Hanson, *Dawn of Apocalyptic* ,71–75, who is followed by E. Achtemeier, *The Community and Message of Isaiah 56—66* (Minneapolis: Augsburg, 1982), 17–26.

(prophets) and shepherds (kings) who knew nothing of God's guidelines for righteous behavior. Their social worldview allowed them to be greedy and live in drunkenness (57:10–12). These people were not godly defenders of the righteous (57:1–2), but sorcerers and adulterers. They deceived people, worshiped other gods, offered child sacrifices, became involved with pagan sexual rites, and ended up in a hopeless condition (57:3–10); therefore, their "righteous" deeds will receive exactly what they deserve—destruction (57:11–13). Hanson's rejection of this as an accurate picture of the wickedness of the Zadokite hierocratic party is not convincing. This is more than an exaggerated argument by the disillusioned and powerless followers of Isaiah who disagree with Ezekiel's restoration program.[92]

Isaiah 58:1–5 and 59:1–15a expanded this description. The wealthier people (58:3, those with servants) came to the temple and pretended to enjoy being near God (58:2). They came to the day of fasting with strife in their hearts. They were more interested in their own pleasures; they did not care about the poor and homeless (58:5–7, 13). Thus God did not hear their prayers.

This record of past and present sins legitimated God's anger (57:16–17) and justified the prophet's call for the people to transform their social understanding of life, to repent, to release the oppressed, to feed the hungry, and to delight in the Lord (58:6–14). The prophet lamented their sins and confessed that God's blessings did not come because of their sins (59:9–15a).

Then the prophet offered encouragement to the righteous, for judgment will not last forever. God will go before them to guide them and raise up the ancient ruins when the people accept God's plan (58:8–14). In this new theological

92. Hanson, *Dawn of Apocalyptic,* 193–201. If these accusations were not true, it would not be hard to disprove things like excessive drinking, the worship of idols, or killing the righteous; but no counter arguments were given. It would seem that Ezekiel's high demands for holiness were totally in agreement with these criticisms. Hanson is left with the difficult solution that the followers of Isaiah were wrong and that this passage does not truly describe the evils of the Zadokite party.

context God will heal His people and provide a (high)way to restore the nation (57:14–20). As the people practice justice and holiness, even the foreigners will come and worship God (56:1–8).

Further encouragement is provided in the second part of this sermon. It described *the glory of restoration* in God's new kingdom (60:1—62:12). These eschatological salvation speeches refer to a time after darkness has covered the whole earth (60:2) and God has acted in wrath (60:10, 15; 62:4). These oracles point to a new theological setting for the nation when the anointed servant of God (61:1–3; see 42:1; 49:8–9) and the presence of God's glory on earth will bring a transformation to Israel and the nations (60:1–2; see traditions in 2:2–4).

When this new kingdom comes into existence, many nations will join themselves to Israel and bring gifts to God (60:3–9; 61:5; 62:2). Israel's enemies will perish, and the holy city will be glorious with God in its midst (60:10–22). Zion will be a place of salvation and praise for the holy people (62:6–12; 61:4–11). God's plan was a basis for trust.

The conclusion of the sermon dealt with the *final judgment and restoration* (63:1—66:24). It challenged the listeners to make a response of trust in God so that they could avoid God's judgment and enjoy God's blessing. The short condemnation of the nations in 63:1–6 (Edom is a symbol here as in 34:1–15) pictured the Divine Warrior in majestic array trampling out the last vestiges of opposition on His final day of vengeance. In power God will slay them to bring salvation to His people. This oracle confirmed God's ability to provide salvation, justice, protection, and peace. All forces which oppose God will be destroyed.

Israel did not enjoy the kingdom at this time; thus the people lamented and pleaded for God to act now. The prayer remembered God's past acts of mercy toward Israel.[93] Based

93. They remembered the covenant when they were in bondage (63:8; see Ex. 6:1–8); the deliverance from Egypt and the Red Sea (63:11–13, see Ex. 14—15); His presence with them (63:9, see traditions in Ex. 33:15); and their rebellion (63:10; see Ex. 16—17; Num. 11—16; 20). Berger, *Social Construction,* 116–22, shows that repeating past traditions will help to maintain continuity with the group's past history and values.

on their knowledge of how God acted in compassion in the past, the righteous asked God to be their Father and Redeemer, to return them to the days of old (63:15–19). They submitted themselves to God's molding power and requested forgiveness (64:4–12).

God's response to the lament was both negative and positive (65:1—66:24). He remembered their acceptance of foreign patterns of worship and claims to be holy (64:1–5; 66:3, 17). The wicked will be judged (65:6–7, 11–12; 66:4–6), but the faithful servants (66:1–2) will be restored to inherit the land when God creates a new heaven and earth. This new setting will be a place of joy and peace between humans and nature (65:8–10, 13–25; 66:7–14).

Then the nations will see God's acts of judgment and grace; His fame and glory will be known (66:18–19). Some will respond and come to worship God (66:19–23), but others will reject Him and receive their final judgment (66:24).

Theological and Social Implications

Why do people trust God? Is it just a natural instinct or an accident of birth? Why do some have so much difficulty believing God's promises? The prophet Isaiah suggested that some people do not trust God because of pride and their own sense of self-sufficiency. Others depend upon what rationally makes sense. Some would rather trust in people who have money, power, or status. How can you trust God when it could make you look like a fool before your friends?

What can be said to help people trust God? God's messenger today can reorient people's thinking process by introducing them to the incomparable greatness of God (40:12–31). All other powers and sources of trust are nothing when compared to Him. He is the Creator, the First and the Last, the One who controls every nation. A second evidence which legitimates trust is God's past plans. He said what He would do and accomplished it; He planned and did it. The credibility of God's future promises are directly related to His past reputation. Third, God will provide the way to remove sin, the central problem to establishing a trusting relationship with God.

Trust must be based on what cannot be fully understood (55:8–9) and looks forward to a kingdom that is not yet seen; but it is not a blind leap of faith. Trust can not be manufactured by slick programming or empty promises of prosperity; it is the result of meeting God. The messenger who introduces his listeners to God and His word will open the door to trust that confounds human predictability or determination.

Questions for Discussion

1. How would you compare and contrast Ahaz's (chap. 7) and Hezekiah's (36—39): (a) military situation; (b) message from the prophet; (c) trust in God; and (d) results.
2. What persuasive evidence was provided in Isaiah 40—41; 44; and 46 to encourage people to trust in God?
3. What were the roles of the Suffering Servant?
4. What was God's plan for the nations in Isaiah 19, 45, 49, 66?

Chapter 8

Nahum: Where Is God's Goodness and Wrath?

Introduction

People who are victims of family abuse, gang violence, con artists, and war often find it hard to believe in the goodness of God. When someone with greater power, economic resources, or social status forcibly takes advantage of another person, God's goodness is not very evident. We know that people are the source of evil actions, but it seems that God should not allow such things to happen. In wrath, He should destroy them.

In difficult times people tend to ask questions like: Why do these things happen to us, and when will they end? People are seldom able to figure out the answers to the why or how long questions, but in the midst of oppression the prophets and God's messengers today can provide hope based on God's character. God has great power, executes wrath against the wicked, and is good to those who trust Him. These characteristics can give some hope to the discouraged listener who faces a hopeless situation.

Social Setting

The Historical Context

The Book of Nahum does not mention any Judean king to help date these sermons, but the prophecy warns of Nineveh's future destruction (in 612 B.C.). The Assyrians had already destroyed No-Amon, the Egyptian city of Thebes (3:8), so the prophet spoke sometime between 663 and 612 B.C.

The wicked kings Manasseh (2 Kings 21:1–18) and Amon (2 Kings 21:19–26) and the good King Josiah (2 Kings 22–23) ruled Judah during these years. The prophet did not condemn Judah, so it is difficult to place his message during Manasseh's or Amon's reign. Nahum's encouraging word from God about the demise of Nineveh probably came in Josiah's reign after he began to seek the Lord (632 B.C.) and before his reforms in 628 and 621 B.C.

	640	Josiah became king
	632	Josiah sought God
Nahum's prophecy	630	
	628	Josiah began reforms
	627	Ashurbanipal's death
	621	Josiah's great reform
	609	Josiah's death

Nahum's prophecy came before King Ashurbanipal's death when Judah was still under the Assyrian bondage (1:12–13).[1] Around 630 B.C. Josiah needed to hear how

1. R. D. Patterson, *Nahum, Habakkuk, Zephaniah* in *WEC* (Chicago: Moody, 1991), 5–7, and D. L. Christensen, "The Acrostic of Nahum Reconsidered," *ZAW* 87 (1975), 17–30, prefer an early date around 654 B.C. before Thebes was recovered by Egypt (see 3:8); I. Eybers, "A Note Concerning the Date of Nahum's Prophecy," *Biblical Essays* in *OTWSA* (1969), 9–12, dates the book at 630–627 B.C. W. Rudolph, *Micha-Nahum-Habakuk-Zephanja* in *KAT* XIII #3 (Gütersloh: Gütersloher Verlagshaus, Gerd Mohn, 1975), 143, puts the death of Ashurbanipal about 632 B.C. as the latest possible date. E. Achtemeier, *Nahum-Malachi* in *IntCom* (Atlanta: John Knox Press, 1986), 7, dates the book shortly before 612 B.C.

Nahum prophesied the destruction of Nineveh including vivid descriptions of the enemy horse and chariot forces. In the above section of the bronze gates from Balawat, the Assyrian chariot force is depicted in action.

God's goodness could transform the political and religious situation in Judah.

The Structure of Social Order

Nahum said little about social institutions, behavior patterns, or the theology of the people of Judah. Instead Nahum focused on the predominant force that influenced the Judean conception of objective reality: the Assyrian empire. Its culture shaped Judah's political and religious conditions and suppressed economic prosperity (1:13; 2:2).

Most Jewish knowledge about Nineveh was socially conditioned through contact with soldiers and government officials who talked about Assyria's power.[2] Nahum and his audience saw Assyrian troops dressed in scarlet, riding in swift chariots (1:3–4). They probably received a somewhat slanted understanding of Assyria's great fortified cities and large temples, the economic vitality of the nation's merchants, and the size of the king's wealth (1:14; 2:5, 9; 3:14,

2. P. Berger and T. Luckmann, *The Social Construction of Reality*, 34–41, stress the important role that language plays in developing a person's worldview.

16). This imaginative picture of Assyria subtly degraded the "inferior" political and religious culture of Judah.[3] The prophet Nahum attempted to transform this picture of Assyria by giving his audience (Josiah) new information about Nineveh. He imagined a new structure of political power (1:9—2:2). Nineveh would be destroyed, and Judah would celebrate her feasts. This would happen because of God's wrath toward His enemies and His goodness toward His own people.

The Social Location and Role of the Prophet

Nahum said nothing explicit about his family background or social status. The prophet was from Elkosh, probably a small Judean city, not the Israelite city of Capernaum.[4] During primary socialization he gained an understanding of objective reality (the language, culture, social roles, and institutions that ordered life in his village)[5] and the pain of living under Assyrian domination. The vividness of Nahum's vision of Nineveh's fall revealed his knowledge of the horror of war and the city of Nineveh, though he never mentioned going to Nineveh.[6] Through social interactions he gained knowledge of ancient Near Eastern history (3:8–10), the violent tendencies of the Assyrians (3:1–4), the geography of Nineveh (2:6–9), and the needs of his audience.

---

3. J. McKay, *Religion in Judah Under the Assyrians* (Naperville: Allenson, 1973), 20–44, notes that Josiah's reform was primarily against Baalism rather than Assyrian religious practices, but this does not mean that the Assyrians did not have a significant effect on Judean culture and social institutions.

4. See the recent discussion by Patterson, *Nahum, Habakkuk, and Zephaniah* in *WBC* 7 who relies on G. Nestle, "Where Is the Birthplace of the Prophet Nahum to Be Sought?" *PEQ* (1879), 136–38, who identifies Elkosh with Kessijah, a city near Beit Jibrin. See the brief survey of R. L. Smith, *Micah-Malachi* in *WBC* 32 (Dallas: Word Books, 1984), 63.

5. Berger, *Social Construction*, 129–37.

6. The tradition that Nahum's grave was in Assyria near Al-Qush, a city about twenty five miles north of modern Mosul, Iraq, has little value. A. S. van der Woude, "The Book of Nahum: A Letter Written in Exile," *OTS* 20 (1977), 108–26, thinks that Nahum was an Israelite (not Judean) who was exiled to Assyria.

The prophet worked to debunk the slanted view of reality which many Judeans had internalized.[7] The capital city of Nineveh was not indestructible. The Assyrian army was powerless before God. King Josiah received from Nahum a new conception of Assyria from the divine perspective. Isaiah's prophecies of Assyria's demise were true (Isa. 10:5–34). This enabled Josiah to reorder his thinking about God's goodness, reevaluate the nation's political status, and regain hope of instituting traditional worship patterns in Jerusalem (1:15).[8]

As a prophetic orator, Nahum employed literary traditions including a hymn (1:2–8), taunt song (2:11–13; 3:14–17), and woe oracle (3:1–7). The remains of an acrostic hymn in 1:2–8 does not imply that the book was a festival liturgy or that Nahum was a cultic prophet in the temple, it only means that Nahum knew some songs sung at the temple.[9] The strong political overtones of his message suggest that Nahum was a central court prophet who supported Josiah's efforts to reform Judah.[10]

Nahum used theological traditions concerning God's character in the hymn in 1:1–8.[11] Other verses have verbal

---

7. R. Perkins, *Looking Both Ways: Exploring the Interface Between Christianity and Sociology* (Grand Rapids: Baker, 1987), 57, describes debunking as a skeptical questioning of what one has been taught to think. Nahum debunked the Judean view of Assyrian power.

8. Although central prophets usually functioned to maintain the dominant social order and existing worldview, if a king wished to bring about change, the central intermediaries would assist this process by legitimating the desired changes. See R. R. Wilson, *Prophecy and Society in Ancient Israel* (Philadelphia: Fortress, 1980), 83–86.

9. S. J. de Vries, "The Acrostic of Nahum in the Jerusalem Liturgy," *VT* 16 (1966), 476–81. J. J. M. Roberts, *Nahum, Habakkuk, and Zephaniah* in *OTL* (Louisville: Westminster/J. Knox, 1991), 48, thinks Nahum used an existing hymn. Nevertheless, the use of hymnic material did not make Nahum a cultic prophet.

10. Wilson, *Prophecy and Society*, 276–77, sees Nahum as a central intermediary attempting to maintain the nationalistic values of the royal cult and the social structure it supported. If this oracle came from the early years of Josiah, its main purpose was to justify Josiah's attempt to change the pro-Assyrian political and religious policies of Manasseh.

11. God's jealousy (Ex. 20:5; Deut. 4:24); vengeance (Deut. 32:35, 41, 43); slowness to anger (Ex. 34:6); unwillingness to clear the guilty (Ex. 34:6–7); and goodness (Ps. 25:8; 118:1).

and thematic connections with Isaiah's prophecy.[12] Although some doubted Isaiah's words (75 years earlier) about God's strategy to destroy the Assyrians, Nahum supported God's plan for Assyria.[13]

Social Interaction

The Book of Nahum

The oracles of Nahum were written with bold imagery, abrupt changes in the speaker (1:12—2:2), and literary skill.[14] Scholars are divided on the redaction of some verses (1:2–8 and 1:11—2:2), the date of the book, and the cultic use of the text.[15] The book was structured into two sections.

I. The Effects of God's Wrath and Goodness 1:1—2:2
   A. Song of the powerful avenger and savior 1:1–8
   B. God's vengeance on Nineveh, deliverance of Judah 1:9—2:2
II. The Fall of Nineveh 2:3—3:19
   A. The battle for Nineveh will be lost 2:3–13

---

12. C. Armerding, "Nahum," *EBC* 7 (Grand Rapids: Zondervan, 1985), 454–55, focuses on the relationship between Nahum and Isaiah, particularly Isa. 51—52. Other references include: rebuking the sea in 1:4 (Isa. 44:27; 50:2); the overflowing flood in 1:8 (Isa. 8:7–8); God will make a complete end of Assyria in 1:8 (Isa. 10:23); burning of thorns and stubble in 1:10 (Isa. 5:24; 10:17); the Assyrian yoke in 1:13 (Isa. 10:27); the feet of the one who declares good news in 1:15 (Isa. 40:9; 52:7); Nineveh is a lion in 2:11–12 (Isa. 5:29–30).

13. Berger, *Social Construction*, 122–23, 153–55, describes how the repetition of traditional definitions of reality inhibits social change, but in a changed society, older traditions can bring people back to earlier ways of understanding life.

14. O. Allis, "Nahum, Nineveh, Elkosh," *EVQ* 27 (1955), 67–80, gives examples of alliteration, assonance, and repetition.

15. See Christensen, "The Acrostic of Nahum," *ZAW* 87, 17–30, on the hymn in 1:1–8; Smith, *Micah-Malachi* in *WBC* (1984), 66–67, reviewed the cultic theories. M. A. Sweeney "Concerning the Structure and Generic Character of the Book of Nahum," *ZAW* 104 (1992), 364–77, shows the book's structural unity.

B. The reasons for Nineveh's devastation 3:1–7

C. The inevitability of Nineveh's fall 3:8–19

These sermons reflected the prophet's cultural perspective, but he was not limited by this worldview. His new vision explained how God's wrath was confirming Isaiah's words, thereby, transforming the pessimistic thinking of his audience.

I. The Effects of God's Wrath and Goodness 1:1—2:2

The prophet's communication reminded his listeners of the contrasting themes of God's goodness and wrath. This hymnic poem (1:2–8) provided a basis for understanding *God's vengeance on Nineveh and deliverance of Judah* (1:9—2:2).

The Assyrians' social understanding of the world was what one might expect of a world power. They were "thinking, planning" how to maintain their power and continue their affluent life, but ignoring the plans of God (1:9, 11).[16] Isaiah had condemned Assyria's blasphemous pride (10:7–16; 36:1–20; 37:22–29), for Assyria's victories were due to God's "planning" not Assyria's (14:24–27; 37:26). They thought they could control the future through military might (1:12), but Nahum knew that Assyria would soon come to a complete end (1:9). Then Judah would be free from the Assyrians (1:12b–13, 15; 2:2b).

The main purpose of his sermon was to encourage Josiah and his followers to continue to seek God's will. Nahum did not condemn Judah, for Josiah was already convinced of Judah's sinfulness. Josiah needed assurance that God's wrath would eliminate Assyria so that he could continue his reform.[17]

---

16. R. J. Coggins and S. P. Re'emi, *Nahum, Obadiah, Esther* in *ITC* (Grand Rapids: Eerdmans, 1985), 27, 30–32, suggest that 1:9, 11, 14 refer to the sinful in Judah, but it is better to make the evil one in 1:11 and 15b refer to an Assyrian.

17. Berger, *Social Construction*, 108, observes that the worldview that wins when a conflict arises is often the one with the strongest military power to force its beliefs on others. Without political independence from the Assyrian presence, it was difficult for Josiah to change the Judean worldview.

To legitimate his conclusion that God would destroy Nineveh and deliver Judah,[18] Nahum adapted an old acrostic theophany *song of the powerful avenger and savior* (1:2–8).[19] The conception of reality that shaped this song centered on God's character and power.[20] God sometimes acted in the heat of His vengeance against His enemies (1:2; see Ex. 20:5, 7; Deut. 4:24).[21] Past hymns recorded that nothing, not even the mountains or the seas, can withstand the power of God's glorious presence (1:4–6; see Ps. 18:7–15; 97:1–5). God's wrath was tempered only by His patience (1:3; see Ex. 34:6) and by the willingness of mankind to take refuge in God's goodness (1:7; see Ps. 25:8; Jer. 18:1–11). Nahum maintained continuity with these earlier authoritative beliefs and provided a justification for transforming Judah's view of God's sovereign rule over the nations. Because Josiah had not seen God's wrath on Assyria as Isaiah promised (Isa. 10:5–30), he probably felt some inconsistency between his experience and what tradition taught.

Nahum externalized a new theological understanding of Judah's future to persuade his listeners to act. God would completely destroy the Assyrians (1:8–10). Although they were strong, they and their idols would be cut off like grass (1:10, 14).[22] God declared an end to Judah's affliction, a new

---

18. B. S. Childs, *Introduction to the Old Testament as Scripture* (Philadelphia: Fortress, 1979), sees the hymn as having a similar function, but connects it to the canonical shaping of the book rather than the prophet's interaction with his audience.

19. Rather than emending the text, it is better to follow A. van Selms, "The Alphabetic Hymn in Nahum," *Biblical Essays* OTWSA (1969), 35–45, and suggest that Nahum never tried to write an acrostic hymn, but borrowed part of one he knew.

20. See Berger, *Social Construction*, 97, for the role that the symbolic universe plays in integrating and explaining the experiences of an individual.

21. See the study of vengeance in G. Mendenhall, "The Vengeance of Yahweh," *The Tenth Generation* (Baltimore: Johns Hopkins, 1973), 69–104, and J. L. Milelic, "The Concept of God in the Book of Nahum," *Int* 2 (1948), 199–208.

22. Beliel "wicked, worthless one" in 1: 11,15 referred to the Assyrian king who represented the Assyrian goddess of the underworld, Belili. Later apocryphal (Jubilees) and New Testament (2 Cor. 6:15) texts use this word to describe Satan. See E. Achtemeier, *Nahum–Malachi* in *IntCom* (Atlanta: J. Knox, 1986), 16.

day of peace, and joyful worship in Jerusalem (1:12b–13, 15a; 2:2). These words encouraged Josiah.

II. The Fall of Nineveh 2:3—3:19

To emphasize the certainty of this message, Nahum described how *the battle for Nineveh would be lost* (2:3–13). The graphic picture of Nineveh's demise functioned as a persuasive reason to accept Nahum's new view of Nineveh. The troops around Nineveh would madly race around the city (2:3–5), but soon the river would flood, the walls would fall, and foreigners would plunder the city's riches (2:6–10).[23] People would mock Assyria, the great lion of destruction that preyed on the nations (2:11; Isa. 5:29–30), because it would be nothing. God was against it and would end her bragging (2:11–13; see Isa. 36–37 for bragging).

In a mocking woe oracle of lamentation Nahum communicated *the reasons for Nineveh's devastation* (3:1–7). Because of the nation's bloody and violent past, its treacherous lies to other nations, its pillage, and its militarism (2:1, 4), devastation would fill Nineveh. These policies were socially accepted by the Assyrians, but they were inconsistent with the divine design for human relationships. Nahum announced God's intention to disgrace Nineveh by exposing the naked truth (3:5; see Isa. 47:3), by showing the vileness of the nation, and by making it a repulsive spectacle that

23. C. J. Gadd, *The Fall of Nineveh: The Newly Discovered Babylonian Chronicle* (London: British Museum, 1923), 27–30, refers to the the Sicilian historian Diodorus, who quoted a prophet who predicted that the river would play a part in the fall of Nineveh. Then Diodorus told how the river did flood and destroy part of the wall. See also D. J. Wiseman, *Chronicles of the Chaldean Kings (626–556 B.C.)* in the British Museum (London: British Museum, 1956), 16–18. The fulfillment of the prophecy took place in *612 B.C.* when the Medes and Babylonians defeated Nineveh. See the annual of *Nabopolasser* (J. B. Pritchard, ed., *ANET* [Princeton: Princeton Univ. Press, 1954] 304, for a Babylonian account of these events and a description of the plunder from the city. W. A. Maier, *The Book of Nahum* (St. Louis: Concordia Publishing House, 1959), 104–39, surveys accounts of Nineveh's fall.

none would grieve over (3:5–7). All would know its true character. Nineveh would get what it deserved—God's wrath.

In the final paragraph Nahum gave his audience assurances of *the inevitability of Nineveh's fall* (3:8–19). This provided another reason why those in Judah should transform their thinking about Assyria and accept the divine view of the future. To legitimate the transcendent perspective, Nahum reminded his audience of what happened to No-Amon (Thebes), the capital of Egypt (in 663 B.C.). It was situated on a famous river, like Nineveh. It also had walls and many allies (3:8–9), but its people were killed or sent into exile (3:10–11).[24] The fall of Nineveh was as inevitable as the fall of No-amon. Nineveh's fortifications will fall like ripe fruit. Its strong soldiers will run like women, and the city will burn (3:11–13). To emphasize the inevitability of God's decision, Nahum sang a satirical taunt (3:14–19) which gave battle instructions to the Assyrians defending the city. No matter what walls were strengthened (3:14), no matter how many troops were added (3:15b, 17), God would destroy Nineveh (3:15a). Poor Nineveh!

Since Nineveh's wound was incurable and its end inevitable, King Josiah and the people of Judah could choose a new political and theological orientation to the future. Nahum's sermon presented arguments to justify a worldview based on the goodness of God (1:2–8). The prophet's persuasive interaction put social pressure on Josiah to begin his reform movement. He knew that God's wrath would destroy his Assyrian overlords.

Theological and Social Implications

Transforming the way people think and act is not easy, especially when everything seems stacked against you. One may seek to know God's will, but in a time of spiritual persecution, powerlessness, and defeat, a person often does not know what God's plans are. It is difficult to wait for God to

---

24. Pritchard, *ANET*, 295.

act. It is hard to remain hopeful and to believe things will change when all evidence points in the opposite direction.

When people see that someone else believes there is hope, it becomes socially acceptable to think that change is possible. A plausibility structure exists when a support system of two or three is in place. However, the justification for an alternate cultural or theological view of the world will not last if the rationale for it fails. Empty hopes do not support real visions.

Therefore, the prophet Nahum, and God's messengers today, must ultimately ground their preaching and their vision for ministry in the character of God. Few prophets ever knew the exact day that God would act or exactly how God would bless. They only knew that He would be faithful and do what He promised. They knew that His character guided His behavior. They were assured that after unbelievable patience, God would always act in wrath against His enemies and in goodness toward those who trusted Him. Although the present reality of evil may contradict the hope that believers derive from faith, God's character is a sure foundation for trust and encouragement. God's goodness may not fit our limited perspective, but His character does not change.

Questions for Discussion

1. What was the popular view of the Assyrians that Nahum opposed?
2. Why was Nahum's use of the hymn in 1:2–8 so important to his message of hope?
3. What does Nahum teach us about God's sovereignty over the powerful nations of the earth?
4. What social effect did Nahum's detailed description of the defeat of Nineveh have on Josiah?
5. How did Josiah respond to this challenge? Did he believe God and continue his reforms in the following years (see 2 Chron. 34)?

Chapter 9

Zephaniah: Seek God Before the Day of the Lord

Introduction

Although most people want to make their peace with God before the judgment day, some delay getting serious about their relationship with God until the last minute. They may put off this decision because everything is going well or because they see no need to change at the present time. Others refuse to seek God because they want to enjoy life and dislike the discipline of a godly life. The danger of this approach is real. The day of the Lord may come quickly, before they get things right with God.

A central responsibility of the Old Testament prophets, and messengers of God today, is to persuade people to humble themselves before God, repent of their sins, and seek His grace. Sometimes people respond to another person's life-transforming experience, but at other times the preacher needs to present solid arguments that motivate faith and action. Zephaniah's message included both negative arguments about the terrible destruction on the day of the Lord and positive reminders about the joy of living with God. He presented a choice: Seek God's grace now, or risk the danger of facing His destructive power on the day of the Lord. This is one of the most decisive choices a person must make. It is a choice of life or death!

Social Setting

Historical Context

Zephaniah preached in Jerusalem during the reign of Josiah, king of Judah (1:1). Since only a "remnant of Baalism" remained and the ritual honoring the hosts of heaven was now practiced on the housetops (1:4–5), most pagan high places of worship were closed (2 Chron. 34:3). This would put Zephaniah's ministry somewhere after Josiah's early reforms in 628 B.C., but before the great spiritual revival in 621 B.C. (2 Kings 22—23).[1]

	640	Josiah became king
	632	Josiah sought God
	628	Josiah's early reform
Zephaniah's ministry	625	
	621	Josiah's major reform
	609	Josiah's death

The Structure of Social Order

Life in Judah underwent many political, social, and religious changes in the years just before Zephaniah gave his

1. J. P. Hyatt, "The Date and Background of Zephaniah," *JBL* 7 (1949), 25–29, and D. L. Williams, "The Date of Zephaniah," *JBL* 82 (1963), 85–88, place Zephaniah in Jehoiakim's reign (609–597 B.C.), but this view does not fit as well as a date before 621 B.C. No one else has placed Zephaniah as late as 200 B.C. as do L. P. Smith and E. R. Lacheman, "The Authorship of the Book of Zephaniah," *JNES* 9 (1950), 137–42.

prophecies. Two key political events precipitated revolutionary transformations in Judean society. The first event was the death of Manasseh and his son Amon. This made it possible to turn away from the Canaanite cultural worldview of worshiping Baal and the hosts of heaven that Manasseh introduced (2 Kings 21:1–18; 2 Chron. 33:1–9) and return to the traditional worship of Yahweh.[2] Zephaniah and Josiah opposed these Canaanite ways and legitimated a new way of ordering Judah's social and religious life. The second event was the death of the Assyrian King Ashurbanipal and the breakup of the Assyrian Empire around 627 B.C. This removed a heavy tax burden and gave Josiah political freedom from Assyria.

These opportunities for change created major problems. The vacuum of political power (previously controlled by Assyrian officials) was quickly filled by greedy Judean officials and dishonest judges (1:8; 3:1–3). This led to oppression because the political leaders under young King Josiah did not accept God's law as their standard. This new upper class used violence to enrich themselves. Fine homes, vineyards (1:13), and wealth (1:13, 18) were a silent witness to their status and sins.

Josiah's major religious reform did not occur until 621 B.C. (after Zephaniah's message), but some initial unpopular changes in the institutionalized practices associated with the worship of Baal and the hosts of heaven were legislated in 628 B.C. (1:4–5). In spite of these changes, a few Baal priests still functioned in Jerusalem, and some pagan prophets and priests carried out their roles in ways that profaned God's sacred laws (1:5; 3:4). The process of secularization caused others to ignore God rather than trust Him (1:6; 3:2).[3] Some concluded that God was unimportant (1:12), for the plausibility structures that supported the ancient Mosaic worldview were undermined by the pluralistic tendencies of Manasseh.[4]

---

2. In 2 Chron. 33:10–20, Manasseh turned to God, but the nation did not follow his change of heart.

3. P. Berger, *The Sacred Canopy* (Garden City: Doubleday, 1967), 105–25.

4. Ibid., 133–53.

The Social Location and Role of the Prophet

The text does not identify Zephaniah's occupation before he became a prophet in Jerusalem. Achtemeier connects him to a Levitical-prophetic reform group that she claims put the Book of Deuteronomy together. Blenkinsopp concludes that he was a priest, but evidence to connect him to an official role in the temple is minimal.[5] He did use hymns from Psalms, but also ideas from the prophets Amos and Isaiah.[6]

The long genealogy of Zephaniah (1:1) traced his ancestry back to Hezekiah. Since genealogies demonstrated a person's social position by pointing back to an important ancestor, this Hezekiah probably was King Hezekiah.[7] If this is correct, Zephaniah was a central court prophet in Jerusalem. This would explain his criticism of the royal officials who were not wholeheartedly behind the reforms of his relative, King Josiah (1:8–9; 3:3).[8] As a member of the extended royal family, Zephaniah was well educated and from the upper class.

As an orator and prophetic spokesman for God, Zephaniah drew on literary traditions to communicate God's message in a form that was meaningful in his culture. These

---

5. E. Achtemeier, *Nahum-Malachi* in *IntCom* (Atlanta: John Knox, 1986), 62. J. Blenkinsopp, *A History of Prophecy in Israel* (Philadelphia: Westminster, 1983), 140, connects Zephaniah to a priestly role in the temple because his anti-Assyrian oracle in 2:13–15 was similar to the work of Nahum.

6. A. Kapelrud, *The Message of Zephaniah* (Oslo: *Universitetsforlaget*, 1975), 56–72, lists examples of contact with other books. G. Gerleman, *Zephanja* (Lund: Gleerup, 1942), 118–19, claims that Zephaniah was a disciple of Isaiah who opposed Josiah's reform, but this does not fit the book.

7. Kapelrud, *Message of Zephaniah*, 43–45, and W. Rudolph, *Micha-Nahum-Habakuk-Zephanja* in *KAT* XIII 3 (Gütersloh: Gütersloher G. Mohn, 1975), 258–59, do not think this was King Hezekiah. R. R. Wilson, *Prophecy and Society in Ancient Israel* (Philadelphia: Fortress, 1980), 279–80, and Williams, "Date of Zephaniah," *JBL* 82 (1963), 77–88, think Zephaniah was the same person as Zephaniah, the father of Josiah (Zech. 6:10) and Zephaniah, the priest (Jer. 21:1), but these people do not seem to be the prophet Zephaniah.

8. Wilson, *Prophecy and Society*, 280, considers Zephaniah a central prophet.

included: judgment speeches in 1:2–6; a summons to repent in 2:1–3; oracles against foreign nations in 2:4–15; a woe oracle in 3:1–6; and salvation oracles in 3:9–20. He used the phraseology of earlier theological traditions (especially Amos and Isaiah) to legitimate his message and encourage his audience to change their ordered understanding of the world.[9] These authoritative traditions functioned to justify Zephaniah's vision of the future and strengthened his attempts to transform his audience's thinking.

Social Interaction

The Book of Zephaniah

Zephaniah's sermons combined words of judgment with promises of hope. These rhetorical units were skillfully held together by repeated vocabulary.[10] These repetitions served as structural markers that signal the start and end of larger sections in his book ("all the earth" in 1:2; 1:18; 3:8, 20 or "gather" in 2:1; 3:8). Few question the unity and authenticity of the Book of Zephaniah.[11] It can be outlined into three sections:

- I. Judgment on the Day of the Lord 1:1–18
    - A. Complete judgment on the wicked 1:1–6
    - B. Recipients of judgment 1:7–13
    - C. Description of the day of the Lord 1:14–18

---

9. The day of the Lord in 1:7, 14–18 (see Amos 5:18–20; Isa. 13:6–16); principles like those who build houses will not live in them in 1:13 (see Amos 5:11); a call to seek God in 2:3 (see Amos 5:4, 6, 15; Isa. 55:6); all nations will bow down to God in 2:11; 3:10 (Isa. 2:2–4; 45:22–25); I am God, there is no other in 2:15 (see Isa. 45:5, 14, 18, 21); God's deliverance of the weak in 3:19 (see Mic. 4:6); and God's purpose for His people in 3:20 (see Deut. 26:18–19).

10. These include "remove" in 1:2–3; "cut off" in 1:3–4; "bow down" twice in 1:5; "day" in 1:14–16, 18. I. J. Ball, *Zephaniah: A Rhetorical Study* (Berkeley: Bibal, 1988), 281–87, deals with these rhetorical structural markers.

11. J. J. M. Roberts, *Nahum, Habakkuk, and Zephaniah* in *OTL* (Louisville: Westminster/J. Knox, 1991), 163, raises questions about 1:3; 2:4–5, 11; 3:10.

II. Repent before the Day of the Lord 2:1—3:8
   A. Gather Judah to repent 2:1–3
   B. Judgment on the nations will bring repentance 2:4–15
   C. Judgment on Jerusalem for not repenting 3:1–5
   D. Gather all nations for judgment, for none repent 3:6–8

III. Transformation and Joy on the Day of the Lord 3:9–20
   A. Transformation of the sinful 3:9–13
   B. Joy when God dwells among His people 3:14–20

This sermon illustrated how Zephaniah functioned as a prophet, how he legitimated a new way of understanding God's relationship to mankind, and how he persuaded his audience to seek God before the judgment day.

I. Judgment on the Day of the Lord 1:1–18

The prophet began his sermon by describing how God would bring *complete judgment on the wicked* (1:1–6), particularly all those living in Jerusalem (1:7–13). In this process he moved from broad universal inclusive statements to specific predictions about God's judgment on individuals in the various quarters of the capital city of Jerusalem.

Some in his audience worshiped the Canaanite god Baal and bowed down on their roofs to astral deities (the hosts of heaven; compare Jer. 8:2; 19:13). Others swore by the name of Yahweh as well as Milcom, the god of the Ammonites (1:4–6; see 2 Kings 23:13). Many Israelites internalized these religious innovations as part of their belief system during Manasseh's reign (2 Kings 21:1–9). They accepted a socially developed fertility worldview that was inconsistent with Israelite sacred tradition. Covenant laws condemned sacred prostitution and worship of other gods (Ex. 34:11–17; Lev. 20:1–5; Deut. 4:15–19).

The Baalistic temples, priests, prophets, myths, and even Manasseh's government provided a solid plausibility framework to legitimate this Canaanite cultural perspective.[12] It was not surprising that many objected when Josiah initially purged Jerusalem of high places and pagan priests (2 Chron. 34:3–7).

Zephaniah criticized the *recipients of judgment* (1:7–13), particularly the Jewish princes and leaders, the trendsetters in Jerusalem. They led the nation astray by adopting the latest fashions in foreign clothes and practicing violence and deceit[13] instead of justice in government (1:8–9; 3:1–5). Israel's tradition condemned this kind of social behavior (Ex. 20:13–17; Mic. 3:9–10). Somehow these people thought that God would not judge them (1:12). Foolishly, they removed Israel's God from their life (1:6) and created a world controlled by Baalism, their own imagination, the power of their political position, and wealth (1:18). Zephaniah's debunking of this worldview undercut its normative status by defining an alternate view of reality based on a different philosophical conception of the symbolic universe.[14]

He externalized the radical and socially unacceptable idea that God would destroy them for their wickedness. To emphasize the power of God and legitimate his statements, Zephaniah *described the day of the Lord* (1:14–18). Using traditions like Amos 5:18–20; Isaiah 2:6–22; 24:1–23; 63:1–7, he justified the maintenance of a different understanding of God's ways.[15] Indeed, God can and will come like a mighty warrior on a day of wrath and darkness (1:14–15). God will destroy the earth (1:2–3, 18; compare Isa. 24:1–23), remove military fortifications and wealth, and leave the survivors totally confused (1:16–18). The great day of the Lord was near,

---

12. Berger, *Social Construction,* 154–55.

13. Zephaniah 1:9, probably referred to breaking into a house to steal, rather than the foreign worship practice of "leap[ing] on the temple threshold" (*NASB*; see also 1 Sam. 5:5). See R. D. Patterson, *Nahum, Habakkuk, Zephaniah* in *WEC* (Chicago: Moody, 1991), 312–13.

14. Berger, *Social Construction,* 62, 106–07.

15. On the day of the Lord, see G. von Rad, "The Origin of the Concept 'Day of Yahweh,'" *JSS* 4 (1959), 97–108, who connects it to Holy War traditions. M. Weiss, "The Origin of the 'Day of the Lord Reconsidered," *HUCA* 37 (1966), 29–72, relates the idea to the theophany of God. See W.A. VanGemeren, *Interpreting the Prophetic Word* (Grand Rapids: Academic Books, 1990), 214–25.

very near to Judah, not just its enemies (1:7)! Judah would be sacrificed (1:7–8).[16] Jerusalem would be filled with wailing (1:10–11). The rich would not enjoy their riches (1:13, 18, compare Deut. 28:30, 39; Amos 5:11). This day seemed unavoidable, but the prophet offered a way of escape.

II. Repent before the Day of the Lord 2:1—3:8

To appease God's wrath, Zephaniah summoned the leaders *to gather Judah together to repent* (2:1–3) before God's anger could fall on them. To persuade and motivate the people to action, Zephaniah predicted God's judgment both on the nations around Judah (2:4–15) and on the violent leaders in Jerusalem who refused to repent (3:1–8).[17]

It seemed like a hopeless case, but Zephaniah called Judah's leaders to repent of their ways and avoid God's wrath (2:1–3). If they would only gather together at the temple before the day of the Lord, humble themselves, and transform their behavior, God might hide His anger (1:2–3; compare Amos 5:14–15; Isa. 55:6–7). Zephaniah knew that people were free to choose what they believed and how they ordered their social relationships.[18]

To legitimate the wisdom of this choice and encourage his audience to change, Zephaniah told how the *judgment of the nations would bring them to repentance* (2:4–15). God would desolate Philistia (2:4–6), Moab (2:8–9), Ethiopia, (2:12) and Assyria (2:13–15) because of their arrogance and harsh

---

16. Most scholars see Judah as the sacrifice. Achtemeier, *Micah-Malachi* in *IntCom,* 67–68, connects the imagery to the sacrifice which preceded a holy war when the soldiers were consecrated for battle (1 Sam. 13:9; 2 Sam. 15:12).

17. The end of the first section (1:18) and the second section (3:8) have God "devouring all the earth in the fire of his zeal." The beginning of the first section (1:2) and the second section (2:1) have a double use of the same root: "removing I will remove" in 1:2 and "gathering, gather yourselves" in 2:1. These repetitions point to structure.

18. Although Berger brackets freedom from his discussion of social behavior, he does recognize that religious conversions or "alternations" do occur. He saw these as a process of resocialization. Although resocialization is a basic part of a post-conversion experience, the act of believing something new can be a free choice, if it is not coerced by social pressure.

treatment of God's people (2:8, 10, 15).[19] The remnant of Judah would inherit these foreign lands (2:7, 9b), and the remnant of the nations would worship God (2:11). These arguments justified Zephaniah's call to repent.[20] If they refused to transform their lives, God would bring *judgment on Jerusalem for not repenting* (3:1–5). Judah was a shameless, undesirable nation (3:5) with violent and treacherous leaders who abused the legal standards of social order (3:3–4). They refused to follow the patterns of behavior in the nation's traditions (3:2) or to fear Yahweh (3:7). They internalized violent and selfish behavior patterns. They did not accept God's ways as their own (3:1, 7), receive correction, or learn from the disastrous experiences of other nations (3:2,6). Although God hoped that some would seek Him, eventually He would *gather all nations for judgment, for none repented* (3:6–8).

III. Transformation and Joy on the Day of the Lord 3:9–20

The final part of Zephaniah's sermon provided a positive externalization that gave the people another reason to repent. A new utopian setting stood on the horizon for those who would seek God. The day of the Lord would include the unveiling of the glorious kingdom of God. This salvation oracle pictured the *transformation of the sinful people* (3:9–13) and their joy in the presence of God, their King.[21]

---

19. D. L. Christensen, "Zephaniah 2:4–15: A Theological Basis for Josiah's Program of Political Expansion," *CBQ* 46 (1984), 669–82, does not date these oracles late (some thought they represent Judah's attitude toward Moab after the fall of Jerusalem), but feels their purpose was to justify Josiah's political expansion rather than convince the leaders to repent.

20. Berger, *Social Construction*, 156–60, stresses the need for the social legitimization of a new worldview when a transformation of thinking takes place.

21. O. P. Robertson, *The Books of Nahum, Habakkuk, and Zephaniah* in *NICOT* (Grand Rapids: Eerdmanns, 1990), 327, and R. Smith, *Micah-Malachi* in *WBC* 32(Waco: Word, 1984), 141–42, argue that this was part of Zephaniah's message, although earlier C. Taylor, "Zephaniah," *IB* 6 (Nashville: Abingdon, 1956), 1031, feels another later, kinder writer, penned these words.

Foreigners as well as Israelites would be there (3:9–10,12)—all those who would call on the name of God. Their social behavior would be drastically transformed. In this new society, they would speak with pure lips (without deceit as in 1:9), they would be humble (without pride as in 2:3, 10), there would be no rebellion or shame (see 2:1; 3:1), for all would be holy (3:9–13). This transformation would replace death and destruction with *joy when God dwells among His people* (3:14–20). God would be their King; He would love them (3:15, 17). He would gather all those who suffered and would restore the fortunes of the nation. He would bring praise and renown through them, as He originally intended (3:19–20; see Deut. 26:18–19).

Theological and Social Implications

A person does not have to watch television very long or read the newspaper many days to realize that society is full of sinful people who do not think biblically or act responsibly in their relationships to others or God. What will happen to them on the day of the Lord? What can be done to enable them to avoid the distress and destruction of that day? What words of warning, what rational arguments, what hopeful promises might encourage these people to seek God? How can God's messengers communicate the urgency of seeking God now before that day of accountability?

Zephaniah did not ignore these problems; neither should the modern preacher. He was not content to let people just do their own thing. Because he cared about the fate of his audience and knew that their choices would determine their future, he challenged them to reject injustice and the worship of other gods. He offered them a choice: experience the wrath of God on the day of the Lord, or seek God and transform your lives before the day of the Lord. Those who will humble themselves, seek God's mercy, and pursue righteousness will enjoy the pleasures of the glorious kingdom of God.

Questions for Discussion

1. Do people in our culture know about the day of the Lord? Do they know that people will be treated differently based on their beliefs and social relationships with others?
2. What methods of persuasion, what rational argument, what experiential evidence will impact the worldview of people today?
3. How can you call people to repentance without becoming so negative that you lose your audience?
4. Contrast the social conditions in Jerusalem in Zephaniah's day with the future conditions in the kingdom of God (3:9–20).

Chapter 10

Habakkuk: Living by Faith

Introduction

The idea of living by faith may sound exciting and adventuresome at first, but often people find greater appeal in the security of knowing what will happen, in being in control of the future. It can be more comforting to have a good job, a nice home, and some money in the bank than to trust in some invisible hand. Those who are unemployed and homeless, who have had a loved one die, or who live with an incurable disease often wonder if it makes any sense to trust in God.

Habakkuk's writings were not a report of the prophet's public communication to persuade the people of Judah to change their faith or behavior, like most other prophetic books. The Book of Habakkuk is a rare look at the private diary of a confused preacher. Habakkuk had constructed his own view of the way God should rule the world. His understanding was not completely consistent with the way God was acting. The diary exposed his questions and fears. How could the prophet call others to faith in God in such circumstances? How could he rejoice in God's strength when that strength remained invisible? The faith perspective of the prophet needed to change.

Before Habakkuk, or the preacher today, can confidently persuade others to trust God, God must transform that person's understanding of His sovereign ways and produce a heart that is open to the dynamics of a life of faith.

Social Setting

The Historical Context

The superscription of the book (1:1) did not connect the setting of Habakkuk to the reign of any Judean king. The iniquities in 1:2–4 does not fit the period of the righteous king Josiah, so some interpreters placed Habakkuk earlier in the evil days of Manasseh (2 Kings 21:10–16).[1] A more fitting context would be the violence created by the political changes in leadership in Jerusalem in Jehoiakim's reign (609–605 B.C.).[2] Judah was under Egyptian control (2 Chron. 35:20—36:10).

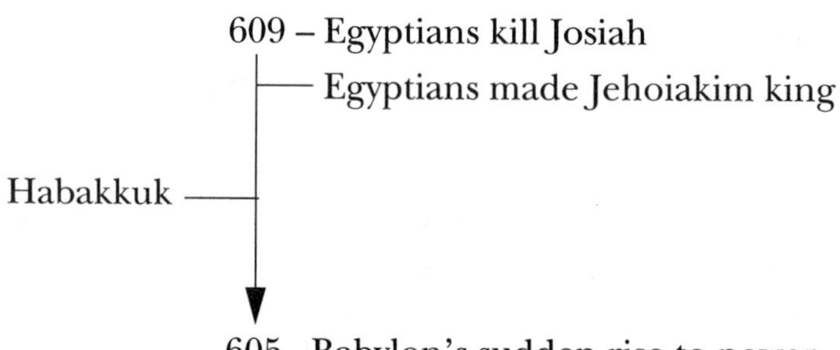

1. R. D. Patterson, *Nahum, Habakkuk, Zephaniah* in *WEC* (Chicago: Moody, 1991), 117, prefers the time of Manasseh. Early rabbinic tradition (*Seder Olam*) placed Habakkuk in the time of Manasseh, while the apocryphal *Bel and the Dragon,* line 33, put him much later and suggested that he took food to Daniel while he was in the lions' den. One manuscript of this apocryphal book claimed that the prophet was a Levite.

2. See J. H. Tullock, "Habakkuk," in *HBD* (Nashville: Holman Bible Publishers, 1991), 590; B. S. Childs, *Introduction to the Old Testament as Scripture* (Philadelphia: Fortress, 1979), 449, believes the oppressors were the Assyrians; J. J. M. Roberts, *Nahum, Habakkuk and Zephaniah* in *OTL* (Louisville: Westminster/J. Knox, 1991), 83, dates the oracles from 605 B.C. to 597 B.C.

In the near future God would surprisingly raise up the Babylonians (1:5). This would put Habakkuk a few years before Nebuchadnezzar defeated Egypt in 605 B.C.

The Structure of Social Order

The Book of Habakkuk is a critique of the prophet's philosophical view of how the world works.[3] The prophet's perception of objective reality included political powers and powerful armies (1:5–11). He knew that one of these nations, the Babylonians, violently attacked other nations (1:7, 11; 2:8, 17). He saw how the economic status of Judah suffered because of the death of King Josiah, the defeat of his army, and the heavy taxation Egypt forced on Judah (2 Chron. 36:3). Political infighting between pro-Babylonian and pro-Egyptian politicians in Jerusalem compounded the problem. A certain level of social disorder accompanied the deposing of Jehoahaz (who reigned only three months) and the enthronement of Jehoiakim as a puppet of Neco, king of Egypt (2 Kings 23:31–35). Murder, stealing, oppression of widows, and shedding innocent blood were everywhere (Jer. 7:5–9).

The Social Location and Role of the Prophet

Habakkuk lived in Judah and had the role of a prophet (1:1; 3:1). His prayers indicate his concern for justice and God's law (1:3–4,13), his beliefs about the character and sovereignty of God (1:12–14), and his familiarity with temple worship (3:1–19). The hymn in chapter 3 (with musical notations) suggests that Habakkuk was one of the Levites assigned to sing for temple services (see 2 Chron. 25:1–8),[4] but

3. P. Berger and T. Luckmann, *The Social Construction of Reality: A Treatise in the Sociology of Knowledge* (Garden City: Doubleday, 1966), 107, calls this the symbolic universe. They emphasize the need for maintaining the legitimations for a symbolic universe when an alternate view of the world is being forced upon a group by unusual events or another social group.

4. See E. Achtemeier, *Nahum-Malachi* in *IntCom* (Atlanta: John Knox, 1986), 33–35; E. Nielsen, "The Righteous and the Wicked in Habaqquq," *ST* 6 (1953), 54–78, suggests the book was used at a New Year's festival, but Childs, *Introduction to the Old Testament as Scripture*, 452, rejects this approach.

nothing indicates that Habakkuk wrote this book as a liturgy for a temple festival. Habakkuk's prayer concerning oppression by the Judean political leaders (1:2–4) shows he was not a central prophet who maintained the perverted views of Jehoiakim's government.[5]

As a prophet and songwriter, Habakkuk used literary and theological traditions to communicate God's message in a cultural form his readers would understand. Literary forms of speech include: laments (1:2–4; 1:12—2:1), a taunt song in the form of five woes (2:6–20), and a hymn (3:1–19).

His prayers maintain continuity with past theological traditions.[6] He knew from tradition that God was everlasting, holy, a rock, and too pure to approve evil in 1:12–13 (see Deut. 32:4; Ps. 11:4–6; 90:2); the Lord came from Mount Paran in 3:3 (Deut. 33:2); and He appeared in a theophany in 3:3–15 (Ps. 18:7–33; 77:11–20).

Although a few scholars have compared the hymn's imagery (3:2–19) with motifs in Babylonian and Ugaritic myths, theophany accounts in the Psalms are a more likely source of these images.[7] The hymnic and theophany traditions point to the prophet's theological background and role in the temple.

---

5. R. R. Wilson, *Prophecy and Society in Ancient Israel* (Philadelphia: Fortress, 1980) 278–79, believes that the prophet's oracles against the nation's enemies (2:6–20) show that he was a central prophet, but it is difficult to see Habakkuk supporting Jehoiakim or serving alongside the central prophets and priests who condemned Jeremiah (compare Jer. 7; 26; 29; 36).

6. Berger, *Social Construction*, 155–56, sees ritual and prayer as two methods of universe maintenance when a person's world is falling apart.

7. W. A. Irwin, "The Mythological Background of Habakkuk Chapter 3," *JNES* 15 (1956), 47–50, looks at Babylonian sources, while W. F. Albright, "The Psalm of Habakkuk," *Studies in the Old Testament,* ed. H. H. Rowley (Edinburgh: T & T. Clark, 1957), 1–18, examines comparisons with Ugaritic poetry.

Social Interaction

The Book of Habakkuk

Interpreters have raised few questions about the unity and authorship of this book.[8] It can be outlined into three sections:

I. Why Does God Allow Injustice to Continue in Judah? 1:1–11
   A. Lament concerning injustice in Judah 1:1–4
   B. Violent Chaldeans will remove the unjust 1:5–11
II. Why Does God Allow the Wicked to Bring Judgment? 1:12—2:20
   A. Lament concerning judgment by the wicked 1:11—2:1
   B. The righteous wait in faith for God's plan 2:2–5
   C. Five woes on the wicked Babylonians 2:6–20
III. Prayer for God's Mercy in Times of Judgment 3:1–19
   A. Prayer for mercy 3:1–2
   B. Theophany of God 3:3–15
   C. Habakkuk's confidence in God's salvation 3:16–19

This diary of the prophet's struggle with God's way of governing the world provided a rare glimpse of his inner theological and sociological frame of reference.

I. Why Does God Allow Injustice to Continue in Judah? 1:1–11

Habakkuk's initial prayer was a *lament concerning injustice in Judah* (1:1–4). Violence, strife, and destructive social relationships between the upper and lower classes dominated Jehoiakim's reign. The courts did not enforce justice;

8. W. Rudolph, *Micha-Nahum-Habakkuk-Zephanja* in *KAT* XII3 (Gütersloh: Gerd Mohn, 1975), 188–94; O. Eissfeldt, *Introduction to the Old Testament* (New York: Harper & Row, 1965), 420.

therefore the righteous suffered (1:2–4). The powerful ignored the civil and religious laws that were supposed to regulate ethical thinking and order social relationships.[9] In contrast to the leaders, Habakkuk's worldview accepted traditional values based on the nation's theological traditions (Ex. 20—23; Deut. 19:11–21) including love, respect, justice, honesty, and loyalty). He looked negatively on the present social disorder, seeing it as wickedness that God should judge (1:3).

Habakkuk identified with the oppressed by lamenting their situation. He did not think God would allow these things to happen. God should defend the righteous and not let the strong pervert justice (1:2; see traditions in Deut. 32:4; Ps. 11:5–7). Could he trust in a God who did not do this?

To encourage faith, God communicated a new vision of the future to Habakkuk. *The violent Chaldeans will remove the unjust* (1:5–11). This new externalization flamed the prophet's imagination and persuaded him to believe that God would judge the wicked. God would remove the violent in Judah by sending the powerful Babylonian army against Judah's unjust leaders.[10] This was a surprise (1:5) because Egypt was the powerful nation that controlled Judah. This was also fearful news, for the Jews had heard about the fierce exploits of Babylon's troops (1:6–10).

II. Why Does God Allow the Wicked to Bring Judgment? 1:12—2:20

God's answer satisfied Habakkuk's concerns over Judah's unjust leaders but raised another problem. Consequently, Habakkuk *lamented concerning judgment by the wicked* (1:11—2:1) and then received another answer from God.

---

9. Achtemeier, *Nahum - Malachi* in *IntCom* 34–3, thinks the law refers to "the whole religious tradition of Israel, including her Deuteronomic law, her traditions of what God has done in her past life, and the ongoing guidance afforded her day by day through the preaching of priests and prophets."

10. The Qumran pesher manuscript on 1:6 read "Kittim" (probably a reference to the Greeks) instead of Chaldeans. W. H. Brownlee, *The Text of Habakkuk in the Ancient Commentary from Qumran* (Philadelphia: JBL Monograph Series 11, 1959), 8.

This second lament was motivated by the divine strategy to use an evil nation (Babylon) to judge a more righteous people (Judah; 1:13). Habakkuk's view of God excluded the possibility of using the wicked Babylonians to bring correction to Judah (1:12b). A related problem was the fate of the people of Judah. They would be sitting ducks, like helpless fish caught in a net (1:14); they would be totally destroyed. This victory would cause the Babylonians to rejoice; it would further their false religious beliefs and encourage their violent activity (1:14–17). If God used Babylon in this way, people would think that God approved of Babylon's evil behavior (1:13). There was dissonance between the concept of justice in Habakkuk's symbolic universe and the way God ruled the earth.[11]

Traditional songs that Habakkuk sang in the temple encouraged faith in God the Rock, the just and righteous One (Deut. 32:4); the holy (Ex. 15:11; Ps. 99:3, 5, 9), and everlasting One (see Ps. 90:2). Other prophets said that the Redeemer, the Holy One of Israel, would deliver His people from Babylon and not let them die[12] (Isa. 41:13–20; 43:14–15; Mic. 4:10). How can a person have faith in a God who tolerates the evil Babylonians and lets them obliterate Judah?

The Lord's answer instructed *the righteous to wait in faith for God's plan* (2:2–5). First, the prophet was to write a message on a tablet (compare Isa. 8:1; 30:8). This public writing had the social function of warning others of what would happen in the future ("it will not fail"), of legitimating the authority of the prophet when the events came to pass, and of assuring the righteous that God honors the faithful and judges the proud (2:2–5).[13] The proud ones who destroyed

---

11. Berger, *Social Construction*, 95–104.

12. O. P. Robertson, *The Books of Nahum, Habakkuk and Zephaniah* in *NICOT* (Grand Rapids: Eerdmanns, 1990), 157, does not follow the emendations of the scribes which reads "You shalt [i.e. God] not die" in 1:12, even though it is parallel to describing God as "everlasting." Instead, 1:12 claimed that God's people will not die. This seems better than R. L. Smith's *Micah-Malachi* in *WBC* 32 (Waco: Word, 1984), 103, decision to accept the scribal emmendation.

13. There was some confusion concerning who or what the word "run" means. Smith, *Micah-Malachi* in *WBC* 32, 106–07, and J. M. Holt, "So He May Run Who Reads It," *JBL* 83 (1964), 298–303, believe the reader will be informed by the tablet and run for his life in light of its message.

many nations were the Babylonians (2:4–5; see Isa. 13—14). The righteous ones were those who faithfully lived according to the standards of behavior God ordered. By faith they believed God's future plan and depended on God for direction during times of chastening.[14]

This brief challenge was followed by a taunting song of *five woes on the wicked Babylonians* (2:6–20).[15] The wicked behavior of the Babylonians justified the divine plan to judge them and legitimated God's call for faith.

These structured woe oracles gave a brief picture of the social behavior of the Babylonian leaders.[16] They took what was not theirs through violence, fraudulent loans, and taxation schemes (2:6–8). They gained wealth, property, security, and high status for themselves by exploiting others (2:2–11). They practiced cruelty (forced labor) and violence to build their empires stronger (2:12–13). They trusted in wood and stone idols that could not teach anything about reality (2:18–19; compare Isa. 44:8–20). This behavior was inconsistent with the divine principles that should guide all social standards of behavior.

Therefore, God will bring a new setting on Babylon. Those who were violently plundered will rise up and plunder Babylon (2:7–8). Babylon will drink the cup of God's wrath (2:16). They will observe God's power and glory and will come to understand His standards for social behavior.

These woes gave Habakkuk an understanding of Babylon's new setting after it judged Judah. They helped the prophet maintain his faith in God. Although this answer did not plumb the mysteries of why God used a wicked nation to

---

14. Hab. 2:4 was used to legitimate a writer's point of view in the New Testament in Romans 1:17; Galatians 3:11; Hebrews 10:38. See P. L. M. Southwell, "A Note on Habakkuk 2:4," *JTS* 19 (1968), 614–17, and O. P. Robertson, "'The Justified (By Faith) Shall Live by His Steadfast Trust'-Habakkuk 2:4," *Presbyterion* 9 (1983), 52–71.

15. Achtemeier, *Nahum-Malachi* in *IntCom,* 49, contends that the woe oracle in this context is more of a curse, not a funeral lament. R. J. Clifford, "The Use of *HOY* in the Prophets," *CBQ* 28 (1966), 458–64, surveys the ways the woe oracle was used in the prophets.

16. Each woe was made up of three verses. These were structured by an identical refrain at the end of the second and fourth woes (2:8b, 17b) and a positive note after the third and last woes (2:14, 20).

The above photo is a portion of the commentary of Habakkuk from the Dead Sea Scrolls. The Qumran community wrote this commentary to apply the words of Habakkuk to their situation.

judge Judah (maybe there were no righteous nations), it assured Habakkuk that God was not rewarding Babylon for its wickedness. Now he can worship before God in silence (2:20).

III. Prayer for God's Mercy in Times of Judgment 3:1–19

This prayer demonstrated that God transformed Habakkuk's faith. The prophet's *prayer for mercy* (3:1–2) was a direct response to God's promise of judgment.[17] While he was praying, Habakkuk either saw a *theophany of God* (3:3–15) or remembered the power of God from one of the nation's traditional hymns (such as Ps. 18:7–15; 77:11–20).[18] This theophany justified Habakkuk's faith in God and legitimated hope. His externalization in this song presented a new view of God.[19]

The theophany account described the appearance of God's splendor at Mount Sinai (3:3; see Deut. 33:2–4; Ps. 68:7–8) and looked forward to His appearance over all the earth. His radiance was like light (3:4; see Deut. 5:22–24); plagues went before Him (3:5; see Ex. 7–11). Nature and people melted before His power (3:6–7; see Ps. 97:3–6). Rivers and armies were nothing before His anger (3:8–10; see Ps. 74:12–17; Ex. 14—15). When the mighty Warrior went forth to fight, God trampled the nations and brought salvation to His people (3:12–15; see Ex. 15:1–18).[20]

This theophany brought the prophet's understanding of God's glory and power into focus. He now had *confidence in God's salvation* (3:16–19). He no longer had questions

---

17. D. D. Garland, "Habakkuk," *BBC* (Nashville: Broadman, 1972), 264, thinks the report (3—15) refers to the deliverance at the time of the exodus from Egypt.

18. Achtemeier, *Nahum-Malachi* in *IntCom*, 53, believes this was a vision.

19. An externalization was a creative new way of imagining a part of reality, independent of the social forces that normally provided meaning to aspects of social reality.

20. T. Hiebert, *God of My Victory: The Ancient Hymn of Habakkuk 3* (Atlanta: Scholars Press, 1986) gives a detailed study of textual, structural, and interpretive problems associated with this song.

about putting his faith in God. His limited cultural perspective was transformed; he willingly submitted himself to the distress that God would bring on the nation. He rejoiced and exalted in the Lord (3:18) because his feet were on sure ground (like the deer in Ps. 18:33) and because God was his source of strength (3:18–19).

Theological and Social Implications

All persons in their private way must learn what it means to walk by faith. David, the man after God's own heart, had questions about wickedness in his days (Ps. 35), and the prophet Habakkuk was no different. Their experiences tell us that we are not that abnormal if we struggle with trusting God completely. We, too, wonder why He does not intervene and prevent violence.

Habakkuk teaches God's messengers to wrestle with God in prayer for a new, transformed conception of His glorious ways before one blindly mouths pious responses that do not meet the needs of God's people. Habakkuk warns us not to be satisfied with pat answers, but to ask for true wisdom from God (Jas. 1:5). Thinking based on God's wisdom may not make sense to the secular, scientific, or philosophical minds of our day, but this is to be expected because it is based on faith in God.

Faith is the acceptance of promises that cannot be humanly verified as certain (Heb. 11:1); yet, without faith, it is impossible to please God (Heb. 11:6). The old man Abraham believed God's promise (Gen. 15:6); Paul saw that faith was necessary for salvation (Rom. 1:16–17; Gal. 3:6–12); and the author of Hebrews knew that faith helped people endure trials (Heb. 10:32–39). The human dilemmas of life pit what is socially acceptable in people's cultural context against their knowledge of what God promises. If a preacher expects to call others to faith, that messenger of God must first learn to act in faith.

Habakkuk asked God for insight, and God gave a new perspective that transformed his life. When the vision of

God's splendor, power over nature, wrath, and salvation were internalized, faith blossomed. Confidence in God's sovereign rule turned to exaltation and praise. This transforming vision of God's power gives hope to those who see it.

Questions for Discussion

1. What should people do when they do not understand why God allows injustices to continue?
2. What was wrong with Habakkuk's view of God? How does your view of God's justice compare with the prophet's?
3. What evidence can we share with a person to encourage an attitude of faith in times of oppression?
4. What does it mean to live by faith?

Chapter 11

Jeremiah: Beware of Deceptive Words!

Introduction

Everyone hates to be deceived. It is hard to believe that a person would spread lies about a trusted friend. People get angry when a business associate betrays their trust and steals money from the company. Nations execute traitors who spy for other nations, and spouses divorce partners who pretend to be loyal, but have another secret romantic relationship.

Deception is a devious sickness. It hides the truth and parades a lie in beautiful words. When a theological illusion is shattered, it devastates believers because they were deceived by "authoritative" religious beliefs that they trusted. Sometimes even a true theological statement by God can become a useless deception if it is misinterpreted or misapplied. A divine promise is usually not an absolute guarantee that applies to everyone. Most promises relate to a specific audience in a special situation. God is not an impersonal force that acts according to a series of theological abstractions. He dynamically interacts with people based on His character and their situations.

A prophet, and God's messengers today, must tell the truth at all costs. An audience may prefer to hear a word of hope or a confirmation of what it already believes, but a half-truth, a one-sided or partial perception of God's view of reality must be recognized as a deception. These illusions may gain acceptance in a values clarification class, widespread inclusion as acceptable cultural norms in society, or official religious sanctions in a sermon but God's messengers are called to resist the temptation of popularity and political correctness. They are to oppose the myths (see 1 Tim. 1:3–4) that twist religious faithfulness into anything other than a dynamic relationship with God.

Social Setting

The Historical Setting

The superscription (1:1–3) and numerous chronological introductions to chapters coordinate Jeremiah's ministry with important events and the Judean kings Josiah, Jehoiakim, Jehoiachin, Zedekiah, and the governor Gedaliah.[1] These stretch from the prophet's call in 627 B.C. (1:2) to Jeremiah's years in Egypt after Jerusalem's destruction (580 B.C.).

The prophet was born in the reign of the wicked King Manasseh when Judah was under Assyrian control. Manasseh encouraged the worship of Baal and the hosts of heaven.[2] He ignored the nation's Yahwistic religious and social traditions (2 Kings 21:1–18; 2 Chron. 33:1–20).

---

1. 21:1; 24:1; 25:1; 26:1; 27:1; 28:1; 29:1–2; 32:1; 34:1; 35:1; 36:1; 37:1; 39:1; 40:1; 42:1; 44:1; 46:1–2; 47:1; 51:59. For a historical overview see D. Redford, *Egypt, Canaan, and Israel in Ancient Times* (Princeton: Princeton Univ. Press, 1992), 430–71.

2. J. McKay, *Religion in Judah under the Assyrians* (Naperville: Allenson, 1973), 28–43, thinks Josiah's reform did not remove Assyrian gods or idols but Canaanite ones.

Jeremiah began his ministry in Josiah's thirteenth year (1:2; 25:3).[3] The evils of Manasseh's era filled the air (Zeph. 1:4–5), but Josiah carried out a brief religious reform in 628 B.C. (2 Chron. 34:3–7) and declared Judah's political independence from Assyria. Later the book of the Law was found as Josiah repaired the temple (621 B.C.). This led to a purging of foreign idolatry and a return to the social standards of behavior in the nation's covenant traditions (Jer. 2—6; 2 Chron. 34—35).

Toward the end of Josiah's reign, Assyria was defeated (612 B.C.). After the Egyptian Pharaoh Neco II killed Josiah in a battle at Megiddo in 609 B.C. (see 2 Kings 23:28–30; 2 Chron. 35:20–27), the Egyptians took control of Judah, required heavy tribute, and put Jehioakim on the throne (2 Kings 23:31–37; 2 Chron. 36:1–5). Jehoiakim was unjust, violent, selfish, and opposed Josiah's revival of Yahweh worship (Jer. 22:13–17; 2 Chron. 36:5). Jeremiah's extended family in Anathoth (11:18–23) and prophets and priests from Jerusalem persecuted Jeremiah in this period (7:4; 8:6,8,11; 14:13–14; 26). After Nebuchadnezzar defeated the Egyptian army at Carchemish, Judah came under Babylonian control (605 B.C.), and the Babylonians deported some Jews to Babylon (Dan. 1:1–3). A few years later Jehoiakim rebelled against Nebuchadnezzar and died in the midst of a Babylonian siege (2 Kings 24:1–17).[4] Jehoiachin ruled for three months until the city surrendered (597 B.C.). The Babylo-

3. J. P. Hyatt, "The Book of Jeremiah," *IB* 5 (Nashville: Abingdon, 1956), 779, and W. Holliday, *Jeremiah: Spokesman Out of Time* (Philadelphia: Pilgrim, 1974) 17–23, conjecture that the thirteenth year of Josiah was the date of Jeremiah's birth, not his calling. C. F. Whitley, "The Date of Jeremiah's Call," *VT* 14 (1964), 467–84, put the call of Jeremiah in 609/608 B.C., the first year of Jehoiakim's reign. These dates were partially based on Jeremiah's silence concerning Josiah's reform. See S. Hermann, *Jeremia* in *BKAT* xii (Neukirchen: Neukirchener Verlag, 1986), 11–23. J. R. Lundbom, *The Early Career of the Prophet Jeremiah* (Lewiston: Millen, 1993), sees the call coming in 627 B.C., acceptance of call in 622 B.C., and a commission reaffirming the call coming also in 622 B.C.

4. J. Bright, *Jeremiah* in *AB* 21 (Garden City: Doubleday, 1965), xlix, thinks Jehioakim was assassinated (Jer. 22:18–19 and 36:30).

nians took the king, his officials, skilled craftsmen, and much gold to Babylon (2 Kings 24:10–16; Ezek. 1:2).[5]

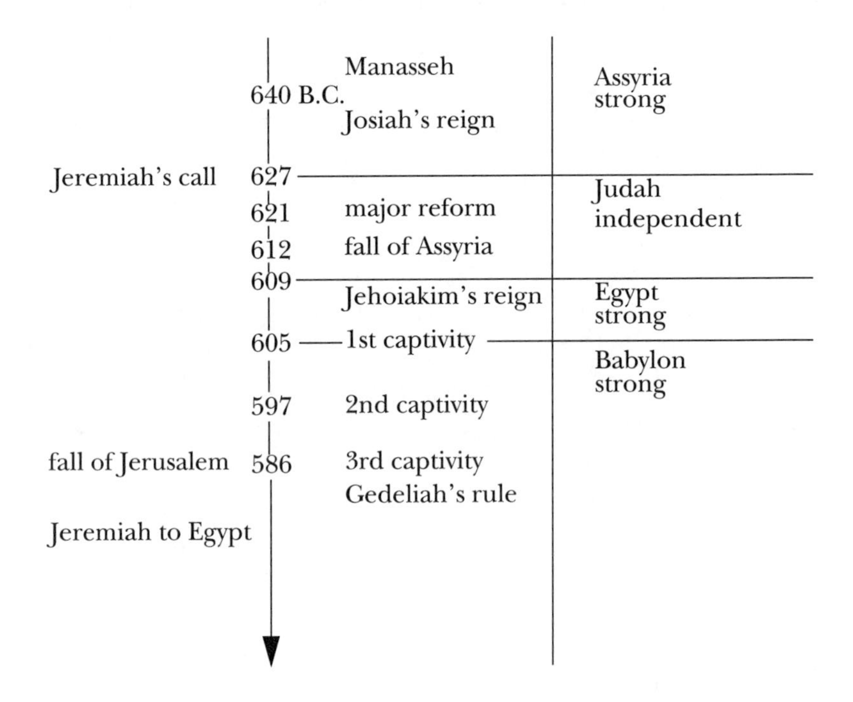

The final king in Judah was Zedekiah (597–586 B.C.; 2 Kings 24:17–20; 2 Chron. 36:10–13). Zedekiah was an ineffective ruler because of his fear of public opinion and the Babylonian deportation of many civic officials (38:5). After he joined a coalition against Babylon (27:1–3),[6] Nebuchadnezzar defeated and burned Jerusalem (39:1–10; 52:1–34; 2 Kings 25:1–21).

Many people went into captivity (52:28–30), but Jeremiah stayed in Palestine (39:10–14; 40:1–5) with Gedaliah, the governor of Judah (40:6–12). Soon Gedaliah was killed (41:1–3), and the remaining people escaped into Egypt to

5. For more details, see J. Bright, *A History of Israel* (Philadelphia: Fortress, 1981), 317–327; Redford, *Egypt, Canaan, and Israel,* 430–71.

6. W. L. Holladay, *Jeremiah 1* in *Her* (Philadelphia: Fortress, 1986), 7, believes this coalition formed in 594 B.C. because there was an internal uprising in Nebuchadnezzar's army. This gave the coalition a rationale for hope (27:1).

avoid another Babylonian attack. Jeremiah and Baruch were forcibly taken with them (43—44). The fate of Jeremiah and this small group of people is unknown, although Jeremiah predicted that they would die in Egypt (43:10).

The Structure of Social Order

The most vivid image of everyday life in Jeremiah's time was the devastation of war (4:5; 5:15; 6:17–19; 8:10–12; 15:2). The Assyrians and Egyptians lost major battles and thousands of troops. Jerusalem was attacked twice, and its homes and businesses were left in total ruin. Social disorder characterized the panic, starvation, and violence of war. After the battle, order was determined by the whim of the stronger army. Rage and revenge replaced normal patterns of morality; assassinations and the captivity of civic officials eliminated traditional authority structures (2 Kings 24—25). Somehow Judah survived this chaos until the death blow in 586 B.C. when Jerusalem was obliterated.

The socially constructed worldview of most Judeans was heavily influenced by prophets who deceived people by promising peace (4:10; 5:12–13; 6:13–14; 14:14; 27—29).[7] Political alliance with Assyria and Egypt supported these delusions (2:18, 36; 37:5–11). Temple priests legitimated this position by saying that God would not let the Babylonians destroy the Jerusalem temple (26:1–19). Jeremiah undermined these humanly created deceptions and exposed God's plans for Judah (7:1–15; 18:1–9; 29:1–14).

Social and economic conditions were directly affected by the nation's political status. Judah enjoyed a few years of social stability and political independence from foreign domination during Josiah's reign (628–609 B.C.), but this did not last. The Egyptians exacerbated Judah's poverty by imposing a large tribute on Jehoiakim (2 Kings 23:33). In the 605 and 597 B.C. exiles, the Babylonians took treasures from

7. P. Berger and T. Luckmann, *The Social Construction of Reality: A Treatise in the Sociology of Knowledge* (Garden City: Doubleday, 1966), 19–34, concluded that worldviews are developed through social interaction with parents and peers, as well as one's own experience.

the king's resources and the temple, skilled craftsmen who could have helped rebuild Judah's economy (2 Kings 24:13–17), and key civic leaders.

Jeremiah condemned King Jehoiakim for abusing people in order to get his large building projects completed. He afflicted the poor, shed innocent blood, and extorted money. (22:13–17). Priests and prophets were also obsessed with greed (6:13; 8:10).

The reformation of Josiah in 627 B.C. rejected the Baalistic worldview and the sacred prostitution popular in Manasseh's day (2 Kings 21—23). The finding of the law book in the temple led to a renewed commitment to the divine covenant. Unfortunately, this revival did not last, for the people forgot the nation's ancient theological traditions during Jehoiakim's and Zedekiah's time (2:4–9; 8:9; 9:13; 11:1–13). The people returned to a ritualistic and syncretistic worship of God at the temple as well as idols at high places (7:1–26). Jeremiah opposed these deceptive beliefs using language similar to Hosea and Deuteronomy.[8]

The Social Location and Role of the Prophet

Jeremiah was the son of Hilkiah, a priest from Anathoth (Josh. 21:13–19), three miles northeast of Jerusalem. He was a descendant of Abiathar's priestly family, which was replaced during the reign of Solomon (1 Kings 2:26–27). Jeremiah was educated in the nation's covenant traditions (11:1–13) and priestly roles, although no evidence exists that he ever functioned as a priest or cultic prophet in the temple as

8. See the comparisons in H. H. Rowley, "The Prophet Jeremiah and the Book of Deuteronomy," *Studies in Old Testament Prophecy* (Edinburgh: T & T Clark, 1950), 157–74, and J. A. Thompson, *The Book of Jeremiah* in *NICOT* (Grand Rapids: Eerdmans, 1980), 81–85. See discussion by F. B. Huey, *Jeremiah* in *NAC 16* (Nashville: Broadman Press, 1993), 26–29. For an attempt to make Jeremiah disappear entirely as an author, see R. Carroll, *Jeremiah* in *OTL* (Philadelphia: The Westminster Press, 1986), 38–50. Compare the critique in P. C. Craigie, P. H. Kelley, J. F. Drinkard, Jr., *Jeremiah 1—25* in *WBC 26* (Dallas: Word Books, 1991), xxxi–xli.

Reventlow suggests.[9] He was not a poor person, for he had his own scribe (Baruch; see 36:4) and was able to buy his relative's field (32:6–15). If his father Hilkiah was the high priest,[10] this would explain his high social status and why Jeremiah was never killed for his treasonous words (contrast 26:20–24).[11] Jeremiah had friends and relatives who held important positions in government.[12] Jeremiah was not married (16:1–4).

The early years after his call (627 B.C.) were somewhat hidden, for he said little about Josiah. His positive words concerning Josiah (22:15–16), lament for Josiah (2 Chron. 35:25), and call for repentance in 2:1–6:30 suggest that he was a central prophet who supported Josiah's reform.[13]

In Jehoiakim's reign Jeremiah boldly condemned the people at the temple for their false security, for thinking that the presence of God in the temple would automatically save them (7:1–15; 26:1–6). He repeatedly opposed the prophets for giving false prophecies of peace (8:8–11; 14:13–16; 23:9–40). Because Jeremiah rejected the popular worldview of his day, relatives plotted to kill him (11:18–23), and the priests and prophets who heard his temple sermon

9. H. G. Reventlow, *Liturgie und prophetisches Ich bei Jeremia* (Gütersloh: Gütersloher Verlaghaus, Gerd Mohn, 1963), 24–77. His role was to oppose most of what was happening in the temple.

10. In 2 Kings 22:4, 8, he was called high priest, but in 2 Kings 22:10, 12, 14, he was just called priest. Jeremiah 1:1–3 did not refer to Hilkiah as the high priest.

11. H. H. Rowley, "The Early Prophecies of Jeremiah in Their Setting," *Men of God* (London: Nelson, 1963), 137–39, lists proponents and opponents (most think he was not the high priest).

12. His uncle Shallum's son, Maaseiah was a keeper of the threshold of the temple (35:4; cf. 2 Chron. 34:8). One of Maaseiah's sons was a priest (21:1; 29:25–26; 37:3).

13. R. R. Wilson, *Prophecy and Society in Ancient Israel* (Philadelphia: Fortress, 1980), 242, concludes that Jeremiah was a peripheral prophet while D. C. Hester, *Authority Claims and Social Legitimation in the Book of Jeremiah* (Doctoral Dissertation at Duke University, 1982), 226, concludes he was a central prophet. Klaus Seybold, *Der Prophet Jeremia: Leber and Werk* (Stuttgart: Kohlhammer, 1993), surveys Jeremiah's life, teachings, and the editing of his work.

threatened to execute him (26:7–19). Pashur, the priest, had Jeremiah beaten and put in stocks to be humiliated publicly (20:1–6). Jehioakim forbade him to enter the temple area (36:5) and forced him into hiding (36:1–4,20–26). During this period Jeremiah functioned as a peripheral prophet who opposed the political and religious policies of the government.

These events had a severe effect on Jeremiah's acceptance of his prophetic role. He wept for the people (4:19–21; 8:18—9:1; 14:14, 19:22) and functioned in the role of intercessor,[14] but he wondered why so much persecution came when God promised to protect him (1:9, 17–19). Why did God let the wicked persecute him (11:18—12:6; 17:12–18; 18:18–23)? Why did God act deceptively against him (15:10–18; 20:7–18)? Jeremiah's prophetic calling seemed rather useless because God refused to listen to Jeremiah's intercession for Judah (14:19—15:9). He was lonely, despised, and depressed (15:10–18). He experienced the fall of Jerusalem and saw friends taken into captivity in 605, 597, and 587 B.C.

Jeremiah's self-understanding of his role was partially explained in prayers of "confession." Some studies of these prayers focused on the prophet's emotional status, rather than the social, theological, and contextual factors which gave rise to his prayers.[15] Jeremiah's thinking emerged through his interaction with God, his audience, and traditional role expectations. The prophet's persecution and confusion over his role influenced his manner of communication (prayer, lament, and autobiography).

The prophet's communicative and persuasive skills are evident in his sermons. Form critics, rhetorical studies, and

---

14. A. B. Rhodes, "The Prophets as Intercessors," *Scripture in History and Theology*, ed. A. L. Merrill and T. W. Overholt (Pittsburgh: Pickwick, 1977), 108–28.

15. Hyatt, "Jeremiah," *IB* 5, 782–83, describes "Jeremiah's Personality" as if it were static over forty years of ministry in very diverse settings. See A. R. Diamond, *The Confessions of Jeremiah in Context* (Sheffield: *JSOT-Sup* 45 1987), 11–16, for a survey of various approaches to the confessions.

statistical analysis have examined the literary characteristics of the prophet.[16] Jeremiah's reflections from other theological traditions reveal his training. In the first few chapters these included the call of Moses in 1:6–9 (see traditions in Ex. 3—4); the wilderness journey in 2:1, 6 (see Deut. 2:7; 8:15); the laws of divorce in 3:1 (see Deut. 24:1–4); and the need to circumcise your heart in 4:4 (see Deut. 10:16). These ideas legitimated Jeremiah's worldview and identified his words with the nation's past sacred traditions.[17]

Social Interaction

The Book of Jeremiah

The text of Jeremiah contains a combination of poetic sermons (type A material), (auto)biographical material in prose (type B material), and sermons in prose (Deuteronomic or type C material). Mowinckel believes these diverse types of literature came from several people in different time periods, being edited together at a much later date.[18] These

16. T. M. Raitt, *A Theology of Exile* (Philadelphia: Fortress, 1977); J. R. Lundbom, *Jeremiah: A Study in Ancient Hebrew Rhetoric* (Missoula: Scholars Press, 1975) focuses on rhetorical markers, and L. Stulman, *The Prose Sermons of the Book of Jeremiah* (Atlanta: Scholars Press, 1986) uses statistical analysis. The prophet used a call narrative (1:4–10); covenant lawsuit (2:1–37); oracle of judgment (5:1–17; 8:4–12; 16:10–13; 28:12–16); lament (11:18—12:6; 15:10–21; 17:14–18; 18:18–23; 20:7–18); summons to repentance (3:12–14; 4:1–4; 7:3–7; 22:3–5; 25:4–6); prayer (14:19–22; 16:19–20); and salvation speeches (3:15–18; 16:10–18; 29:10–14; 30—31; 32:36–44; 33).

17. Holladay, *Jeremiah 2* in *Her*, 35–70, finds reminiscences from the pentateuchal, historical, hymnic, wisdom, and prophetic traditions. See also P. Grech, "Interprophetic Re-interpretation and Old Testament Eschatology," *Augustinianum* 9 (1969), 235–65.

18. S. Mowinckel, *Zur Komposition des Buches Jeremia* (Kristiana: Dybwald, 1914), 20–45, believes the first material came from Jeremiah, the biographic prose came from Egypt around fifty years later (later he concluded it came from Baruch), and the final type of material came from late Deuteronomic redactors. Holladay, *Jeremiah 2* in *Her*, 10–24; 53–63, and Thompson, *Jeremiah* in *NICOT*, 33–56, discuss these problems. Most recently, see M. J. Williams, "An Investigation on the Legitimacy of Source Distinction for the Prose Material in Jeremiah," *JBL* 112 (1993), 193–210. See note 8 in this chap.

interpretations fragment the book and downplay points of continuity that unify the text.[19] The book was topically organized:[20]

I. Deception Is Judged, If There Is No Repentance 1:1—9:29
   A. Jeremiah's call 1:1–19
   B. Repentance or deception 2:1—4:4
   C. Deceptive peace or disaster from the north 4:4—6:30
   D. Amend your deceptive ways 7:1—9:26

II. Judah's Rejection and Jeremiah's Lament 10:1—20:18
   A. Broken covenant and laments 10:1—12:17
   B. Total rejection brings laments 13:1—15:21
   C. No lament for Judah, only Jeremiah 16:1—17:18
   D. The Potter's ways and a lament 17:19—18:23
   E. Pottery judgments, persecution, and laments 19:1—20:18

III. Judgments against Leaders and Nations 21:1—25:38

---

19. On the basis of a linguistic study Bright, *Jeremiah* in *AB* 21, lxvii–lxxiii, concludes that the "Deuteronomic" material was early (not post-exilic) and not contradictory to Jeremiah's thinking. T. W. Overholt, "Remarks on the Continuity of the Jeremiah Tradition," *JBL* 91 (1972), 457–62, sees a similar treatment of the theme of "falsehood" throughout Jeremiah, while W. L. Holladay, "Prototypes and Copies: A New Approach to the Poetry and Prose Problem in the Book of Jeremiah," *JBL* 79 (1960), 351–67, shows a dependence between the poetic and prose sections.

20. A helpful discussion of Jeremiah's structure is D. A. Dorsey, "Broken Potsherds at the Potter's House: An Investigation of the Arrangement of the Book of Jeremiah," *EJ* 1 (1983), 3–16.

IV. Prophetic Deceptions Oppose Jeremiah's Words 26:1—29:32

V. Promises of Restoration 30:1—33:26

  A. Poetic promises of a new day 30:1—31:40

  B. Prose promises of restoration 32:1—33:26

VI. Narratives of Jeremiah's Rejection 34:1—45:5

  A. Rejection before the fall of Jerusalem 34:1—38:28

  B. Rejection after the fall of Jerusalem 39:1—43:7

  C. Rejection after going to Egypt 43:8—45:5

VII. Oracles against Foreign Nations 46:1—51:64

VIII. An Appendix: The Fall of Jerusalem 52:1–34

These sermons and biographical accounts of Jeremiah's ministry record how the prophet interacted with and unmasked the deceptive theological beliefs of his audiences. To our surprise, Jeremiah's own deceptive construction of reality was exposed in his laments.

I. Deception Is Judged, If There Is No Repentance 1:1—9:29

According to the superscription (1:1–3), Jeremiah's ministry extended from the thirteenth year of Josiah to the fall of Jerusalem (627–587 B.C.).[21] *Jeremiah's call* (1:4–19) coincided with two key events: Josiah's declaration of independence from Assyria and his purging of Judah's pagan high places (2 Chron. 34:1–7). These royal initiatives began to transform the political and religious norms established during Manasseh's reign (2 Kings 21). God set apart the unborn child Jeremiah for the prophetic task of announcing His new plans for destroying and rebuilding the nations (1:4–10).

21. Holladay, *Jeremiah 1* in *Her*, 4, 17, concludes that 627 B.C. was the date of Jeremiah's birth since 1:5 said that Jeremiah was called from his birth. This helped to explain why Jeremiah said almost nothing about Josiah, but few have accepted this interpretation. See note 3 above.

God's vision for Jeremiah was initially rejected in rather Mosaic fashion (see Ex. 3:10–12),[22] but God promised His presence, direction, power, and word would transform this inexperienced man's self-perception. The call and its two visions (1:11–14) had the social function of authenticating to Jeremiah and his audiences that God would watch over His words to fulfill them (1:12).[23] The prophetic role involved delivering God's message in a credible way to a hostile audience. It required fearless courage in times of social disapproval and an internalization of God's protecting presence (1:16–19).[24]

Jeremiah's sermons in Josiah's reign (3:6) contrasted two choices. The people's worldview could be directed by *repentance or deception* (2:1—4:4). Jeremiah argued that Baalism had deceived the people (2:1—3:5) and then he called the nation to true repentance (3:5—4:4). He used the logic of a covenant lawsuit to contrast logically the people's denial of sinfulness with their syncretistic practices.[25] The ideal relationship for Judah and God involved loving devotion, total commitment, holy living, and God's protection (2:2–3). The people's identity as the "bride of God" was lost when they forgot about God's deeds of mercy in the wilderness and His gift of the land (2:6–7; compare Deut. 8). The social opinion-makers (kings, priests, and prophets) ignored God, and the nation began to accept a Baalistic cultural worldview (2:8). Jeremiah's audience was deceived and claimed innocence of

22. See N. Habel, "The Form and Significance of the Call Narratives," *ZAW* 77 (1965), 297–323, on structural factors and Holladay, *Jeremiah: Spokesman Out of Time,* 16–18, on comparisons with Moses and Samuel.

23. There is no sign that this is a public ordination ritual for a cultic prophet as Reventlow, *Liturgie und prophetisches,* Ich 24–77, suggests or that this was merely a literary device and not a private experience of Jeremiah as R. Carroll, *Jeremiah* in *OTL,* 100, suggests.

24. Berger, *Social Construction,* 129, sees internalization as the social process of accepting another person's meaningful interpretation of this world as one's own.

25. K. Nielsen, *Yahweh as Prosecutor and Judge: An Investigation of the Prophetic Lawsuit (Rib–Pattern)* (Sheffield: Sheffield Press, 1978) discusses the structure and theology behind covenant lawsuits.

any sins (2:35). They said they were not devoted to Baal (2:23) and were free to do what they wished (2:31).[26] Jeremiah claimed the people:

(a) changed gods, substituting the stagnant water of idolatry for the fresh spring water of God (2:11–13),

(b) made alliances with other nations and did not depend on God (2:14–16), and

(c) were obsessed with degenerate Baal rituals (2:20–28).

Therefore, God will judge Judah for harlotry, just as He judged Israel about 100 years earlier. Some initial reforms began in 628 B.C., but many people did not transform their deceptive syncretistic thinking (3:6–10).

Surprisingly, in the middle of his sermon, Jeremiah turned his back on Judah and called the exiled Israelites (the northern tribes) to repent of their sinful ways (3:12–14) and participate in God's glorious transformed kingdom (3:14–19). They could be part of a new world of prosperity, intimate worship at God's throne, and commitment to divine patterns of behavior by Jews and Gentiles. Some recognized their unfaithfulness, the deceptive nature of Baal worship, and in shame confessed their sins (3:21–25). Jeremiah assured Israelites (4:1–2) and Judeans (4:3–4) of God's blessing if they truly turned from their old ways and let righteousness guide them.

These sermons brought conflicting responses. Some prophets contradicted Jeremiah and scoffed at his wild predictions because they rejected the possibility of divine retribution. Jeremiah's next sermon contrasted the options of *deceptive peace or disaster from the north* (4:5—6:30). Jeremiah externalized a new vision of Judah:[27] a vividly illustrated vi-

---

26. Bright, *Jeremiah* in *AB* 21, 17–18, finds the changes from the second masculine plural pronominal suffix (2:4–13, 29–32) to second feminine singular (2:1–3,4–28, 33–37) identifies two different sermons that were joined together, but such changes may be based on the group addressed (Israel is singular in 2:1–3, while "all the families" in 2:4 is plural).

27. Berger, *Social Construction,* 104, sees externalization as the social process of bringing new meanings to life which are not derived from social forces in one's environment.

sion of war by an army from the north bringing great desolation in Judah (4:5–8, 13, 16, 29; 5:14–17; 6:1–12). There was hope if the people would repent (4:14), but most did not seek justice and truth (5:1). The audience did not know God's teachings, but practiced oppressive and deceitful social relationships to gain greater wealth for themselves (5:5, 7–8, 25–28). Kings, priests, and prophets predicted God's protection and peace for Jerusalem. They claimed that war would not destroy Jerusalem (4:9–10; 5:12–13; 6:13–14; see Isa. 36—37).[28] Jeremiah realized how they deceitfully twisted divine promises based on a faithful and loving relationship to God into absolute guarantees of God's grace that were not dependent on their devotion to God.[29] His prophetic role was to refine and test the popular thinking in Judean culture (6:27–30). He was overcome with anguish and lamented over their impending destruction (4:19–22).

The next sermons came in Jehoiakim's reign shortly after Josiah's death in 609 B.C. Jehoiakim did not continue Josiah's reform movement, so the people began to syncretize Baal and temple worship again (2 Kings 23:31–24:7). Jeremiah called the people to *amend their deceptive ways* (7:1–9:26). The prophet unmasked the people's deceptive trust in the temple (7:1–15; compare 26:1–19). The audience practiced injustice against the weak, stealing, murder, sacrificing to Baal, and then came to the temple to proclaim divine deliverance. The socially accepted ritual confession "The temple of the Lord" was just a magical slogan of empty temple theology. Yes, God's glory did dwell in the temple (Ps. 132:12–13) as the priests taught, but this was not an unconditional guarantee of safety. God's presence would dwell in that place (the temple) and the people would dwell in their place

---

28. R. E. Clements, *Jeremiah* in *IntCom* (Atlanta: J. Knox, 1988), 43, thinks that God's deliverance of Hezekiah from Sennacherib only reinforced their absolute confidence in God's promises of an eternal Davidic dynasty in Jerusalem (see 2 Sam. 7).

29. Berger, *Social Construction*, 89–90, calls this false view of reality a reification. It de-humanizes reality and creates an unreal facticity out of a mirage.

(Jerusalem) only if they amended their ways and truly worshiped God (7:3–5). If they did not change, God would destroy the temple, like He destroyed the tabernacle at Shiloh (7:12–15).

Equally deceptive was the worship of the Queen of Heaven, the mother goddess (7:17–20),[30] offering sacrifices to God while stubbornly refusing to practice acceptable behavioral patterns (7:21–26), and burning children at the high place called Tophet (7:30–34).[31] Jeremiah's audience maintained their deceitful ways and refused to repent (8:4–7). Their leaders claimed to be wise and know God's law, but actually they rejected the law. They were more concerned about making money and telling people that all would work out fine (8:8–12).

This evidence logically justified God's decision to turn Jerusalem into an empty wasteland for birds and wild beasts, a place of wailing women, great shame, and death (8:13–17; 9:10–22). Jeremiah announced this news with great sorrow in his heart. He cried out for mercy and wondered why there seemed to be no balm that could restore the broken nation (8:18—9:2).[32]

Jeremiah ended this rhetorical unit with a final verdict that has something of a wisdom flavor.[33] If people want to avoid the deception of the values of popular culture (riches, wealth, or strength), they must trust in God and order their lives around His values of justice, lovingkindness, and righteousness (9:23–24).

---

30. She is probably Ashtarte. See M. Weinfield, "The Worship of Molech and of the Queen of Heaven and its Background," *UF* 4 (1972), 149–54.

31. Craigie, et, al., *Jeremiah 1—25,* in *WBC* 26, 125 connect this child sacrifice with Baalism (2 Kings 21:6; Jer. 19:5; 32:25), for archeologists found the remains of many children at the Phoenician temple at Carthage.

32. Carroll, *Jeremiah* in *OTL,* 235–36, concludes that the wounded people in the city lamented, but there is no sign of their repentance. Clements, *Jeremiah* in *IntCom,* 59, properly identifies the lamenter as Jeremiah.

33. Thompson, *Jeremiah* in *NICOT,* 318.

II. Judah's Rejection and Jeremiah's Lament 10:1—20:18

This section has four cycles. Each contain sermons and a lament. These came in Jehoiakim's reign when Jeremiah faced severe persecution and strong doubts about his prophetic role.

The first section dealt with Judah's *broken covenant and Jeremiah's laments* (10:1—12:17). The Judeans returned to idol worship in Jehoiakim's reign, so Jeremiah's sermon warned them not to internalize the deceptive custom of following man-made gods of wood and silver. He mocked the impotence of idols which cannot speak or do anything; they are a delusion, worthless pieces of wood (10:2–5, 8–9, 14–15). People should fear Yahweh who has incomparable power. He is the King, the living and everlasting God who wisely created the earth, sent rain to care for it, and will destroy all false gods (10:6–7, 10, 12–13).[34]

Jeremiah's persuasive appeal for action was strengthened by his personal identification with the plight of the people in a lament. He deeply cared about the coming incurable wounds of destruction that Judah's leaders brought on the nation (10:17–22). He also interceded for God to graciously correct His people and judge other pagan nations with wrath (10:23–27). Jeremiah set the example; maybe others would reject idolatry, grieve over Judah's coming destruction, and intercede for mercy.

The sermon on deceptive idols supported Jeremiah's claim that the people broke their covenant relationship with God (11:1–17). To convince his audience in Jerusalem of the validity of their guilt, Jeremiah described their original covenant relationship with God using traditions from Deuteronomy.[35] God promised to be the people's God and gave them

---

34. The works of M. Margoliot "Jeremiah X.1–16: A Re-Examination," *VT* 30 (1980), 295–308, and T. W. Overholt, "The Falsehood of Idolatry: An Interpretation of Jer. X.1–16," *JTS* 16 (1965), 1–12, outline the structure and unifying themes.

35. Craigie, et al., *Jeremiah 1—25,* 168–69, lists connections with Deuteronomy as well as phrases that frequently occured in Jeremiah, but which were not characteristic of Deuteronomy.

a land if they would commit themselves to Him (11:4–5). God saw the rejection of Josiah's reform and the return to idolatry in Jehoiakim's reign as a conspiracy not to internalize what He said (11:10, 13, 17). God will bring unescapable disaster on the nation (11:11).

This section ended, like the other cycles in Jeremiah 10—20, with Jeremiah lamenting. Two personal cries of anguish (11:18–20; 12:1–4) questioned why God allowed people to persecute him for faithfully declaring God's word.[36] Jeremiah's relatives in Anathoth, the priests who should provide social plausibility to his teaching and action, responded to his preaching with a plan to kill him to keep him from speaking his socially unacceptable ideas (11:21).[37] Jeremiah was astonished and fearful. He asked for God's vengeance, and God promised to punish the perpetrators (11:20–23). Jeremiah questioned why God allowed these wicked "religious" people to prosper; why did He not side with Jeremiah and destroy them (12:1–3)? God gave three answers. First, Jeremiah should quit complaining and get ready for the difficult days ahead; second, God would desolate Judah as He said; and third, He would have compassion on Judah and the Gentile nations if they would reject idolatry (12:5–17). These written laments authenticated the prophet's role and revealed his own weakness. They vindicated the prophet's message and God's rejection of Judah's leaders.[38]

In the second cycle God's *total rejection brings laments* (13:1—15:21). This portion included symbolic acts (13:1–

36. Reventlow, *Liturgie und Prophetische Ich* (Grand Rapids: Eerdmans, 1988), and Carroll, *Jeremiah* in *OTL,* 276–78, concludes that this was a community lament at a worship service. In it they recognize the disintegration of their world and cry out to God. It seems better to follow W. Brueggemann, *Jeremiah 1—25: To Pluck Up, To Tear Down* in *ITC* (Grand Rapids: Eerdmans, 1988), 109 and Holladay, *Jeremiah 1* in *Her,* 358, who see these as personal laments.

37. Berger, *Social Construction,* 121, finds one method of universe maintenance (the socially accepted world of the priests in Anathoth) was to liquidate (kill) the person presenting a deviant view of life (Jeremiah).

38. Brueggemann, *Jeremiah 1—25* in *ITC,* 112. Diamond, *Confessions of Jeremiah,* 22–51, examines the form, diction, redaction, interpretation, aim, and setting of each of these laments.

27), Jeremiah's intercession over God's rejection of Judah (14:1—15:9), and a lament by Jeremiah (15:10–21).

The symbolic action Jeremiah did was fairly simple, but it carried a powerful political message. He bought a loincloth, hid it in water, then found it later in a ruined condition (13:1–7). The worthless cloth symbolized the proud Judeans who worshiped other gods; they were totally worthless (13:10). The worthless cloth was contrasted with the original loincloth. Judah was to cling to God like a loincloth clings to a man to bring praise and honor to God, but now they were worthless (see Deut. 26:18–19).[39] A second symbolic act of smashing jugs of wine symbolized God smashing Judah's drunken political and religious leaders (13:12–14). The audience should reject pride and humble themselves before God (13:15–16). If they refused to change, they would weep bitterly as they were exiled in shame (13:17–27).

Later when a drought hit Judah (14:1–6), Jeremiah socially identified with those suffering in Judah and tried to persuade God to be merciful. He interceded by confessing Judah's sins and asking God not to forsake them (14:7–9). God affirmed His rejection of Judah and told Jeremiah not to pray for them (14:11–12). The prophet interceded again and blamed the nation's condition on the social acceptability of the deceptive words of the false prophets. God reaffirmed His rejection of the false prophets and the people who followed their deceptions (14:13–16). Then Jeremiah lamented the horrors of war and passionately questioned whether God had completely rejected Judah (14:17–22). The answer was final. God would send sword, famine, and captivity. He would not listen even if Moses or Samuel asked for mercy (15:1–9). These laments and intercessory prayers increased the people's ability to accept Jeremiah as a legitimate prophet. He was not against Judah; he was on their side. Jeremiah did not enjoy giving God's words of destruction; he wept and pleaded for God's mercy.

---

39. Since the distance to the Euphrates was about 400 miles, some believe another place was meant or else it was a parable or dream that the prophet told. See Carroll, *Jeremiah* in *OTL*, 295.

This ultimatum for Judah (death) and Jeremiah (no prayer will help) caused the prophet to question if he could continue to function as a prophet (15:10–18). God had promised to protect him and make him strong (15:11–12; see 1:18–19), but instead God sent strife (15:10, 15), loneliness, and no joy. He gladly accepted God's call to be a prophet (15:16), but God's total rejection of Judah (15:13–14) left him without a meaningful function.[40] God deceived him; God did not protect him and would not hear his prophetic intercession. Jeremiah could withstand social rejection of his identity as a prophet for a time, but now God, Jeremiah's ultimate legitimator, had modified his identity out of existence.[41] God rejected the prophet's complaint, called for repentance, reaffirmed his identity, and promised to protect him (15:19–20).

The third cycle has *no lament for Judah, only Jeremiah* (16:1—17:18). By not marrying, having children, or attending funeral banquets, Jeremiah symbolically communicated the end of God's compassion for idol worshipers. In the coming war people will die, and no one will lament for them (16:1–13). This symbolic action carried a high price, for without a marriage partner Jeremiah cut himself off from the social support of a wife and extended family. By not attending important community functions like funerals, Jeremiah ostracized himself from the community support of dependent relatives.[42]

Jeremiah's sermons did not leave his audience hopeless. He externalized the divine vision of a later day when Judah would return from exile (16:14–15 used exodus tradition), God would judge the nations (16:16–18), and some would

40. The significance of the two quotations of God in vv. 11–12 and 13–14 are explained in G. V. Smith, "The Use of Quotations in Jer. XV 11–14," *VT* 29 (1979), 229–31.

41. Berger, *Social Construction*, 30–34, 173–80, sees identity as a social defining process. It is related to typification systems within society. Thus Jeremiah no longer saw himself fitting the social type called prophet.

42. Ibid., 150–52. Berger describes how a significant other impacts a person and how conversation with others affects social identity and one's worldview.

recognize the deception of idols and turn to Yahweh (16:19–21).[43]

Though this future hope existed, Jeremiah's concern was to persuade the people that Judah's immediate future of exile was determined by the undisputable sinfulness of their Baal altars and idolatrous hearts (17:1–4). People will be cursed if they trust themselves, but God will bless those who trust in Him (17:5–8; see Ps. 1). A deceitful heart cannot fool God. He keeps a record of those who trust and those who forsake Him (17:9–13).

This cycle ended with another lament (18:14–18) and a final exhortation about observing the Sabbath (17:19–27). Jeremiah lamented those who mocked his prophecies of judgment and persecuted him (17:15, 18), confessed his commitment to God (17:16), and asked God to save him in the day of trouble (17:14, 17). God's response did not address Jeremiah's lament; instead, Jeremiah was instructed to call the people to leave their economic concerns on the Sabbath day so that normal covenant worship and political life may continue. If the covenant Sabbath was not kept, God would destroy Jerusalem (17:19–27).[44]

In the fourth cycle Jeremiah learned the *potter's ways and lamented* (17:19—18:23). When Jeremiah visited a potter, God showed him how making pottery compared to God's work. Jeremiah preached that God dynamically interacted with people according to their relationship to Him. Two principles apply. God may decide to destroy an evil nation, but if the people repent, He will have compassion on them (18:7–8). On the other hand, God may plan to bless that nation at another time, but if the people do evil, He will judge them instead (18:9–10). Judah was in the second situation and needed to repent. Since they stubbornly refused

---

43. Brueggemann, *Jeremiah 1—25* in *ITC*, 148–50, has this interpretation, while Thompson, *Jeremiah* in *NICOT*, 410–12, thinks vv. 16–18 referred to the judgment of Judah.

44. See M. Tsevat, "The Basic Meaning of the Biblical Sabbath," *The Meaning of the Book of Job and Other Studies* (New York: KTAV, 1980), 39–52.

From the mid-2000s B.C., a limestone statue of a potter working at his potter's wheel. See Jeremiah 18:3.

to transform their ways and reject their worthless gods, Yahweh would reject them (18:11–17). Jeremiah's hostile audience saw his deviant words as contradictory to the worldview of the present leadership in Judah; therefore they discredited him (18:18).[45] Jeremiah lamented their oppression and evil plans. In righteous indignation he asked God to punish them severely (18:19–23).

The final cycle of this section included *pottery judgments, persecution, and laments* (19:1—20:18). Jeremiah relentlessly

45. Berger, *Social Construction,* 104–21, describes social methods of dealing with conflicting views of reality. Some will not consider the validity of the idea, but simply call it a heresy or deviance that should not be taken seriously. Sometimes the social structures in power may destroy the messenger.

continued to preach warnings of destruction to Judah. He used the symbolic act of smashing a piece of pottery to illustrate to his audience how God would utterly smash Jerusalem and its stiffnecked people. Those who would see Jerusalem's ruins would be astonished at the results of the savage siege (19:1–15). The audience response was violent. Pashur, the priest with official control of the opinions taught at the temple area, had Jeremiah beaten and put in stocks to jeer and humiliate him. In spite of public persecution, Jeremiah maintained that Babylon would defeat Judah and carry the people (and Pashur) into captivity (20:1–6).

Jeremiah's final laments (20:7–13, 14–18) revealed the depth of his despair over his social rejection. He felt it was impossible to maintain his theological position because of the violent threats of his "trusted" friends (his social support group) and the mockery of others (20:7,10). It seemed that God had tricked him;[46] he was in a no-win situation. As much as he might want to avoid the persecution, he could not quit being a prophet of doom. There was such deviance between Jeremiah's expectations of his prophetic role and reality that he wished he had never been born (20:14–18).[47]

III. Judgments Against Leaders and Nations 21:1—25:38

The sermons in this unit have no following persecution or laments by Jeremiah. Jeremiah's sermons contrasted God's decision to destroy unjust kings, false prophets, and the people of Jerusalem with His opposite decision to

46. The root *pth* is translated "persuaded" by D. J. A. Clines and D. M. Gunn, "'You Tried to Persuade Me' and 'Violence! Outrage' in Jer. XX 7–8," *VT* 28 (1978), 20–27, and Craigie, et al., *Jeremiah 1—25* in *WBC* 26, 273, agree; but Holladay, *Jeremiah* 1 in *Her*, 552, prefers the traditional translation of "deceived," as does D. R. Jones, *Jeremiah* in *NCBC* (Grand Rapids: Wm. B. Eerdmans Publishing Co., 1992), 272–73.

47. Berger, *Social Construction*, 127, maintains that all deviant worldviews need group support to provide an objective base, but does not consider the possibility of a divine objective base. Jeremiah felt that both support structures were inadequate.

bless another king and the people exiled from Jerusalem (23:1–8; 24:4–7). These sermons were intended to undermine the audience's social approval of King Zedekiah and his military policies.

During Nebuchadnezzar's final siege of Jerusalem (588 B.C.), King Zedekiah put social pressure on Jeremiah to intercede and bring news of God's grace to Jerusalem (21:1–2). Jeremiah contradicted the king's wishes and externalized news of a time when God's anger and outstretched arm will come against them (21:5; contrast Ex. 6:6).[48] The Divine Warrior would have no pity or compassion on the king, the people, or the city unless they did what was socially unacceptable; that is, surrender to Babylon (21:6–10).

The king did not fulfill his social role of administering justice, delivering the oppressed, and caring for the weak, but instead ignored the covenant with God (21:11–22:8). Jeremiah mourned the death of the good King Josiah (22:10) and recognized that Shallum (22:11; Jehoahaz in 2 Kings 23:30–34) would not return to the throne. Instead, Jehoiakim ruled with injustice, used forced labor to build lavish buildings for himself, did not care for the weak, and shed innocent blood (22:12–17). He will not be mourned, but exiled (22:24–30). These accusations delegitimated the rule of Jehoiakim by showing that he did not function in the roles God designed for kings.

Judah's kings did not tend God's sheep according to the divine ideals, and thus God will scatter them into exile. This hopeless situation will one day be corrected when God gathers His people back to the land and gives them a new Davidic king, the Messianic Branch (23:3–8, see traditions in Isa. 9 and 11).[49] He will fulfill the divine role of kings by

48. Ibid., 104. Berger sees externalization as a process of creating a new understanding of reality. Jeremiah rejected the worldview of the king and was considered a traitor.

49. Carroll, *Jeremiah* in *OTL*, 446–47, has the unlikely interpretation that this is an inaugural celebration of Zedekiah's legitimate rule, but Holladay, *Jeremiah* 1 in *Her*, 617–20, argues for a messianic interpretation of the "legitimate scion." See Huey, *Jeremiah* in *NAC*, 211–12.

ruling with justice and wisdom, so that Israel and Judah may dwell securely in their land. In this positive promise Jeremiah did not suddenly turn into a false prophet of peace. His vision contrasted the future justice of the ideal king with the injustices of Judah's present kings (21:12; 22:3, 13–17; 23:2, 5).

A second group of social leaders carried primary responsibility for the destruction of Judah, the false prophets (23:9–40). Jeremiah's frontal attack undermined their social authority to determine public opinion by claiming the popular prophets and priests brought evil into the temple. The prophets prophesied by Baal, spoke messages of peace out of their imagination. They played the role of prophet, but never stood in the divine council, were not sent by God, and did not receive a message from God. They falsely claimed "this is an oracle from the Lord." Jeremiah unmasked their devious ways, reckless boastings, and outright lies and announced God's anger toward them.[50] They will be humiliated when their words are proven wrong, for they will not be able to hide from God or the social scorn of their fellow Judeans.

After the Babylonians took Jehoiakim and thousands of people into exile in 597 B.C. (2 Kings 23:10–17), Jeremiah's audience in Jerusalem developed an optimistic view of their situation because they had escaped God's punishment of exile (24:1–10). Jeremiah's vision report contrasted the good and the bad figs. To the surprise of Jeremiah's audience, those in exile were the good figs God will plant and transform, so that they will wholeheartedly follow Him. The rotten figs which God rejected were those still left in Jerusalem (24:8–10). Jeremiah reversed the theological implications of exile. In this case social and political humiliation would lead to divine blessing.

This section closed with a summary sermon which described God's wrath on Judah, their seventy years of exile in

---

50. T. W. Overholt, *The Threat of Falsehood* (Naperville: Allenson, 1970), 49–71, deals with Jeremiah 23.

Babylon, and God's wrath on the nations around Judah (25:1–38).[51]

IV. Prophetic Deception Opposes Jeremiah's Words 26:1—29:32

These narratives describe the popular prophets' opposition to Jeremiah's ministry. Jeremiah gave his temple sermon (26:1–19) at the beginning of Jehoiakim's reign in 609–608 B.C. Jehoiakim and the people openly rejected Josiah's earlier reforms and returned to Baal worship (2 Kings 24:3–9). Jeremiah's sermon challenged the people to amend their ways. If they did not, God would destroy the Jerusalem temple, for He was not unconditionally tied to the temple (26:1–7; see 7:1–15). Jeremiah's message threatened the security of the socially developed belief in the unconquerability of Jerusalem and its temple.[52] The prophets and priests rejected Jeremiah's worldview and threatened Jeremiah with death. Jeremiah maintained his unpopular view of future social conditions in spite of strong social opposition. Finally, a city elder legitimated a positive response to Jeremiah's words based on Hezekiah's earlier positive response to Micah's threats against Jerusalem (26:17–19; see Mic. 3:12). During that same time, the prophet Uriah was killed for similar words, but Jeremiah was protected by the powerful political influence of Ahikam, an earlier advisor to Josiah (26:24; 2 Kings 22:12–14).

About ten years later during the optimistic first year of Zedekiah's reign, Jeremiah's symbolic action of wearing a wooden ox yoke around his neck visualized to Judah and the conspiring leaders from the surrounding nations that God, the Creator, would put their lands under Babylon's yoke (27:1–8). This contradicted the popular prophets, diviners,

---

51. The Greek translation of the Hebrew text has the oracles against the foreign nations in Jeremiah 46—51, after chap. 25.

52. W. Brueggemann, *To Build and to Plant: A Commentary on Jeremiah 26—52* in *ITC* (Grand Rapids: Eerdmanns, 1991), 6, sees this as a royal-temple ideology, but in this case the royal officers did not agree with the prophetic and priestly opposition to Jeremiah.

and dreamers who falsely predicted that the temple vessels would soon return. They encouraged Judah not to serve Babylon (27:9–10, 14–18). The prophet Hananiah rejected Jeremiah's deviant perspective by predicting in a public context that God would return the temple vessels, the exiles, and King Jehoiachin within two years (28:1–4).[53] When a respected person in a sacred role says so, this can be a powerful legitimator, even if there is no rational justification for the position.[54] To counteract this affront, Jeremiah publicly expressed his wish that Hananiah's words were true, but exhorted all to notice how time would soon prove who was the false prophet. In defiance Hananiah broke Jeremiah's wooden yoke (27:10–11). Soon Jeremiah wore an iron yoke, and Hananiah was dead as Jeremiah predicted (27:12–17).

Jeremiah also had conflict with the Jerusalem priests and prophets after he wrote a letter to the exiles and told them to settle down in Babylon, pray for the city where they lived, wait seventy years until God would return them to their land, and ignore the false prophecies of their exilic prophets (29:1–32). Later the exilic prophet Shemaiah exhorted Zephaniah, who had the high status of overseer of the temple, to stop Jeremiah's crazy ideas and punish him.[55]

V. Promises of Restoration 30:1—33:26

During the final siege of Jerusalem at the end of Zedekiah's reign, when the socially constructed world of the

---

53. R. P. Carroll, "Prophecy, Dissonance, and Jeremiah XXVI," *A Prophet to the Nations*, eds. L. G. Purdue and B. W. Kovacs (Winona Lake: Eisenbrauns, 1984), 381–91, sees the false prophet's change from no exile before to only a short exile after 597 B.C. as a reaction to the dissonance between reality and their former predictions.

54. Berger, *Social Construction*, 85–88, 108–28, discusses how divergent worldviews supported by professionals lead to conflict that is often reduced by the liquidation of one expert or by assigning a negative definition (false prophet) to one speaker.

55. Ibid., 66, 115. Berger suggests that another approach to deviance was to designate it as moral depravity, ignorance, or a mental disease. By classifying Jeremiah as a madman, Zephaniah tried to marginalize the prophet's opinions.

prophets was shown to be bankrupt, Jeremiah surprisingly began to preach sermons about God's future plans for Israel and Judah in a series of *poetic promises of a new day* (30:1—31:40).[56]

His sermons did not provide false hope like the deceptive prophets. At the time Jerusalem endured terror, pain, and an incurable problem (30:4–7, 12–15). Now that history was proving that Jeremiah's hopeless prophecies from God were true, the people were finally persuaded to internalize his depressing view of reality for Jerusalem. But in the future God would deliver them from bondage, send their Davidic King, destroy their enemies, and compassionately restore the people to their land (30:8–11, 16–24). Destruction was not the end of God's plan for His people. Jeremiah externalized a new world for the future that was not developed out of the people's present worldview. He challenged them to transform their thinking, to imagine the possibility that God's original promises could still be fulfilled in the future. What could legitimate such a belief? God's commitment to be their God and their covenant commitment to Him (31:1). God's everlasting love and compassion, God's act of bringing back the exiles, and His rich blessing on the land would bring joyful dancing back to Samaria and Zion (31:3–14). When God hears the sorrowful weeping of His chastised people who repent, then there will be hope. Jeremiah constructed a new vision of the future which included both Judah and Israel being built up and planted in the land. A new covenant would establish a close, revitalized relationship. God would forgive their sins, and they would know and follow God's patterns for life (31:31–34; see traditions in Deut. 4:13; 30:5–6).[57] Jeremiah pressed the people to accept God's promise

56. Holladay, *Jeremiah 2* in *Her*, 156–59, believes several sections in 30—31 came from Jeremiah's early preaching in the northern nation of Israel, but Clements, *Jeremiah* in *IntCom*, 175–76, argues for a Judean audience late in Zedekiah's reign.

57. The Qumran community thought that they were the people of the new covenant. Early Christians believed the new covenant was made possible by the death of Jesus (see Luke 22:20; 1 Cor. 11:15; Heb. 8:8—9:28).

for the future in spite of their present hopeless situation, for it was absolutely as sure as day and night—nothing could change it (31:35–40).

A second series of *prose promises of restoration* (32:1—33:26) repeated these divine promises less than a year before Nebuchadnezzar captured Jerusalem. While Jeremiah was in prison for predicting a Babylonian victory over Jerusalem, God told him to buy his relative's field in Anathoth (32:1–5). Jeremiah did have a family responsibility to redeem the field (see Lev. 25:25–32), but it made no sense to waste his money on it. This field was in enemy territory, and Jeremiah knew Judah would go into exile for seventy years (29:10). Nevertheless, he openly followed the institutionalized legal practices involved in the purchase of land, because he believed God's promise that people would again live in Judah (32:15). This public act was a powerful legitimator of his preaching.[58] He not only preached that the people would return after the city was destroyed, he was so sure of it he invested his money in Judah immediately.

Jeremiah's monetary testimony of faith was accompanied by a prayer which justified his beliefs to the Jews who witnessed his purchase of the land. Jeremiah's act was based on his theological convictions about God (part of his symbolic universe).[59] His decision of faith was justified because God created the world, has unlimited power, and in justice brings both punishment and lovingkindness. God is wise and demonstrated these character traits both when He brought Israel out of Egypt and when He brought Babylon to destroy Judah (32:16–25). The reestablishment of the covenant, the transformation of their hearts, and their new joy will come from God's powerful lovingkindness (32:36–

58. People probably discounted many of his words, but when Jeremiah put his money where his mouth was, it demonstrated that he believed God's promises in spite of the hopelessness of Jerusalem's military situation.

59. Berger, *Social Construction*, 95–99, sees the symbolic universe as a theoretical abstraction of reality that integrates the objective and subjective meanings people give to parts of reality. This abstract world is socially created through interaction with traditions, people, and life experience.

44). In spite of Judah's terrible situation, Jeremiah could envision a day when the nation will finally call on God. God will heal them, pardon their sins, restore their prosperity, give them joy, send the Davidic Messianic Branch, and restore the normal worship patterns. God's unbreakable oath supported Jeremiah's bold act and should have sparked faith in his audience (33:1–26).

VI. Narratives of Jeremiah's Rejection 34:1—45:5

Jeremiah faced *rejection before the fall of Jerusalem* (34:1—38:28), in Jehoiakim and Zedekiah's reigns, because his words were so out of line with the socially accepted views that developed in Jerusalem. Jeremiah compared the Rechabite's total commitment to obey the instructions of their forefathers (not to drink wine, dwell in houses, plant crops)[60] with the unwillingness of the people of Jerusalem to obey any of God's instructions (35:1–19).

In Jehoiakim's fourth year (just before Babylon took its first captives in 605 B.C.; 36:1; Dan. 1:1–3) Judah totally rejected Jeremiah's preaching and did not even allow him to speak in the temple.[61] Therefore, he dictated his earlier messages to his scribe Baruch so that he could read them to those gathered for worship at the temple. Possibly some would be persuaded by what they would hear about God's plan for Jerusalem and repent (36:1–7). When the temple officials heard what Baruch read, they reported it to King Jehoiakim who eventually burned the scroll (36:9–26). Jeremiah and Baruch went into hiding, were socially ostracized and feared for their lives . They rewrote and added more sermons to a new scroll (36:19, 27–32).

Later, during the siege of Jerusalem, Zedekiah and the wealthy class made a covenant to release all slaves from bond-

---

60. J. T. Cummings, "The House of the Sons of the Prophets and the Tents of the Rechabites," *Studia Biblica* 1978 (Sheffield: JSOT Press, 1979), 119–26.

61. Berger, *Social Construction*, 118–19, indicates that some groups maintain their worldview through force (Jehoiakim), ignoring the logic or evidence for a conflicting perspective (Jeremiah's).

age according to the traditional Mosaic law, possibly to gain God's favor (34:6–10; see Ex. 21:2–6; Lev. 25:3–7; Deut. 15:12–18).[62] When the Egyptians came to rescue Zedekiah, the Babylonians lifted their siege for a short time (34:22; 37:1–16).[63] At this point the leaders reversed their decision and forced their slaves back into bondage. Jeremiah condemned those who profaned God's name by not honoring their covenant to release their slaves (34:11–22). Selfish economic gain motivated their action.

Great joy and optimism returned in Jerusalem when the Babylonians briefly lifted their siege of Jerusalem. Everyone thought the war was over and they were saved; but Jeremiah opposed this popular optimism and warned Zedekiah not to be deceived, for the Babylonian army would soon return (37:1–10). This unpopular position led to Jeremiah's arrest and imprisonment when he was falsely accused of being a traitor to the Babylonians (37:11–21). A short while later the king's officials threw Jeremiah into a muddy cistern to die because he encouraged the king to surrender to Babylon (38:1–6). Later Zedekiah gave Ebed-melech, a brave Ethiopian eunuch who saw the unjust way Jeremiah was treated, permission to rescue Jeremiah from death (38:7–13). For his act of kindness God promised to protect Ebed–melech from the Babylonians (39:15–18). Even though Zedekiah secretly committed himself to protecting Jeremiah, the prophet did not change his prediction about the Babylonians to please the king (38:14–28).

Jeremiah also faced *rejection after the fall of Jerusalem* (39:1—43:7), even though the fall of Jerusalem demonstrated that his prophesies were correct. In Zedekiah's eleventh year the wall was breached, the fleeing king was caught near Jericho, captives were taken, and the city was burned (39:1–10). Ironically, the Babylonian officials recognized that Jeremiah was a true prophet, so they gave him some food and a

62. Carroll, *Jeremiah* in *OTL*, 647, lists possible reasons why the slaves were released.

63. Thompson, *Jeremiah* in *NICOT*, 606, hypothesizes this setting was a motivation for canceling the covenant to release the slaves.

gift and let him choose to stay in Jerusalem if he wished (39:11–14; 40:1–6). Jeremiah stayed in Judah at Mizpah where Gedaliah, the new governor, and the poorest people of the land gathered. Gedaliah ignored a warning of insurrection; but before long Ishmael, the Ammonite, viciously killed him, the Babylonian soldiers with him, and eighty innocent worshipers (41:1–10). Fearing for their lives, the remaining Jews headed for Egypt to escape the wrath of Babylon (41:11–18). Before entering Egypt, the group asked Jeremiah to function as a prophet and intercede for them. The small group that suffered through the destruction of Jerusalem appeared to have a major alternation in their worldview.[64] They took an oath to do whatever God said, submitting themselves to obey God's direction for their lives (42:1–6). Jeremiah externalized an amazing vision of the future for these fearful people. In spite of their social instability and military helplessness, God would build them up and protect them from the king of Babylon if they would stay in the land and trust God. If they rejected God's promises and ran for protection in Egypt, God would pour out His anger on them and destroy them (42:7–22).

Evidently, the people did not really alter their commitment to do whatever God said, for they accused Baruch of deceiving Jeremiah so they would be killed by the Babylonian army. The fleeing people then forcibly took Jeremiah and Baruch to go with them to Egypt (43:1–7).

The final section recorded Jeremiah's *rejection after going to Egypt* (43:8—45:5). Jeremiah's sermon in Egypt addressed the deceptive worldview of those who thought they were safe from Babylon in Egypt. He warned that Nebuchadnezzar would destroy Egypt, burn its temples, and kill the Jews in Egypt because the Jews had repeatedly rejected God's word through the prophets and were now burning sacrifices to the gods of Egypt (43:8–44:14; this happened in 582 B.C.). The women (and their husbands) justified their rejection of Jer-

64. Berger, *Social Construction,* 157–59, sees alternation as a process of primary resocialization in which a person converts from the worldview of one group to another.

emiah's word and sacrificed to the Queen of Heaven as they did before the fall of Jerusalem (44:17–19; see 7:17–25), because then they were well-off. What Jeremiah considered the cause for God's judgment, the people considered the cause for their prosperity. One experience viewed in opposite ways justified contradictory views of history.[65] When Jeremiah failed to persuade the people, he reexplained the logic of God's action; He made Jerusalem an abandoned ruins covered by His curse because the people worshiped false gods. (44:20–30). In a similar way God will destroy all but a few Jews in Egypt when Babylon defeats Pharaoh.

This section closed with a brief lament by Baruch (45:1–5). After Jeremiah and Baruch were forced into hiding for reading the scroll in the temple (36:1–19 in 605 B.C.), Baruch felt the pain of social rejection, admitted his physical weariness, and called out to God for mercy. God assured Baruch that His words of judgment and restoration would be fulfilled. He warned Baruch not to let social disapproval affect his view of himself or his responsibilities. Baruch played a key supportive role by creating a social plausibility structure for Jeremiah's ministry.[66]

VII. Oracles against Foreign Nations 46:1—51:64

These sermons were structured into three groups: oracles against Egypt (46); smaller nations which may have formed a coalition with Judah against Babylon (47—49); and Babylon (50—51). These messages communicated to the leaders of Judah that God has power over all nations. Judah should not fear their enemies or trust in political alliances to save them from other nations.

---

65. Carroll, *Jeremiah* in *OTL,* 737–38, observes that a person's existing faith interprets experience for both Jeremiah and the Jews. Experience should have legitimated one alternative, but it deceptively supported two opposite worldviews. Berger, *Social Construction,* 19–27, describes how the experiences of everyday life organize a worldview.

66. Berger, *Social Construction,* 154–55, sees the importance of social safe havens (a spouse, friend, or group) where the plausibility of a person's worldview is accepted as normal.

The oracles against Egypt relate to its war against Babylon at Carchemish in 605 B.C. (46:1–13) and a later war with Egypt (possibly 587 B.C.; see 37:6–10). The pro–Egyptian politicians associated with Jehoiakim in Judah from 609–605 B.C. saw Egypt as a pivotal ally and expected Egypt to win the battle at Carchemish. Jeremiah's sermon dashed the hopes of the royal house with the unpopular news that the Lord will defeat Egypt's army (46:1–12). Jeremiah maintained that God was the powerful King who ruled the nations. He would cause the Egyptian army to stumble, to want to return home. God would destroy Egypt, their gods, and all who trust in Pharaoh. The final verses explained the purpose of this oracle. Judah should not fear armies, but trust God who will save them and destroy all nations (46:27–28; see 30:10–11).

In the undated oracles against smaller nations (47–49)[67] Jeremiah was persuading his audience to internalize into their political philosophy that God sovereignly controlled the history of all nations.[68] They should accept God's plan to destroy the nations (49:20) and not fall for the popular political strategy of trusting in alliances to oppose Babylon (27:1–7; 47:4).

Philistia, Moab, Ammon, Edom, Damascus, Kedar, and Elam should not be trusted, because their proud boasts of strength, wisdom, and riches were arrogant self-exaltations that put them in conflict with the plan of God (48:26–30, 42; 49:4, 16).[69] Judah would be foolish to count on people destined for destruction. With graphic rhetorical imagery Jeremiah legitimated this perspective by describing the rumbling war chariots, the ruin of lush valleys and great cities, the shame of total defeat, the humiliation of having deceptive gods, the horror of becoming the laughingstock of the ene-

67. Only the Elam oracle (49:34) was dated to the beginning of Zedakiah's reign in 597 B.C. This agrees with the date of the coalition attempts in 27:1–3.

68. Brueggemann, *Jeremiah 26—52* in *ITC*, 246–48, emphasizes this purpose.

69. Jeremiah used authoritative traditions concerning Moab and Edom (Isa. 15—16; Obad. 1–6) to support his present message.

my, even the wailing of grown men, and the loss of all joy and hope. Although God will restore a remnant of some nations at a later time (46:26; 48:47; 49:6, 39), it is senseless to foolishly oppose God's plans and purposes.

The final chapters include a complex series of oracles about the demise of the Babylonian Empire under Nebuchadnezzar (50:17; 51:34).[70] The prophesy has similarities with the false prophets' deceptive hopes for the destruction of Babylon, so some commentators do not believe these were Jeremiah's words.[71] These fit Jeremiah's other message which foresaw the fall of Jerusalem, the eventual defeat of Judah's enemies, and the restoration of Judah (compare 29—33 and the sign act of Seraiah in Babylon in 51:59–64).[72] If these words accompanied Jeremiah's sermons of hope (30—33) late in Zedekiah's reign when Judah had no hope of survival, they would legitimate the prophet's claim that the people would one day return from their seventy-year exile. When they were delivered by Seraiah in Babylon, they would have encouraged the Jews in exile to maintain their faith in God's plan to defeat Babylon and bring them home to Jerusalem.

From listening to Jeremiah's sermons, some in his audience probably either thought that Jeremiah taught that God was on Babylon's side or implied from Jerusalem's defeat that the gods of Babylon were stronger than Israel's God, or wondered if God would ever forgive them and return them to their land. Jeremiah taught that:

(a) God's people in Judah and Israel were scattered among the nations (50:3, 17, 33),

---

70. K. T. Aitken, "The Oracles against Babylon in Jeremiah 50—51: Structure and Perspective," *TB* 35 (1984), 25–62, finds a structure of situation, intervention, and outcome.

71. Holladay, *Jeremiah 2* in *Her,* 401, concludes that these were a *priori* ideological conclusions not based on linguistic evidence.

72. Carroll, *Jeremiah* in *OTL,* 816, strongly sensed contradictory aspects, but if God's treatment of Judah can change over time, certainly He can help them do His will and then bring an appropriate judgment at a later time.

(b) in vengeance God would bring a nation against the arrogant and violent Babylon to destroy it (50:9–16, 21–32, 35–46; 51:1–4, 6–14, 20–33, 37–44, 54–58), and

(c) the Jews would return and enter an everlasting covenant with God (50:4–5, 19–20, 34; 51:6, 10, 45–46, 50–51).

This was God's plan, and His wisdom and power would fulfill it (50:20, 45; 51:11, 15, 29). Every Babylonian god would be seen as a worthless illusion (50:2; 51:17–19; see 10:14–16; 51:44, 47, 52). This news was an encouragement to those who questioned the bright promises of 30—33.

VIII. An Appendix: The Fall of Jerusalem 52:1–34

This historical record of the fall of Jerusalem was not part of Jeremiah's scroll (51:64), but a later addition parallel to 2 Kings 24:18—25:30. It covered more details than the biographical approach of 39—40. It carefully recorded what happened to the people, temple objects, and rulers of Judah. It ended with a mysterious story about a Babylonian king's kindness to the exiled Judean King Jehoiachin (52:31–34).

Theological and Social Implications

Jeremiah's life casts a long shadow that contradicts many modern philosophies of ministry, and his sermons are like truth serum that reveals the shameful deceptions that parade as sermons. Indeed, the heart is deceitful, cultural expectations of a successful ministry without conflict is appealing, widespread public acceptance can be alluring, and the status and power of being "God's messenger" can be exhilarating; but God's calling and His plans give priority to listening to Him, sharing His words, and serving Him. Like Jeremiah, all of God's messengers begin ministry with cultural expectations of what the people want them to say and how people want them to act, but have little idea about what God wants. Some have the illusion that they both want the same things, that one can please both God and mankind, that people want to hear God's word and transform their lives.

Jeremiah's life casts the dreaded threat that faithful messengers of God may suffer rejection by leaders and the laity, instead of status and popularity. He did not spend his time administering programs, but cared enough about his audience to spend time weeping for them and intently interceding for God's mercy. His message constantly pointed out the danger of accepting the deceptive theology of his day. He had the courage and honesty to disagree with the prophets and priests who enjoyed preaching frothy peace and prosperity messages. They did not take the time out of their busy schedule to understand what God was saying. Jeremiah was willing to reflect on how cultural and social norms had gradually replaced earlier moral standards. The faithful messenger gave words of hope, as well as words of judgment, even when they seemed inappropriate and used whatever means possible (sermons, books, drama, parables) to persuade some.

Such honesty and devotion to God's truth may even create internal doubts and questions about God's care and protection. Is it all worth it? Why should I have to take such disrespect and political manipulation? Why do I feel so alone and rejected? The greatest struggle will not be the deceptive beliefs of others, but a messenger's struggle to maintain a personal walk with God.

Questions for Discussion

1. What theology of suffering can be developed from Jeremiah's experiences?
2. What were the deceptive factors in Judah's theology of the temple, God/the gods, and the exile (see 7; 10; 24)?
3. What is the role of an intercessor?

4. How did Jeremiah's laments for the nation affect the audience's view of Jeremiah?
5. What was the basis for Jeremiah's hope in such hopeless situations (see chap. 32 or 42)?

Chapter 12

Joel: Call on the Lord for His Day Is Near!

Introduction

People react in different ways when a special day arrives. The anticipation of the first day of college fills new students with excitement and expectation. The students' parents often dread such days because they know their children will face new ideas and peer pressure that could get them in trouble. Similar tension arises on the day that a couple is married, a person interviews for a new job, or a family buys their first house. Certain days dramatically change the events that follow.

How should a person react to the announcement that God's day is near? Is it a time of hope and joy or a threat of danger? Is there hope for an individual or a nation when God comes? Should they call out for mercy or look forward to that day? What should God's messengers today say about the day of the Lord? Should one say there is nothing to worry about or take a pessimistic view?

Social Setting

The Historical Context

Joel mentioned no kings and only a few historical events. He described a great locust plague (1:1–12), but did not specify when it happened. The fasting and offering of sacrifices at the temple (1:13–14; 2:15–17) indicate that Joel lived before the temple's destruction in 586 B.C.

The historical information does not point to an exact date, thus weaker arguments from silence (e.g. no mention of a king) were introduced to suggest a date for the prophet.[1] Some date Joel in Uzziah's reign (around 780 B.C.),[2] but many opt for a post-exilic date after the temple was rebuilt (500 B.C.),[3] or after Nehemiah rebuilt Jerusalem's wall (440–400 B.C.).[4]

A better alternative would put Joel around 595–590 B.C.[5] The threat from the "northern" foe (2:20) on the day

1. Arguments from silence like a) no reference to any Judean king, b) no reference to the Assyrians or Babylonians, c) no mention of Baalism, or d) no naming of the northern nation of Israel have no value. It is difficult to determine if verses in Joel that are parallel to verses in other prophetic books were copied from or by Joel. Linguistic or stylistic features are used by all sides.

2. R. D. Patterson, "Joel," *EBC* 7 (Grand Rapids, Zondervan, 1985), 231–32. The book's placement with other early books (Hosea and Amos), their quotation of verses in Joel, and historical circumstances suggest this date.

3. D. A. Hubbard, *Joel and Amos* in *TOTC* (Downers Grove: InterVarsity, 1989), 23–27; G. W. Ahlstrom, *Joel and the Temple Cult of Jerusalem* in *VT-SUP* 21 (Leiden: Brill, 1971), 111–29, and T. J. Findley, *Joel, Amos, Obadiah* in *WEC* (Chicago: Moody, 1990), 8; L. C. Allen, *The Books of Joel, Obadiah, Jonah, and Micah* in *NICOT* (Grand Rapids: Eerdmans, 1976), 24. The reference to the Greeks, late Hebrew vocabulary, the historical allusion to the fall of Jerusalem (3:1–2), and arguments from silence (no Jewish king is given, the Babylonians are not Judah's enemies) support this date.

4. J. Limburg, *Hosea-Micah* in *IntCom* (Atlanta: John Knox, 1988), 58, and H. W. Wolff, *Joel and Amos* in *Her* (Philadelphia: Fortress Press, 1977), 4–6, agree with those who date the prophet at 500 B.C. but felt that the reference to the wall in 2:7–9 pointed to a date after Nehemiah rebuilt Jerusalem.

5. A. S. Kapelrud, *Joel Studies* (Uppsala: Lundequistska Bokhandeln, 1948) dates the book around 600 B.C., but W. Rudolph, *Joel-Amos-Obadja-Jona* in *KAT* XIII 2(Gütersloh: Gütersloher Verlagshaus Gerd Mohn, 1971), 133–41, puts Joel between 597 and 587 B.C.

of the Lord was still future, thus Joel (like Jeremiah and Zephaniah) was warning of Babylon's destruction of Jerusalem in 586 B.C.[6]

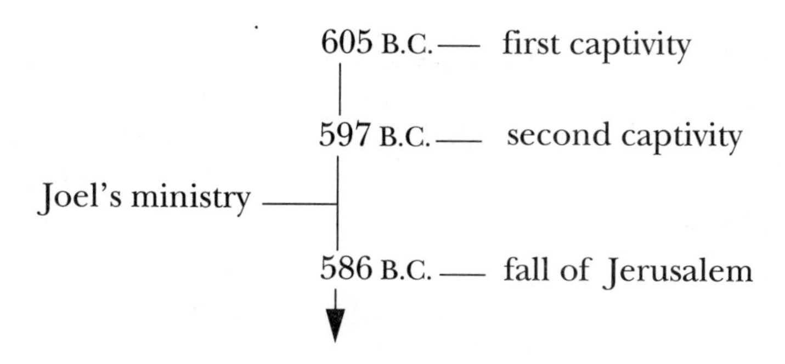

The impassioned tone of the prophet's call to repentance (2:12–17) implies that the threat was imminent.[7] The Jews from Judah who were already scattered among the nations (3:2) were those exiled by Babylon in 605 and 597 B.C.

The Structure of Social Order

The prophet did not critique inequities within the social system in Judah or condemn perversion of role relationships like other prophets. The locust plague, a precursor of the day of the Lord, destroyed the people's usual way of looking at the world. The earth did not provide grass, wine, fruit, or grain as it usually did. The behavior of drunkards changed because there was no wine (1:5); the farmers' harvest ended when the barley was destroyed (1:11). The priest's role of offering sacrifices at the temple stopped (1:10). Elders were at the fast (1:2, 14; 2:16, 28) but their leadership role was not described.[8]

The enemy threatening Jerusalem was pictured as an army. Divided into ranks, it marched forward in orderly lines

---

6. D. Stuart, *Hosea–Jonah* in *WBC* 31 (Waco: Word, 1987), 226, puts Joel before one of the three battles in 701, 598, and 588 B.C..

7. Wolff, *Joel and Amos* in *Her*, 42, thinks the enemy was an apocalyptic army.

8. The elders were tribal or family leaders who had political and religious functions which probably changed during different periods of Israel's history.

no one could stop. Its enormous power will destroy everything in Judah. The normal order of things in the heavens and the earth will be transformed on the day of the Lord (2:2–10).

Joel also addressed social structures in the distant future. These will include a new outpouring of the Spirit on those who call on the Lord—people from every age, sex, nation, and social status (2:28–32). God will transform the political order between nations. He will destroy the enemies of His people, restore exiled Jews to Jerusalem, and give His people rain, good harvests, and protection from enemies (2:18–27; 3:18–21).

The key social institution that affected the future was the temple. It had the traditional sacrifices and priests and was a national meeting place for fasting in times of grave danger. Joel encouraged the people to confess their sins, lament, and trust in God's mercy at this fast (1:13–14; 2:12–17).

The Social Location and Role of the Prophet

Joel's writings employed imagery taken from agricultural, military, and temple life. His prophetic role in Jerusalem was unique. In contrast to most prophets, he never accused the people of any specific evil or condemned temple worship (2:12–17).[9] Kapelrud thinks Joel functioned as a cultic prophet. Joel promoted temple theology and scornfully attacked the people for weeping for Baal, their impotent Canaanite fertility god.[10] Ahlstrom finds a strong cultic flavor to Joel's language and believes he was opposing Canaanite syncretism in Judah in the post–exilic era.[11] It seems better to follow Wolff who rejects these views, since there was no direct reference to Baalism.[12] Joel believed

9. The call to "return to Me with all your heart" in 2:12 suggested that there may be a need to return, but the text could be an admonition to turn to God for mercy without any implied suggestion of repentance.

10. Kapelrud, *Joel Studies*, 17–43.

11. Alstrom, *Joel* in *VTSUP*, 35–61.

12. Wolff, *Joel and Amos* in *Her*, 29–30.

that God was sovereignly in control of nature,[13] but this was not a veiled attack on Baalism.[14]

Hanson viewed the book as a social protest against the exclusive claims of the Zadokite priests. Joel undermined their authority position by arguing for direct communion with God by all people.[15] This interpretation is problematic because Joel's main thrust was to encourage the priests.

As an orator, Joel used traditional literary forms of speech to communicate his ideas. The lament, judgment speech, call to repentance, and promise of salvation conveyed Joel's message in a persuasive manner. Within these messages, Joel legitimated ideas by quoting traditions from earlier authoritative prophets. These included ideas about the day of the Lord (Isa. 13:6; Zeph. 1:7, 14), Yahweh alone is God (Isa. 45:4–5), God's coming to Zion to judge (Amos 1:2), and God's blessings of fertility (Amos 9:13).

Social Interaction

The Book of Joel

A few scholars question the authenticity of parts of Joel (the prose section in 3:4–8), but most see a unity and balance within the structure of the book.[16] Motifs were repeated in different contexts (the sun darkened in 2:10, 31; 3:15) to build on the central theme of the day of the Lord.[17] The Hebrew text has four chapters with 2:28–32 being 3:1–5, and

---

13. R. Simkins, *Yahweh's Activity in History and Nature in the Book of Joel* (Lewistown: E. Mellon, 1991), 3–75.

14. Kapelrud, *Joel Studies*, 17–43, and Ahlstrom, Joel in *VTSUP*, 38–53, identifies many features in Joel with the Baal fertility cult. Wolff, *Joel and Amos* in *Her*, 29, does not accept this view.

15. P. D. Hanson, *The People Called* (New York: Harper, 1986), 313–14.

16. O. Loretz, *Regenritual und Jahwetag in Joelbuch* (Altenberg: CIS Verlag, 1986) finds eight layers of tradition in Joel, but Allen, *Joel, Obadiah, Jonah, and Micah* in *NICOT*, 39–43, analyze the balanced, unified text. See recently W. S. Prinsloo, "The Unity of the Book of Joel," *ZAW* 104, (1992), 66–81.

17. F. E. Deist, "Parallels and Reinterpretation in the Book of Joel: A Theology of the *Yom Yahweh*," *Text and Context* in *JSOTSup* 48, ed. W. Classen (Sheffield: JSOT, 1988), 63–79.

3:1–21 being 4:1–21. The outline of the second half of Joel reversed the negative effects of the Day of the Lord in the first part:[18]

- I. Lament, for the Day of the Lord Is Here 1:1—2:17
  - A. Lament because of the present locust plague 1:1–20
    1. The devastating locusts 1:1–12
    2. Lament, call on God's name at the temple 1:13–20
  - B. Lament because of the future enemy 2:1–17
    1. The devastating army 2:1–11
    2. Lament, call on God's name at the temple 2:12–17
- II. God's Salvation on the Day of the Lord 2:18—3:21
  - A. Salvation from the locust plague 2:18–32
    1. Material blessings restored 2:18–27
    2. Spiritual blessings outpoured 2:28–32
  - B. Salvation from the enemy armies 3:1–21
    1. Restoration of the exiled 3:1–8
    2. Enemies judged and Zion restored 3:9–21

Within these sermons Joel interacted with his audience's theological perspective. He attempted to transform their view of the locust plague and use it as a model for understanding the near and future day of the Lord.

I. Lament, for the Day of the Lord Is Here 1:1—2:17

After identifying the divine source of his words in the superscription (1:1), Joel called the people to *lament because of the present locust plague* (1:1–20).[19]

---

18. Simkins, *Yahweh's Activity*, 203–8, and D. A. Garrett, "The Structure of Joel," *JETS* 28 (1985), 289–97, see the major break coming after 2:27 rather than 2:17 because 2:17–27 were not eschatological, but a positive response to the locust plague in 1:1–12. They ignore the contrast between the lament form (1:1—2:17) and God's answer (2:18—3:21).

19. Wolff, *Joel and Amos* in *Her*, 20, puts 1:5–14 together because of the common lament form, but Allen, *Joel, Obadiah, Jonah, and Micah* in *NICOT*, 57, divides the material 2–12, 13–20.

The prophet's goal was to convince his listeners that the locust plague was a warning of the approaching day of the Lord for Judah (1:15). If they understood the theological significance of this "natural" event, they might be motivated to come to the temple to fast, lament, and cry out for God's mercy (1:13–14). Joel gained credibility by identifying with the people's sense of loss.[20] This locust plague was a history-making event that would be remembered for centuries (1:2). Every imaginable kind of locust was devouring vegetation (1:4).[21]

Surprisingly, and with some irony in his tone, Joel warned the heavy drinkers that they would soon be kicking the habit.[22] They would transform their behavior, because the powerful jaws of the locusts had stripped the vineyards bare (1:5–7). This call to lament the plight of the drunkards gained little sympathy, but it enabled Joel to point to the massive destruction of agricultural resources. The grain, fruit, and wine were dried up, robbing the people of their economic stability and religious security (1:8–12).

What was the purpose of this great plague? Joel's dramatic presentation externalized the belief that God was using the locust and the drought to warn people of a much more severe judgment in the future.[23] The people knew other prophetic traditions about the day when God would powerfully intervene in the course of history and destroy the wicked and save the righteous (Amos 5:18–20; Isa. 2:1–21;

---

20. B. E. Bradley, *Fundamentals of Speech Communication: The Credibility of Ideas* (Dubuque: Brown, 1974), 134–52, and K. Burke, *A Rhetoric of Motives* (New York: Prentice-Hall, 1950), 55, stress the importance of identifying with the audience to gain credibility.

21. For a discussion of the nature and habits of the locusts, see Simkins, *Yahweh's Activity*, 102–20, and B. P. Uvarov, *Grasshoppers and Locusts* 2 vols. (Cambridge: Cambridge Univ. Press, 1977).

22. Although 5–7, 8–10, 11–12, appear to be laments, they do not include some characteristics of the laments in the psalms, including an address to God, a plea for deliverance, a confession of trust, a declaration of innocence, or a vow to praise.

23. Berger, *Social Construction*, 104, thinks that people create new meanings to explain reality, externalizations that are not part of society's present understanding of phenomena.

13:1–16; Zeph. 1:14–18; Jer. 46:1–12).[24] Most Judeans thought they would be blessed by God's miraculous deliverance on the day of the Lord, but Amos and Zephaniah had shown that this was a deceptive social reification.[25] There was no absolute guarantee of Jewish salvation on that day.

Joel called the priests, elders, and common people to lament and call on God at the temple (1:13–20). The leaders must solidify social opinion so the people will internalize a change in their behavior. The priest should set the example by lamenting all night in sackcloth (1:13). They should encourage the people to cry out to God for mercy at the temple (1:14). God's hand of justice was about to act against them (1:15–18). Joel ended the lament with his own prayer for God's compassion.

In the second sermon Joel *lamented because of the future enemy* (2:1–17). Its structure was similar to the first message, with a description of the devastating army (2:1–11) and a call to lament to avoid the destruction on the day of the Lord (2:12–17).

Watts identifies the armies in this section as the locusts in chapter 1, while Simkins sees chapter 2 as a reference to a continuation of the locust plague in the following years.[26] Wolff's conclusion that Joel pictured an army makes more sense, for the Babylonian army was about to destroy Jerusalem.[27]

---

24. W. S Prinsloo, *The Theology of the Book of Joel* in *BZAW* 163 (Berlin: W. de Gruyter, 1985), 35–36, and Ahlstrom, *Joel and the Temple Cult*, 62–97, review the extensive literature on the day of the Lord.

25. Berger, *Social Construction*, 89, defines reification as the apprehension of human-created reality as a non-humanly conditioned fact of history. Thus the day of the Lord became a given fact, a day when God would deliver Judah, rather than a day when God would deliver the Judeans who were righteous.

26. J. D. W. Watts, *The Books of Joel, Obadiah, Jonah, Nahum, Habakkuk and Zephaniah* in *CBC* (Cambridge: Cambridge University Press, 1975), 24, and Simkins, *Yahweh's Activity*, 154–55.

27. The nearness of the day of the Lord argues against Wolff's conclusion (*Joel and Amos* in *Her*, 42). R. Dillard, "Joel," *The Minor Prophets*, ed. T. McComiskey (Grand Rapids: Baker, 1992), 277–78, sees chap. 2 as an appearance of a divine theophany and God's army in an eschatological context. It is inappropriate to use Revelation 9:1–11 to interpret Joel who spoke hundreds of years earlier. Stuart, *Hosea-Jonah* in *WBC*, 241–42, finds an historical enemy, probably the Babylonians.

With great rhetorical fervor, echoing thoughts of the locust plague on Egypt (Ex. 10:5–15) and the day of the Lord on Babylon (Isa. 13),[28] Joel requested that someone blow the trumpet to warn the people of an impending military catastrophe (2:1; see Zeph. 1:16). He externalized a new and ominous perspective on the future. On their doorstep stood a massive gathering of mighty people (2:2–3). This disciplined and unstoppable military machine will methodically drive forward, destroying the lush Garden of Eden-like landscape and the walled cities in its path (2:3–9). The socially accepted cultural belief in the invincibility of Zion was delegitimated (Ps. 46—48; Jer. 7:1–7), for this force was God's army. He will disrupt the cosmic and earthly structures that stabilized religious and social life (2:10–11).[29]

Joel appealed to the audience's basic desire for self-preservation to motivate them to action. Joel supported this behavioral response by recalling God's graciousness to the people at Sinai (Ex. 34:6–7). The cultural means of expressing full commitment to God was through heartfelt confession, sacrificing, fasting, and praying for mercy (2:13–17). The priests, elders, children, and newlyweds must gather at the temple to weep and intercede, so that people will not mock God's reputation (2:17; see Ex. 32:12; Ps. 79:4–10). If the people would truly turn to God, there was a possibility of compassion.

II. God's Salvation on the Day of the Lord 2:18—3:21

Joel suddenly made a dramatic shift from lamentation to hope.[30] At some point God will reverse His treatment of the nation and bring *salvation from the locust plague* (2:18–32) and the enemy armies (3:1–21). Judgment did not mean the

---

28. Wolff, *Joel and Amos* in *Her*, 47, identifies the linguistic connection with Isaiah 13.

29. Allen, *Joel, Obadiah, Jonah and Micah* in *NICOT*, 73–74, connects 2:10–11 to a theophany. The language was similar to other theophany accounts, but there was no indication that the Lord Himself would be seen, only His power and works were evident.

30. This was similar to the movement from complaints to statements of confidence in lament psalms (60:8–10; 85:9–14).

end of God's plans for His people. After the judgment, material and spiritual blessings were available for those who called on God's name.

Some commentators assume the nation responded to God's challenge, repented, and received God's blessing just before this message. It is better to see these blessing as eschatological.[31] These promises rhetorically function as motivations to repent because there was hope if the people responded positively.

The unending cycle of human sin and divine judgment will stop, and a new era will begin. In terms similar to Isaiah (Isa. 32:14–15; 44:3), Joel legitimated his confidence in this transformation of social relationships and human history by pointing to an unusual new outpouring of God's Spirit on all people, regardless of age, sex, status, or nationality (2:28; see Acts 2:17–21).[32] The Spirit will outwardly manifest His presence through visions and prophecies. People will see new evidence of God's power in miraculous heavenly signs (2:30–32). This hope of salvation should persuade some in Joel's audience to transform their thinking, repent, and call on God for mercy. God would not only restore the nation's devastated material and spiritual condition, He would restore their political status by providing *salvation from their enemies' armies* (3:1–21).

Joel addressed two present military problems: the threat of Babylonian conquest and some local slave trade. The Babylonians took Jews and some gold utensils from the temple into exile in 605 and 597 B.C. (see Dan. 1:1–2; 2 Kings 24:10–17), and the Greeks bought Jews as slaves. Joel tried to

---

31. Findley, *Joel, Amos, Obadiah* in *WEC*, 60–61, and Allen, *Joel, Obadiah, Jonah and Micah* in *NICOT*, 86–87, believe God's reversal happened during Joel's lifetime, but Stuart, *Hosea-Jonah* in *WBC* 31, 258, thinks the Hebrew perfect verbs were prophetic perfects. This allowed the prophet to describe the future as if it had already happened. Since 2:26–27 twice repeated "My people will never be put to shame again" and pointed to the nation's acceptance of God, it must be describing eschatological events.

32. Hanson, *The People Called*, 313–14, finds an "egalitarian impulse characteristic of early Yahwism" which condemned the pompous institutionalized exclusivity of the Zadokite priests, but this reconstruction has little support.

convince his audience that the nation's political situation was determined more by spiritual realities than military capabilities. God would protect those who called on His name and defeat their enemies. He would judge those nations; the Philistines, Phoenicians, and Babylonians would receive their just reward (3:2–8).[33]

God would also declare Holy War on His enemies at the end of time. God would challenge the nations to gather together for a decisive battle in the Valley of Jehoshophat, and then He would tread them under His feet (3:9–13).[34] This will be the day of the Lord for these nations. The sun will no longer shine on them; their world will end. On the day of the Lord, God will dwell in Zion, roar against His enemies, and give the land back to His people (3:16–17; Obad. 15–17). Then agricultural conditions will be ideal (3:18; see Amos 9:13). Judeans will put down permanent roots in Jerusalem (3:19–21).

Theological and Social Implications

Radicals have always walked around proclaiming that the world was about to end. Preachers have raved about the last judgment and scared people with threats of the coming of the day of the Lord. Because of all these abuses, it is tempting just to avoid this topic. No one wants to be seen as a weird crazy person or a religious fanatic.

Yet many Old and New Testament preachers did make use of the coming day of the Lord to motivate people to repent (Matt. 24:1–31; 2 Thess. 2:2; 2 Pet. 3:10–12). They were respected because the day of the Lord did come on Babylon as Isaiah predicted (Isa. 13), on Israel as Amos forewarned

---

33. Wolff, *Joel and Amos* in *Her*, 74, believes 4:4–8 and 4:18–21 were later additions, but Stuart, *Hosea-Jonah* in *WBC* 31, 206, treats the chapter as a unit.

34. Simkins, *Yahweh's Activity*, 221, thinks the whole chapter was a divine warrior hymn. Wolff, *Joel and Amos* in *Her*, 74, calls 4:9–14 (3:9–13) a summons to battle, but Dillard, "Joel," *The Minor Prophets*, 300, identifies it as a lawsuit.

(Amos 5:18–20), and on Judah as Zephaniah prophesied (Zeph. 1:7–18). Although many preferred to listen to the positive words of the false prophets who proclaimed peace, these were deceptive words (Jer. 6:14).

This suggests that the question should not be: Should God's messengers talk about the day of the Lord? The question is: How can one faithfully communicate God's message about the day of the Lord in a way that will motivate people to respond appropriately? The messenger can weep (rather than rant and rave) for those who will endure the judgment of the day of the Lord, encourage people to lament for their sins, and call on God's name. One can assure people that God is compassionate and slow to anger.

Questions for Discussion

1. What should one say about the day of the Lord today?
2. How does Joel's theological perspective connect God's work in history with His work in nature?
3. How did later generations interpret Joel's prophecy of the coming of the Spirit (see Acts 2)?

Chapter 13

Obadiah: Can Proud Oppressors Escape Judgment?

Introduction

The world has many grade school bullies, violent gang members, merciless businessmen, and oppressive nations. People all over the world have suffered because of the proud tongue of a superior or the abusive hands of someone who was stronger. When you end up on the receiving end of this kind of behavior, you wish that a third party would do something to stop what is happening. Discouragement and despair can set in because no one sees the pain or cares enough to confront the guilty party.

What should the messenger of God do for these oppressed people? What words of comfort and assurance can provide hope for the future? Does God care about them? Will He let the proud oppressors escape, or will they be judged?

Social Setting

The Historical Context

The Book of Obadiah is not dated to the reign of any king. It does refer to a period before Edom was defeated (3:9) and shortly after Jerusalem was invaded, looted, and destroyed (10:14). The Edomites were part of an earlier coalition against Babylon (Jer. 27:3; around 594 B.C.), but when the Babylonian attack came a few years later, the Edomites, descendants of Esau, did not come to the aid of the Israelites, the seed of Jacob. From the Edomite vantage point of safety, wealth, and political alliances (3:7), they watched as an army devastated Jerusalem.

Although Armerding connects these events to the reign of Jehoram (840 B.C.; 2 Kings 8:20–22) and Allen opts for a post-exilic date (500 B.C), Wolff and Stuart provide convincing evidence for a date a few years after the fall of Jerusalem in 586 B.C.[1] Another strong argument for this date is the parallelism between Obadiah and Ezekiel's description of Edom's vengeful behavior toward Israel after the fall of Jerusalem (Ezek. 25:12–14; 35:1–36:5; Ps. 137:7; Lam. 4:18–22).[2]

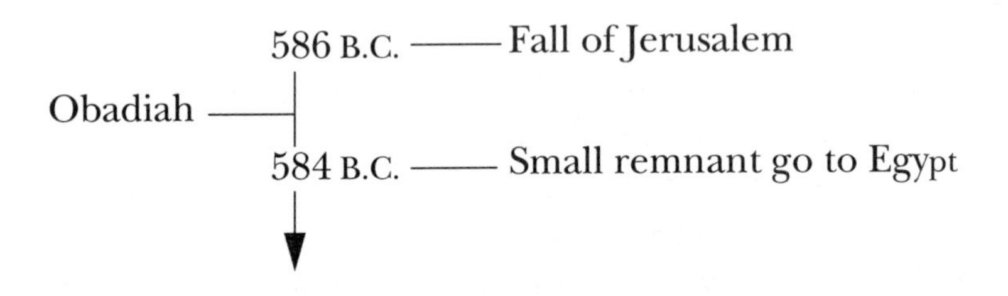

1. C. Armerding, *Obadiah* in *EBC* (Grand Rapids: Zondervan, 1985), 350–51; L. Allen, *Joel, Obadiah, Jonah, and Micah* in *NICOT* (Grand Rapids: Eerdmans, 1976), 131; H. W. Wolff, *Obadiah and Jonah: A Commentary* in *CC* (Minneapolis: Augsburg, 1986), 18; D. Stuart, *Hosea–Jonah* in *WBC* (Waco: Word, 1987), 404.

2. For a review of the history of Edom, see J. R. Bartlett, "The Rise and Fall of the Kingdom of Edom," *PEQ* 104 (1972), 36–37, or J. R. Bartlett, "The Moabites and Edomites," *Peoples in Old Testament Times* (Oxford: Clarendon, 1975), 243–44.

Obadiah's audience was a small group of people in Jerusalem. They were broken, discouraged, and wondering why the Edomites behaved the way they did. They experienced shock, that feeling of numbness that comes when a person suffers a severe loss of a loved one, a home, or a business. This agony was reflected in the laments they sang (see Lam. 1—4). Would God let these proud Edomite oppressors escape, or would He judge them for their spiteful hatred? Was there any hope for the Jews who escaped the destruction of Jerusalem? Would God's glorious kingdom ever be established in Judah?

The Structure of Social Order

The prophet's message focused on the Edomites' optimistic view of their political and social situation. They were a self-confident and proud people who lived on the east side of the Arabah, south of the Dead Sea. They lived in a dry, hot, and mountainous area south of the Moabites. No army could overpower Edom, for the entrance to that area (Sela, modern Petra) was limited to a narrow crevice in the mountains. The city was easily guarded by a few troops stationed at the top of this rock formation (3:4). The Edomites took advantage of their strategic location to gain economic wealth from taxes on goods traveling on the King's Highway from or to the Red Sea (5:6). The stability of Edom was insured because of numerous political alliances, its decision not to oppose Babylon, and its wise leaders (7:8).

The political security of Edom led to a proud attitude of invincibility (3, 12). Their historical animosity toward Judah (Num. 20:14–21; 2 Sam. 8:13–14; 1 Kings 9:26–28; 2 Chron. 20:1–2; 25:11–12) developed into a hatred of the Jews. Social norms were abandoned, and anarchy reigned as they looted Jerusalem and robbed the defenseless Judean survivors (13:14). They tried to claim Jewish land for themselves (Ezek. 35:36).

Jerusalem's devastation left the nation with little sense of social or political order. Jeremiah's description of Gedeliah's assassination and the people's subsequent flight to

Egypt (Jer. 40—44) collaborates the anarchy and hopelessness of this time.

The Social Location and Role of the Prophet

Early Jewish tradition (Bab. Talmud, *Sanhedrin*, 39b) guessed that Obadiah was Ahab's steward (1 Kings 18:3–16), while Watts and Wolff think Obadiah was a cult prophet preaching at a worship service, possibly at a lament ceremony commemorating the destruction of Jerusalem.[3] Obadiah used traditions about Edom (compare Jer. 49:7–16), the day of the Lord, and an oracle against a foreign nation; but these do not prove that he was a professional cult prophet. Discussion of these topics was not limited to worship contexts.[4]

Obadiah was a Jewish prophet from Jerusalem who survived the Babylonian destruction of Judah. His vivid description of events in and around Jerusalem recollected the experiences of those who suffered under Edom's hatred. Obadiah identified with his Jewish audience's conception of reality and their frustration over Edom's brutality, because he suffered with the rest of the refugees.[5] Obadiah offered a ray of hope in Judah's darkest days. Obadiah functioned as God's messenger of comforting news. God would not forget Judah's suffering or allow the proud oppressors from Edom to escape without punishment. On the day of the Lord, God will square accounts with the Edomites and return His people to their land.

---

3. J. D. W. Watts, *Obadiah* (Grand Rapids: Eerdmans, 1969), 24–27; Wolff, *Obadiah and Jonah* in *CC*, 19–21, 42.

4. R. R. Wilson, *Prophecy and Society in Ancient Israel* (Philadelphia: Fortress, 1980), 287; Stuart, *Hosea-Jonah* in *WBC* 31, 407, and Allen, *Joel, Obadiah, Jonah, and Micah* in *NICOT*, 136, do not believe that Obadiah was a cultic prophet.

5. S. W. Littlejohn and D. M. Jabusch, *Persuasive Transactions* (Glenview, Ill.: Scott, Foresman and Co., 1987), 130–31, describe how the power of relational identification with another person can increase persuasion.

Social Interaction

The Book of Obadiah

Some commentators question the unity of this prophecy and suggest that the final verses (15a, 16–21 or just 19–20) were from another person at a later time, but others attribute the whole prophecy to Obadiah.[6] Obadiah 1–5 are almost identical to Jeremiah 49:9,14–16, but it is impossible to tell who originally received this message.[7] Obadiah's short sermon can be outlined into three sections:

I. God Will Remove Edom's Sources of Security and Pride 1–9

II. Edom Should Not Have Oppressed Judah on That Day 10–14

III. Edom Will Not Escape, for Judah Will Possess Zion 15–21

Obadiah's interaction with his audience had the goal of transforming the thinking of the people left in Jerusalem after its destruction. Their terrible social situation determined their bleak and hopeless vision of the future, but it did not take into consideration Obadiah's news that God would punish Edom on the day of the Lord.

I. God Will Remove Edom's Sources of Security and Pride 1–9

Obadiah began his sermon by justifying the source of his message (1:1). He received a message from God like other prophets. He externalized ideas about Edom that contradicted Edomite propaganda which many Jews had

6. Wolff, *Obadiah and Jonah* in *CC*, 19–22, finds later additions, while Stuart, *Hosea-Jonah* in *WBC* 31, 413, and T. J. Findley, *Joel, Amos, Obadiah* in *WEC* (Chicago: Moody, 1990), 348–49, maintain the book as a unified whole.

7. Stuart, *Hosea–Jonah* in *WBC* 31, 415–16, compares the Hebrew texts in detail and found 55 percent of the words to be identical and 10 percent almost identical. He feels both prophets independently used a third source.

internalized.[8] It appeared that Edom had a great future, but the foundation stones which supported its self-image would crumble. Judeans should recognize that God will destroy Edom (vv. 1–2).

How was this possible? How could Obadiah persuade them to transform their thinking about Edom and themselves? Since God did not save the nation from the hands of the Babylonians, why would He now rescue them from the Edomites?

Obadiah legitimated his faith in God by recounting four things that God would take away from the proud Edomites. First, God would remove the Edomites security in their location high in the rugged mountains. God can reach this so-called "untouchable nesting place high among the stars of heaven" and make it an insignificant and despised place (vv. 2–4). The Edomites had a false illusion of invincibility. Second, Edom's riches will be ransacked with greater thoroughness than a grape harvester who leaves a few clumps of grapes for the poor to glean (vv. 5–6). Nothing will remain; all their gold and hidden wealth will vanish. Third, Edom's peaceful and trusted military and trade allies will betray them (v. 7). Fourth, God will remove the cunning wisdom that enabled Edom's leaders to maintain a strong military force. When these wise men fail, Edom's strength will crumble. Then all its people will die (vv. 8–9); it will be worse off than Judah.

The prophet's message from God began to transform the thinking of Obadiah's Jewish audience because point by point it demolished the pillars of Edomite superiority. Obadiah's persuasive evidence supported the claims he was making.[9]

---

8. P. Berger and T. Luckmann, *The Social Construction of Reality* (Garden City: Doubleday, 1966), 104, see externalization as the human process of projecting one's own understandings of reality which others may accept and internalize into their thinking if there is sufficient evidence to support it.

9. H. W. Simmons, *Persuasion: Understanding, Practice, and Analysis* (Reading, Mass.: Addison-Wesley, 1976), 192–223, compares the similarities between logic and rhetorical proof.

II. Edom Should Not Have Oppressed Judah on That Day 10–14

The prophet enhanced his rhetorical case against the dominant hopelessness in Jerusalem in the second part of his sermon by emphasizing God's condemnation of Edom's oppression on Judah's "day of disaster" in 586 B.C. God has justifiable reasons for not allowing Edom to escape punishment.

God will cut off the Edomites because they did a shameful thing. They stood by and did nothing to help their Jewish brothers (Jacob and Esau were blood brothers; Gen. 25:22–26) when the Babylonians attacked and looted Jerusalem (2 Kings 25; Jer. 52). By benign neglect and inaction, the Edomites participated in the violence against their brothers (vv. 10–11). They were as guilty as the Babylonians who actually wielded the swords.

The prophet then changed his indirect descriptive approach (vv. 2–11) to a more direct emotional address to convey the intensity of God's reprimand for Edom's calloused and perverted behavior (vv. 12–14).[10] A brother should not gloat, boast, or rejoice when a family member loses everything![11] When a brother's home is destroyed, family members do not laugh and walk through the rubble trying to loot for themselves (v. 13). When family members come for safety after a disaster, a brother should not steal from them or kill them (v. 14)! This is outrageous! People do not do these things to a brother.

III. Edom Will Not Escape, for Judah Will Possess Zion 15–21

Obadiah concluded his sermon by externalizing the surprising news that God will give Edom exactly what it deserves.

---

10. Wolff, *Obadiah and Jonah* in *CC*, 53, calls this section "living speech" while Allen, *Joel, Obadiah, Jonah, and Micah* in *NICOT*, 156, see this as a reliving of the pathos of the experience.

11. I. Beit-Arieh, "New Light on the Edomites," *BAR* 14 (1988), 41, finds evidence of an Edomite presence at this time in a site not far from Hebron.

What Edom did to Judah, the same thing will happen to Edom (vv. 15–16). This was not part of the worldview of the Edomites or the Hebrews; it was a divine message about new divine action that would transform the political status quo. Although Edom oppressed the survivors of Jerusalem and took possession of some Israelite land on their "day of the Lord," God would totally reverse their situation. God will not let Edom, or other nations who attacked God's holy city of Jerusalem, escape punishment. Then they will be like helpless stubble before a flaming fire on the day of the Lord.[12] God will also bring His people back to Zion, let them take possession of the land, and restore the territory that Edom and other nations took away. God has not abandoned them, and He will not let the proud oppressive Edomite escape His punishment.

Theological and Social Implications

Obadiah's brief message carries two lasting principles that relate to acts of oppression and violence. It has a word of warning to the proud and powerful who oppress the weak: you will reap what you sow, your evil will come back to haunt you. Another message was to the oppressed who suffered the humiliation of defeat and the agony of despair: God sees your troubles and will establish His kingdom after judging the proud oppressors.

Like the Edomites, a secure position in a big company, a safe home in a quiet neighborhood, several month's expenses in a savings account, and lots of good friends can make life very enjoyable. These factors can easily seduce people to a false sense of well-being and pride (like the Edomites). Those who have positions of power over others (parents, older siblings, teachers, bosses, and police) need to be particularly careful about how they deal with those under them. Attitudes of superiority can become deadly.

12. D. Stuart, "The Sovereign's Day of Conquest," *BASOR* 221 (1976), 159–64.

God's messengers today need to stand against these attitudes and delegitimize such behavior. They are not acceptable to God. The worldview that accepts pride and oppression as normal social behavior will not escape God's punishment. Knowing this, the preacher can offer hope to those who know the hopelessness of oppression. God establishes justice, and He will crush the forces of evil when He sets up His kingdom.

Questions for Discussion

1. What made Obadiah's message so convincing to his audience? How well did Obadiah know his audience's needs?
2. What examples of proud oppression do you see in society today? What can be (or is being) done about it?
3. What encouragement does Obadiah bring to his audience?

Chapter 14

Ezekiel: When Will You Acknowledge God?

Introduction

Daily life is full of the mundane habits of getting up, getting dressed, eating, going to work, attending to the usual responsibilities, coming home, going to bed, and many other routine activities. Sometimes it is not easy to see God's involvement in the daily affairs of life. In this secular world, science explains the weather on the basis of air pressure, winds, and humidity, while doctors heal diseases by understanding genes, DNA, and the nervous system. Politicians and diplomats negotiate to influence international relations while economic conditions are controlled by government policy and semi-rational market forces. For many people, God has nothing left to do. Humans have filled all His traditional responsibilities. Humans now understand how nature works. People do not acknowledge a need for God, because they think that they can handle life by themselves.

The messenger of God today, like the prophet Ezekiel, will meet people who have given up on God because of misconceptions about His role. Some believed in God when they were children but became disillusioned when they grew older. Some think God has rejected them, while others cling to deceptive ideas about what God will or will not do. How does one communicate effectively to those who are not ready to acknowledge God and recognize His role in their lives?

Social Setting

Historical Context

Ezekiel was born in Judah during Josiah's reign, thirty years before he was called to be a prophet (1:1). When Ezekiel was still a child, Josiah carried out political and religious reforms (628 and 621 B.C.; 2 Chron. 34). This gave Judah a new lease on life and independence from the foreign domination of Assyria. These positive changes were shattered when King Josiah was killed in a battle against the Egyptian King Neco (609 B.C.; 2 Kings 22:28–29). The Egyptian domination of Judah lasted only four years, for the Babylonian King Nebuchadnezzar defeated Egypt at Carchemish and took Daniel and many other Jews into exile before Ezekiel was twenty years old (Dan. 1:1–2; in 605 B.C.).

The Babylonian control of Judah was never well accepted, so in a few years Judah rebelled. After a long siege, Jehoiachin surrendered Jerusalem to the Babylonians in 597 B.C. (2 Kings 23:36—24:16). The Babylonians took the political leaders, the skilled craftsmen, military commanders, and Ezekiel to a place near Nippur in Babylon (Ezek. 1:1—3). Ezekiel never mentioned Judah's last king by name, but after the prophet went into exile the Babylonians made Zedekiah king. When Zedekiah rebelled, the Babylonians destroyed the city, burned the temple, and took more people into exile (586 B.C.; 2 Kings 25; Ezek. 33:21).[1]

1. W. Zimmerli, *Ezekiel* 1 in *Her* (Philadelphia: Fortress Press, 1979), 9–16, provides a detailed discussion of the historical situation in Jerusalem, but most of this took place before Ezekiel began to prophesy.

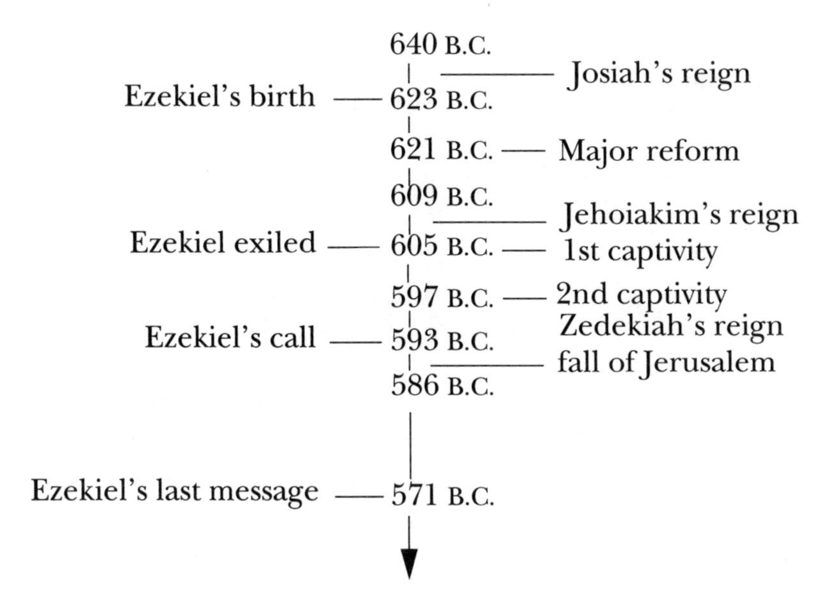

Ezekiel gave his sermons to people in Babylonian exile,[2] but little is known about the historical events that affected their life in Babylon. Jeremiah's letter to the exiles encouraged them to settle down, plant crops, and seek the welfare of the city where they lived (Jer. 29:1–14). This suggests that many Jews managed fairly well in captivity. King Nebuchadnezzar provided political and economic stability for Babylon throughout this period (605–562 B.C.), and there is little evidence of persecution (except Dan. 3). Surprisingly, Ezekiel's prophecies related to events in Jerusalem, not to the daily or political events in Babylon where he lived. Ezekiel dated many prophecies, the first in his fifth year of exile (593 B.C. in 1:2) and the last in the twenty-seventh year of exile (571 B.C. in 29:17). Only a few of these dates can be connected to key historical events (like the siege or fall of Jerusalem).[3]

2. W. H. Brownlee, *Ezekiel 1—19* in *WBC* 28 (Waco: Word, 1986), xxii–xxvii, suggests that Ezekiel was at Gilgal, but C. G. Howie, *Date and Composition of Ezekiel* (Philadelphia: Society of Biblical Literature, 1950) provides stronger evidence for an exilic location for the prophet, even though he did speak about things in Jerusalem.

3. See K. S. Freedy, "The Dates in Ezekiel in Relation to Biblical, Babylonian, and Egyptian Sources," *IEJ* 90 (1970), 462–85, or M. Greenberg, *Ezekiel 1—20* in *AB* 22 (Garden City: Doubleday, 1983), 8–11.

The Structure of Social Order

The Babylonians determined political policies, the places where the exiles lived, and what they could do. They trained and gave important government responsibilities at the national and provincial levels to some Jewish exiles, like Daniel and his three friends (Dan. 1:3–4, 17–21; 2:48–49; 3:12). Life in Babylon was so good that many exiled Jews decided to stay when Cyrus allowed them to return to Jerusalem (Ezra 1—2). They were comfortably settled and had profitable businesses in Babylon.

Tribal and family social relationships involving unique cultural practices enabled the exiles to maintain their Jewish worldview. A written register of Jews helped maintain their distinctive identity (13:9; Ezra 2). They built their own houses, had children, and were involved in the civic activities in Babylonian cities (Jer. 29:5–7). The elders of Israel maintained some social functions of leadership and prophets continued to give God's word to those who would listen (Ezek. 8:1; 14:1).

In spite of being in Babylon, in many of his messages Ezekiel described what was going on in Jerusalem. He had much more to say about the violence and idolatry in Jerusalem (Ezek. 8:7–18; 22:6–12; 34:1–10) than the political events in Babylon. When Ezekiel's sermons addressed issues in Jerusalem, one can assume that exiles from Jerusalem had some of the same problems and misconceptions about what God would do in Jerusalem.[4]

The theological beliefs of the exiles were a mixture of traditions handed down from their priests and parents, and numerous deceptive misconceptions about God's relationship to the exiles in Babylon. In the call narratives, the exiles were characterized as a rebellious and hard-hearted people who had not listened to God in the past and would not pay much attention to Ezekiel (2—3). These people believed that God dwelt in the temple at Jerusalem and that His all-

4. Greenberg, *Ezekiel 1—20*, 17, argues for little contrast between the theology of the two groups. This is true of some issues, but being in exile did give the people in Babylon a somewhat unique worldview.

powerful presence was a protection against any enemy. The people did not want to acknowledge the serious evil going on in Jerusalem, so Ezekiel gave a detailed description of the abominations of Judah's leaders and priests (8:5–18). These sins defiled the holiness of God; therefore Ezekiel repeatedly predicted the fall of Jerusalem (4:1—7:27). Many people continued to cling to the false hope that this destruction would not happen for a long time, if at all (12:21–28). These illusions were fostered by false prophets who deceived the people (13:1—14:11). The exiles thought God had not treated them justly, that they were punished for their fathers' sins, not their own (18:2, 25). The exiles felt cut off from the land, forsaken by God, not able to worship, and hopeless pawns controlled by stronger nations (33:10; 37:11).[5] Some hoped that foreign nations would help defeat Babylon (25—32). Central to all these misunderstandings was the people's failure to acknowledge Yahweh as their holy God.

The Social Location and Role of the Prophet

Ezekiel was from a priestly family, but was taken into exile at age twenty-five, a few years before he could begin official duties in the temple (1:1). His writings do not mention whether he had children; but nine years after entering Babylon, while Jerusalem was under siege, his wife died (24:1, 15–24). Since there was no temple in exile, his main role was to give God's words to the people in Babylon (2:1–7). God appeared to him in a theophany on a Babylonian plain near Nippur in his fifth year in Babylon.[6] As a prophet, his social function was to be a watchman who warned people of impending danger (3:17–21). He cannot be considered a cen-

5. E. F. Davis, *Swallowing the Scroll: Textuality and the Dynamics of Discourse in Ezekiel's Prophecy* (Sheffield: The Almond Press, 1988), 85–90, does not think that one can understand Ezekiel's audience from his quotation of them, but Zimmerli, *Ezekiel 1* in *Her*, 36, advances stronger arguments for taking these quotations as authentic representations of exilic thinking.

6. R. R. Wilson, "Prophecy in Crisis: The Call of Ezekiel," *Int* 38 (1984), 121–22.

tral prophet, for he refused to cooperate with the elders of Israel in his home (14:3; 20:3) and did not support the popular exilic prophets (Ezek 13; see Jer. 28—29) or the government in power in Jerusalem.[7] His vision of the future ministry of the Zadokite priesthood (40—44) did not bring him support while in exile.[8] He functioned as a sign (12:6, 11; 24:24), a silent example to those who observed his dramas. There is little evidence for Lang's theory that Ezekiel was a prophetic politician who argued against a pro-Egyptian group that was encouraging Zedekiah to rebel against Babylon.[9]

Ezekiel's vocabulary included words common to priests, and his emphasis on holiness, morality, God's glory, and temple activities reveal his early training in Leviticus.[10] He was broadly educated about smelting silver, building ships, and the thinking of people in foreign nations (22; 25—32). He had a literary gift for creating parables, rewriting history, and skillfully probing and disemboweling the dead theology of the exiles. To communicate these messages in a way that would arouse the interest of hardened rebels, the silent prophet dramatized several symbolic acts (4—5). He also sent a powerful message by not following the cultural norm of lamenting his wife's death.

Ezekiel functioned as an unusual visionary whose messages required a radical transformation of traditional thinking. His powerful vision of the glory of God appearing in Babylon, the glory leaving the Jerusalem temple because of

---

7. R. R. Wilson, *Prophecy and Society in Ancient Israel* (Philadelphia: Fortress, 1980), 283, sees him as a central Zadokite prophet but finds disturbing Deuteronomic influences.

8. P. D. Hanson, *The People Called* (San Francisco: Harper and Row, 1986), 216–24, sees Ezekiel as a champion of the Zadokites' cause, but there is little evidence that this future vision was supported by other exilic priests.

9. This approach by B. Lang, *Kein Aufstand in Jerusalem* (Stuttgart: Verlag Katholisches Bibelwerk, 1978), 158–59, was critiqued by Davis, *Swallowing the Scroll*, 64–67.

10. See W. Eichrodt, *Ezekiel: A Commentary* in *OTL* (Philadelphia: Westminster, 1980), 28–30, for a discussion of the priestly theology of Ezekiel.

pagan worship, and the return of God's glory to an ideal temple of the future challenged popular theology (1; 8—11; 43). God is holy, glorious, and the all-powerful One who will not spare the temple, but will graciously restore worship for all who acknowledge Him.

Ezekiel's visions plus his bizarre behavior have confounded modern interpreters. Some thought he suffered with psychosis, hallucinations, and schizophrenic mental disorders.[11] It is better not to put limitations on what can happen in visionary revelations. Ezekiel's silence and dramatic signs were the best method of communicating with an unreceptive audience of confused exiles. A unique aspect of Ezekiel's prophetic role was that people could not come to him to inquire of God (14:3; 20:3).[12]

As an orator and writer, Ezekiel used traditional prophetic forms of speech which were well known to his audience. These included the lament (19), vision report (1), oracles against foreign nations (25—32), disputations (11; 18; 33), parables (17; 21), and salvation oracle (36:22–38). To legitimate his claims, Ezekiel sometimes appealed to ancient theological traditions or the sayings of recent prophets.[13] Regardless of the technique used, Ezekiel's strange silence, unusual actions, and unique visions left an uncomfortable feeling that called the stubborn audience to pay attention.

---

11. R. W. Klein, *Ezekiel: The Prophet and His Message* (Columbia: Univ. of South Carolina, 1988), 7–10, does not accept these conclusions, but his suggestion that many of these unusual aspects were merely literary creations is unsatisfactory.

12. Davis, *Swallowing the Scroll*, 24–28, 47–67, searches for a literary function operative in Ezekiel's environment in exile to explain how the prophet chose to communicate his message. She concludes he wrote his prophecies.

13. K. W. Carley, *Ezekiel among the Prophets* in *SBT* 2:31 (Naperville: Allensons, 1975) draws lines of connection between Elijah and Elisha, Leviticus and Deuteronomy, and Hosea and Jeremiah.

Social Interaction

The Book of Ezekiel

Ezekiel's social involvement with his audience was recorded in first person narratives and poetic oracles against foreign nations. Commentators have argued over Ezekiel's location (in exile or Palestine), whether Ezekiel, later writers, or an Ezekelian school wrote the book.[14] Recent commentaries by Allen and Greenberg believe Ezekiel wrote the book in Babylon. The messages were grouped in three sections.[15]

I. Acknowledge that God Will Destroy Jerusalem 1:1—24:27
   A. The visionary call to be a watchman 1:1—3:27
   B. Signs of Jerusalem's end 4:1—7:27
   C. Visions of the temple's desecration 8:1—11:25
   D. Destroying false hopes 12:1—14:23
   E. Metaphors of God's justice with Israel 15:1—19:14
   F. The profaning of Jerusalem 20:1—24:27

II. Acknowledge that God Will Destroy the Nations 25:1—32:32
   A. Oracles of judgment on the nations 25:1–17
   B. Judgment of Tyre 26:1—28:24
   C. Hope for Israel 28:25–26
   D. Judgment of Egypt 29:1—32:32

III. Acknowledge that God Will Restore Israel 33:1—48:35
   A. The watchman defended God's justice 33:1–33
   B. Restoration of Israel 34:1—37:28

---

14. J. W. Weavers, *Ezekiel* in *NCBC* (London: Nelson, 1969), 22–30, found five stages in the literary evolution of the book while Zimmerli, *Ezekiel 1* in *Her*, 68–74, hypothesizes the later redactional work of Ezekiel's disciples in a school.

15. L. C. Allen, *Ezekiel 20—48* in *WBC* 29 (Dallas: Word, 1990), xxv, and Greenberg, *Ezekiel 1—20* in *AB* 22, 18–27.

C. Protection from future enemies 38:1—39:29
D. Restoration of the temple 40:1—46:24
E. Restoration of the land 47:1—48:35

In these sermons Ezekiel interacted with the socially developed worldview of the exiles. His innovative methods of communication confronted a rebellious people who did not know God. They did not realize the seriousness of profaning God's holiness.

I. Acknowledge that God Will Destroy Jerusalem 1:1—24:27

Ezekiel's *visionary call to be a watchman* (1:1—3:27) legitimated his claim to be a prophet and explained his silence. In the vision he experienced God's presence in Babylon and acknowledged God's authority over his life. The prophet struggled to find adequate words to communicate the obscurity and majesty of God's visible appearance. Ezekiel saw four living beings with wings, hands, and multiple faces (1:5–14).[16] Beside the living creatures were spinning wheels with beautiful gems, and above the creatures was a gleaming platform with a throne. On the throne was a brilliant burning shape surrounded by fantastic colors, an indescribable representation of God's glory (1:15–28). The vision left Ezekiel awestruck with his face to the ground in humility.

This event impacted Ezekiel's audience as well, for it brought into question their perspective that God had abandoned them in Babylon (11:15). Ezekiel externalized a new view of Israel's holy and sovereign God.[17] He was not limited by the land of Israel, the temple building in Jerusalem, or the

16. Greenberg, *Ezekiel 1—20* in *AB* 22, 55–56, sees a connection between Ancient Near Eastern (ANE) pictures of deities and parts of Ezekiel's vision.

17. P. Berger and T. Luckmann, *The Social Construction of Reality: A Treatise in the Sociology of Knowledge* (Garden City: Doubleday, 1966), 104, do not see people as socially determined robots but as worldview creators. This revelation allowed Ezekiel to introduce a new, innovative understanding of God to a confused and dejected audience.

Babylonian gods. The glory of the God of Israel was with them in Babylon.

God's immediate purpose was for His Spirit to transform a young priest into a committed prophetic watchman. Ezekiel needed to transform his natural self-identity and goals to internalize God's plan to send him to a rebellious people. He should not fear his audience, nor base success on the people's response; he should focus on speaking God's words (2:1–11, see Jer. 1). He would not have the luxury of group acceptance within the plausibility structures of exilic society, so he must be impervious to ridicule or apathy.[18] He was God's watchman to warn those in danger. If he failed to fulfill his task, he would be held accountable (3:16–21). This whole affair left him stunned and socially ostracized from the people. God closed the prophet's mouth so that he could not speak words of hope or rebuke of his own free will. He could only speak to the people what God communicated to him (3:24–27).[19]

But how could a silent prophet communicate effectively with a society that had heard too many prophetic messages? Ezekiel presented dramatic *signs of Jerusalem's end* (4:1—7:27), with only minimal prophetic commentary (4:7; 5:5–12; 6:3–13; 7:2–9).[20] He prefigured a mock siege of Jerusalem using a brick (4:1–3), representing Israel and Judah bearing the guilt for their sins by laying on his side 390 days and 40 days (4:4–8)[21], announced a famine during Jerusa-

---

18. Berger, *Social Construction*, 154, emphasizes the tenuousness of social patterns and belief structures that were not shared or supported by other important individuals.

19. Brownlee, *Ezekiel 1—19* in *WBC* 28, 54–55, inappropriately emphasized Ezekiel's suffering. Greenberg, *Ezekiel 1—20* in *AB* 22, 102, concludes that Ezekiel only spoke when God spoke. This was better than Zimmerli, *Ezekiel 1* in *Her*, 161, who limits Ezekiel's dumbness to a brief period before the fall of Jerusalem and treats 3:25–27 as a later redactional addition.

20. Bearing his arm and unbinding his tongue were connected in 3:25–26, but what he said is not recorded and not that important.

21. Klein, *Ezekiel*, 43, compared these forty years to the forty years wandering in the wilderness (Num. 14:33–34) and adds 390 and forty to get 430, the time spent in Egypt (Ex. 12:40–41), but these comparisons seem insignificant.

lem's siege by eating bits of bread cooked over dung (4:9–17), and predicted the death and exile of people still in Jerusalem by burning, cutting up, and hiding hairs from his beard and head (5:1–17). Ezekiel agreed with the prevailing theological belief that Jerusalem had a central place in God's eyes (5:5; see Deut. 12:11; Ps. 132:13–14), but he thought the people's rebellion against God's rule and covenantal behavior patterns would cause God to destroy Jerusalem (5:5–12; see similar curses in Lev. 26:14–39).[22] Ezekiel expressed the deviant view that God would not spare them from His wrath, for they profaned the temple with idols. The exiles reified God's connection to Jerusalem into a guarantee of blessing, rather than a conditional relationship based on love for God and commitment to His ways.[23]

God will destroy the Baal high places and the Judeans who worshiped idols there (6:1–7). Experience will teach the remnant of Judah who will later enter captivity that these idols were nothing, for they would not protect their dead worshipers. God's wrath on Jerusalem would legitimate a symbolic universe that acknowledges Him as their God.[24] Then they will recognize that the sovereign and holy controller of their lives did not vainly warn them with covenant curses (6:8–14). The audience thought that the prophetic warnings of judgment on the day of the Lord would be delayed for many years (12:22–25; see Amos 5:18–20; 8:2),[25] but Ezekiel externalized a new idea of the end that was radically different from the social norms in exile and the common beliefs in Jerusalem. It is near! It is now, not in the distant future! The disaster of the end is coming shortly (7:5–7)! God had seen all the arrogance, violence, and evil that He

---

22. Greenberg, *Ezekiel 1—20* in *AB* 22, 124.

23. Berger, *Social Construction*, 89–91, observes that when reification takes place people think that personal responsibility and involvement in determining the future are removed.

24. Berger, *Social Construction*, 92–128, thinks that the abstract symbolic world was directly related to daily life.

25. For different views on the origin of this day, see M. Weiss, "The Origin of the 'Day of the Lord' Reconsidered," *HUCA* 37 (1966), 29–41; K. S. Cathart, "Day of Yahweh," *Anchor Bible Dictionary* ed. D. N. Freedman (New York: Doubleday, 1992), 2, 84–85. Its military aspect is clear in this context.

could take (7:10–11, 23)! He will not save His people or His land on the day of the Lord; He will judge them without pity. When the trumpet blows and the war begins, the people of Judah will not be able to fight because of fear and shame. Their riches will not save them, for God will give them into the hands of wicked foreigners. They will yearn for peace and look to their social leaders for hope, but the deceptions propagated by the prophets, priests, and kings will not help (7:14–27). The people will no longer be able to maintain their old worldview, for the destruction will force them to recognize that a holy God has judged them for their sins.

A year later Ezekiel received *visions of the temple's desecration* (8:1—11:25) that further legitimated his contention that God would destroy the Jerusalem temple. While the elders of Judah were at Ezekiel's house, the prophet suddenly saw the same fiery brightness he saw earlier in chapter 1. God transported him to Jerusalem where he saw the glory of God at the temple (8:1–4). There in the temple court was an idol that outraged God (8:3–5). The sculptured image of the Baal fertility goddess, Ashtarte, like the image Manasseh made, was put back in the temple after Josiah's reform was over (2 Kings 21:7; 2 Chron. 33:7, 15).[26] Amazingly, underneath the sanctuary were chambers where the seventy elders of Israel, the leaders of Jerusalem, were worshiping carved images of wild monsters which represented pagan gods (8:7–12; possibly Egyptian gods).[27] Added to all this, on the north side of the temple, women were weeping for the god Tammuz. According to mythology, he died and went to the underworld at the end of the spring rains.[28] Finally, between the altar for

---

26. Greenberg, *Ezekiel 1—20* in *AB* 22, 202, thinks this worship was from Manasseh's time, which Ezekiel imagined in his vision and projected into a later time. This interpretation is wisely rejected by J. Blenkinsopp, *Ezekiel* in *IntCom*(Louisville: John Knox, 1990), 55, for Jeremiah also referred to the people worshiping pagan gods (Jer. 7:17–20, 30–8:3; 19:3–6, 13; 32:34–35; 44:15–19). For a pre-millennial interpretation of the glory, see L. Cooper, *Ezekiel* in *NAC 17* (Broadman Press, 1994), 113–42.

27. P. C. Craigie, *Ezekiel* in *DSB* (Philadelphia: Westminster, 1983), 61.

28. T. Jacobson, *Toward the Image of Tammuz and Other Essays* (Cambridge: Harvard Univ. Press, 1970), 100, describes the myth and accompanying weeping by women.

sacrifices and the porch of the temple were twenty-five men worshiping the sun (8:14–16). Such vile actions and horrid worship justified God's intense anger with the people who defiled His holy temple. The leaders' attitude was that God would not see anything they were doing because He had forsaken the land (8:12; 9:9). God saw it all, and Ezekiel saw Judah's abominations. God had not forsaken the land yet. No, the people had forsaken God. Because of these vile sins, God will not pity His people!

At this point the glory of God left the temple so that executioners could defile the temple and the city by killing every man, woman, and child. Only a small remnant of righteous people who wept over the sinfulness of Judah were marked to escape the slaughter (9:1–8). As the slaughter began, a man in linen scattered on Jerusalem coals of fire from between the wheels of God's chariot throne. Then the wheels, cherubims, and glory of God left the temple and went to the east gate (10:1–19). The bloodshed overcame Ezekiel as he watched the massacre, so he cried out for mercy, for they were killing almost everyone (9:8).

Ezekiel had this same response in 11:13 when he saw one of Jerusalem's leaders struck dead right before his eyes. This man and other deceptive leaders would die because they plotted evil and gave bad advice to the people. They claimed that it was not time to build houses. The city of Jerusalm was protecting them like a pot, and they were like choice meat protected from the Babylonians (11:3).[29] God disputed this false perception of reality that was socially accepted by the brutal murderers in Jerusalem. They were not the choice meat, and they would not be protected by the pot (Jerusalem); they would be killed (11:5–13).

The people in Jerusalem thought God rejected the people in exile so they inherited their relatives' land. God de-

---

29. The translation and interpretation of this quotation is uncertain. Most commentators do not agree with Brownlee, *Ezekiel 1—19* in *WBC* 28, 157, who follows the *LXX* and interprets the men to say it was a good time to build. This and most other's interpretations see the speakers as overly optimistic about Jerusalem's future.

clared that these arrogant people in Judah misunderstood God's intentions. God would not destroy the remnant of Judah. He Himself would bring the exiles back to Jerusalem and transform their hearts and behavior (11:14–21). At that point the cherubims moved the glory of God to the mountain just east of Jerusalem, the visions ended, and Ezekiel told his audience what he saw (11:22–25).

When Ezekiel shared this vision with his exilic audience, it confirmed his prophetic identity as God's messenger in Babylon. The transportation of the prophet into the inner recesses of the Jerusalem temple in the vision gave an authentic report on the secret sins of Jerusalem's leaders. Such first-hand reporting legitimated the seriousness of God's accusations and justified the severity of God's response. God's abandonment of the temple and the city explained how it was possible for an enemy to destroy that place. If God was not there, then the city and temple were not impregnable. The callous self-interests of the present leadership in Jerusalem demonstrated that they were not the chosen people whom God would use to restore the nation and fulfill His purposes. No, hope remained only for the discouraged exiles, for God would gather them back to the land, bring a great spiritual renewal, and restore His covenant again. This vision argued for a new way of looking at Jerusalem, God, and themselves.[30] When all these things take place, the people in exile will acknowledge that He is God.

Ezekiel's audience had difficulty internalizing his prediction of the destruction of the Jerusalem temple for two reasons. First, they heard God's message, but stubbornly refused to accept what was said.[31] Secondly, they were influenced by their social interaction with false prophets who had

30. Berger, *Social Construction*, 106–07, describes how the theoretical framework of a group's symbolic universe supports and maintains their worldview. When Ezekiel removed the underpinnings of this tenuous socially constructed approach to reality (by claiming that Jerusalem would be destroyed and the exiles were the chosen ones), change was possible.

31. Ezekiel 12:3 held out a slight hope that the people might understand and change.

Exiles with their packs of belongings on their backs are prodded by a conquering soldier in this relief from the palace of Ashurbanipal at Nineveh. See Ezekiel 12:1–16.

a different worldview. Before Ezekiel could transform their thinking, he had to *destroy false hopes* (12:1—14:23).

Two sign actions dramatized the true nature of what would happen in Jerusalem. Just as Ezekiel publicly packed his bags and escaped through a hole in a wall one evening,[32] so the people and ruler of Jerusalem (Zedekiah) would exit the city for exile in Babylon (12:1–16). Ezekiel's second act illustrated the starvation and thirst for water in Jerusalem during its siege (12:17–20). These signs argued against the common false hope that Jerusalem would not be destroyed.

Ezekiel attacked a popular exilic proverb that the day of Jerusalem's judgment was a long way off, that the prophetic visions of doom would fail (12:21–28). This saying was false and misleading, for the day of fulfillment was now. God would prove the bankruptcy of this false hope by doing what He said He would. He would prove their false prophets wrong. They reported false visions, divinations that God did not send.[33] These fools misled the people; they were like jackals scavenging the ruins of Judah, rather than helping the people prepare for the day of the Lord (13:4–5).[34] They thought Jerusalem would have peace (13:10, 16), but instead God would destroy the imaginary wall of protection they constructed around Jerusalem. These charlatans would not be numbered among those who would return to the land after exile (13:9).

In addition, female fortunetellers and sorcerers made a living by putting magical cloth or veils on people to protect some and bring death curses on others (13:17–23).[35] God would destroy these false prophets because these practices disheartened the righteous people, encouraged more wick-

---

32. Greenberg, *Ezekiel 1—20* in *AB* 22, 209, notes that "in their sight" occurred seven times here to prove that they would see, but not see (12:1).

33. Berger, *Social Construction,* 114, describes the technique Ezekiel used to deny the worldview of the false prophets as nihilation. Nihilation denies the reality of deviant views and gives them a negative ontological status.

34. Greenberg, *Ezekiel 1—20* in *AB* 22, 236. These prophets did not intercede for the people or warn them of God's judgment.

35. Zimmerli, *Ezekiel 1* in *Her,* 297, discusses possible interpretations of these strange magical practices.

edness, and caused people not to acknowledge God's control of their lives.

Even the elders of Israel who came to Ezekiel in exile were setting up idols in their hearts.[36] Drawing on ideas from Leviticus 17,[37] Ezekiel destroyed the leaders' hope to inquire of God while in this sinful state. He called them to repent of their sin and change the way they looked at divine power. Then they could come to find God's will, and He would answer (14:6–7). It was also a false hope to think that the few righteous people left in Jerusalem (compare Gen. 18:22–33), or that intercession by great righteous men like Noah, Job, or Daniel, would stop the destruction of Jerusalem (14:12–20).[38] Ezekiel attempted to persuade his audience to look at their world in a new way by undermining the false hopes of the people.

Ezekiel also tried to redefine who God's people were and what their relationship to God was in a series of *metaphors of God's justice with Israel* (15:1–19:14). A vine was useless for making furniture and even more useless if it was partially burned in a fire. But Judah, the nation which thought of themselves as a noble vine of God (Ps. 80:8–11; Isa. 27:2–6), was identified as a burned vine, for God would destroy the nation with fire because of their unfaithfulness (15:1–8).[39] Ezekiel reconceptualized the history of Israel by emphasizing the Gentile background of their ancestors, their rejection by others, and God's undeserved care for this

---

36. Greenberg, *Ezekiel 1—20* in *AB* 22, 253, does not believe Ezekiel was referring to the syncretistic worship of idols but their unregenerate state of mind, but Blenkinsopp, *Ezekiel* in *IntCom* 71 compares this to the Egyptian exiles who worshiped other gods in Jeremiah 44.

37. Zimmerli, *Ezekiel 1* in *Her*, 302–03, points out numerous connections in vocabulary and thought with Leviticus 17.

38. H. H. P. Dressler, "The Identification of Dnil with the Daniel of Ezekiel," *VT* 29 (1979), 152–61, discusses whether Ezekiel knew Daniel or whether he was referring to another Dnil.

39. Berger, *Social Construction*, 91, discusses the reification of identity, the estimation of one's value and role on the basis of absolute positive (you are beautiful) or negative (you are ugly) characteristics, rather than human behavior. The identity of God's people was based on their faithfulness, not that they were the seed of Abraham or lived in Jerusalem.

helpless young girl. God graciously made her beautiful and married her, but she trusted in her beauty and became a prostitute by trusting other gods and the military might of other nations (16:1–34). Therefore, God will uncover her shameful behavior before her many lovers, so that they may stone this woman caught in adultery (see traditions in Lev. 20:10; Deut. 22:23–24). She forgot God's grace in her youth, and now she will get her just reward. Although this woman Judah was worse than her sisters Samaria and Sodom (16:44–52), in the future God will graciously restore a remnant from Sodom and Samaria, and reestablish the everlasting covenant He made with Judah in her youth (16:53–63). If Ezekiel's audience would accept this allegory, it would reorient their thinking about God's past and future grace and the justice of His punishment on the nation.[40] They must come to the place where they acknowledged Him as their covenant God.

Judah's recent history was also depicted in an allegory of two great eagles. The king of Babylon took vines from Judah and planted them in his own lands, but when the other eagle appeared (the king of Egypt), the vine foolishly reached out to it (17:1–10). This was a warning for the followers of Zedekiah not to reach out to the Egyptian Pharaoh for help, even though King Nebuchadnezzar had already taken Jehoiachin into Babylonian exile in 597 B.C. This trust in Egyptian horses was breaking a political covenant, and not trusting in God was breaking His covenant (17:11–21). The nation's only hope must rest on the twig that God plants. That king will prosper, everyone will be under his care, and other nations will recognize God as the real power behind him.[41]

---

40. Ibid., 60, 64, 67, 92–99. Berger explains how each person's or group's biography gives meaning to reality. One's view of experience legitimates a philosophy of life or symbolic universe. The reinterpretation of the past throws into question the meaning of past events and the validity of present conceptions of reality.

41. Brownlee, *Ezekiel* in *WBC* 28, 273, thinks this twig was Zerubabbel, but it seems better to follow Craigie, *Ezekiel* in *DBS*, 130–31, and Zimmerli, *Ezekiel 1* in *Her* 368, who see this as a messianic promise.

Ezekiel not only dealt with the exile's misunderstanding of the way God would justly judge those left in Jerusalem, he also addressed the deep-seated feeling that God was not fair with those in exile. The socially accepted explanation popular among the exiles was they were suffering for their parents' sins, that God did not treat them justly (18:2, 25, 29; 18:4, see Ex. 20:5). Ezekiel's sermon argued against the exiles theological perspective, for God justly judges only sinners (see Deut. 24:16; Jer. 31:29). If a son followed proper social behavior with regards to women, the poor, lending money, practicing justice, and did not worship other gods, his father's wickedness or righteousness would not affect God's blessing on his life (18:5–18). Ancient covenant traditions in Leviticus 18:19–20; 19:13; 25:35–37; and Deuteronomy 24:16 legitimated Ezekiel's view of just social behavior. They must repent, transform their conduct, and change their heart attitude, for God does not want to judge anyone (18:30–32). Ezekiel emphasized each person's individual responsibility for their own action.

Ezekiel finished this section with a lament of a lioness who had two cubs (King Jehoahaz and King Jehoiachin) who were captured and taken to Egypt and Babylon (19:1–9). Then he lamented the destruction of a vine (Judah) which was fruitful and strong, but now was withered and consumed with fire. These laments undermined the false hopes of those who thought that God would not destroy Judah or her leaders (19:10–14).

The long series of oracles against Jerusalem ended with additional confirmations of the *profaning of Jerusalem* (20:1—24:27). In 591 B.C., in the prophet's seventh year in exile, Ezekiel rehearsed the darker side of Israel's salvation history to the elders of Israel in Babylon. God chose Israel to be His people and promised to bring them out of Egypt and give them a beautiful land (see Ex. 6:2–8). This relationship required Israel to reject Egypt's gods, but at Mount Sinai they built a golden calf. God had mercy on them and did not destroy them (Ex. 32:1–9, 11–14), but gave them

His behavioral guidelines and sabbaths to help them be holy (20:11–12; see Ex. 20:1—23:33). They rebelled again in the wilderness and defiled God's sabbath, but God was merciful again. Throughout the story Ezekiel reversed the people's positive views of their history by emphasizing their idolatry, rebellion, defilement, uncleanness, detestable pagan practices, and blasphemous treachery against God. Their few positive days were nothing compared to the utter depravity and corruption of their sins. They profaned Jerusalem, so God will destroy them in His anger. He will not pity them, and then they will understand that He truly is God (20:18–29).

Should Ezekiel's audience continue these sinful ways (20:30–31)? No! God's people should not and will not be like other nations (20:32), for in the future God will be their King. There will be a new exodus, a new wilderness, a new group that will not profane God's holiness, a new people to serve God, a new Israel that will acknowledge that He is God. Ezekiel's sermon externalized a hope for the hopeless.[42] God was determined to make His people distinct from the nation's, and He was committed to sanctifying His name. This was a radically new view of God's future dealings with the exiles.

Ezekiel saw that God's sword would cut off the righteous and wicked in Jerusalem, so he groaned, wailed, and struck his thigh in anguish before the exiles. He also clapped his hands like the victorious enemies would when they defeated Jerusalem (21:1–17).[43] He portrayed Nebuchadnezzar looking at road signs and using pagan methods of divination to decide to attack Jerusalem instead of Ammon (21:18–24; Ammon is judged in 28—32).[44] Nebuchadnezzar will seize

42. Berger, *Social Construction*, 60–61, 104, sees externalization as the social process of introducing new subjective meanings into reality that were not part of the existing worldview of the audience. Both Ezekiel's historical review and his future hope explore the boundaries of traditional thought among the exiles.

43. Zimmerli, *Ezekiel 1* in *Her*, 184, explains the clapping of the hands.

44. Ibid., 443–44, discusses the nature of the divination used by the Babylonians.

the people, humble the wicked prince of Judah (Zedakiah), and make the city a ruin. This judgment from God will come on the guilty who shed the blood of the innocent, oppressed the orphan and widow, worshiped idols, slandered people, sexually abused others, financially cheated people, and forgot God (22:1–12). God cannot stand these acts, so He will scatter them among the nations and purify out the dross of the nation in a fiery furnace.

Why has this happened? The prophets deceived the people, the priests did not teach people how to be holy, the leaders did not establish justice in the land; therefore the people were oppressed, and there was no social leader to intercede to God for mercy (22:23–31). The political leaders in Samaria (Oholah) and Jerusalem (Oholibah) trusted in alliances with Assyria, Babylon, and Egypt, but they will turn against Judah and betray her (23:1–30). These acts were like unfaithful and lewd harlotry, and they resulted in profaning God's holy temple.

To further demonstrate to this audience that the people profaning Jerusalem deserved destruction, Ezekiel used a parable of a boiling pot to announce that the siege of Jerusalem was beginning (in 588 B.C.; see 24:1). The happy song or story about the pot vigorously boiling choice meat for a meal (24:3–5) was reversed into a negative picture of God boiling the "choice" people in bloody Jerusalem and cleansing it by burning out all impurities.[45] As a final dramatic sign, Ezekiel did not mourn the death of his wife, because the people in Jerusalem would die and have no one to mourn them (24:15–24). This antisocial behavior would speak volumes to the exiles and raise questions in people's minds. Why did Ezekiel behave in such a deviant manner? Why would he not mourn the loss of his beloved wife?

45. D. I. Block, "Ezekiel's Boiling Cauldron: A Form-Critical Solution to Ezekiel xxv 1–14," *VT* 51 (1991), 12–37, concludes that this was a disputation speech.

II. Acknowledge that God Will Destroy the Nations 25:1—32:32

The *oracles of judgment on the nations* (25:1–17) included the judgment of Ammon (25:1–7), Moab (25:8–11), Edom (25:12–14), and Philistia (25:15–17).[46] These nations laughed when Judah was forsaken and Jerusalem's temple was profaned (25:3, 6, 8, 12, 15). Therefore, God will vindicate His holiness and desolate these lands so they will acknowledge that Yahweh truly is God (25:5, 7, 11, 17). Ezekiel persuasively communicated a message of comfort to the exiles, for they would see God's justice.[47] Ezekiel's sermon on the *judgment of Tyre* (26:1—28:24) included an announcement of judgment and lament on the mainland city of Tyre (26:1–21; 27:1–36) and an announcement of judgment and lament on the proud king of Tyre (28:1–10; 28:11–19). When Babylon was destroying Jerusalem,[48] Tyre remained powerful and gloated over their new economic opportunity to control trade around the world (26:3). To convince the exiles that Nebuchadnezzar could destroy Tyre, Ezekiel recreated in their imagination a realistic portrayal of the battle scene. A great Babylonian army of horses, chariots, and soldiers would siege the city, bring down its walls, and dump them in the sea. They would kill the people of Tyre, take her riches, and leave the place a bare rock (26:3–14). Other coastal cities that traded with Tyre would lament the fall of Tyre (26:15–18).

Ezekiel strengthened the exiles' ability to internalize this prediction and accept God's sovereignty by voicing his own lament for the island city of Tyre (27:1–36). The eulogy contrasted Tyre's own wonderful self-portrait (27:3–9) and

---

46. Klein, *Ezekiel*, 130, connects these oracles as a response to events in 594/593 B.C. when they and Judah rebelled against Babylon (see Jer. 27:3), but a date after 586 B.C. is more likely.

47. Craigie, *Ezekiel* in *DSB*, 188–91, sees Ezekiel teaching the exiles about the universal sovereignty of God. These judgments were fulfilled by Nebuchadnezzar in 582 B.C.

48. L. Allen, *Ezekiel 20—48* in *WBC* 29, 71, dates this oracle in the twelfth year after the fall of Jerusalem, rather than the eleventh year in the Hebrew text.

the praises of her trading partners (27:10–25) with the bitter end of Tyre (27:26–36). Tyre was like a beautiful ship in the sea, strongly built, filled with great riches, and sailed by a wise crew.[49] Tyre was known as the richest and best trading partner, but this ship will sink, lose its valuable cargo, and sailors.

Lest any exile doubt God's plans for Tyre, Ezekiel also condemned the arrogant king of Tyre, Ethbaal II. The mythology was that this king had almost divine authority and wisdom to help the nation gain its riches. In reality this proud king was just a man. He would die a shameful death, and his splendor and wisdom would vanish (28:1–10).[50]

In the center of this long series of destructive oracles was a pivotal sermon of *hope for Israel* (28:25–26). Ezekiel reminded the exiles that God would fulfill His promises. He would manifest His holiness before all the nations by gathering His people. Then everyone will acknowledge that He is God.

The oracles against the nations ended with a *judgment of Egypt* (29:1—32:32). These sermons were all (except 29:17–21) given in the eleventh and twelfth years of exile when Jerusalem was being besieged by Babylon (587–586 B.C.).[51] These seven oracles repeatedly refer to the pride and power of Egypt (29:3; 30:6, 18; 32:12), Nebuchadnezzar's destruction of Egypt (29:18; 30:10, 24–25; 32:11), how Egypt's great river will dry up and kill its sea monster (29:4; 30:12; 32:2–4), and its inhabitants will go into exile (29:13; 30:18,26). God, not Pharaoh, made Egypt and the Nile (29:9); He gave strength and could take it away (30:20–26). The day of the

49. For a discussion of this extended metaphor of the ship, see E. M. Good, "Ezekiel's Ship: Some Extended Metaphors in the Old Testament," *Semitics* 1 (1970), 79–103, or C. A. Newsom, "A Maker of Metaphors—Ezekiel's Oracles Against Tyre," *Int* 38 (1984), 151–64.

50. Allen, *Ezekiel 20—48* in *WBC* 29, 92–96, discusses the difficult issues related to the interpretation of the king of Tyre.

51. See K. S. Freedy, "The Dates of Ezekiel in Relation to Biblical, Babylonian and Egyptian Sources," *JAOS* 90 (1970) 462–85, for a fuller discussion of the history of this period. Compare D. Redford, *Egypt, Canaan, and Israel in Ancient Times* (Princeton: Princeton Univ. Press, 1992), 467–71.

Lord was near for Egypt (30:1–5). Ezekiel lamented the death of the Pharaoh (32:1–16) and wailed because Egypt will join the other nations in Sheol (32:17–32). Ezekiel's rhetorical purpose was to undermine popular beliefs among the exiles, and convince them that Egypt will not save Judah from the Babylonians in 587 B.C. (29:16; see Jer. 37). He sought to demonstrate that their future was in God's hands and to explain that these events will cause both Judeans and Egyptians to internalize the belief that Yahweh truly is God (29:6, 9, 21; 30:8, 19, 25; 32:15). Judean political alliances with Egypt will not save Jerusalem (19:2–4).

III. Acknowledge that God Will Restore Israel 33:1—48:35

Ezekiel began the third phase of his ministry when a refugee from Judah came to the exiles to announce the fall of Jerusalem (33:21–22). This dreaded news marked the fulfillment of Ezekiel's earlier prophecies, the end of Ezekiel's dumbness (see 24:25–27), and the conclusion of his role as a watchman for the exiles.[52] Soon Ezekiel would have a new role;[53] he could offer hope to the people (33:30–33). Before he took up that role the *watchman defended God's justice* (33:1–33) by recapitulating the past, legitimating his prophetic status before the exiles, and calling the people to transform their thinking in light of what happened.

Ezekiel publicly explained to the exiles his role for the last several years (33:1–9).[54] He functioned as a watchman who warned the people to turn from iniquity before God's judgment would come (see 3:17–21). The audience responded with a desperate cry that they were hopelessly rot-

52. Zimmerli, *Ezekiel 2* in *Her*, 183, thinks of this as another call or recommissioning. There is no doubt that Ezekiel can now speak freely, but these oracles look back to evaluate the past rather than projecting a new role for Ezekiel.

53. Berger, *Social Construction*, 72–75, connects role to typical actions and stereotyped statements, so when Ezekiel changed his behavior and vocabulary, he forced the people to look at him in a new way.

54. Klein, *Ezekiel*, 28–32, thinks 3:17–21 was a private communication to Ezekiel while 33:1–9 was a public announcement of his role.

ting away in exile because of their sins (33:10). Ezekiel reminded them of his earlier message about God's just treatment of the sinner and the one who repents (18:1–30). Ezekiel saw that the audience's socially developed worldview misunderstood how God works.[55] God is not only a judge of sinners; He is a deliverer of those who turn from their sin. He treats people fairly, for the one who repents will live (33:10–20). They had no need to be hopeless.

Ezekiel also rejected the idea that Judeans who remained in Jerusalem after the captivity could claim the property of the dead and the exiled. They were the seed of Abraham, but that did not justify taking their land (33:24).[56] These people who kill, worship idols, and commit adultery will not possess Judah, for God will give this ownerless land to wild beasts (33:25–29).

The chapter ends with a warning to Ezekiel. Although many exiles will come to hear what he has to say and everyone will be talking about him, Ezekiel must not allow popularity to deceive him (33:30–33). These people will not be faithful disciples. They will come to be excited or to make a profit off of Ezekiel's next prophecy. They will look at him as an entertainer and enjoy his talks, but not do what he says. Ezekiel must not be swayed by the audience; he must be a prophet in their midst.

Once Ezekiel's exilic audience knew that Jerusalem was destroyed, their hopes were dashed. God had judged Judah for its sins, abandoned His temple, and given up on His people. Feelings of hopelessness were inevitable. Why did God let it happen, and would He ever gather the nation back to Jerusalem like earlier prophets promised (Isa. 2:1–4; Mic. 4—5)? Ezekiel's audience needed an explanation for God's actions and some insight into His plans for the *restoration of Israel* (34:1—37:28).

---

55. It seems that the exiles reified their status. Hopelessly condemned, they could do nothing to change their predicament. See Berger, *Social Construction*, 90–92.

56. The same problem existed in 11:15 after the captivity of Jerusalem in 597 B.C.

God allowed Babylon to destroy Judah and scatter the people in exile because the shepherd kings of Judah ignored the people, destroyed them, and did not protect them from predators (34:1–10; see Jer. 23:1–8). To encourage his listeners to internalize this hope, Ezekiel assured them that the scattered people were His people, sheep in His flock. Jerusalem's destruction allowed Him to remove these evil leaders. One day God will care for the sheep, bring them back from foreign nations into the pleasant and peaceful land, feed them, and nurse the sick (34:11–16). God will judge between the good and the evil who treat others unjustly (34:17–22).[57] Then God will set one king over them, the messianic seed of David who will serve God. His eternal covenant of peace will bring material fruitfulness to the land, security, and a heartfelt acknowledgment of God's relationship to them (34:23–31; compare Lev. 26:4–13; Hos. 2:17–23; Jer. 30–31). With this vision of the future Ezekiel was trying to convince the exiles to believe in what God would do, in spite of their discouraging situation in exile.

One stumbling block to accepting Ezekiel's imaginative picture of the future was Edom. What would God do about this nation that took advantage of Judah after Babylon destroyed the nation (35:1–15; see 25:12–14; Obad. 10–14; Ps. 137:7). The Edomites tried to claim Judah and Israel as their land. They rejoiced when Jerusalem fell. They acted in hatred and anger and arrogantly boasted about their new possession. Ezekiel assured his audience that God would desolate Edom and any other nation that tried to appropriate His land (36:1–5). His fruitful land will be occupied by His people. The foreign nations will never insult His people again, and everyone will acknowledge that this was the work of God (36:6–15).[58] This oracle convincingly illustrated how

57. Blenkinsopp, *Ezekiel* in *IntCom,* 159, relates this to economic and political exploitation during the time of Gedeliah (Jer. 41), but this narrows the application too specifically. For a pre-millennial view of the new covenant, see L. Cooper, *Ezekiel* in *NAC* 17, 287–346.

58. Allen, *Ezekiel 20—48* in *WBC* 29, 169–74, discusses the political relations between Edom and Judah when Jerusalem was destroyed.

God's promise would apply to a concrete situation which recently had brought great humiliation to the Jews.

Ezekiel repeated his claim that God would deliver His people from these nations, cleanse them from evil, pour out His Spirit on them, renew the covenant, and bring blessings on them. This happened not because the people deserved it, but to vindicate and reclaim the glory of God's holy name (36:22–32). The regenerative power of God will transform their social behavior, rejuvenate the desolate land, and increase their numbers so much that even the nations around them will acknowledge this is an act of God (36:33–38).[59] This great idea of reviving the nation was pictured as a dramatic reanimation of dry bones into a huge multitude of breathing people who were filled with God's Spirit (37:1–14). Those exiles in Ezekiel's audience who thought the nation was dead and completely cut off were wrong (37:11), for God will bring the nation back to life.[60] This creative work of God will cause the doubters to acknowledge that He is God.

Ezekiel put two sticks together to symbolize God's future reunification of Judah and Israel (37:15–28). They will be one nation with one king, and they will not defile themselves again. The Messianic Servant from the line of David will be king. They will all have one eternal covenant of peace. All will worship God together at one temple. They will be God's people, and the nations will acknowledge this as an act of God.[61]

To assure the doubter in the audience, Ezekiel promised that God would provide security and *protection from future enemies* (38:1—39:29). No matter who the unknown enemy may be who might devise plans to take Israel's land and plunder it,[62] God would stand against them in all His fury and an-

59. R. M. Hals, *Ezekiel* in *FOTL* XIX (Grand Rapids: Eerdmans, 1989), 265–66.

60. D. I. Block, "Beyond the Grave: Ezekiel's Vision of Death and Afterlife," *BBR 2* (1992) 113–41, argues for an Israelite belief in life after death in this and earlier prophetic texts.

61. Allen, *Ezekiel 20–48* in *WBC* 29, 192–96, emphasizes this theme of unity and oneness with God and each other.

62. See Zimmerli, *Ezekiel 2* in *Her,* 301, on the possible identification of Gog with an ANE figure, but this is a mysterious superpower of the future.

ger. He would destroy them and magnify His name in the sight of all nations. Then the doubters among God's people will internalize and acknowledge God's power and holiness. When the nations see this demonstration of God's glory in His dealings with Israel, all nations will recognize His renown.

In Ezekiel's twenty-fifth year in exile (573 B.C.) he saw a vision concerning the *restoration of the temple* (40:1—46:24), an amplification of his brief reference to a temple in 37:24–28. The future temple would allow Yahweh's glory to dwell among the people (contrast 10:4, 18; 11:23) so that worship could return. It promised a new day of acceptance by God. The people in exile would no longer be rejected. There really was hope in the future!

The details of the walls, windows, gates, steps, pillars, chambers, altars, carvings, furniture, and porches provided realism to the vision which Ezekiel saw, just like the detailed picture of the defeat of Tyre brought the event to life (27—28). This account has similarities with earlier temple architectural traditions in Exodus 25—31, but Ezekiel was most concerned with the return of God's glory (43:2–9). This new era would mark the end of defiling God's holy name (43:7), the end of going out the east gate of the temple (44:2),[63] the end of improper sacrifices and worshipers (44:6–8), the end of unqualified priests (44:9–31), and the end of oppressive and unjust princes (45:7–12).[64] This picture of the future envisaged a world radically different from the world the exiles knew before the exile. The people and the rulers will worship God at feasts and sabbaths with sacrifice following regular Levitical procedures (45:13—46:15). Everything will be orderly according to God's instruction. This was the future time the exiles dreamed about. Ezekiel's vision rekindled their faith in God.

63. Ibid. Zimmerli emphasizes that the closed gate symbolized how God once and for all times was taking possession of the temple and would never leave it.

64. Hals, *Ezekiel* in *FOTL* XIX, 286–89, notes the negative formulation of the message. The errors of the past will not plague the nation again.

God's plan not only included a new eschatological temple, but also the *restoration of the land* (47:1—48:35). In this new world a fresh water river would flow from the temple where God dwelt. It would transform the barren Judean desert into a fertile land with ever–bearing fruit trees and leaves that healed (almost a new garden of Eden.[65]) This river would transform the Dead Sea into a fresh lake teeming with many fish (47:1–12; see Joel 3:18; Rev. 22:1–2)).

All of Israel was equally divided into idealistic horizontal strips of land and inherited by the tribes of Israel as God swore to the patriarchs (this contrasted with the division of the land in Num. 34). An area dedicated to God's temple, the priest, the prince, and the city called "the Lord is there" would be situated in the center of the tribes (48:8–20).[66] These promises encouraged the landless exiles to believe that one day God's people would have their land back and would be able to acknowledge God in their worship at the new temple.

Theological and Social Implications

Like Ezekiel, the messenger of God today must deal wisely with those who think that God does not care what they are doing, who do not want to admit their own failures, and who refuse to acknowledge God's holiness. Sometimes more sermons will not get their attention, and more accusations will not change their attitudes. The more they operate on the basis of false perceptions of reality, the more they become alienated from God's transforming power. They may feel rejected, misunderstood, and without hope; but God may have a redemptive plan for their lives.

---

65. J. Levenson, *Theology of the Program of Restoration of Ezekiel 40—48* (Missoula: Scholars Press, 1976), 28–29, and Blenkinsopp, *Ezekiel* in *Int-Com*, 231, sees a connection between this river and the ones in Gen. 2:10–14. For a literal interpretation of the millennial temple, see Cooper, *Ezekiel* in *NAC* 17, 347–424.

66. Allen, *Ezekiel 20—48* in *WBC* 29, 282–83, includes a drawing of the tribal territories and the central area where the temple will be.

Like Ezekiel, God's messengers today must be willing to communicate with people through powerful and personal symbolic acts that can speak far stronger than words. Through such acts it may actually be possible to get through to those who refuse to listen to normal preaching. It is always difficult to oppose what people believe, but it is far more loving to destroy false hopes than to perpetuate the pious lies of "religious" people. God is holy and just. He does not defend those who profane His name or maintain highly regarded religious institutions where His glory is not acknowledged. He can abandon those who abandon Him.

The central aim of every messenger involves persuading one's listeners to acknowledge who God is, submit their lives to His will, and glorify His name. Allegories, parables, life histories, dramatic presentations, disputations, and promises of future hope gave spice and bite to the prophet's delivery, but the challenge was to not let the medium destroy the power of the message. Modern methods of reaching people can help bring variety and culturally relevant forms to the communication process, but audience sensitivity must never overpower the fundamental task of communicating God's word. The thing that counts in the end is: Does the audience acknowledge God's claim on their life and seek to glorify His holy name?

Questions for Discussion

1. Why did Ezekiel's audience in exile need to know what was really happening in Jerusalem? How would this change their thinking? What are some misconceptions people have today?
2. How does the picture of the glory of God in Ezekiel 1 fit the modern conception of God?
3. How is a prophet like a watchman (Ezek. 33:1–9)?
4. How can a messenger's externalization of hope impact an audience's willingness to reevaluate their hopeless condition?

Chapter 15

Daniel: Who Rules the World?

Introduction

In the last century the world has fought two world wars, several large wars between neighboring nations, numerous ethnic or tribal battles within a nation, and a multitude of coups d'état. For some people this is a search for freedom from oppression from a stronger oppressor, but at other times these movements are a foolish rebellion by power-hungry leaders who do not want to submit to a higher authority. In the search for respect, riches, and control of territory and people, thousands of soldiers are killed, and the lives of thousands of innocent civilians are disrupted. Homes are burned, places of worship are defiled, businesses are destroyed, law and order degenerates into the law of the jungle, and people are forced into foreign territories. Fear and hopelessness overwhelm those caught in the cross fire. Survival becomes the main goal of life.

Whether these endless wars are under the control of military strategists or senseless gangs on city streets, God's people in the past and today want to know who has the ultimate say on which kingdoms (or gangs) rise to power and which fall into oblivion. God's messengers can assure His people who suffer through wars and their aftermath that these events are not beyond His control. They may bring persecution and death, but in the end God will establish His kingdom and destroy the forces of evil. Then everyone will recognize that God is the ruler over all nations, peoples, tribes, and individuals.

Social Setting

The Historical Context

Daniel was born during the reign of the righteous King Josiah, but during his teens the Babylonian army took Daniel and many other Judeans into captivity in the third year of King Jehoiakim (605 B.C.; 1:1; see 2 Kings 24:1; Jer. 25:1–12).[1] Those in captivity lived under King Nebuchadnezzar, a great builder and the military ruler over a vast empire. Nebuchadnezzar gave Daniel and his three friends positions of leadership in important government offices (1:17–20; 2:48–49) because God gave Daniel special wisdom and revelations about the interpretation of the king's dreams. Later, King Nabonidus rejected the worship of Babylon's popular god Marduk and left the throne to his son Belshazzar while he went on a military trip to Tema.[2] The Medo–Persian King Cyrus defeated Belshazzar and ended the Babylonian Empire (539 B.C.; 5:1–31) while Nabonidus was away.

---

1. A. R. Millard, "Daniel 1—6 and History," *EvQ* 49 (1977), 68–69, explains the difference between the third year of Nebuchadnezzar in Daniel 1:1 and the fourth year in Jeremiah 25:1 by suggesting that one system considered the first year as the accession year and the next year as year one, while the other counted the accession year as year one. Another solution was to suggest that two different calendars were used in the two books: one began the new year in the spring, while the other began the year in the fall.

2. W. H. Shea, "Nabonidus, Balshazzar, and the Book of Daniel: An Update," *AUSS* 20 (1982), 133–49, bases this conclusion on the Harran Inscription, the Nabonidus Chronicle, and the Verse Account of Nabonidus. This explained Belshazzar's offer to make someone the third ruler in the land (his father was first, and Belshazzar was second).

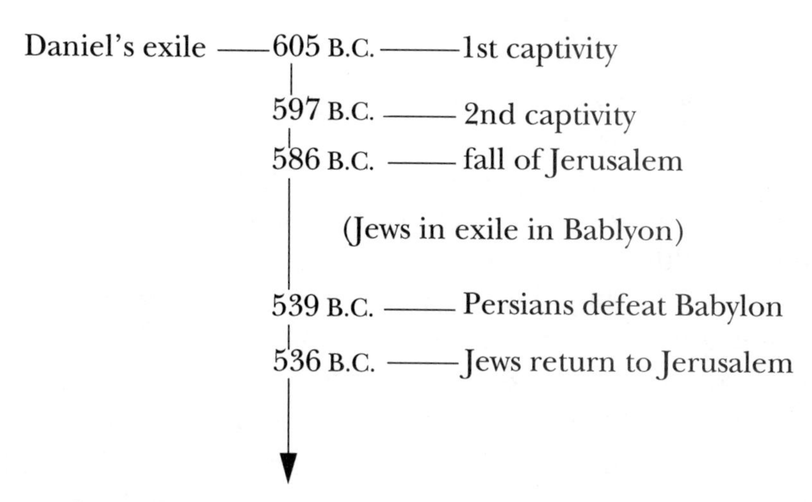

Cyrus had a very tolerant policy toward the nations which the Babylonians deported to different parts of their empire. He repatriated many groups in Babylon to their native lands, including the Jews under the leadership of their governor Sheshbazzar and high priest Joshua (Ezra 1:1–11). Daniel stayed in Babylon and was given the political responsibility to be one of three commissioners over the 120 satraps that ruled the Persian Empire (6:1–3).

The Structure of Social Order

Social order was determined by the powerful armies of the Babylonian and Medo–Persian Empires. The Babylonians defeated nations like Judah and deported skilled craftsmen and educated government officials to assist in building the beautiful city of Babylon. Jeremiah's letter to those in exile (Jer. 29) indicated that some exiles had a fair bit of personal freedom, but when people were forced to live outside of their country, the social ordering of life was unavoidably altered by foreign customs. A person's identity and status is altered when defeated by foreigners; new economic and political conditions reorient people's views of objective reality.[3]

Events surrounding the interpretation of the Babylonian king's dreams portray him as an absolute monarch who

3. P. Berger and T. Luckman, *The Social Construction of Reality: A Treatise in the Sociology of Knowledge* (Garden City: Doubleday, 1966), 107–09, sees that powerful tend to impose their view of the world on the weaker.

controlled the life and prosperity of his subjects (2:5, 46—49). He could act humbly and graciously or in fits of anger and irrationality. The Persian kings were bound by law (6:12, 15). These cultures believed the gods revealed their will through dreams, so the king employed many wise men to advise him on their interpretation. Although the dreams related to cultural phenomena within the Babylonian world (symbols, dividing history into periods), the wise men's inability to interpret them pointed to a limited knowledge of their deeper secrets and application.

Some commentators conclude that the social order of war and severe persecution in 7—12 came from a circle of wise men in a Judean context when the Maccabees were revolting against the persecution and defilement of the temple by Antiochus Epiphanes (198–165 B.C.).[4] They maintain that these stories reflected the intertestamental conflict with the Greek social and religious perspective and the imagery and ideas that were popular in apocalyptic literature of that era. Lacoque thinks that Daniel's reactions against these foreign ideas came from the worldview of the Hasidim, but Collins demonstrates the discontinuity between the fighting Hasidim and the persecuted masses in Daniel.[5] Other scholars maintain a unified setting in Babylon for the book and see 7—12 as prophetic projections of a future sociopolitical period instead of an historical account of the past.[6]

---

4. J. J. Collins, "Daniel and His Social World," *Int* 39 (1985), 137–40, finds two different worlds behind 1—6 and 7—12. E. M. Yamauchi, *Persia and the Bible* (Grand Rapids: Baker, 1990), provides background for Daniel's life during the Persian period.

5. A. Lacoque, *The Book of Daniel* (Atlanta: J. Knox, 1979), 11; Collins, "Daniel and His Social World," *Int* 39 (1985), 132–33.

6. J. Baldwin, *Daniel* in *TOTC* 21 (Leicester: InterVarsity, 1978), 35–46, bases her conclusion on the belief that the book is a unified whole. Since 1—6 were from the Babylonian period, the rest must be. See also A. J. Ferch, "The Book of Daniel and the 'Maccabean Thesis,'" *AUSS* 21 (1983), 129–41; S. Miller, *Daniel* in NAC 18 (Nashville: Broadman and Holman Press, 1994); Kenneth L. Barker, "Premillennialism in the Book of Daniel," *MSS* 4 (1993), 25–45.

The Social Location and Role of the Prophet

Daniel and his three friends lived in and around the royal court, a world very different from most exiles. These young boys were well fed, educated, upper class individuals who already had a solid perspective on the world from their Jewish upbringing in Jerusalem. New externalizations about the Babylonian world were mediated to them over a three-year period by government officials who taught them Babylonian literature and wisdom, instructed them on how to serve the king, and controlled their diets and living conditions (1:4–20).[7] Once they were fluent in Aramaic and met the king's expectations, Daniel functioned as the head over the wise men who advised the king, while Shadrach, Meshach, and Abed-nego served as administrators over the province of Babylon. These social positions of authority and status brought conflict when Babylonian customs and laws clashed with Jewish convictions. This conflict resulted in a negotiated exception to the king's command in regard to Jewish food laws (1:9–13), an angry and uncompromising confrontation concerning worshiping Babylonian idols and expressions of absolute loyalty to the king (3:8–23), and hope for the safety of a trusted friend when the king was tricked into making a bad law (6:6–15). These events demonstrated that the worldview accepted by these Jewish men during primary socialization in Jerusalem was not eradicated during their Babylonian training or service.[8] The stories do not reveal how these men interacted with the social order promoted by Babylonian diviners, wise men, and astrologers, but do reveal how Babylonian and Persian kings were led to accept a Jewish perspective on key issues. The authorial perspective that was legitimated through the experiences of Daniel was that other Jews did not need to submit to

7. Berger, *Social Construction*, 104, sees externalizations happening when a person projects a new meaning of reality which is not a part of the existing view of the world.

8. Ibid., 135–43. Berger finds secondary socialization in specific roles and sub-universes of knowledge that pertain to specific occupations, but this does not involve the emotional identification with a worldview that is characteristic of primary socialization.

foreign pressure or persecution, for the Babylonians and Persians could not deny the wisdom and power of Daniel's God.

The accounts in 7—12 were Daniel's insight into the future political and social order of his own people. Daniel also functioned as an intercessor and prayed that God would fulfill His promise to return His people to Jerusalem after seventy years of captivity (9:1; see Jer. 25:12; 29:10). He also externalized God's insight into future international conflicts which would involve the persecution of Jews. These enemies will kill many, defile the temple, oppose God, and change religious and social laws; but in the end God will destroy them and resurrect His own to everlasting life (12:1–3). As these revelations became known to his Jewish audience, Daniel's prophetic role was recognized.

Daniel was not a typical prophetic orator who persuaded the masses to submit to God. Initially (2; 4; 6) his role was to interpret and persuade the king to believe his mysterious dreams or the handwriting on the wall. Secondarily, his written record of these stories were a powerful testimony to his Jewish readers that God rules over all nations. These prophecies were an encouragement to the readers to persevere and maintain their Jewish piety in spite of future times of severe persecution.

Social Interaction

The Book of Daniel

Daniel 1:1—2:4a and 8:1—12:13 are in Hebrew, while 2:4b—7:28 are in Imperial Aramaic.[9] Collins classifies the book as an historic apocalypse, with the literary forms of symbolic dream visions in 7—8, an angelic discourse in 10—11, a midrash in 9, and court tales of conflict in 1—

---

9. G. F. Hasel, "The Book of Daniel and Matters of Language: Evidence Relating to Names, Words, and the Aramaic Language," *AUSS* 19 (1981), 211–25, concludes that the Aramaic text of the Job Targum from Qumran was later (second or third century B.C.) than Daniel's Aramaic.

6.[10] In these apocalyptic scenes, heavenly messengers revealed hidden secrets about history, the final judgment, and God's salvation of the righteous in strange and mysterious symbolic messages. The visions include dramatic presentations of great conflicts to come in the future, with vivid images of earthly events and hints of heavenly turmoil. These messages were organized into two major sections:[11]

I. God Rules Nations and His servants 1:1—6:28
   A. God gave His servants favor and wisdom 1:1–21
   B. God revealed mysteries of the kingdoms 2:1–49
   C. God delivered those who trusted Him 3:1–30
   D. God humbled and raised up a king 4:1–37
   E. God weighed and will divide Babylon 5:1–31
   F. God delivered the one who trusted Him 6:1–28
II. God Rules over His People in Evil Times 7:1—12:13
   A. The kingdom will come after persecution 7:1–28
   B. Persecution by the little horn 8:1–27
   C. Prayer about the end of the seventy years 9:1–27
   D. War and persecution before the end 10:1—12:13

Daniel did not preach like the typical prophet, but when he shared his wisdom with a king, it had a powerful transforming effect. When his fellow exiles heard or read these words, they were a great encouragement in difficult days.

---

10. J. J. Collins, *Daniel* in *FOTL* XX (Grand Rapids: Eerdmans, 1984), 6–10, 42. He rejects Lacoque's view (*The Book of Daniel 1*) that the book was a midrash. For a recent study of Daniel, see A. S. Van der Woude (ed.), *The Book of Daniel in the Light of New Findings* in *BETL*; (Leuven: Leuven University Press/Peters, 1993), 106.

11. D. W. Gooding, "The Literary Structure of the Book of Daniel and Its Implication," *TB* 32 (1981), 43–79, finds a pairing of chaps. 2—3, 4—5, 7—8, 9—12.

I. God Rules Nations and His Servants 1:1—6:28

In the first conflict *God gave His servants favor and wisdom* (1:1–21). Nebuchadnezzar's Babylonian worldview led him to believe that if he chose some good-looking, intelligent, and courteous Jewish men, they would be loyal servants in the king's court. He tried to resocialize these men by educating them in the language and wisdom of Babylon for three years. He gave them quality food from his own table, but Daniel and his friends thought this food would defile them.[12] God caused the Babylonian official to let them eat other food. A credible and limited ten-day test, which an official would evaluate, legitimated Daniel's request to eat different food. God gave Daniel and his friends good health, and more wisdom than all the king's advisors. Daniel was able to interpret dreams.[13]

This story encouraged exilic Jewish readers to maintain their commitment to a pious lifestyle and legitimated their trust in God's sovereign power to protect them when their beliefs conflicted with pagan practices.[14]

Later *God revealed mysteries of the kingdoms* (2:1–49) to Nebuchadnezzar in a dream. The Babylonian diviners, chanters, and Chaldeans got into a conflict with the king because they could not externalize the new dream or interpret it for the king.[15] The bankruptcy of their wisdom was unmasked, for they did not know what the gods said and had no way of communicating with the gods in heaven (2:5–12).[16] Nebuchadn-

12. L. Wood, *A Commentary on Daniel* (Grand Rapids: Zondervan, 1973), 37, thinks this food was defiled because it might include unclean food and might be offered to a pagan god. Baldwin, *Daniel* in *TOTC* 21, 83, suggests that Daniel refused the food because it committed him to a covenant relationship of allegiance, loyalty, and dependence on the king.

13. Daniel 1 should not be considered a midrash on Joseph's life as suggested by Lacoque, *Book of Daniel*, 32.

14. Berger, *Social Construction*, 106–11, recognizes that every humanly created universe of meaning is unstable when threatened by another worldview, and sees that a person's theological view of how God relates to humans as a great defense against alternate cultural perspectives.

15. Ibid., 104. Berger contends that people are able to create new meaning to make their cultural experience meaningful (externalizations), but the wise men lacked a source for creating the meaning of the dream (contact with God).

ezzar ordered their executions but Daniel and his friends prayed, and God made known the mysteries of the dream.

Daniel humbly admitted that his wisdom was limited, but God in heaven had given him knowledge of the dream (2:26–30). Daniel revealed the extraordinary characteristics of the statue in the king's dream and interpreted the gold head as a symbol of King Nebuchadnezzar (2:31–38). Later kingdoms will follow, but they will be destroyed by a divinely sent instrument. This stone will introduce the final kingdom of God (2:44–45).[17] Daniel's explanation persuaded the king, so Daniel was promoted and his God was honored (2:46–48). Daniel humbly asked the king to give some of these responsibilities to his three friends.

When exiles in Babylon read Daniel's account, it convinced them of God's wisdom and power and persuaded them to not accept all the Babylonian rhetoric about their gods. The dream assured the Jewish reader that God would one day defeat the human forces that controlled their lives and establish His eternal kingdom. The behavior of Daniel legitimated their humble piety and dependence on God in the midst of a turbulent Gentile world.

In the next episode the political careers of Daniel's three friends were endangered, but *God delivered those who trusted Him* (3:1–30). This conflict arose when Nebuchadnezzar required his satraps, judges, magistrates, governors, and counselors to bow down to a statue and confess their loyalty to Nebuchadnezzar and his god (3:2–7).[18] The socially ac-

---

16. R. Perkins, *Looking Both Ways: Exploring the Interface Between Christianity and Sociology* (Grand Rapids: Baker, 1987), 58–59, sees the unmasking of false views of reality as a sociological task, but Daniel also debunked their social claims as wise men to the king by undermining their theological claims to knowledge.

17. J. Goldingay, *Daniel* in *WBC* 30 (Dallas: Word Books, 1989), 60, does not think that Daniel interpreted the rock messianically but recognizes that later New Testament writers connected the rock in this and other passages to Jesus. See also E. F. Siegman, "The Stone Hewn from the Mountain (Daniel 2)," *CBQ* 18 (1956), 364–79.

18. W. H. Shea, "Daniel 3: Extra-Biblical Texts and the Convocation on the Plain of Dura," *AUSS* 20 (1982), 29–52, relates this event to a political revolt against Nebuchadnezzar in 594/593 B.C. This is possible, but this commitment was a politico-religious loyalty that involved worship of the king's god, possibly Bel as Goldingay, *Daniel* in *WBC* 30, 70, suggests.

cepted Jewish beliefs of Shadrach, Meshach, and Abed-nego forbid this deviant behavior. These men stubbornly maintained their Jewish belief system,[19] for God could even deliver them from death. Nebuchadnezzar angrily threw them into a extremely hot furnace, but an angelic being delivered them from the flames (3:25–27). This miraculous deliverance legitimated the men's claims about God and persuaded the king to internalize part of their view of God (3:28–30).

This story encouraged the Jewish readers in exile to maintain their loyalty to God and not bow to social pressures to worship other gods. God is able to deliver those who trust Him.

Some years later King Nebuchadnezzar had a dream about a great tree and learned how *God humbled and raised up kings* (4:1–37). Again the wise men and diviners could not, or would not, interpret the dream. Daniel (or Belshazzar) told the king that he was the tree that everything gathered around. In the future God would remove him from the throne, and he would behave like an animal until he recognized that the Most High God rules over all mankind (4:17, 25). Nebuchadnezzar was a proud and powerful earthly king who did whatever he wished, so it was difficult to internalize this foreign perspective. Everyone else treated the king like a glorious absolute monarch, so Daniel was the only support group for this new kind of kingship (4:27). Eventually the dream was fulfilled: the king acted like an animal and then was restored when he gave glory to God (4:28–34).[20]

These events led to proclamations of praise to Daniel's God that were read in all the provinces of Babylon (4:1–3, 34—37). The conversion of a Babylonian king to a Jewish worldview was an event that must have encouraged the exiles to believe God. Over twenty years later on the evening that the Persian troops captured Babylon (539 B.C.), a mysterious

19. Berger, *Social Construction*, 92–97, would call this belief system their symbolic universe. It justified behavior and integrated the parts of their orderly world of meaning.

20. Collins, *Daniel* in *FOTL* 20, 62, and Lacoque, *Book of Daniel*, 74–75, think that the Qumran "Prayer of Nabonidus" was the background for things attributed to Nebuchadnezzar, but Baldwin, *Daniel* in *TOTC* 21, 116–18, gives good reasons to reject this view.

hand wrote on the wall that *God weighed and will divide Babylon* (5:1–31). This happened at Belshazzar's feasts when he defiled the gold vessels from Jerusalem's temple by drinking wine from them (5:2, 23).[21] The Chaldean wise men could not interpret the writing, so Daniel interpreted the message. His interpretation was legitimated by his past insight, ability to interpret other dreams, his godly spirit, and the recommendation of the queen mother (5:10–16).[22] To persuade the king of the seriousness of the message, Daniel drew on the experience of Belshazzar's great-grandfather who was judged for his pride (5:18–21). Belshazzar's proud defilement of God's temple vessels did not glorify God, so God numbered the days of his kingdom (*MENE*), weighed it in his balance and found it lacking (*TEKEL*), and will divide it up and give it to the Medes and Persians (*PERES*). This happened that very night (5:25–30).[23]

In the Persian period a plot against Daniel demonstrated that *God will deliver the one who trusts Him* (6:1–28).[24] A conflict arose because other political officials were jealous of Daniel's political wisdom and the king's plan to give Daniel greater authority (6:3). These officials could not find any corruption or fault in Daniel's political behavior, so they decided to attack Daniel's commitment to pattern his life after God's law. These officials tricked the king into enacting an unchangeable law that made it illegal for people to pray to anyone except the king (6:7). In contrast to this law, the religious beliefs in Daniel's cultural group allowed people to pray only to God. These were a higher legitimator of behavior than the king's secular law, so Daniel did not change his usual practice of openly praying in his private home. Soon

21. See Shea, "Nabonidus, Belshazzar, and Daniel," *AUSS* 20, 133–49, for a discussion of the historical problems surrounding these two kings and the end of the Babylonian Empire.

22. Berger, *Social Construction,* 119, refers to the importance of experts to strengthen the legitimacy of a group's social view of reality.

23. Goldingay, *Daniel* in *WBC* 30, 107, summarizes several ANE documents that comment on circumstances surrounding the fall of Babylon.

24. J. H. Whitcomb, *Darius the Mede* (Grand Rapids: Eerdmans, 1959), summarizes attempts to identify Darius the Mede with a general, the Babylonian governor, or Cyrus himself.

he was condemned to death in a lion's den, for the Persian culture did not allow the king to change even a bad law (6:16–17). The king externalized the belief that Daniel's God could deliver him,[25] and in the morning he found Daniel alive, protected by an angel from God (6:22). This experience caused the king to internalize Daniel's view of God and destroy those who falsely accused Daniel.

This story strengthened the exile reader's faith in God's deliverance in times of persecution. It legitimated a policy of uncompromising commitment to God's law in a hostile culture. Daniel's experience exemplified the rewards of honest work and showed that a political role did not have to destroy one's faith.

II. God Rules over His People in Evil Times 7:1—12:13

Daniel's visions in the second half of the book were not insights related to a conflict with a king as in 1—6. They were private revelations that Daniel wrote to warn his fellow Jews. In the future, foreign kings will persecute God's people, but they must stand firm in their commitment to follow God.

The first vision has some similarities with Nebuchadnezzar's dream in chapter 2, but this vision emphasized that *the kingdom will come after persecution* (7:1–28). In this vision Daniel's view of the eschatological day of the Lord was transformed. He knew that four other nations would come and that God would judge the nations and set up His kingdom (see 2:36–45), but this vision changed his understanding of the final earthly kingdom and the coming of God's kingdom.

The proud boasts and destructive nature of the fourth kingdom, along with the little horn that grew out of it disturbed Daniel. The horn waged war against the saints of God (like Daniel was persecuted) until the Ancient of Days destroyed the horn and gave the kingdom to the saints (7:7–8,

---

25. This externalization was the creation of a new meaning that was not part of the king's Persian culture, an idea that Daniel may have planted by telling the king about God's deliverance of His people in the past.

19–22). This king (the horn) will verbally attack God, crush the saints,[26] and change laws for three-and-a-half years.

Later the Ancient of Days, the eternal and holy God, who sits on His throne surrounded by thousands of worshipers, will destroy the beast and horn (see theophany traditions in Ps. 50:32; 97:1–5; Isa. 6; Ezek. 1). Then the Ancient of Days will give dominion over His kingdom to the Son of Man who comes from heaven. This person is not a personification of the saints, but a ruler of the world, the Messiah (Ps. 2; Jer. 23:1–8; Ezek. 37:24–28).[27]

A similar vision of *persecution by the little horn* (8:1–27) came a few years later. Two animals, symbolizing Media-Persia and Greece, preceded the appearance of a small horn. This horn attacked the beautiful land of Palestine and the hosts of heaven, claimed to be equal with God, and stopped regular sacrificing at the temple for over three-and-a-half years. These little horns in 7 and 8 acted in similar ways, but some identify the horn in 8 with the blasphemous Greek ruler Antiochus Epiphanes who desecrated the temple in the Intertestamental Period around 165 B.C.[28]

These two similar visions were a warning to Daniel's readers to be prepared for greater persecution in the future. They also engendered hope in God's sovereign power over

---

26. G. F. Hasel, "The Identity of 'The Saints of the Most High' in Daniel 7," *Bib* 56 (1975), 173–92, thoroughly examines the thesis of M. Noth that the saints were angelic beings and demonstrates that these were humans not angels. Lacoque, *Daniel,* 126–27, accepts this conclusion, but J. Collins, *The Apocalyptic Vision of the Book of Daniel* (Missoula: Scholars Press, 1977), 123–47, concludes that the term referred to angels.

27. Lacoque, *Daniel,* 146, concludes this figure was "the perfect image of the righteous individual." Although the kingdom was given to the saints in 7:27, some see this Son of Man as a collective symbol of the saints. Baldwin, *Daniel* in *TOTC 21,* 147–54, demonstrates that this figure has messianic roles. See G. R. Beasley-Murray, "The Interpretation of Daniel 7," *CB 2* 45 (1983), 44–58. In the NT Jesus is identified as the Son of Man (John 8:28, 53; 9:36; 12:36).

28. Baldwin, *Daniel* in *TOTC* 21, 162; E. J. Young, *The Prophecy of Daniel* (Grand Rapids: Eerdmans, 1949), 276; and Wood, *Daniel,* 215, distinguish between the two little horns.

any kings who might oppose God, His people, or the religious laws of God.

Before Daniel explained other visions about this future persecution, he inserted a prayer he made in the first year of Cyrus's reign, before his decree to allow the exiles to return to Jerusalem. Daniel *prayed about the end of the seventy years* (9:1–27) of exile in Jeremiah's prophecy, for this period of time was almost complete (Jer. 29:10). He knew from texts like Leviticus 26:34–45 that God would restore His people to their land only when the people confessed their sins. Therefore, Daniel fasted and prayed a communal prayer of confession.

The angel Gabriel reapplied the seventy years of exile to seventy future weeks of years. In these weeks God will remove all sin, bring an end to sin, and fulfill all prophecies (9:24; soteriological and eschatological). Initially Jerusalem will be rebuilt, and an anointed (messianic) leader will arise; but then Jerusalem and the temple will be destroyed, and the anointed leader will be killed (9:25–26). In the final week a covenant with the Jews will be broken. Sacrificing in the temple will stop when an abominable thing is put in the temple, but in the end the person that causes all this persecution will be defeated (9:27). Some Bible students hypothesize a fulfillment in the Maccabean era (165 B.C.). Others look to the time of Jesus' death, but still others contend that the final week referred to eschatological events.[29]

Daniel's final visions in the third year of Cyrus expanded on earlier themes of *war and persecution before the end* (10:1—12:13). Daniel received another angelic vision assuring him that his prayers were answered but that the angel was delayed because of a continuing battle with angelic powers from Persia and Greece (10:10–21).[30] The vision was a de-

---

29. See the discussions in Goldingay, *Daniel* in *WBC* 30, 257–63; Baldwin, *Daniel* in *TOTC* 21, 167–77; Wood, *Daniel,* 243–63. Matt. 24:15 placed Daniel's abomination (9:27) in the future and connected it to end time events.

30. Collins, *Apocalyptic Vision,* 108–18, thinks these angelic beings were a sign of the mythical system that the Hebrew borrowed from their neighbors, but Goldingay, *Daniel* in *WBC 30,* 284–85, finds numerous verbal connections between this passage and other prophetic and hymnic texts.

tailed account of future wars by northern and southern kings against each other and the people in Judah, the Beautiful Land (11:1–45). At the end of this time a proud king who opposes God desecrates the temple with an abominable idol, stops sacrifices, and changes temple laws (11:31–39) will be defeated. This persecution will bring death to some, but the wise people who understand what Daniel wrote will explain what this all means to others and lead many to follow God's righteous ways (11:33; 12:3).

Some of this vision was beyond Daniel's understanding and was sealed up until the end of time (12:4, 8–9). In spite of all the terrible persecution that will take place in these final days, the wise person (like Daniel) will persevere knowing that God will raise the righteous to everlasting life and the wicked to everlasting disgrace (12:1–2).[31]

Theological and Social Implications

God's people who live in a pagan cultural setting will inevitably be faced with conflicts between the dominant socially developed culture and their own religious beliefs and practices. These conflicts may relate to what one eats or drinks, how a person acts in a political context, how one advises a superior with humility and honesty, or a person's regular practice of religious patterns of behavior.

When persecution, ridicule, or intimidation comes, it raises many questions. What shall I do? Is this really wrong to bend on this issue? Am I really responsible if I am just following orders? What is insubordination going to cost me? Will God protect me and provide another job if I stand up for what is right and I end up losing my job? Who controls what happens to me—others, myself, or God?

Daniel and God's messengers today can encourage those who struggle with ethical and faith decisions. When

---

31. Goldingay, *Daniel* in *WBC 30*, 306, thinks this was "a flight of the imagination, not a 'fully developed' belief in resurrection," but there seems no reason to deny a belief in the resurrection in this passage. See Baldwin, *Daniel* in *TOTC* 21, 203–5.

their beliefs and practice conflicts with demands in their social setting, they need not submit to social pressures to perform unacceptable practices. God is in control of their situation. He rules over all people and nations. He can deliver those who trust Him. Although God will not remove all source of threat and will even allow some believers to die for their faith, He will not forget them, but will raise them up to everlasting life.

Questions for Discussion

1. Why would God reveal His will to an unbeliever like Nebuchadnezzar?
2. Contrast the worldviews within chapters 3—6.
3. How did the climax in the last few verses of chapters 1—7 support Daniel's main theological theme?
4. How should a person respond to the threat of persecution?

Chapter 16

Haggai: What Are Your Priorities?

Introduction

The process of making decisions involves choosing one option instead of another, making one thing more important than anything else. When people go for a walk rather than get some work done, they have a priority of relaxing or exercising. After working for four hours, they may need a change of pace so that they will be more effective when they get back to work.

A priority is done first; it is the most urgent, the most critical basis for success. A priority is a necessity that cannot be ignored. It may bring hardship, but a priority is the driving force that controls thinking and action. Nearly impossible goals can be reached if they are given top priority.

Unfortunately, many people just respond to the immediate demands around them and do not analyze what is controlling their behavior. The prophet Haggai challenged people to think about key priorities, particularly their spiritual priorities. God's messengers today can also challenge people to think about how they juggle the earthly responsibilities of earning a living with the heavenly priorities of serving God.

Social Setting

The Historical Context

The prophet Haggai (and Zechariah) spoke to people in Jerusalem during the post-exilic Persian era, in the second year of Darius's reign (520 B.C.). Years earlier the Persian king Cyrus allowed the Jews to return to Jerusalem (539 B.C.),[1] but only about fifty thousand made the long trip back from Babylon (Ezra 1—2). They tried to rebuild the temple under the leadership of the high priest Joshua and the governor Zerubbabel, but when the Jews rejected the help of the local people in Palestine, the Persians stopped temple reconstruction (Ezra 3—4).[2]

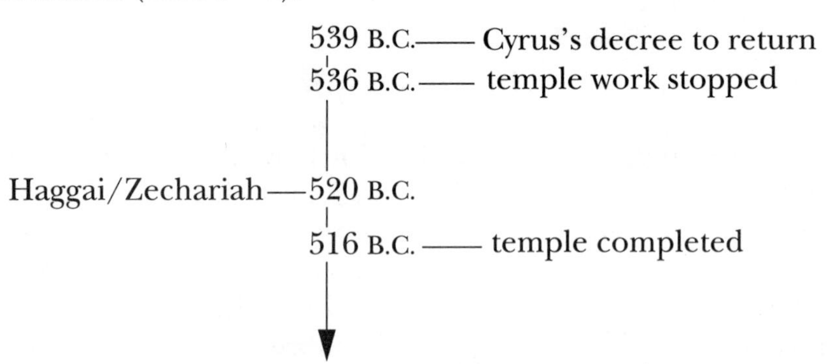

This discouraging situation continued until the second year of Darius (about 15 years) when Haggai and Zechariah encouraged the people to make temple rebuilding a priority (Ezra 5).

---

1. Archaeologists found Cyrus's general decree that allowed many exiled people in Babylon to return to their countries (see J. B. Pritchard, ed., "The Cyrus Cylinder," *ANET,* 316). The specific decree concerning the building of the temple in Jerusalem is found in Ezra 6:1–5.

2. D. L. Petersen, *Haggai and Zechariah 1—8* in *OTL* (Philadelphia: Westminster, 1984), 19–27, has an extensive discussion of the historical context of this time. See also E. M. Yamauchi, *Persia and the Bible* (Grand Rapids: Baker Book House, 1990).

The Behistun Inscription shown above records the political situation under Darius I of Persia (see Hag. 1:1; Zech. 1:7).

The Structure of Social Order

Social interaction in Jerusalem was ordered by the Persians, by the socioeconomic difficulty of living in a land that was in ruins, and by the religious traditions the people inherited from their forefathers. The people in Jerusalem found themselves within the sympathetic and benevolent Persian Empire. It allowed cultural and religious freedom, provided financial support, and gave legal authority for the rebuilding of the temple in Jerusalem (Ezra 1, 6). Jerusalem was in the satrapy/province of "Beyond the River" (west of the Euphrates) ruled by Tattenai, a governor who collected taxes and administered local policies. He seemed to oppose the rebuilding of the temple in Jerusalem (Ezra 5:3). The local Jewish governor Zerubbabel was probably newly appointed by Darius. He lacked initiative and confidence as a leader and was not anxious to challenge his superiors concerning rebuilding the temple. The older men in the community were major opinion-shapers (2:3), but the priests and the prophets (Haggai and Zechariah) were also highly respected (1:12; 2:10–14).

Daily life in Jerusalem was difficult because the city did not have a secure wall or a strong police force. Fields were overgrown with many years of disuse; roads, houses, and wells needed repairing. There were relatively few Jews to do all this rebuilding, and the newcomers were not welcomed by those who lived in the area before the exiles arrived in Jerusalem.[3] One of the main social structures was the "father's household" (Ezra 2:59; 8:1). Social groups in Judah included the people of the land (Ezra 9:1), priests, Levites, princes (9:1), and the sons of Solomon's slaves (2:55).[4] Mak-

3. On the nature of this struggle, see articles by K. Hoglund "The Achaemenid Context," and D. L. Smith, "The Politics of Ezra: Sociological Indicators of *Postexilic* Judean Society," *Second Temple Studies 1. Persian Period* (Sheffield: JSOT, 1991), 54–97.

4. Petersen, *Haggai and Zechariah 1—8* in *OTL*, 30–31, summarizes studies of the economic situation and the social organization of people into "father's households" which existed in parts of the Persian Empire. See J. Weinberg, *The Citizen-Temple Community* (Sheffield: JSOT, 1992) for a detailed demographic and linguistic study of the social setting in the post-exilic era. J. Blenkinsopp, "Temple and Society in Achaemenid Judah," *Second Temple Studies 1. Persian Period* (Sheffield: JSOT, 1991), 22–53, questions and confirms some of Weinberg's conclusions.

ing a living was not easy, although some had quite nice homes (1:4). Agricultural life was made worse by a drought that reduced the harvest (1:10; 2:17).

The people's sense of religious order was connected to the temple area and the priests who officiated at the altar (1:2; 2:10–14). Evidence for the "citizen-temple community" that Weinberg proposes was weak in Haggai's time, but it strengthened after the temple was built. The people were aware of earlier traditions about the Exodus (2:5) and had expectations about what God would do when they returned to Jerusalem (Isa. 40—66). Their original spiritual priorities of worshiping God in the rebuilt temple soon took second place when political pressures and economic struggles reduced their hopes of success.

The Social Location and Role of the Prophet

Haggai functioned in the role of prophet (1:1, 3, 12; 2:2, 10) or messenger of the Lord (1:13). Beuken's idea that Haggai was a Judean farmer who never went into exile is questionable,[5] although Ezra's list of those who returned from exile did not include his name. On the other hand, the view that he was an older man who returned with the Babylonian exiles is not proved simply because he understood the complaints of the old men who saw the temple before it was destroyed (2:3).[6] Blenkinsopp concludes that Haggai was a cultic prophet, and Hanson believes Haggai and Zechariah were prophetic supporters of the Zadokite priests' restoration program; but these ideas hypothesize far more than the text supports.[7] Haggai was a central prophet who did not try

---

5. W. Beuken, *Haggai-Sacharja 1—8* (Assen: Van Gorcum, 1967), 221–29. H. W. Wolff, *Haggai: A Commentary* in CC (Minneapolis: Augsburg, 1988), 17, agrees with this conclusion.

6. J. Baldwin, *Haggai, Zechariah, Malachi* in *TOTC* (Downers Grove: InterVarsity, 1972), 28.

7. J. Blenkinsopp, *A History of Prophecy in Israel* (Philadelphia: Westminster, 1984), 232; P. Hanson, *The People Called: The Growth of the Community* (San Francisco: Harper, 1986), 257–62. P. R. Ackroyd, "Apocalyptic in Its Social Setting," *Int* 30 (1976), 413–21, rejects many of Hanson's views. Wolff, *Haggai* in *CC*, 17, does not think Haggai was a cultic prophet. Recently, D. S. A. Clines, "Haggai's Temple, Constructed, Deconstructed, and Reconstructed," *SSOT* (1993), 51–77, discusses the social reality behind the text.

to oust the leaders in Jerusalem, but challenged them to act boldly.[8] His rhetorical skills in preaching effectively augmented the Spirit's work in his audience's hearts (1:14). He asked questions, emphasized themes by repetition, quoted earlier authoritative traditions, and used a dialogical illustration at one point (2:10–12). He understood his audience's worldview and provided persuasive arguments to legitimate some new priorities.

Social Interaction

The Book of Haggai

Issues related to the composition of Haggai center around the relationship of the editorial dating of each sermon and a few verses in some sermons.[9] Some relocated 2:15–19 to chapter 1 and put 1:15b as part of the introductory formula for chapter 2.[10] Each sermon was marked by its date.

I. The Priority of Building the Temple 1:1—2:9
   A. Should you build your house or God's house? 1:1–15
   B. Should you build an inferior temple? 2:1–9
II. The Priority of Holiness 2:10–19
III. The Priority of the Davidic Hope 2:20–23

These sermons show how Haggai addressed the weaknesses within the worldview of the struggling community in Jerusalem. By legitimating new priorities, he motivated them

8. R. R. Wilson, *Prophecy and Society in Ancient Israel* (Philadelphia: Fortress, 1980), 288, thinks Haggai was a central prophet, but not a priest or cultic prophet.

9. Beuken, *Haggai-Zecharja 1—8*, 231–32, argues for a Chronistic editor who added the dates, because there are common themes in Haggai and Chronicles, but R. Mason, "The Purpose of the 'Editorial Framework' of the Book of Haggai," *VT* 27 (1977), 413–21, sees a connection between Haggai and Deuteronomic themes.

10. See P. R. Ackroyd, "Some Interpretive Glosses in the Book of Haggai," *JJS* 7 (1956), 163–67.

to action that solidified the community's religious and social identity, strengthened leadership, and glorified God.

I. The Priority of Building the Temple 1:1—2:9

During the second year of the Persian King Darius I: Hystaspis (522–486 B.C.), Haggai addressed the Jewish leaders and the laypeople who interrupted their grape and fig harvest to celebrate the new moon festival at the temple (the first of the month; see Num. 28:11).[11] Haggai knew there was social pressure not to rebuild the temple at this time (1:2). Rebuilding did not make sense because national and provincial officials were against it (Ezra 4:4–5), and the people did not have the money to finance the rebuilding because of droughts (1:10). The prophet boldly asked his audience: *Should you build your house or God's house* (1:1–15)? Since the poor people were not paneling their homes with cedar wood, this biting question about their decorated homes and God's desolate house confronted the priorities of the wealthier leaders, including Zerubbabel and Joshua.[12] Haggai externalized a perspective on the nation's situation that was deviant from the common view of Judah's leaders.[13] It was wrong to conclude that the drought and financial struggles were a reason not to rebuild the temple. They were the reason why they should rebuild. If they did not rebuild, God would curse their crops because of misplaced priorities (1:9–11; see the covenant traditions in Lev. 26:26; Deut. 28:22–24,

---

11. Baldwin, *Haggai, Zechariah, Malachi,* 37, saw this as the setting. C. L. Meyers and E. M. Meyers, *Haggai, Zechariah 1—8* in *AB* 25B (New York: Doubleday, 1987), 6, 20, concludes that these sermons were dated for the theological purpose of linking them with the end of Jeremiah's seventy years and encouraging the people to build the temple by that time.

12. Baldwin, *Haggai, Zechariah, Malachi,* 40, and Meyers, *Haggai, Zechariah 1—8,* in *AB* 25, 23, focus on the roofing of the people's homes, but E. Achtemeier, *Nahum-Malachi* in *IntCom* (Atlanta: John Knox, 1986), 98, and P. R. Ackroyd, *Exile and Restoration* in *OTL* (Philadelphia: Westminster, 1968), 155, stress the ornamentation of the wealthy homes.

13. Berger, *Social Construction,* 52, 104, sees externalization as the human projection of new meanings concerning reality, not just a restatement of widely held social perspectives.

38–40). Haggai's solution was to set a new priority: to please and glorify God by rebuilding the temple (1:8).[14]

The social leaders, Zerubbabel and Joshua, and the rest of the people feared God and internalized what God said through Haggai (1:12–15).[15] Haggai was careful not to suggest that his skillful rhetoric persuaded the people. God deeply stirred their hearts, transformed their wills, and promised that His abiding presence would help overcome the people's fear.

A month later, after the people finished celebrating the Day of Atonement and the Feast of Booths in Jerusalem (see Lev. 23:3–36), it was time to continue work on the temple (2:1). Haggai again challenged the community leaders, Zerubbabel and Joshua, and the rest of the people to work. This was necessary because some of the older people were comparing Solomon's temple with the new one and were asking: *Should you build an inferior temple* (2:1–9)? By comparing the smaller size of the overall complex, the chipped stones, and the lack of gold, the people felt this structure was an embarrassment. The first meager results were far from their high and unrealistic expectations. It was such an artistic disappointment that the people wanted to quit. If they could not build it right, they should not do it at all.

The prophet's sermon acknowledged this sentiment among his audience and called the people to work because God would bring great glory to this temple (2:4–9). Zerubbabel and Joshua must face this task with courage and provide a plausibility base for thinking the temple can and should be built (like Joshua in Josh. 1:6), then the rest of the people will courageously follow.[16]

---

14. The *niphal of qbd* does not refer to God's glory coming to the temple. See Petersen, *Haggai and Zechariah 1—8* in *OTL*, 51. For the opposite position, see P. A. Verhoef, *The Books of Haggai and Malachi* in *NICOT* (Grand Rapids: Eerdmans, 1987), 67.

15. Berger, *Social Construction*, 129, sees internalization as the process of accepting another person's subjective meaning of reality as your own.

16. Ibid., 154. Berger believes if some humans think an idea or action is plausible and makes sense, others will accept it and not think it is crazy.

Their acts of courage will make sense if they transform their perspective and accept God's promises and vision for the temple. God will be with them. His Spirit that helped the people when they came out of Egypt (Ex. 29:45) was still available to protect them. God will shake up the political forces that might oppose them. He will provide much gold from other nations to beautify the temple (see the fulfillment in Ezra 6) and fill this temple with glory and peace. Apparently the people responded and internalized a new view of the temple, for Ezra recorded that the temple was completed a few years later (Ezra 6:15).

II. The Priority of Holiness 2:10–19

Two months later, Haggai delivered a message to the whole community (not the Samaritans,[17]) without any reference to its leaders. His sermon began with an illustration on how the people socially constructed their view of purity and uncleanness (2:10–12). The priests, who taught the law and gave authoritative interpretations on holiness (see Lev. 10:10; Mal. 2:5–7), confirmed that an object does not become holy just by touching something holy (Lev. 6:27). However, ritual uncleanness was passed on by contact with something unclean (Lev. 11:28). These illustrations related to Haggai's audience. They thought that contact with the temple would make them holy, but that was not true. They concluded that their sin would not make them unholy, but it did. Apparently the people repented,[18] for in 2:15–19 Haggai predicted there would be a tremendous change in agri-

---

17. Although Baldwin, *Haggai, Zechariah, Malachi* in *TOTC*, 51, thinks it did refer to the Samaritans, the arguments against this position are more persuasive. See Petersen, *Haggai and Zechariah 1—8* in *OTL*, 80–81, or Verhoef, *Haggai and Malachi* in *NICOT*, 112–13.

18. Commentators deal with 2:15–19 in very different ways: Ackroyd, *Exile and Restoration* in *OTL*, 159, relocated 2:15–19 after 1:12–15 because the change of heart assumed in 2:15–19 is described in 1:12–15. In contrast, Petersen, *Haggai and Zechariah 1—8* in *OTL*, 89, suggested that these verses reflected the ceremony of laying the foundation stone for the temple (note the reference to the stone, this day and the founding of the temple in 2:15–18).

cultural production. Before they received little, but now God would bless them with much.

III. The Priority of the Davidic Hope 2:20–23

Haggai's last sermon was a word of encouragement to Zerubbabel. As the new governor of Judah, he was not able to fulfill his political role because he had minimal financial resources, no army to protect his people, and little ability to meet aggressively the expectations of the people. In language similar to 2:6–7, Haggai encouraged the governor to reevaluate his identity and role,[19] for God would use His power to shake up the political powers that controlled the world. Zerubbabel's identity should be based on his function in God's eyes, not his peers or critics. He was God's chosen servant, and God would put His signet ring on his finger. He was in the line of David, the grandson of Jehoiachin, so his return to power marked a new era in Judah's history. When God destroyed Judah, He took His signet ring from the Davidic King Jehoiakim (Jer. 22:24), but now God was returning His sign of approval to Zerubbabel. He was the legitimate heir to David's throne, and God would work to bring about His plans through him.

Theological and Sociological Implications

In the midst of the pressures for time, energy, and commitment, it is easy to lose sight of what is most important. The urgent gets done, but the important waits. When priorities get out of line, loved ones are taken for granted, spiritual responsibilities are ignored, and excuses are multiplied. People who desire to be God's people cannot put their wishes and comforts above God's glory (1:1–11) or negative comparisons above God's glorious plans (2:1–9). They cannot allow good religious activity to replace true holiness (2:10–15) or allow negative thoughts about their abilities or role to

19. Berger, *Social Construction,* 100, 173, describes how a person's identity is formed on the basis of social interaction and fulfilling set roles.

cloud how God can use His chosen servants (2:20–23). These social evaluations by others and ourselves can lead to misplaced priorities, bad theology, no action, and no confidence. When this happens, God's leaders will not act courageously, His work will not be done, and God will not be pleased or glorified.

Questions for Discussion

1. How might the priorities addressed in Haggai relate to strengths or weaknesses in the church today?
2. Contrast the leadership of the prophet Haggai with the leadership of Joshua and Zerubbabel.
3. What are some of the keys of Haggai's success in persuading the people to transform their priorities?

Chapter 17

Zechariah: What Are God's Purposes?

Introduction

People often wonder why things happen the way they do. Why did I lose my job? Why did a friend get cancer? Is there a purpose behind what happens, or is it all bad luck? Does God have a plan for what happens?

The prophet Zechariah, and God's messengers today, have the task of understanding God's action in the past, helping people discover God's purpose and direction today, and discerning God's plans for the future (1:6; 8:13–15). This responsibility involves giving words of warning, advice, and encouragement. No one can fully know the mind of God or begin to understand all His purposes, but on some issues His plans are known. When His purposes are understood, God's vision of the present and the future brings strength, as well as humble submission.

Social Setting

The Historical Context

The prophet Zechariah (and Haggai) spoke to the people in Jerusalem in the post-exilic Persian period, in Darius's second (1—6) and fourth (7—8) years (520–518 B.C.). Earlier the Persian King Cyrus allowed the exiles to return to Jerusalem (539 B.C.), but the people could not rebuild the temple because of local opposition (Ezra 1—4). No progress was made until Darius's second year (520 B.C.) when Haggai convinced the people to rebuild the temple.

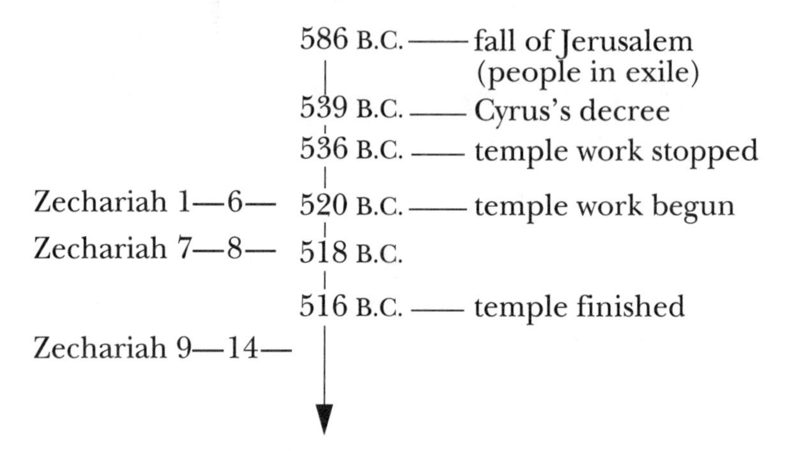

The undated prophecies in 9—14 are not set in a specific historical context. Some Bible students think they presume the conquest of Alexander the Great in 330 B.C. or the Maccabean period around 165 B.C. because of events described in 9:1–10, but it is possible to imply a date between 500–480 B.C.[1] These oracles have no direct references to the

1. R. K. Harrison, *Introduction to the Old Testament* (Grand Rapids: Eerdmans, 1969), 949–57, surveys the various theories on dating portions of Zechariah. P. Hanson, *The Dawn of Apocalyptic* (Philadelphia: Fortress, 1975), 27, 400, argues for a date between 550 and 475 B.C. The most extensive review of this period is found in C. L. Meyers and E. M. Meyers, *Zechariah 9—14* in *AB* 25C (Garden City: Doubleday, 1993), 18–28. A. E. Hill, "Dating Second Zechariah," *HAR* 6 (1982), 105–32, gives extensive linguistic evidence for a date around 500–475 B.C.

audience's setting, so it is best to focus on their general rhetorical function. They gave encouragement to a struggling people confused about God's purposes. God's plan was to defeat Judah's enemies, have compassion on His people, and establish His kingdom.

The Structure of Social Order

The international disorder associated with the Persian conquest of Egypt, the death of the Persian king Cambyses, and the later rise of the Greeks affected the way political superiors treated Judean authorities. Jewish life was caught between King Cyrus, who allowed the Jews to build the temple in 539 B.C. (but later rescinded permission) and the satrap over the "Province beyond the River" who distrusted any signs of Jewish nationalism (Ezra 4:3–5). This undermined the leadership of Judah's political and religious leaders, Zerubbabel and Joshua. There were few ways they could influence the structure of social order, initiate new policies, or fulfill the duties their roles assumed (Zech. 3—4).

Life in Judah was also difficult because there were so few people to do the rebuilding and so much work to do. Judah had some economic diversity and social stratification of the people (princes, priests, sons of Solomon's slaves, people of the land; see Ezra 2), but most people were organized into social units called the "father's households" (Ezra 2:59; 8:1).[2] These extended families provided identity, shared economic resources, protection from external oppression, and the assurance of cultural and religious purity. The disadvantage of these close knit groups was that they could become so internally oriented that it was difficult for the larger community to initiate joint projects. There is minimal evidence of

---

2. J. Weinberg, *The Citizen-Temple Community* (Sheffield: JSOT, 1992) discusses the citizen-temple social organization. His views are critiqued by several authors in P. R. Davies, *Second Temple Studies: 1. Persian Period* (Sheffield: JSOT, 1991), but all see the father's household as the basic social unit.

the conflict between the Zadokite and Levites that Hason hypothesized.[3]

Zechariah provided some information about the people's religious worldview. Commentators have emphasized the importance of the temple, but ironically, it was not important enough for the people to get it built (Hag. 1—2:9).[4] They misunderstood the idea of holiness (Hag. 2:10–14), treated people unjustly (Zech. 5:1–4), fasted for themselves, not God (7:6), and needed to repent of their sins (1:1–6). Their spiritual leader, Joshua the high priest, lacked confidence in his role as mediator between God and mankind (3:1–10) and did not provide dynamic leadership in the temple rebuilding. In contrast, Zechariah envisioned God's purposes for Judah's enemies, her leaders, and the worshiping community (8:13–15). This plan provided the basis for a transformation of their perspectives.

The Social Location and Role of the Prophet

Some evidence suggests that the prophet (1:1, 7) was also a priest, or at least from a priestly family. He may be the Zechariah who headed the priestly household of Iddo (Neh. 12:4, 10, 16). He helped those who came to the temple area to receive advice on fasting (7:1–3), was well acquainted with the role of the high priest, and used the language of forgiveness, repentance, and uncleanness (1:3; 3:9; 5:3–11). He challenged the thinking and inaction of the leaders in Jerusalem, but he seemed to function as a central prophet.[5]

As an orator who declared God's messages, Zechariah persuasively motivated his audience to look at their present

---

3. P. Hanson, *The People Called* (San Francisco: Harper, 1986), 257–68, thinks that Haggai and Zechariah were strong supporters of the Zadokite restoration program. His views are criticized by R. Carroll, "Twilight of Prophecy or Dawn of Apocalyptic?" *JSOT* 14 (1979), 3–35.

4. J. Baldwin, *Haggai, Zechariah, Malachi* in *TOTC* (Downers Grove: InterVarsity, 1972), 18–21, discusses the theology of the temple, but fails to show that Zechariah's audience accepted this theology or acted on this perspective.

5. R. R. Wilson, *Prophet and Society in Ancient Israel* (Philadelphia: Fortress, 1980), 289.

and future in light of God's purposes. The eight highly symbolic visions in chapters 1—6 were grouped in pairs (2—3, 4—5, 6—7), with parallels developed between the first and last vision. Zechariah did not explain all the imagery in the visions, but he did understand the theological message for his audience.

The "burdens" in 9—14 repeat themes of the destruction of Judah's enemies, the nation's response to their Messiah, and the restoration of Judah in a complexly organized manner using language that has similarities with apocalyptic eschatology.[6] The prophet alluded to ideas in earlier prophets to connect the future with the past and legitimate his messages.[7]

Social Interaction

The Book of Zechariah

The dated visions in 1—8 attributed to Zechariah and the undated anonymous burdens in 9—14 treat similar themes (judgment of the nations, the Messiah, and the restoration of Judah), but each section is quite unique. On the basis of a different historical period, content, style, and theology, some scholars attribute parts of 9—14 to later authors, and a few hypothesize a pre-exilic author for 9—11. It is possible to maintain the unity of the whole book.[8] These messages were organized into three major section.[9]

I. Visions of God's Purposes for Jerusalem 1:1—6:15

---

6. See the discussion of alternate views in the survey in R. L. Smith, *Micah-Malachi* in *WBC* 32 (Waco: Word, 1984), 173–75.

7. Meyers and Meyers, *Zechariah 9—14* in *AB* 25, 35–45, provide an extensive catalog of connections with other biblical traditions.

8. Most commentators emphasized the disunity between Zechariah 1—8 and 9—14, but Baldwin, *Haggai, Zechariah, Malachi*, 78–83, in *TOTC* and P. Lamarche, *Zecharie i–xiv: Structure, Litteraire, et Messianisme* (Paris: Gabalda et Cie, 1961) suggest an early date with great unity between the two sections.

9. M. Butterworth, *Structure and the Book of Zechariah* (Sheffield: JSOT, 1992) provides an extensive discussion of various approaches to analyzing the structure of this book.

   A. Call to repentance 1:1–6
   B. Visions for Jerusalem 1:7—6:8
   C. Joshua's symbolic role 6:9–15
II. What Is the Purpose of Fasting? 7:1—8:23
III. Burdens about God's Purposes for the Future 9:1—14:21
   A. The first burden 9:1—11:17
   B. The second burden 12:1—14:21

Zechariah's social interaction with his audience persuaded Judah's leaders to reexamine God's purposes for Judah in a new light. He motivated the people to transform their ways.

I. Visions of God's Purposes for Jerusalem 1:1—6:15

Zechariah gave these sermons in the same year that Haggai encouraged the nation to rebuild the temple (520 B.C., Darius's second year). His initial sermon was a *call to repentance* (1:1–6). Zechariah legitimated a change in behavior by pointing to the failed experience of their fathers. They did not internalize prophetic calls to repent (see Jer. 25:4–5; 35:15), so many died in exile. The curses for rejecting God and His statutes were fulfilled (see Deut. 28:15). In response, Zechariah's audience repented and changed.[10]

Next, Zechariah encouraged the people with news of God's plan to change Judah's political, social, and theological situation. The eight *visions for Jerusalem* (1:7—6:8) externalized God's vision of the present and the future to counteract the gloomy popular social construction of reality

10. C. L. Meyers and E. M. Meyers, *Haggai, Zechariah 1—8* in *AB* 25B (New York: Doubleday, 1987), 96, relate this turning to the people's change in behavior concerning rebuilding the temple in Haggai 1:12–15, while D. L. Petersen, *Haggai and Zechariah 1–8* in *OTL* (Philadelphia: Westminster, 1984), 134, thinks the prophet was referring to the repentance of his audience's fathers.

among the returnees.[11] The revolts against Darius in 522–521 B.C. were now over, and there seemed no hope of escaping Persian authority. The people questioned whether God cared about them.

The first vision (1:7–17) changed the audience's view of God. The patrol that the angel of the Lord led demonstrated that God knew what was happening throughout the world. The angel's prayer for compassion on Jerusalem at the end of seventy years assured the listeners that they had a powerful advocate before God.[12] God's answer also assured them that He was determined to act vigorously. God was angry with the nations at ease and was compassionate toward Zion. His plan was to rebuild His temple and Jerusalem and to increase the number of people in the city.[13] This vision showed that God had not abandoned them as some thought.

The second (1:18–21) and third visions (2:1–13) formed a pair and expanded the first vision. How would God's anger affect the nations at ease in 1:15? The second vision illustrated how four strong nations (the horns) that defeated and scattered God's people would be defeated (by the craftsmen). The people also wanted to know more about God's compassion on Jerusalem. The third vision (2:1–13) projected a greatly expanded rebuilt city with an enormous number of people.[14] God's glory will be in Jerusalem and He will protect them from danger. Jews and Gentiles will recog-

---

11. P. Berger and T. Luckmann, *The Social Construction of Reality* (Garden City: Doubleday, 1966), 104, refer to the human process of giving meaning to reality and creating a worldview. Most worldviews come from social contacts with others in that culture, but it is possible to give new meanings (externalizations) that are not determined by one's social setting.

12. Smith, *Micah-Malachi* in *WBC* 32, 191, surveys different interpretations of the seventy years. Here the number must refer to the years between the destruction and building of the temple.

13. Baldwin, *Haggai, Zechariah, Malachi* in *TOTC*, 101–3, emphasizes the covenantal nature of God's action.

14. Petersen, *Haggai and Zechariah 1—8* in *OTL*, 168–72, demonstrates a number of connections between Zechariah's vision and Ezekiel 40—48. In Zechariah's vision, the city was bigger than in Ezekiel.

nize the One sent by God against the nations.[15] Together they will joyfully worship God.

The next pair of visions challenged Joshua the high priest (3:1–10) and Zerubbabel the governor (4:1–14) to reevaluate their own self-identity. The vision of the cleansing of Joshua before God's throne assured the high priest that God had forgiven his sins and made him an acceptable high priest (3:1–6). He needed to reject any societal role limitations[16] and to accept God's identification of him as a forgiven priest. He could function as an intercessor before God. As he fulfilled this role, God would fulfill His promises. God would one day bring the Messiah the Branch, watch over the temple stones, cleanse the nation, and bring prosperity to all (3:8–10).[17] Joshua was not an insignificant figure in God's plan.

The complementing vision in 4:1–13 pictured a candlestick drawing oil from two olive trees. It symbolized how the community was relying on Joshua and Zerubbabel's leadership. This vision challenged Zerubbabel the governor to depend on God's Spirit for strength to lay the top stone of the temple. Zerubbabel must internalize the belief that God can make this mountainous problem into a molehill, that God's eyes were watching over everything, that God did not despise small beginnings. Many Jews, and Zerubbabel himself, may have doubted whether it was possible to finish the temple, or questioned the value of such a small temple (see (Hag. 2:3); but God's purpose was to see Zerubbabel finish it.

The last pair of visions (5:1–4, 5–11) confronted the sinful people in Judah with God's plan to remove evil (sins against God and sins against others) from the land.[18] The

15. Zech. 2:8, 9, 11, refer to this person as "me," but it seems unlikely that this could be the prophet Zechariah as some commentators suggest. Could it be the angel of the Lord?

16. Berger, *Social Construction*, 130–34, describes how social roles and identity are prescribed during socialization.

17. For the numerous different ways of interpreting 3:8–10, see Meyers, *Haggai, Zechariah 1—8* in *AB* 25B, 198–213.

18. Not the whole earth, as suggested by Petersen, *Haggai and Zechariah 1—8* in *OTL*, 249.

covenant curses written on the flying scroll will come upon the evil and destroy them (see Deut. 28). The next vision pictured the removal of evil to Babylon to purify the land (5:5–11).

The series of visions ended with a message that paralleled the first vision (compare 6:1–8 and 1:7–17). Zechariah assured his audiences that all these purposes could be realized, because God's forces controlled all nations, especially Judah's enemies.

A final message explained how *Joshua's symbolic role* (6:9–15) was related to the nation's future. Zechariah and some returnees from Babylon made an elaborate crown and symbolically put it on Joshua, the high priest. This ceremony and the crown reminded the people of their hope that the Davidic Messiah (the Branch) would some day be crowned king and function as priest (see traditions in Ps. 110:4).[19] All this would take place if the people conform to God's will for their lives (6:15).

II. What Is the Purpose of Fasting? 7:1—8:23

Two years later two men from Bethel asked Zechariah if the people should continue to fast and commemorate the burning of Jerusalem and the temple (7:1–3; see 2 Kings 25:8). Since the new temple was about half rebuilt, some thought the fasts should end.

Zechariah questioned whether their fasts were for God's benefit or their own.[20] Were they maintaining these institutionalized rituals to feel sorry for themselves or to humble themselves before God? Did they remember that God asked their forefathers to practice justice and stop oppressing the weak (see Jer. 7:5–6; 22:3)? Did they think about why God de-

---

19. E. Achtemeier, *Nahum-Malachi* in *IntCom* (Atlanta: John Knox, 1986), 130–32, has a messianic interpretation fulfilled in Jesus. There is little reason to follow Petersen, *Haggai and Zechariah 1—8* in *OTL*, 276, who concludes Zerubbabel, not Joshua, was crowned.

20. Smith, *Micah-Malachi* in *WBC* 32, 225, concludes that 7:7–10 was Zechariah's quotation of earlier prophets, but other commentators also see 7:5–6 as part of what earlier prophets said.

stroyed the city? It was because they would not listen to God's instructions concerning proper social behavior (7:8–14).

If the people would learn these lessons from their fasting, there was hope for the future. God intensely wanted to transform Zion. He wanted to return to His holy mountain, to establish Zion as a city of truth (8:1–3; see 1:14, 16). The prophet's symbolic universe included a future utopian kingdom full of children, old men, and many people returned from exile.[21] The social situation of Zechariah's audience was very different from this, but they must not doubt God's promises. The prophet persuaded his listeners to see the future with faith and courage (8:9, 13, 16) as they did two years earlier when they began to rebuild the temple (Hag. 1). If they transform their lives and avoid behavior that God hates, God's purposes for Jerusalem will happen (8:14–17). Their fasts will be turned to feasts of gladness, and many foreigners will come to worship the God of Israel (8:19–23).[22]

III. Burdens about God's Purposes for the Future 9:1—14:21

In two burdensome messages, Zechariah developed a new perspective on the future of Israel and the nations.[23] Zechariah's *first burden* (9:1—11:17) recognized difficult days ahead and proposed that the future was either a product of God's powerful purposes or their rejection of His ways.

God's purposes will be fulfilled on earth because His eyes will see what happens on the earth, especially what will happen in Jerusalem (9:1, 8). He is the supreme power and

21. Berger, *Social Construction,* 95–99, sees the symbolic universe as a mental picture which orders and integrates life. Zechariah's view was not based on his present social situation in Jerusalem, but externalized ideas from God that were known to other prophets (Isa. 2:2–4; 66:18–21; Jer. 3:17; Ezek. 36:23).

22. Meyers, *Haggai, Zechariah 1—8* in *AB* 25B, 433–34, suggests possible events remembered in these additional days of fasting.

23. Smith, *Micah-Malachi* in *WBC* 32, 242–49, and Butterworth, *Structure of Zechariah,* 166–237, summarize and critique the structural approaches of Lamarche, Otzen, Hanson, and Willi-Plein.

the ultimate Warrior who will end wars between peoples.[24] God will destroy Judah's neighbors and make a remnant of the nations, His own people (9:1–8). A central figure in these events will be the Messiah, the One who will deliver Judah, rule the whole earth, and bring true peace (9:9–10, see Isa., 9:6–7; 11:1–5; Jer. 23:4–6).[25] This King will not fit the role expectations of many, for He will be humble, not proud like other rulers.

God will free His people who are still in exile because He has a covenant with them. The Divine Warrior in a vivid theopany will trample their enemies into the ground. God will save His people, for they are His precious jewels (9:16–17).

Before continuing these themes in 10:3—11:3, the prophet briefly paused to warn his audience not to be fooled by the political, social, or religious worldview of false prophets, diviners, or political leaders (shepherds) who might try to persuade them to view their future in a different way. These were illusions, lies that were false.[26] The people must depend on God, for He is the only One who can meet their needs (10:1–2). God will punish the evil leaders and replace them with reliable leaders (having the positive characteristics of a cornerstone or battle bow). In spite of people's hopeless view of the future, God will strengthen His people and have compassion on them (10:6). He will bring many back to the land in a new exodus (10:10; see Isa. 11:11–15).

---

24. Hanson, *Dawn of Apocalyptic*, 293, concludes that this Divine Warrior Hymn gave the expectations of the visionaries who were against the Zadokite priests in Jerusalem, but Hanson's political approach does not deal adequately with the dependence of 9—14 on 1—8 or adequately analyze 9:1–17 (see Butterworth, *Structure of Zechariah*, 196).

25. The New Testament writers thought this prophecy was fulfilled when Jesus rode into Jerusalem on a donkey on what is now called Palm Sunday (Matt. 21:5 and John 12:15). See Achtemeier, *Nahum-Malachi* in *IntCom*, 150–54.

26. Berger, *Social Construction*, 114, describes one way of socially delegitimating a deviant worldview by giving its conception of reality a negative ontological status. It is false.

He will cut off the proud foreign oppressors and strengthen all who follow God's ways (10:11—11:3).[27]

In the final section of the first burden (11:3–17), God punished the worthless political leaders who destroyed God's flock. Zechariah symbolically played the role of a good shepherd king who ruled with graciousness to bring unity to the people (see Ezek. 37:15–23). When the people rejected this good king and followed an evil leader (11:15–17), the good shepherd was paid next to nothing, and unity ended (11:10–14). This graphic drama was a warning not to let bad leaders deceive them or reject the messianic king God would send to unify the nation.[28]

The *second burden* (12:1—14:21) described how a dramatic change in Judah's attitude will precede God's final destruction of the nations and establishment of His reign on earth. God will transform the people's attitude and cause them to look at reality in a new way (compare Ezek. 36:25–26). Drawing on images of the wounded one in Isaiah 53:5,[29] the prophet referred to a future day when the people will come to a new understanding of the One they pierced (the rejected shepherd of 11:4–14 according to Achtemeier).[30] Then people from every family in Israel will mourn and confess their sins (12:10). Idolatry and false prophets will be rejected (13:2–6). The people will recognize the Lord as their God, and He will count them as His people (13:9).

This miraculous transformation of Judah will coincide with great changes in Judah's relationship to the nations. Judah will be attacked by strong nations from throughout

27. There is no indication that this oracle opposed priestly leaders as suggested in Hanson, *Dawn of Apocalyptic*, 347.

28. Achtemeier, *Nahum-Malachi* in *IntCom*, 155–59, follows this messianic interpretation confirmed in Matthew 26:15; 27:9–10, while Smith, *Micah-Malachi* in *WBC* 32, 272, rejects any messianic reference by its original author. Paul Redditt, "The Two Sheperds in Zechariah 11:4–17," *CB* 255 (1993), 676–86, analyzes the sociological roles of the sheperds.

29. D. R. Jones, *Haggai, Zechariah, Malachi* in *TBC* (London: SCM, 1962), 163.

30. Achtemeier, *Nahum-Malachi* in *IntCom*, 161. John 19:37 saw this verse fulfilled in Jesus.

the earth (12:1–2; 14:1–3), but God will appear in power to rescue His people (12:1–6; 14:3–5, 12–15). A new world order will be established: new light, new water, new king, new land, new peace, new worship in Jerusalem by foreign nations, and a new holiness among mankind (14:6–11, 15–21). This externalization gave hope to those who were struggling under weak internal leadership (8:1–2) and the weight of foreign domination.

Theological and Social Implications

Political and spiritual leaders can lose sight of God's plans, His power to fulfill His purposes, and their own ability to persuade people to act in faith. God's people need good leaders who understand God's purpose for people and have insight into God's plans for the future. These chosen servants need to accept their leadership responsibilities and understand the spiritual resources that God gives them (Zech. 3—4). These purposes become the source of a leader's vision for ministry and the framework for developing action plans. This vision cannot be based on human values which depreciate small beginnings (4:10) or on the supposition that God cannot use forgiven sinners (3:1–7). When discouragement arises and political circumstances are bleak, God is still zealously longing to fulfill His plans (1:14–16). A good shepherd leader may be rejected, but eventually God will even use such rejection to fulfill His plan. Human failures, delays, and opposition will not change God's purpose of establishing His kingship over all the earth. This hope motivates action today and gives courage to those who desire to fulfill His purposes.

Questions for Discussion

1. How did God's plan for Jerusalem and the nations (1:6—2:13) differ from the people's social and political perspectives?

2. How did Zechariah's vision about Zerubbabel in chapter 4 help the governor understand God's purposes for him?

3. How do chapters 9, 11, 12 compare with other messianic passages?

Chapter 18

Malachi: Whom Do You Honor?

Introduction

A person's social relationships with other people are heavily influenced by each person's conception of the audience to whom they are talking to. Sometimes people will get a bad impression of someone because a person stands for something (political view, social policy, or religious belief) which is not accepted. On the other hand, people will honor students when they graduate from college, give special recognition to the top salesperson, or publicly acknowledge those who contribute to civic projects.

When a group honors a person, it says something about what is valued. If great musical ability is valued, the musician may be asked to play at a special event. If ten years of volunteer work at the hospital is valued, a service banquet may honor a great humanitarian. People are honored for character traits and behavior that is appreciated. Honoring someone involves saying why they are special. The practice of honoring people says something about the people showing appreciation, too. They notice the good things and affirm these valuable contributions.

The prophet Malachi raised a series of probing questions about whether it makes any difference if one honors God. If one decides it is important, it is necessary to ask: What should one do to honor God? How can God's messengers today honor Him?[1]

Social Setting

Historical Context

This prophecy was not overtly connected to any kings in Israelite history; instead, a governor was ruling the people (1:8). This implies that the prophet preached after the people returned from exile (after 539 B.C.) when the Persians appointed governors. Since the temple was in use (1:7–14) and the people were quite lax concerning temple worship, these sermons came years after Haggai and Zechariah encouraged the nation to finish building the temple (516 B.C.; Ezra 6:14–15).

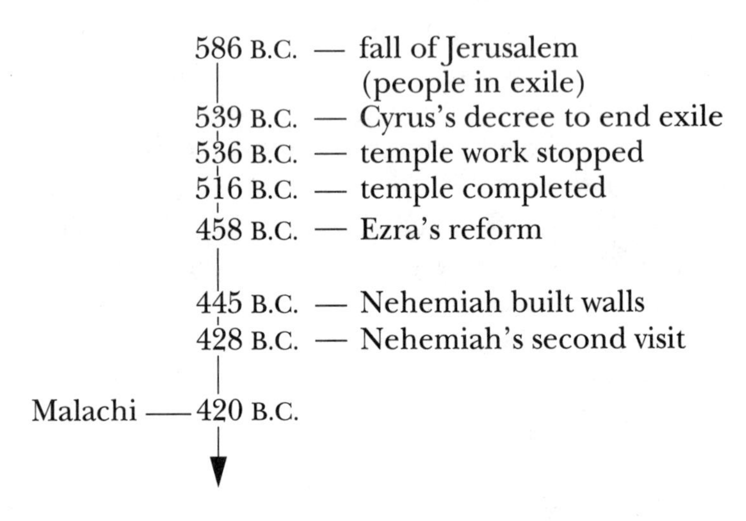

1. B. Glazier-McDonald, *Malachi: The Divine Messenger* (Atlanta: Scholars Press, 1987), 2, recognizes the centrality of honoring God in Malachi's massages.

Many commentators think the prophet spoke around the time of Nehemiah, because both books refer to problems with mixed marriages (Ezra 9—10; Neh. 13:23–29; Mal. 2:10–12), lack of tithing (Neh. 10:32–38; 13:10–14; Mal. 3:6–12), corruption of the priesthood (Neh. 13:7–9; Mal. 2:1–9), and oppression of the poor (Neh. 5; Mal. 3:5). Although Dumbrell places Malachi before Nehemiah (before 445 B.C.) and Kaiser puts him between Nehemiah's two visits (after 433 B.C.; see Neh. 13:6–7),[2] it is better to date Malachi after Nehemiah's second visit (possibly 420 B.C.). The mixed marriage problem in Ezra and Nehemiah was solved by encouraging people to divorce their pagan spouses, but Malachi was fighting a later problem of too much divorce (2:14–16). In Malachi's day, the people had so liberalized this practice that they were even divorcing their Jewish spouses.[3]

The Structure of Social Order

The worldview of the people in Palestine was not strongly affected by the experiences of their parents and grandparents who returned from exile over one hundred years earlier (539 B.C.). Their ancestors struggled to clear the land, resettle in their old homes, build the temple (516 B.C.), and repair the walls of Jerusalem (445 B.C.); but this generation was well established in the land. Jewish priests functioned in the temple, and sacrifices were offered, so there were no major crises that subverted religious expression.[4]

Hanson sees a conflict in the post-exilic community between the corrupt ruling Zadokite priests that returned from the exile and the sons of Levi,[5] but O'Brien demonstrates that

2. W. J. Dumbrell, "Malachi and the Ezra-Nehemiah Reforms," *RTR* 35 (1976), 42–52; W. C. Kaiser, *Malachi: God's Unchanging Love* (Grand Rapids: Baker, 1984), 16–17; or G. L. Klein, "An Introduction to Malachi," *CTR* 2 (1987), 23–26.

3. G. V. Smith, "Malachi," *ISBE* III (1986), 226–28.

4. See Glazier-McDonald, *Malachi, 10—13,* on Persian policies.

5. P. Hanson, *The People Called: The Growth of the Community in the Bible* (San Francisco: Harper, 1986), 253–90; Dumbrell "Malachi and the Ezra-Nehemiah Reforms," *RTR* 35 (1976), 43.

the priests and Levites were not two different groups.[6] If this conflict did not exist, then the tension was between Malachi's theological views of appropriate covenant behavior and the socially developed views of the priests and people in Israel.

Malachi described a secularizing trend.[7] People were more concerned with the practical matters of making a good living in the midst of an agricultural plague (3:11) than worrying about what God wanted. The normal regulations that governed sacrificial offerings were ignored (1:6–14), and tithing became an optional practice (3:7–12). It was not a problem if people intermarried with non-Jews or divorced their Hebrew wives (2:10–16). Many questioned whether it was really all that important to observe all the picky Jewish laws of the past (3:13–15). People began to practice sorcery, adultery, and oppression of the poor. The priests did not strictly observe covenant laws and did not teach the people to honor God (1:6) or believe in His justice (2:17).

The Social Location and Role of the Prophet

Numerous scholars conclude that "Malachi" was not the name of the prophet who wrote this book. Instead they translate 1:1 "the word of the Lord to Israel through my messenger."[8] They suggest that a later editor took the term "my messenger" from 3:1 and introduced it in 1:1, but it is unlikely that an editor would claim that the future messenger of 3:1 had already come.[9] The Targum added after the words "my messenger" the qualifier "whose name was Ezra," and the

---

6. J. M. O'Brien, *Priest and Levite in Malachi* (Atlanta: Scholars Press, 1990), 24–48.

7. C. R. Wells, "The Subtle Crisis of Secularization: Preaching the Burden of Israel," *CTR* 2 (1987), 39–62. P. Berger, *The Sacred Canopy* (Garden City: Doubleday, 1967), 107, defines secularization as the process of removing parts of culture from the dominion of religious institutions or symbols.

8. J. A. Soggin, *Introduction to the Old Testament* (Philadelphia: Westminster, 1976), 343, used this translation since there was no mention of the prophet's ancestory or place of birth like other introductions.

9. T. C. Vriezen, "How to Understand Malachi 1:11," *Grace upon Grace* (Grand Rapids: Eerdmans, 1975), 128–31, and E. Achtemeier, *Nahum-Malachi* in *IntCom* (Atlanta: John Knox, 1986), 171, thinks that it does not make sense to see the prophet as the forerunner of 3:1.

LXX implied that this was not the name of a prophet. Childs and Verhoef find these witnesses unconvincing and feel that Malachi was the prophet's name.[10]

Achtemeier hypothesizes that the prophet took on the role of a priest (the priest was called God's messenger in 2:7) and brought the issues raised in the book before a Levitical court to argue each case.[11] It seems better to relate the disputational method of the prophet's sermons to the role of a public orator.[12] The prophet's rhetorical skills are evident in the regularized structure and logical argumentation of these short sermons. Each section has:

(a) an initial assertion;

(b) the people's objection to this statement;

(c) evidence to support the initial claim; and

(d) a concluding promise, threat, or encouragement.[13]

Malachi's opposition to the established priesthood suggests that he was not a central prophet.

Social Interaction

The Book of Malachi

Most maintain the unity of the text of Malachi, but some scholars have questioned a few verses, particularly 4:4–6.[14]

---

10. B. S. Childs, *Introduction to the Old Testament as Scripture* (Philadelphia: Fortress, 1979), 390–92.

11. Achtemeier, *Nahum-Malachi* in *IntCom,* 172.

12. P. A. Verhoef, *The Books of Haggai and Malachi* in *NICOT* (Grand Rapids: Eerdmans, 1987), 166; C. Westermann, *Basic Forms of Prophetic Speech* (Philadelphia: Westminster, 1967), 201, also discusses disputations.

13. Verhoef, *Haggai-Malachi* in *NICOT,* 171, calls the third element a motivation, while E. R. Clendenen, "The Structure of Malachi: A Textlinguistic Study," *CTR* 2 (1987), 3–7, follows Longacre's discourse approach and develops a different structure.

14. J. M. O'Brien, *Priest and Levite in Malachi* (Atlanta: Scholars Press, 1990), 51–56.

The somewhat regular structure of the disputations help define the book's outline:[15]

- I. Do You Know that God Loves You? 1:1–5
- II. Do You Honor God in Worship? 1:6—2:9
  - A. Do you honor God with your sacrifices? 1:6–14
  - B. The priests do not honor God. 2:1–9
- III. Do You Honor God in Your Marriage? 2:10–16
- IV. Do You Believe in God's Justice? 2:17—3:6
- V. Do You Honor God with Your Tithe? 3:7–12
- VI. Do You Honor God by Serving Him? 3:13—4:3
- VII. Concluding Exhortation 4:4–6

In these sermonic disputations, Malachi persuasively argued for a transformation of the priests' and people's theology and behavior. A continuation of the present secularization process would radically change the identity of the nation and bring the refiner's fire (3:2).

I. Do You Know that God Loves You? 1:1–6

The prophet began his sermon by challenging the people's view of God. Malachi's claim that God loved them was met with skepticism, for God did not have a key role in their secularly constructed objectifications.[16] The evidence that proved the validity of God's love came from the different ways God treated Jacob and his descendants (the audience Malachi addressed) and Esau and his descendants (the Edomites). God chose Jacob and not Esau (Gen. 25:23). He brought the Israelites back to their land after the exile, but made Edom desolate because they abused the Jews when the city of Jerusalem was destroyed (Obad. 10–16; Ps. 137:7; Ezek. 36).[17] Evidently, Malachi's reasoning did not persuade

---

15. The Hebrew text has only three chapters, thus 4:1–6 were 3:19–24 in the Hebrew. Our outline follows the English numbering.

16. P. Berger and T. Luckmann, *The Social Construction of Reality* (Garden City: Doubleday, 1966), 28–34, describe the way the cultural perspective of each group is developed through social interaction.

17. The date of the destruction of Edom is still unknown. See Glazier-McDonald, *Malachi,* 38–41, for the possible influence of Nabonidus or the Nabateans in destroying Edom.

many, but he concluded that some day in the future God's people would see God's acts in other nations and realize they could not eliminate God from their worldview. Then they will confess that God is alive and worthy of praise (1:5).

II. Do You Honor God in Worship? 1:6—2:9

The second disputation initially challenged the priests with the question: *Do you honor God with your sacrifices* (1:6–14)? Malachi claimed that the priests did not honor God as a heavenly father or master. The priests rejected Malachi's charge, but the prophet argued that the priests failed to honor God when they offered sacrifices at worship. They were despising God's name by ignoring the Levitical traditions concerning bringing only the best animals to God (Lev. 1:3, 10; 3:1, 6; 4:3; 22:17–25). Did they actually think God would accept lame, blind, and sick animals that were socially unacceptable to their earthly political authorities? If they were so bored with honoring God, it would be less hypocritical just to close the temple completely. Malachi twice repeats his conclusion (2:11,14): on a future day many nations will fear God their King and honor His name (see Isa. 2:1–4, 49:6; Amos 9:12; Jer. 3:15–19).[18] They will reject the secular worldview of Malachi's audience.

God's curse will come on these religious leaders because *the priests do not honor God* (2:1–9) by keeping the covenant with Levi.[19] God's covenant with the Levites (Ex. 32:26–29; Num. 25:11–13; Deut. 33:8–11) required certain personal qualifications and social functions of the priests. God's blessing of peace would be on them if the priests honored God's name, taught God's law (Lev. 10:11; Deut. 17:10–11), reject-

18. Verhoef, *Haggai and Malachi* in *NICOT*, 225–31, and Glazier-McDonald, *Malachi*, 57–61, discuss the arguments for and against defining the people who will honor God in 1:11 and 14. Some thought Malachi referred to the (a) heathen in the messianic era, (b) proselytes, or (c) Jews in exile.

19. O'Brien, *Priest and Levite in Malachi*, 27–48, demonstrates that the Levites and priests were the same group. This is better than Hanson's interpretation, which makes a sharp distinction between the corrupt Zadokites and the Levites. See Hanson, *The People Called*, 282.

ed injustice, walked with God, and turned people away from sin. If they would internalize these role behaviors, then they would have the social function of maintaining the divine perspective among the people.[20] Through their teaching, they would be God's messengers (2:5–8).

The priests rejected these roles and turned people away from God with their instruction and legal decisions (2:8). Therefore, God began to send a curse upon them (2:2). Malachi tried to persuade the priests to transform their ways[21] or else God would bring social rejection by people, Levitical rejection because of uncleanness, and a greater divine curse (2:2–3, 9).

III. Do You Honor God in Your Marriage? 2:10–16

Malachi interacted with a group of people who married non-Jewish spouses (2:10–12) and some who divorced their Jewish wives (2:13–16). Malachi based this disputation on two theological assumptions that his audience would accept. The Jewish sense of identity and social cohesiveness was founded on the conviction that they had one father and one God (2:10).[22] The unfaithful marriages with people who worshiped other gods profaned their sacred covenant with God and threatened to destroy the unity of the group (see Deut. 7:1–7). God will cut these people off, even though some worshiped in the temple (2:12).[23]

---

20. Berger, *Social Construction*, 117–18, 152, discusses how conversation (teaching) by full-time experts (the priests) helps maintain a pure social construction of reality in the face of competing worldviews.

21. J. Baldwin, *Haggai, Zachariah, Malachi* in *TOTC* (Downers Grove: InterVarsity, 1972), 232, recognizes the possibility of repentance.

22. As Glazier-McDonald, *Malachi*, 86, maintains, the prophet is not announcing the universal brotherhood of all people, for this passage is focused on the unity of the Jewish people under one God and one father. Verhoef, *Haggai and Malachi* in *NICOT*, 265, believes the father was God, but it seemed Malachi based his conclusions on both the theological and genetic unity of the nation. See Baldwin, *Haggai, Zechariah, Malachi* in *TOTC*.

23. Many think the difficult terms "the one who calls and answers" was an idiomatic way of saying "everyone." Glazier-McDonald, *Malachi*, 95–98, hypothesizes a sexual connotation "the one who is aroused and the lover" to fit the marriage context.

Ezra and Nehemiah had earlier encouraged people to divorce their non-Jewish spouses (Ezra 9—10; Neh. 13). In this pluralistic setting the traditional norms surrounding the institution of marriage were changing and becoming unglued from religious standards.[24] Secularism and social preference caused some in Malachi's audience to divorce their Jewish wives (2:13–16). They were unfaithful to the Jewish marriage covenant they made before God. Later these people were greatly distressed and dumbfounded because God would not accept their sacrifices. Malachi maintained that spiritual people who hope to raise godly children do not do this, for God hates this kind of behavior and will not bless it.[25] Malachi was persuading these people to reevaluate their unfaithful action, to reassess their spiritual priorities in light of their tragic consequences, and to not make divorcing a Hebrew wife normative behavior (see Deut. 24:1; Matt. 19:3).

IV. Do You Believe in God's Justice? 2:17—3:6

Some people, and even some priests in Malachi's audience (3:3), became disillusioned and cynical about religion. They claimed that God dealt with people unjustly. It seemed to them that God was actually showing favoritism to the evil people in society (2:17). Deviance between the theological principles in their symbolic universe (God is just) and social reality around them (evil is not judged) undermined their faith in God.[26]

The prophet reaffirmed the justice of God. He reminded his audience that earlier prophets said that God would send a messenger to prepare the way before He came back to rule His kingdom and that one day His glory would again

---

24. Berger, *Sacred Canopy*, 144–47, describes the undermining of religious traditions in a pluralistic context.

25. For the textual problems and a survey of interpretive issues in 2:15 see Verhoef, *Haggai and Malachi* in *NICOT*, 275–81.

26. Berger, *Social Construction*, 92–98, deals with the symbolic universe and on 106–07, addresses the problem of maintaining a symbolic universe when actual experience points in a different direction.

fill the temple (Isa. 40:1–11; Ezek. 43).[27] God's character did not change. On the day of the Lord, He will refine and purify the Levitical priests and bring justice on the adulterers and oppressors who do not honor God (3:2–6).

V. Do You Honor God with Your Tithe? 3:7–12

During an agricultural plague, Malachi's audience was not following God's covenant norms by bringing 10 percent of their earnings to the temple (see Lev. 27:30).[28] They were robbing God. The prophet challenged the people to repent, to honor God by bringing their tithe to the temple. If they would do this, God would turn His favor toward them and bless them.

VI. Do You Honor God by Serving Him? 3:13—4:3

The last disputational message indicated just how far the secularization process had changed the worldview of one group of people in Judah.[29] An arrogant group claimed that it did not make any difference if a person served God. Earlier they had mourned and repented of past failure, but this religious activity never resulted in any advantage for them (3:14). In fact, they could point to cases where the wicked seemed to be blessed (3:15). Why should they bother with God if it did not make any difference?

---

27. D. L. Peterson, *Late Israelite Prophecy: Studies in Deutero-Prophetic Literature and Chronicles* (Missoula: Scholars Press, 1977), 42, suggests that the messenger in 3:1 was the prophet Malachi, but this does not fit earlier tradition or the history of Malachi's time. Matthew 11:10–14 identified the messenger with John the Baptist. C. Blomberg, "Elijah, Election, and the Use of Malachi in the New Testament," *CTR* 2 (1987), 99–118, deals with the fulfillment of 3:1. The messenger of the covenant compares to the angel of the Lord associated with the Mosaic covenant (Ex. 23:20–23; Gal. 3:19; Acts 7:38). In light of the everlasting covenant with the seed of David (Isa. 55:3; Ezek. 34:25; 37:24–26) many identify this person with the Messiah.

28. The issue of giving tithes today was addressed by G. B. Davis, "Are Christians Supposed to Tithe?" *CTR* 2 (1987), 85–98.

29. Verhoef, *Haggai and Malachi* in *NICOT*, 318, concludes that these were not heathen people but Jews.

Malachi could not claim that God's justice immediately brought a blessing on the righteous and a judgment on the wicked, for experience proved otherwise. Possibly he would not be able to persuade these hardened cynics who had rejected God, but he could encourage those who still feared God. A righteous group of people talked to one another, reaffirming the plausibility of their behavior (3:16).[30] Malachi assured these people that it made sense to fear God, even though there was no immediate payback, because God was keeping a record of everyone who honored His name. The prophet assured them they had a special identity in God's eyes; they were His people, His special prized possessions (see Ex. 19:5), His deeply loved sons. This evidence supported the claim that God will one day distinguish between the righteous and the wicked (3:16–18). On that day the arrogant evildoers will burn in judgment, but those who honor God will be healed and delivered in a time of great joy.[31]

VII. Concluding Exhortation 4:4–6

The book concluded with a brief exhortation to let God's instructions in the Mosaic writing be a guide for life, a reminder of His promise to send another great prophet before the day of the Lord (the messenger of 3:1), and a promise that their spiritual restoration would include a new social ordering of relationships between people.

Theological and Sociological Implications

The secularization of religion in Malachi's day was probably only a pale precursor to the enormous godless perspec-

30. Berger, *Social Construction*, 154, outlines the importance of having a social support group which validates that it is okay to think the way you think. Without a plausibility group, a person would begin to think their ideas are crazy and would change due to social pressure.

31. Different interpretations of the "sun of righteousness" are described in Verhoef, *Haggai and Malachi* in *NICOT*, 327–30. Although the speaker may have drawn on the ANE symbol of the winged sun disk, the focus of attention should be on its source (from God), character (righteous), and function (healing).

tive of many today. People still doubt that there is such a thing as God's love in this violent and inhumane world. How can one hypothesize the justice of God when the powerful get stronger and the weak get militarily, economically, and racially trampled? Does it really pay to serve God and honor His name? The secular worldview of reality without God seems to make logical sense, and it is accepted by educated people.

The modern messenger of God faces an uphill battle with the forces of secularism. It affects people in three ways. Some bow to social pressure and join a social group which does not give God a significant place in their perspective. Many have tried religion as a child, but no longer think it has any value (see 3:13–15). By implication, they arrogantly conclude that it is all a waste of time. Another group practices the socially accepted religious customs, but is actually bored and undisciplined about honoring God. Even religious leaders go through the motions, but have no burning desire to transform people's lives (see 1:6—2:9). A third group fears God and looks forward to that eschatological day of vindication (see 3:16–18).

How can one credibly speak to these distinct groups? One has to listen to and understand each audience's worldview so that it can be addressed. Malachi knew what people were saying and thinking; thus he avoided being boring and irrelevant. He also used an untypical method of communicating these issues in a fairly direct and logical disputational approach. He called a spade a spade and boldly suggested the astonishing idea of closing down the temple. He tackled the tough social and moral issues of marriage and money. Central to his rhetorical skill was his ability to bring the discussion back to the main issue of how their action related to their beliefs about God. If he could only convince people to fear God, the Creator, Ruler, and Judge of all the nations of the earth, they would automatically honor His name with their behavior.

Questions for Discussion

1. How does the role of the priest compare to the messenger of God today (2:4–9)? List similarities and differences.
2. What are the key theological characteristics of God developed in this book? Give one practical implication that can be drawn from those characteristics.
3. How do Malachi's instructions on marriage (2:10–16) and tithes (3:7–12) relate to practices today?

Chapter 19

Prophetic Ministry

The written records of the prophets portray them as normal people, preaching to diverse audiences, in a wide variety of settings. Each fulfilled God's calling by communicating a life-transforming message that required a reevaluation of the way their audiences conceived the phenomena in the world. This reordering impacted the dominant socially defined ways of understanding God/the gods, themselves, nature, economic and political life, their relationship to God, and their relationships to others. With one voice the prophets opposed the seductive and deceptive explanations social groups developed to order their cultural patterns of thinking and behaving. The prophetic goal was to faithfully give God's new meaning to life and the world, to communicate it in a persuasive manner that would be meaningful to the listener, and to transform the worldview and behavior of their audiences. They saw themselves as messengers who communicated God's word to an audience that needed God's love, wisdom, power, and grace.

The Prophetic Message

The central theological perspective of prophetic preaching was that Israel's God was in control of all people, nature, and power in heaven and earth. God is the first and the last (Isa. 48:12); the One who created the world of nature and human beings (Isa. 44:24; 45:12). He established the nations and controls them (Isa. 40:15–17; 44:7). God planned both the former things that happened in the past and the things to come in the future (48:3–6). God raised up ruling kings and will destroy wicked kings and their nations in the future (Jer. 25; Dan. 4). God is the sovereign King of the hosts of heaven and earth (Isa. 6; Dan. 7; Mal. 1:14). All other gods are deceptions; all armies are nothing; all who trust in human power, wisdom, and wealth are senseless (Jer. 9:23–24). If the prophet's audience would not internalize the belief that God ruled the world, they had little reason to fear or obey Him.

The prophets described God's rule over nature and people in two ways: a) He acted in justice, and b) He acted freely in accordance with His plans. Because God is holy, His justice orders His relationships to people and the lands where they live. God's justice will bring judgment to those who rebel, are unfaithful, and disobey His instructions (Isa. 6). He judges nations' and individuals' pride, violence, and oppressive use of power (Isa. 2:6–21; 13—23; Obad.1–4; Mic. 3:1–4; Hab. 1—2; Nah. 1—3:8), but justly blesses those who repent of sin, act justly, and seek God (Jer. 3:12–18; Amos 5:14–15; Jonah 3:5—4:2; Joel 2:12–14). God's justice applied to the pagan nations as well as the covenant communities of Israel and Judah. God's justice was particularly hard on political, social, and religious leaders who abused their privileged positions of trust and power. When they did not rule justly and righteously as God's vice-regents on the earth, their power and position of leadership were removed.

God did not always act justly, for many times He freely acted according to His wise plans. These acts were more mysterious because God never told the prophets what governed these acts. God's sovereign plans included the wise creation of the world (Isa. 40:12–12), the loving choice of individuals and nations to serve His purposes (Isa. 42:1; 44:1; 49:5–6; Ezek. 2—3), the compassionate sending of a messenger to warn undeserving nations (Jer. 1; Jonah 3), and the decision to pour out the Spirit in an unusual manner in the future (Joel 2:28; Ezek. 11:18–20). These acts were outside the parameters of reward and punishment. God miraculously and freely worked to accomplish His purposes without regard to whether His acts were justified by the human recipients. Although God is dependable, His ways are beyond what humans can fully understand from this earthly perspective.

Each of the prophetic messages was news of God's sovereign desire to interact with the audience so that: (a) the rebellious might transform their misunderstandings of life and decide to fear and serve Him, or (b) the righteous might be encouraged to maintain their hope in God's power and His plan to establish His kingdom. The prophets communicated principles that were known from earlier traditions in the Torah or earlier prophets to legitimate what they said. They also gave imaginative new externalizations that ran counter to the cultural worldview of their audiences. Their teachings were often based on past revelation in the law, but they were not limited by ideas formulated to apply to people in an earlier cultural context.

The Communication of the Message

The method of communication had an important part to play in the process of transforming the thinking of the audience. When Amos and Hosea spoke to the people in Israel, they thought about how they could convince their listeners to look again at what they were doing and transform their behavior. Under God's direction, Amos largely ignored the Baal worship in Israel and focused on their unjust treatment of others (2:6–8; 3:9–10; 4:1–3; 5:10–13; 8:4–6), their unacceptable worship (4:4–5; 5:21–24), and their misunderstanding of true Israelite traditions (3:1–2; 5:18–20; 9:7–10). A few years later Hosea spoke to some of the same people and chose a completely different tactic. He centered his preaching on Israel's syncretistic joining of Baal and Yahweh worship. Both prophets creatively used major problems in their audiences' cultural context to challenge sinful religious and social behavior. Both methods were legitimate. Hosea designed his sermons after the literary structure of a lawsuit in the courts, but Amos used war and woe oracles, visions, and disputations that were common in his culture. Both prophets were interested in communicating persuasively, in framing their messages in formats that were meaningful to their audience.

Similar differences exist when comparing Jeremiah's preaching in Jerusalem with Ezekiel's messages in exile. Ezekiel was frequently silent. Since the people would not likely listen if he did speak, drama became an intriguing method of gaining a hearing (Ezek. 4—6). When Ezekiel did speak, he described mysterious visions of the glory of God (Ezek. 1; 8—11; 43) or untraditional parables and allegories that creatively addressed old problems in a unique way (Ezek. 15—17; 19—20). In contrast, Jeremiah saw no visions of God's glory, performed few dramas (Jer. 13; 19) and spoke few parables (Jer. 24). He repeatedly lamented and interceded for the nation (Jer. 8:18—9:2; 14:1–9, 13, 19–22) and lamented about the persecution he received (11:18—12:6; 15:10–21; 20:7–18). Yet both Ezekiel and Jeremiah attacked their audiences' misunderstanding of the invincibility of Jerusalem, the vileness of Judah's sins, and the deceptive teaching of false prophets. These were different people who experienced life in alternative ways. Both prophets received God's messages and were faithful to their calling, but they had the freedom to communicate the divine word in a way that was appropriate to the Judean audience they addressed.

The prophets talked about all aspects of life. They had things to say about money, sex, and power. They did not avoid attacking issues of worship, war, or women. They were not afraid to condemn power-hungry kings, dishonest court officials, gouging landlords, or wicked priests. The prophets' honesty, their accurate depiction of their situation, their identification with those who suffered, their courage, and their rhetorical skill gave them credibility with their listeners. Most spoke in poetic style with a liberal use of imagination and creative flare. At different times their messages were sarcastic (Amos 4:4–5), filled with emotionally distraught gloom (Jer. 14), vibrant and overjoyed with excitement (Isa. 40:12–31), reasoned with logical deductions (Mal. 2:1–9), or wildly visionary (Dan. 7—8). They communicated God's message, but their own emotional and literary styles were stamped on the way each was delivered.

The Transformation of the Audience

The prophets effectively communicated God's message with their audiences because they knew what their listeners believed, how they thought, and the framework in which these ideas interacted (their objective reality). Ezekiel heard people using the popular proverb that suggested that they were wrongly suffering for their parents' sins (Ezek. 18:1–3) Nahum knew that Josiah would not be able to carry out his reforms if God did not remove the Assyrian control of Judah. Amos employed a modified form of the war oracle like the ones he heard at the military fortress in Tekoa (Amos 1—2). Hosea and Jeremiah illustrated their sermons with the sexual overtones of the Baal worship that was popular in their day (Hos. 4; Jer. 2); Malachi knew that some people in his postexilic setting questioned God's love and justice (Mal. 1:1–5; 2:17—3:5).

The prophets had a cultural perspective on laws, social roles, and religious duties different from those who listened to them, but these differences did not prevent people from understanding what the prophets were saying. When the prophets externalized their messages, they were generating new ways of looking at reality, ways different from, and not a part of, the dominant cultural understandings of their audiences. For example, Israel was at the height of her military strength under Jeroboam II when Amos told them the unimaginable and unpopular news that the nation would be destroyed and exiled (Amos 7:7–17). Ezekiel's externalization about the glory of God leaving the Jerusalem temple and appearing on Babylonian soil blew apart the exiles' cultural perspective which limited God's protecting power to the Jerusalem temple (Ezek. 1; 8—11). If God were with them in Babylonian exile, that would mean that He had not totally forsaken them as many thought. When Sennacherib was about to attack Hezekiah in 701 B.C., logic said to make a treaty with the Egyptians (Isa. 30—31) or make a bargain with the Assyrian general Rabshakah (Isa. 36), but the prophet Isaiah externalized the view that an Egyptian alliance would be of no profit and that God would destroy the proud Assyrian king (Isa. 30—33; 37:22—29). Each prophet proposed a new way of understanding life from God's point of view. These challenges required the audience to give up a frame of reference that their friends and associates accepted as self-evident truth. Hope required the transformation of the mind, a willingness not to be pressured to conform to the socio-cultural interpretations of this world, and a faith acceptance of God's way of thinking.

Effective communication did not just mean that the prophets spoke in a culturally comprehensible manner and faithfully externalized God's message in an unfriendly setting. It also meant they did everything possible to persuade the audience to internalize the message. This was not an easy task, for the audience frequently had a socially developed worldview that contradicted the prophetic perspective. Zechariah used heavenly visions to convince the discouraged Governor Zerubabbel not to depreciate small things, but to trust in the Spirit's power to help him finish rebuilding the post-exilic temple (Zech. 4). He encouraged Zerubabbel by reminding him that God's eyes were sovereignly watching over this project and by promising him that he would put the top stone on the temple amidst great rejoicing.

Obadiah encouraged the Jews left after the destruction of Jerusalem in 586 B.C. by convincing them that God would judge the Edomites' pride, punish them for their violence against Judah during and after the conquest of Jerusalem, and return all of Judah's land to them (Obad. 1–21). The prophet's claims about what God would do were supported by logical evidence, traditions that outlined what God had required in the past, the testimony of past experience, and the promises of God. This information did not prove anything to the unreceptive listener, the blind skeptic, the scheming power brokers, or the stubborn rebels; but these persuasive ideas did generate repentance in the brokenhearted and hope in the eyes of those who would dare to believe.

Theological and Social Implications

Whoever is wise,
let them understand these things.
Whoever has insight,
let them know them.
Indeed, the Lord's ways are right,
the righteous live by them
but the rebellious die because of them. (Hos. 14:9)

Glossary of Terms

Deviance: A thought or action that is outside the realm of what is acceptable for a specific group.

Externalization: The process of introducing new views of reality to another person or group.

Institutionalization: A group process of defining and accepting pre-defined ways of acting in a specific context as normative for human behavior.

Internalization: The process of accepting another person's thoughts or behavior as one's own.

Legitimation: The process of explaining or justifying a point of view or action. Reason, experience, tradition, and the symbolic universe justify a person's actions.

Objectification: The process of becoming aware of the subjective meaning that another person has given to phenomenon in the world.

Phenomenology: An approach to understanding reality based on the phenomena available to the senses. God, freedom, and ultimate questions cannot be addressed by this method.

Plausibility structures: A group of people who accept a common view of the world. Their existence allows a person to believe that this approach to life makes sense.

Reification: The process of attributing an absolute or unalterable characteristic to what is actually a human creation that can be changed.

Socialization: The process of instilling in a person the sociocultural characteristics of a group.

Social function: The part or role a person's activity plays in a group of people.

Subjective reality: What a person thinks about the world.

Symbolic universe: The abstract philosophical beliefs about how economics, society, politics, and religion work. This information explains and integrates the part of reality at an abstract level.

Worldview: The way a person views the world. It includes the meaning that people give to all phenomenon, social relationships, and the symbolic universe.

Bibliography

Communication

Baird, J.E. *Speaking for Results: Communication by Objectives.* New York: Harper & Row, 1981.

Bradley, B.E. *Fundamentals of Speech Communication: The Credibility of Ideas.* Debuque: Brown, 1974.

Burke, K. *A Grammar of Motives.* Cleveland: Meridan, 1962.

———. *A Rhetoric of Motives.* New York: Prentice-Hall, 1950.

Craft, C. *Communication Theory for Christian Witness.* Nashville: Abingdon, 1983.

Cronkhite, G. *Persuasion: Speech and Behavioral Changes.* New York: Bobbs-Merrill, 1969.

Dodd, C.H. *Perspectives on Cross-Cultural Communication.* Debuque: Kendall, Hunt, 1977.

Ehninger, D. *Influence, Beliefs and Argumentation: An Introduction to Responsible Persuasion.* Glenview: Scott, Foresman, 1974.

Ehninger, D. et al. *Principles and Types of Speech Communication.* Glenview: Scott, Foresman, 1986.

Gangel, K.O. and S. Canine, *Communication and Conflict Management in Churches and Christian Organizations.* Nashville: Broadman, 1992.

Gergen, K. Toward *Transformation in Social Knowledge.* New York: Springer-Verlag, 1982.

Hesselgrave, D.J. *Communicating Christ Cross-Culturally.* Grand Rapids: Zondervan, 1991.

Hazel, H. *The Power of Persuasion.* Kansas City: Sheed and Ward, 1989.

Littlejohn, S.W. and D.M. Jabush, *Persuasive Persuasion.* Glenview: Scott, Foresman, 1987.

McClelland, D. *Human Motivation.* Glenview: Scott, Foreman, 1985.

Ross, J.F. "The Prophet as Messenger," *Israel's Prophetic Heritage.* eds. B. W. Anderson and W. Harrelson, 98–107. New York: Harper and Row, 1962.

Toulmin, S. *The Uses of Argument.* New York: Cambridge University Press, 1964.

Sociology

Berger, P. *Invitation to Sociology: A Humanistic Perspective.* Garden City: Doubleday, 1963.

———. *The Sacred Canopy.* Garden City: Doulbleday, 1967.

Berger, P.L. and T. Luckmann, *The Social Construction of Reality: A Treatise in the Sociology of Knowledge.* Garden City: Doubleday, 1966.

Collins, R. *Conflict Sociology.* New York: Acedemic Press, 1975.

Douglas, J.D. *The Sociologies of Everyday Life.* Boston: Allyn and Bacon, 1980.

Elliot, J.H. *What Is Social-Scientific Criticism.* Minneapolis: Fortress, 1993.

Fredrichs, R. *A Sociology of Sociology.* New York: Free Press, 1970.

Gottwald, N. *The Hebrew Bible: A Socio-Literary Introduction.* Philadelphia: Fortress, 1985.

Hanson, P.D. *The Dawn of Apocalyptic.* Philadelphia: Fortress, 1975.

Herion, G.A. "The Impact of Modern and Social Science Assumptions on the Reconstruction of Israelite History." *JSOT* 34 (1986), 3–33.

Hewitt, J.P. and M.L. Hewitt, *Introducing Sociology*. Englewood Cliff, N.J.: Prentice-Hall, 1986.

Mannheim, K. Ideology and Utopia, *An Introduction to the Sociology of Knowledge*. New York: Harcourt, Brace, 1936.

Perkins, R. *Looking Both Ways: Exploring the Interface between Christianity and Sociology*. Grand Rapids: Baker, 1987.

Petersen, D.L. *The Role of Israel's Prophets*. In JSOTSup. Sheffield: JSOT, 1981.

Ritzer, G. *Toward an Integrated Sociological Paradigm*. Boston: Allyn and Bacon, 1981.

———. *Contemporary Sociological Theory*. New York: Knopf, 1983.

Rodd, C.S. "On Applying Sociological Theory to Biblical Studies," *JSOT* 19, 95–106.

Rogerson, J.W. "The Use of Sociology in Old Testament Studies," *SVT* 36 (1983), 245–56.

Stark, W. *The Sociology of Knowledge*. Glencoe: Free Press. 1958.

Weber, M. *The Sociology of Religion*. Boston: Beacon, 1964.

Wilson, R.R. *Prophecy and Society in Ancient Israel*. Philadelphia: Fortress, 1980.

———. *Sociological Approaches to the Old Testament*. Philadelphia: Fortress, 1984.

Introduction to Prophecy

Amos

Anderson, F. and D.N. Freedman, *Amos*. In AB. Garden City: Doubleday, 1989.

Barton, J. *Amos's Oracles Against the Nations*. Cambridge: Cambridge Univ. Press, 1980.

Finley, T. *Joel, Amos, Obadiah*. In WEC. Chicago: Moody, 1990.

Hasel, G. *Understanding the Book of Amos: Basic Issues in Current Interpretation*. Grand Rapids: Baker, 1991.

Hayes, J.H. *Amos, the Eighth-Century Prophet: His Times and His Preaching.* Nashville: Abingdon, 1988.
Hubbard, D.A. *Joel and Amos.* In *TOTC.* Downers Grove: InterVarsity, 1989.
Limburg, J. *Hosea-Micah.* In IntCom. Atlanta: John Knox, 1988.
Mays, J. *Amos.* In OTL. Philadelphia: Westminster, 1969.
Paul, S. *A Commentary on Amos.* In *Her.* Minneapolis: Fortress, 1991.
Smith, G.V. *Amos: A Commentary.* Grand Rapids: Zondervan, 1989.
Stuart, D. *Hosea-Jonah.* In WBC. Waco: Word, 1987.
Wolff, H.W. *Amos the Prophet: The Man and His Background.* Philadelphia: Fortress, 1973.
———. *Joel and Amos.* In *Her.* Philadelphia: Fortress, 1977.

Hosea

Anderson, F. and D.N. Freedman, *Hosea.* In AB. Garden City: Doubleday, 1980.
Brueggemann, W. *Tradition in Crisis: A Case Study in Hosea.* Richmond: J. Knox, 1968.
Davies, G.I. *Hosea.* In NCBC. Grand Rapids: Eerdmans, 1992.
Limburg, J. *Hosea-Micah.* In IntCom. Atlanta: John Knox, 1988.
Mays, J. *Hosea.* In OTL. Philadelphia: Westminster, 1969.
Rowley, H.H. "The Marriage of Hosea," *Men of God,* 66–97. London: Nelson, 1963.
Stuart, D. *Hosea-Jonah.* In WBC. Waco: Word, 1987.
Wolff, H.W. *Hosea.* In *Her.* Philadelphia: Fortress, 1974.

Jonah

Allen, L.C. *Joel, Obadiah, Jonah, and Micah.* In NICOT. Grand Rapids: Eerdmans, 1976.
Fretheim, T.E. *The Message of Jonah.* Minneapolis: Augsburg, 1977.

Landes, G.M. "The Message of the Book of Jonah," *Int* 21 (1967), 3–31.

Limburg, J. *Hosea-Micah.* In IntCom. Atlanta: J. Knox, 1988.

———. *Jonah.* In OTL. Louisville: J. Knox, 1993.

Magonet, J. *Form and Meaning: Studies in the Literary Techniques in the Book of Jonah.* Sheffield: Almond, 1983.

Sasson, J. M. *Jonah.* In AB. Garden City: Doubleday, 1990.

Stuart, D. *Hosea-Jonah.* In WBC. Waco: Word, 1987.

Wolff, H.W. *Obadiah and Jonah.* In CC. Minneapolis: Augsburg, 1986.

Micah

Allen, L.C. *Joel, Obadiah, Jonah, and Micah.*In NICOT. Grand Rapids: Eerdmans, 1976.

Hagstrom, D.G. *The Coherence of the Book of Micah.* Atlanta: Scholars Press, 1988.

Hillers, D. *Micah.* In *Her.* Philadelphia: Fortress, 1983.

Mays, J. *Micah: A Commentary.* In OTL. Philadelphia: Westminster, 1976.

Smith, R.L. *Micah-Malachi.* In WBC. Waco: Word, 1984.

Willis, J.T. "The Structure of the Book of Micah," *SEÅ* 34 (1969), 5–42.

Wolff, H.W. *Micah the Prophet.* Philadelphia: Fortress, 1981.

Isaiah

Achtemeier, E. *The Community and Message of Isaiah 56–66.* Minneapolis: Augsburg, 1982.

Childs, B.S. *Isaiah and the Assyrian Crisis.* London: SCM, 1967.

Clements, R. *Isaiah 1—39.* In NCBC. Grand Rapids: Eerdmans, 1980.

Erlandsson, S. *The Burden of Babylon: A Study of Isaiah 13:2—14:23.* Lund: Gleerup, 1970.

Gitay, Y. *Prophecy and Persuasion: A Study of Isaiah 40—48.* Bonn: Linguistica, 1981.

Kaiser, O. *Isaiah 1—12.* 2nd ed. In OTL. Philadelphia: Westminster, 1983.
———. *Isaiah 13—39.* 2nd ed. In OTL. Philadelphia: Westminster, 1983.
Leupold, H.C. *Exposition of Isaiah.* Grand Rapids: Baker, 1968.
McKenzie, J.L. *Second Isaiah.* In AB. Garden City: Doubleday, 1968.
Melugin, R.F. *The Formation of Isaiah* 40—55. In *BZAW* 141. Berlin: de Gruytes, 1976.
Muilenburg, J. *Isaiah 40—66: Introduction and Exegesis.* In *IB.* Nashville: Abingdon, 1952.
Oswalt, J. *The Book of Isaiah: Chapters 1—39.* In NICOT. Grand Rapids: Eerdmans, 1986.
Rowley, H.H. "Hezekiah's Reform and Rebellion," *Men of God,* 98–132. Edinburg: Nelson, 1963.
———. "The Servant of the Lord in Light of Three Decades of Criticism," *The Servant of the Lord and Other Esaays,* 1–57. London: Nelson,1952.
Seitz, C.R. *Isaiah 1—39.* In IntCom. Louisville: J.Knox, 1993.
Thompson, M.E.W. *Situation and Theology: Old Testament Interpretation of the Syro-Ephraimite War.* Sheffield: Almond, 1982.
Watts, J.D.W. *Isaiah 1—33.* In WBC. Waco: Word, 1985.
———. *Isaiah 34—66.* In WBC. Waco: Word, 1987.
Wegner, P.D. *An Examination of Kingship and Messianic Expectations in Isaiah 1—35.* Lewistown: Mellon, 1992.
Westermann, C. *Isaiah 40—66.* In OTL. Philadelphia. Westminster, 1969.
Wildberger, H. *Isaiah 1—12.* In CC. Minneapolis: Augsburg, 1991
Young, E.J. *The Book of Isaiah.* 3 vols. In NICOT. Grand Rapids: Eerdmans, 1965–72.

Nahum

Achtemeier, E. *Nahum-Malachi.* In IntCom. Atlanta: J.Knox, 1986.

Baker, D. *Nahum, Habakkuk, Zephaniah.* In TOTC. Downers Grove: InterVarsity, 1988.

Maier, W. *The Book of Nahum.* In St. Louis: Concordia, 1959.

Patterson, R.D. *Nahum, Habakkuk, Zephaniah.* In WEC. Chicago: Moody, 1991.

Roberts, J.J.M. *Nahum, Habakkuk, and Zephaniah.* In OTL. Louisville: Westminster/J. Knox, 1991.

Robertson, P. *The Book of Nahum, Habakkuk, and Zephaniah.* In NICOT. Grand Rapids: Eerdmans, 1989.

Smith, R.L. *Micah-Malachi.* In WBC. Waco: Word, 1984.

Zephaniah

Achtemeier, E. *Nahum-Malachi.* In IntCom. Atlanta: J.Knox, 1986.

Baker, D. *Nahum, Habakkuk, Zephaniah.* In TOTC. Downers Grove: InterVarsity, 1988.

Ball, I.J. *Zephaniah: A Rhetorical Study.* Berkeley: Bibal, 1988.

Kapelrud. A. *The Message of Zephaniah.* Oslo: Universitetforlaget, 1975.

Patterson, R.D. *Nahum, Habakkuk, Zephaniah.* In WEC. Chicago: Moody, 1991.

Roberts, J.J.M. *Nahum, Habakkuk, and Zephaniah.* In OTL. Louisville: Westminster/J. Knox, 1991.

Robertson, P. *The Book of Nahum, Habakkuk, and Zephaniah.* In NICOT. Grand Rapids: Eerdmans, 1989.

Smith, R.L. *Micah-Malachi.* In WBC. Waco: Word, 1984.

Habakkuk

Baker, D. *Nahum, Habakkuk, Zephaniah.* In TOTC. Downers Grove: InterVarsity, 1988.

Hiebert, T. *God of My Victory: The Ancient Hymn of Habakkuk.* Atlanta: Scholars Press, 1986.

Patterson, R.D. *Nahum, Habakkuk, Zephaniah.* In WEC. Chicago: Moody, 1991.

Roberts, J.J.M. *Nahum, Habakkuk, and Zephaniah.* In OTL. Louisville: Westminster/J. Knox, 1991.

Robertson, P. *The Book of Nahum, Habakkuk, and Zephaniah.* In NICOT. Grand Rapids: Eerdmans, 1989.

Smith, R.L. *Micah-Malachi.* In WBC. Waco: Word, 1984.

Jeremiah

Bright, J. *Jeremiah.* In AB. Garden City: Doubleday, 1965.

Brueggemann, W. *Jeremiah 1—25: To Pluck Up, to Tear Down.* In ITC. Grand Rapids: Eerdmans, 1988.

———. *Jeremiah 26—52: To Build and to Plant.* In ITC. Grand Rapids: Eerdmans, 1991.

Carroll, R. *Jeremiah.* In OTL. Philadelphia: Westminster, 1986.

Clements, R.E. *Jeremiah.* In IntCom. Louisville: Westminster/J. Knox, 1989.

Craigie, P.H. et al. *Jeremiah 1—25.* In WBC. Dallas: Word, 1991.

Diamond, A.R. *The Confessions of Jeremiah in Context.* Sheffield: In JSOT, 1987.

Harrison, R.K. *Jeremiah and Lamentations.* Downers Grove: InterVarsity, 1973.

Holliday, W. *Jeremiah: Spokesman Out of His Time.* Philadelphia: Pligram, 1956.

———. *Jeremiah 1.* In *Her.* Philadelphia: Fortress, 1986.

———. *Jeremiah 2.* In *Her.* Philadelphia: Fortress, 1989.

Huey, Jr. F. B. *Jeremiah, Lamentations.* In NAC. Nashville: Broadman, 1993.

Lundbom, J.R. *Jeremiah: A Study in the Ancient Hebrew Rhetoric.* Missoula: Scholars Press, 1975.

McKane, W. A *Critical and Exegetical Commentary on Jeremiah.* Vol 1. In ICC. Edinburgh: T & T Clark, 1986.

Overholt, T.W. *The Threat of Falsehood: A Study in the Theology of Jeremiah.* New York: Schocken, 1970.

Thompson, J.A. *The Book of Jeremiah.* In NICOT. Grand Rapids: Eerdmans, 1980.

Joel

Allen, L.C. *Joel, Obadiah, Jonah, and Micah.* In NICOT. Grand Rapids: Eerdmans, 1976.

Ahlstrom, G.W. *Joel and the Temple Cult of Jerusalem.* In VTSup. Leiden: Brill, 1971.

Dillard, R. "Joel," *The Minor Prophets.* ed. T. McComiskey. Grand Rapids: Baker, 1992.

Finley, T. *Joel, Amos, Obadiah.* In WEC. Chicago: Moody, 1990.

Hubbard, D.A. *Joel and Amos.* In TOTC. Downers Grove: InterVarsity, 1989.

Limburg, J. *Hosea-Micah.* In IntCom. Atlanta: John Knox, 1988.

Simkins, R. *Yahweh's Activity in History and Nature in the Book of Joel.* Lewistown: Mellon, 1991.

Stuart, D. *Hosea-Jonah.* In WBC. Waco: Word, 1987.

Wolff, H.W. *Joel and Amos.* In *Her.* Philadelphia: Fortress, 1977.

Obadiah

Allen, L.C. *Joel, Obadiah, Jonah, and Micah.* In NICOT. Grand Rapids: Eerdmans, 1976.

Bartlett, J.R. "The Rise and Fall of the Kingdom of Edom," *PEQ* 104 (1972) 32–44.

Finley, T. *Joel, Amos, Obadiah.* In WEC. Chicago: Moody, 1990.

Stuart, D. *Hosea-Jonah.* In WBC. Waco: Word, 1987.

Watts, J.D.W. *Obadiah.* Grand Rapids: Eerdmans, 1969.

Wolff, H.W. *Obadiah and Jonah.* In CC. Minneapolis: Augsburg, 1986.

Ezekiel

Allen, L.C. *Ezekiel 20—48.* In WBC. Dallas: Word, 1990.

Block, D.I. " Beyond the Grave: Ezekiel's Vision of Death and Afterlife," BBR 2 (1992) 113–41.
Brownlee, W.H. *Ezekiel 1—19.* In WBC. Waco: Word, 1986.
Cooper, L. E. *Ezekiel.* In NAC. Nashville: Broadman, 1994.
Eichrodt, W. *Ezekiel, A Commentary.* In OTL. Philadelphia: Westminster, 1970.
Greenberg, M. *Ezekiel I-XX.* In AB. Garden City: Doubleday, 1983.
Hals, R.M. *Ezekiel.* In FOTL. Grand Rapids: Eerdmans, 1989.
Klein, R.W. *Ezekiel: The Prophet and His Message.* Columbia: Univ. of South Carolina, 1988.
Levenson, J. *Theology of the Program of Restoration of Ezekiel 40—48.* Missoula: Scholars Press, 1976.
Stuart, D. *Ezekiel.* Dallas: Word. 1989.
Taylor, J. *Ezekiel.* In TOTC. Downers Grove: InterVarsity, 1969.
Zimmerli, W. *Ezekiel 1.* In *Her.* Philadelphia: Fortress, 1979.
———. *Ezekiel 2.* In *Her.* Philadelphia: Fortress, 1983.

Daniel

Baldwin, J. *Daniel.* In TOTC. Downers Grove: InterVarsity, 1978.
Collins, J.J. *Daniel with an Introduction to Apocalyptic Literature.* In FOTL. Grand Rapids: Eerdmans, 1984.
Goldingay, J.E. *Daniel.* In WBC. Dallas: Word, 1989.
Gooding, D.W. "The Literary Structure of the Book of Daniel and Its Implications," *TB* 32 (1981) 43-79.
Hartman, L.F. and Dilella, A.A. *The Book of Daniel.* In AB. Garden City: Doubleday, 1978.
Hasel, G. The Identity of 'The Saints of the Most High' in Daniel," *Bib* 56 (1975) 173-92.
Lacoque, A. *The Book of Daniel.* Atlanta: J.Knox, 1979.
Miller, S. *Daniel.* In NAC. Nashville: Broadman, 1994.
Wood, L. *A Commentary on Daniel.* Grand Rapids: Zondervan, 1973.
Walvoord, J.F. *Daniel: The Key to Prophetic Revelation.* Chicago: Moody, 1971.

Whitcomb, J.H. *Darius the Mede.* Grand Rapids: Eerdmans, 1959.

Young, E.J. *Commentary on Daniel.* London: Banner of Truth, 1949.

Haggai

Achtemeier, E. *Nahum-Malachi.* In IntCom. Atlanta: J.Knox, 1986.

Baldwin, J. *Haggai, Zechariah, Malachi.* In TOTC. Downers Grove: InterVarsity, 1972.

Beuken, W. *Haggai-Sacharja 1—8.* Assen: Van Gorcum, 1967.

Meyers, C.L. and E.M. Meyers. *Haggai and Zechariah 1—8.* AB. Garden City: Doubleday, 1987.

Petersen, D.L. *Haggai and Zechariah 1—8.* In OTL. Philadelphia: Westminster, 1984.

Smith, R.L. *Micah-Malachi.* In WBC. Waco: Word, 1984.

Verhoef, P.A. *The Books of Haggai and Malachi.* In NICOT. Grand Rapids: Eerdmans, 1987.

Wolff, H.W. *Haggai: A Commentary.* In CC. Minneapolis: Augsburg, 1988.

Zechariah

Achtemeier, E. *Nahum-Malachi.* In IntCom. Atlanta: J.Knox, 1986.

Baldwin, J. *Haggai, Zechariah, Malachi.* In TOTC. Downers Grove: InterVarsity, 1972.

Butterworth, M. *Structure and the Book of Zechariah.* Sheffield: JSOT, 1992.

Beuken, W. *Haggai-Sacharja 1—8.* Assen: Van Gorcum, 1967.

Meyers, C.L. and E.M. Meyers. *Haggai and Zechariah 1—8.* In AB. Garden City: Doubleday, 1987.

———. *Zechariah 9—14.* In AB. Garden City: Doubleday, 1993.

Petersen, D.L. *Haggai and Zechariah 1—8.* In OTL. Philadelphia: Westminster, 1984.

Smith, R.L. *Micah-Malachi.* In WBC. Waco: Word, 1984.

Malachi

Achtemeier, E. *Nahum-Malachi.* In IntCom. Atlanta: J.Knox, 1986.

Baldwin, J. *Haggai, Zechariah, Malachi.* In TOTC. Downers Grove: InterVarsity, 1972.

Glazier-McDonald, B. *Malachi: The Divine Messenger.* Atlanta: Scholars Press, 1987.

Kaiser, W.C. *Malachi: God's Unchanging Love.* Grand Rapids: Baker, 1984.

O'Brien, J.M. *Priest and Levite in Malachi.* Atlanta: Scholars Press, 1990.

Smith, R.L. *Micah-Malachi.* In WBC. Waco: Word, 1984.

Verhoef, P.A. *The Books of Haggai and Malachi.* In NICOT. Grand Rapids: Eerdmans, 1987.

Introduction to Prophecy

Achtemeier, P. J. and J. L. Mays eds. *Interpreting the Prophets.* Philadelphia: Fortress, 1987.

Armerding, C. E. and W. W. Gasque, eds. *A Guide to Biblical Prophecy.* Peabody: Hendrickson, 1989.

Blenkinsopp, J. *A History of Prophecy in Israel.* Philadelphia: Westminster, 1983.

———. *Prophecy and Canon: A Contribution to the Study of Jewish Origins.* Notre Dame: University of Notre Dame Press, 1977.

Brueggemann, W. *The Prophetic Imagination.* Philadelphia: Fortress, 1978.

Bullock, C. H. *An Introduction to the Old Testament Prophetic Books.* Chicago: Moody Press, 1986.

Carroll, R. *When Prophecy Failed: Cognitive Dissonance in the Prophetic Traditions of the Old Testament.* New York: Seabury, 1979.

Clements, R. E. *Prophecy and Tradition.* Atlanta: John Knox, 1975.

Crenshaw, J. L. *Prophetic Conflict: Its Effects upon Israelite Religion.* Berlin: de Gruyter, 1971.

Gottwald, N. K. *All the Kingdoms of the Earth: Israelite Prophecy and International Relations in the Ancient Near East.* New York: Harper & Row, 1964.

Johnson, A. R. *The Cultic Prophet and Israel's Psalmody.* Cardiff: University of Wales, 1979.

Koch, K. *The Prophets.* 2 vols. Philadelphia: Fortress, 1982, 1984.

Lindblom, J. *Prophecy in Ancient Israel.* Philadelphia: Fortress, 1962.

McKane, W. *Prophets and Wise Men.* London: SCM, 1965.

Newsome, J. D., Jr. *The Hebrew Prophets.* Atlanta: John Knox, 1984.

Neumann, P. H. A. *Das Prophetenverstandnis in der Deutschsprachigen Forschung seit Heinrich Ewald.* Darmstadt: Wissenschaftliche Buchgesellschaft, 1979.

Petersen, D. L. *The Roles of Israel's Prophets.* In JSOTSup 17. Sheffield: JSOT, 1981.

———. ed. *Prophecy in Israel: Search for an Identity.* Philadelphia: Fortress, 1987.

Vangemeren, W. A. *Interpreting the Prophetic Word.* Grand Rapids: Zondervan, 1990.

Von Rad, G. *The Message of the Prophets.* New York: Harper & Row, 1965.

Ward, J. *The Prophets.* Nashville: Abingdon, 1982.

Westermann, C. *Basic Forms of Prophetic Speech.* Philadelphia: Westminster, 1967.

Whitley, C. F. *The Prophetic Achievement.* Leiden: Brill, 1963.

Zimmerli, W. *The Law and the Prophets: A Study of the Meaning of the Old Testament.* New York: Harper & Row, 1965.

Index of Subjects

V

W

Z

Index of Names

D

E

F

G

H

J

K

L

M

N

O

P

R

S

T

V

W

Y

Z